Oxford Studies in European Law

General Editors: Paul Craig and Gráinne de Búrca

CULTURE AND EUROPEAN UNION LAW

Culture and European Union Law

Edited by

RACHAEL CRAUFURD SMITH

OXFORD
UNIVERSITY PRESS

This book has been printed digitally and produced in a standard specification in order to ensure its continuing availability

OXFORD
UNIVERSITY PRESS

Great Clarendon Street, Oxford OX2 6DP

Oxford University Press is a department of the University of Oxford. It furthers the University's objective of excellence in research, scholarship, and education by publishing worldwide in

Oxford New York

Auckland Cape Town Dar es Salaam Hong Kong Karachi Kuala Lumpur Madrid Melbourne Mexico City Nairobi New Delhi Shanghai Taipei Toronto

With offices in

Argentina Austria Brazil Chile Czech Republic France Greece Guatemala Hungary Italy Japan South Korea Poland Portugal Singapore Switzerland Thailand Turkey Ukraine Vietnam

Oxford is a registered trade mark of Oxford University Press in the UK and in certain other countries

Published in the United States by Oxford University Press Inc., New York

Reprinted 2007

ISBN 978-0-19-927547-2

GENERAL EDITORS' PREFACE

Culture has received relatively scant attention from Community lawyers compared with many other aspects of the subject, notwithstanding the fact that it has been an operative Title of the EC Treaty since 1993. An assessment of its impact is therefore timely, in particular since the connection between Community law and culture goes back considerably further, to the origins of the EEC Treaty. The very fact that culture will often have a commercial value and be an object of trade has meant that national treasures have not infrequently been the subject matter of actions concerning the free movement of goods, as Member States have sought to protect their valuable artefacts from the operation of the unfettered free market. It is equally apparent that the notion of culture is far broader, more complex, and more eclectic than the single category of national treasures. This volume does not, however, seek to address directly the contested meaning of culture, but rather to explore the ways in which cultural arguments are used in the EU, and to consider the forces, whether political, social, or economic, which have shaped EU cultural policy.

The rich set of essays contained in this volume attests to the diversity of the subject matter embraced by the notion of culture. Part 1 examines the early stages of Community law in relation to culture, and the motivations underlying the adoption of the key Treaty provision, Article 151. This is followed in Part 2 by chapters that address in varying ways the relationship between culture and commerce, including in this respect the connection between labelling and culture, the place of cultural arguments in the commercialized world of modern sport, and the capacity of Member States to limit trade in cultural goods in order to protect their cultural heritage. The focus then shifts in Part 3 to the role of the mass media, language, and education in the communication of culture and the formation of identity, and the differing nature and degree of Community involvement in these areas. This provides a natural bridge to the topics dealt with in Part 4, where there is an examination of the extent to which Article 151 can and has been used to foster a common European identity, and the way in which Community initiatives in the spheres of asylum and immigration might affect notions of nationality and identity. The final part of the book is concerned with the role played by culture in the EU's external relations, followed by a conclusion drawing together a number of the common themes in the preceding chapters.

The book provides a fascinating insight into the plethora of ways in which EU law has an impact on culture, and will be of interest to all those concerned with the interrelationship between the EU and national cultural traditions.

Paul Craig
Gráinne de Búrca

ACKNOWLEDGEMENTS

I would like to thank the Europa Institute at the University of Edinburgh for sponsoring the workshop on culture and identity, held at Edinburgh in September 2001, which was the springboard for this edited collection. My colleagues at the Institute, in particular Professor John Usher and Dr Niamh Nic Shuibhne, have throughout been extremely supportive of this project. Margaret Beechey and Myra Reid from the Research Office at Edinburgh University provided highly professional assistance in relation to the organization and management of the initial workshop. The team at Oxford University Press who worked on the book, among them, John Louth, Gwen Booth, Geraldine Mangley, and Catherine Minahan, not only provided valuable strategic advice on how best to put the work together but also ensured that it was edited with great care and professionalism. I understand that there were three external readers at the submission stage and I would also like to thank them for their helpful suggestions and comments, many of which have been taken on board. Matthew East from the European University Institute in Florence came in at the last minute to work on the various tables for the volume and his efficient, careful work has helped to make this book considerably more user friendly than it would have been otherwise. Generous support from the European University Institute in the form of a Jean Monnet Fellowship gave me time to work on the text prior to printing. Lastly, I would like to thank both the contributors for their considerable patience during the gradual transformation of this project—I hope that it has not left too many walking wounded—and my husband, Sean Smith, for his unfailing and constant support.

Rachael Craufurd Smith
April 2004

TABLE OF CONTENTS

Part IV: Culture, Identity, and European Integration

Part V: Culture and the European Union's External Relations: Trade and Aid

Part VI: Concluding Observations

LIST OF CONTRIBUTORS

Andrea Biondi is Senior Lecturer and Co-Director, Centre of European Law, King's College London; Professor, College of Europe (Natolin), and Member of 2 Harcourt Building Chambers, London.

Rachael Craufurd Smith is a Senior Lecturer at the School of Law, University of Edinburgh, and a member of the Europa Institute at Edinburgh University.

Joshua Holmes is a Legal Secretary at the European Court of Justice and Lecturer in Law at University College London.

Paul Kearns is a Lecturer in Law at the Manchester School of Law, University of Manchester.

Theodora Kostakopoulou is Reader in European Law and European Integration at the Manchester School of Law, University of Manchester.

Julian Lonbay is a Senior Lecturer at the School of Law, University of Birmingham. He is currently visiting Commerzbank Professor at the Bucerius Law School in Hamburg and Chairman of the Training Committee of the Council of the Bars and Law Societies of the European Union (CCBE).

Joseph A. McMahon is Professor of International Trade Law at the Queen's University of Belfast.

Niamh Nic Shuibhne is a Lecturer in EC Law at the School of Law, University of Edinburgh, and a member of the Europa Institute at Edinburgh University.

Stephen Weatherill is the Jacques Delors Professor of European Community Law at the University of Oxford. He also serves as Deputy Director for European Law in the Institute of European and Comparative Law, and is a professorial fellow at Somerville College, Oxford.

Olaf Weber is Rechtsanwalt at Gleiss Lutz. His doctoral thesis at Heidelberg concerns issues of EC and WTO law. He practised law at the European Commission's legal service and for a private TV operator.

Bruno de Witte is Professor of EU Law at the European University Institute, Florence.

TABLES OF CASES

ALPHABETICAL

Court of Justice

Court of First Instance

European Court of Human Rights

Rulings by Other Courts and Tribunals

Court for Arbitration in Sport (Lausanne)

France

Germany

Ireland

Italy

The Netherlands

Spain

UK

United States

World Trade Organisation

NUMERICAL

Court of Justice

Court of First Instance

European Court of Human Rights

TABLES OF EC/EU TREATY PROVISIONS

European Community Treaty (EC)

Article Numbers (current)

Treaty on European Union

TABLES OF EC LEGISLATIVE INSTRUMENTS

Regulations

Directives

Decisions

TABLES OF OTHER INTERNATIONAL INSTRUMENTS

Council of Europe

European Community Cooperation Agreements

United Nations/Unesco

World Trade Organisation

Other

TITLE XII OF THE EUROPEAN COMMUNITY TREATY[1]

CULTURE

Article 151

1. The Community shall contribute to the flowering of the cultures of the Member States, while respecting their national and regional diversity and at the same time bringing the common cultural heritage to the fore.
2. Action by the Community shall be aimed at encouraging cooperation between Member States and, if necessary, supporting and supplementing their action in the following areas:
   —improvement of the knowledge and dissemination of the culture and history of the European peoples,
   —conservation and safeguarding of cultural heritage of European significance,
   —non-commercial cultural exchanges,
   —artistic and literary creation, including in the audio-visual sector.
3. The Community and the Member States shall foster cooperation with third countries and the competent international organizations in the sphere of culture, in particular the Council of Europe.
4. The Community shall take cultural aspects into account in its action under other provisions of this Treaty, in particular in order to respect and to promote the diversity of its cultures.
5. In order to contribute to the achievement of the objectives referred to in this Article, the Council:
   —acting in accordance with the procedure referred to in Article 251 and after consulting the Committee of the Regions, shall adopt incentive measures, excluding any harmonization of the laws and regulations of the Member States. The Council shall act unanimously throughout the procedure referred to in Article 251;
   —acting unanimously on a proposal from the Commission, shall adopt recommendations.

[1] A consolidated version of the Treaty establishing the European Community is available at OJ [2002] C 325/33.

1

Introduction

*Rachael Craufurd Smith**

Personne ne conteste que notre continent est le foyer d'une civilisation exceptionelle. Cette civilisation est aussi bien marquée par des traits et des caractères culturels communs que par une extraordinaire diversité. Cette double dimension explique les deux grands objectifs qui soustendent l'action culturelle de l'Union européenne: d'une part, mettre en valeur et promouvoir les caractéristiques communes de nos sociétés culturelles; d'autre part, respecter, faire respecter et promouvoir la diversité culturelle concept qui rejoint ceux de multiculturalisme et de multilinguisme tant en Europe que par le monde.[1]

Why a book on European Union law and culture? The very fact that it is necessary to address such a question serves to highlight the still limited appreciation of the scope and remit of European Union, and more particularly European Community, law.[2] Books on European Community trade or competition law

* School of Law, University of Edinburgh.

[1] Mme Viviane Reding, Commissioner for Education and Culture, speaking on the theme of 'Multilinguisme et multiculturalisme: des défis pour l'éducation en Europe', at St-Germaine-en-Lay, 14 March 2003 (Speech/03/128): 'No one would disagree that our continent is the seat of an exceptional civilization. This civilization is distinguished as much by its common cultural traits and characteristics as by its extraordinary diversity. This double aspect explains the two main objectives which underpin the European Union's activities in the cultural field: on the one hand to highlight and promote the common characteristics of our cultural societies; on the other, to respect, to ensure respect for, and to promote cultural diversity, a concept which is linked to those of multiculturalism and multilingualism both at a European and worldwide level.' (Author's translation.)

[2] The contributions in this book are, for the most part, specifically concerned with European Community law, and the majority of references are therefore to 'Community' rather than 'European Union' law. The use of the term 'European Union law' in the title, and at various points in the book, serves, however, as a reminder that cultural issues may arise outside the immediate confines of European Community law. E.g., Article 6(3) of the TEU specifically provides that the *Union* 'shall respect the national identities of its Member States', while Article 7 TEU enables the Council to oversee compliance by the Member States with the principles set out in Article 6(1) TEU, namely, liberty, democracy, and respect for human rights and fundamental freedoms and the rule of law. It may also be noted that citizens under Article 17 EC are citizens of the European Union, not the European Community, and that the term 'European Union' is now generally used to refer to the geographical area covered by the Member States.

rarely start by asking why it is necessary to explore the topic in question, though they might consider what distinguishes their particular contribution from other works in the field. Yet, since November 1993, Title XII of the European Community Treaty (the 'EC Treaty') on culture has been in operation, alongside the more familiar titles relating, for example, to agriculture or the free movement of goods. Ten years after its introduction, some assessment of the impact of the culture title would therefore seem to be in order.

But the interaction between culture and European Union law is, of course, considerably more long-standing than this, and can be traced back to the origins of the European Economic Community (the 'EEC Treaty') in 1957. Culture frequently has a commercial value, is the subject of trade, or can act as a catalyst for the sale of other goods and services. In consequence, the rules established in the European Economic Community relating to the free movement of goods, services, and persons, customs duties, and competition quickly began to have an influence on the cultural sphere. National rules and anti-competitive business practices in the cultural field came under challenge, along with established consumer expectations and attitudes.

Those who drafted the EEC Treaty certainly had some understanding of its potential cultural impact: Article 36 (now Article 30 EC), for example, allows Member States to restrict the free flow of goods in order to 'protect national treasures possessing artistic, historic or archaeological value'. Article 36 was, however, something of an exception and it is probable that the original contracting states expected Community intervention in the cultural field to be fairly marginal. Indeed, it is unlikely that, in the immediate aftermath of the Second World War, the cultural ramifications of economic integration would have been regarded as a particularly important or pressing issue.[3] The general perception was that cultural issues would be left to other international organizations with an explicit cultural remit, notably UNESCO and the Council of Europe, operating along traditional inter-governmental lines.

The contributions to this book, which explore the interaction between European Union law and culture, illustrate why these expectations proved to be so wrong. The topic broached is clearly a vast one, not assisted by the chameleon-like nature of the concept of culture itself, and coverage is by no means comprehensive. The chapters have been grouped to highlight certain

[3] The international community was, however, clearly committed in the immediate post-war period to restoring the damage caused to Europe's cultural heritage, as well as to promoting understanding of Europe's cultural diversity. This is evident from the cultural remit of UNESCO, established in 1945, and the Council of Europe, established in 1949, under whose auspices the European Cultural Convention was agreed in 1954.

issues, but there is considerable overlap among the different parts and certain chapters could equally well have been located in one part as another. It is also important to realize that it is not the purpose of this book to add directly to the extensive literature on the meaning of culture; rather it focuses on why and how cultural arguments are used in European Union law, and on the political, social, and economic forces which shape the development of European Union cultural policy. Ultimately, it is hoped that the varied chapters in this volume will offer new perspectives on the role of law in the process of European integration and, in so doing, stimulate further debate on the scope and objectives of European Union law.

Part I provides an introduction to the topic. It considers not only the early stages of European Economic Community intervention in the cultural field, but also the possible motivations behind the adoption of Title XII of the EC Treaty, and with it the key culture Article, Article 151, which is set out in full in the frontispiece. Initially, the economic freedoms guaranteed in the EEC Treaty were used by traders to hammer away at national rules designed to exclude foreign goods and services on cultural grounds. Though framed in terms of a conflict between economic and cultural interests, these disputes were ultimately about the legitimacy, from the Community's perspective, of Member State attempts to preserve cultural practices by legal means. National rules of this type result in a form of cultural closure, impeding foreign goods and services from obtaining access to the domestic market. The economic liberalism enshrined in the Economic Community is not only a cultural manifestation in its own right, but has latent within it certain cultural preferences. Economic integration can lead to more culturally diverse societies, but, to be successful, also requires that those societies be culturally open. Framing the early Community law challenges to domestic standards in terms of a clash between economic and cultural values may thus obscure the cultural prerequisites which lie behind the operation of the internal market.

From the beginning, therefore, Community law was suspicious of any attempt to close off national markets through legal means. By knocking down domestic regulation of this type, and encouraging cross-border trade, Community law exposes the individual to a new environment of choice. Any consequent demise in traditional goods or services can then be justified on the basis of consumer preferences, provided always that the consumer has access to the information necessary to make an informed decision—a requirement which explains the Community's active involvement in the field of product labelling. There can thus be no doubt that European Community law, from its inception, posed a challenge not only to the economic but also to the cultural policies of the Member States.

The theme of culture and commerce is developed in Part II, in which Niamh Nic Shuibhne ventures into the area of labelling and considers whether cultural diversity should be afforded greater prominence in the context of the free movement of goods, above and beyond its present status as an offshoot of consumer protection; Stephen Weatherill explores how Community institutions have responded to cultural arguments in the increasingly commercialized field of sport; and Andrea Biondi considers what leeway has been afforded Member States to restrict the trade in cultural goods in order to preserve their cultural heritage.

The initial stage of Community intervention in the cultural field may have constituted a direct assault on the use of law in an attempt to preserve indigenous traditions, but this was tempered by a growing recognition on the part of the Community institutions, and in particular by the Court of Justice, that certain domestic regulations pursued legitimate policy objectives and were not simply designed to protect domestic economies. The maintenance of such rules nevertheless ensured continuing barriers to cross-border trade and encouraged the Community itself to enact legislation to approximate national laws in these areas. Particular Community measures indicate some awareness that the market will not always further choice and that, whether or not supported by domestic regulation, distinctive goods and services may come under threat in the wider internal market. A number of Community regulations passed in the 1990s were, for example, designed to ensure that culturally specific goods, associated with a particular geographic area, would not be devalued through poor quality imitations.[4] But producers may themselves decide to modify their products in order to reach a larger and more diverse market, leading to homogenization and a loss of authenticity. Traditional French, Greek, and Italian food is, for instance, popular throughout Europe, but is often modified for external consumption, or produced abroad in a modified form. In consequence, although Europeans now have access to a greater diversity of produce, much of it has an ersatz, synthetic quality: multiculturalism packaged for the mass market.

Consideration of Community law and its impact on what we eat highlights the difficulty of establishing simple cause and effect in the cultural context.

[4] Council Regulation (EEC) No 2081/92 on the Protection of Geographical Indications and Designations of Origin for Agricultural Products and Foodstuffs, OJ [1992] L 208/1; and see also Council Regulation (EEC) No 823/87 Laying down Special Provisions Relating to the Quality of Wines Produced in Specified Areas, OJ [1987] L 84/59. The European Community is now seeking to ensure protection for such foods, e.g. Parma Ham, also at the international level.

The Community clearly has the capacity to exert considerable influence in this area, by, for example, altering production patterns through common agricultural policy subsidies; offering protection to commercial rights along the lines indicated above; or through health and hygiene regulations that affect how goods are produced or sold. But the survival of authentic goods and services is clearly dependent on the operation of a complex range of forces which operate both above and below the Community level: on the continuing willingness of national or local authorities to support small businesses, whether producers or distributors, and to take into account their needs in the planning context; as well as on the purchasing and sales strategies of the large supermarket and multinational food production companies. Above all, in an increasingly affluent society, the survival of authentic products will depend on consumer preferences and life-style choices. As Felipe Fernández-Armesto notes: '[a]n artisanal reaction is underway. Local revulsion from pressure to accept the products of standardized taste has stimulated revivals of traditional cuisines . . . The priorities of fast food already seem as outmoded as futurism or vorticism: they belong to an already bygone era, which was exhilarated by the novelties of speed.'[5]

Though traditional cuisines may not yet be a thing of the past, an awareness on the part of the public that membership of the European Economic Community was affecting certain of the familiar fundamentals of everyday life led to growing suspicion of further European integration. From the late 1970s onwards, the Community's pro-European élite, and in particular the Commission, began to consider the potential consequences of this alienation and explore how individuals might be encouraged to identify more closely with Europe's political institutions and policies, perhaps even to go beyond this and develop a distinct European identity. It is the theme of European identity that forms the focus of Parts II and III of this book.

Part III explores the role of the mass media, language, and education in the communication of culture and formation of identity. It considers the impact of Community law on existing domestic policies, and the coherence and clarity of Community objectives in these areas. Member States are keenly aware of the importance of the media, language, and education in the construction and consolidation of identity, and are extremely wary of any Community initiative which could weaken or marginalize national identity. The impact of these concerns is particularly apparent in the educational field, where Member States have proved reluctant to develop their domestic curricula in

[5] Fernández-Armesto, F, *Food, A History* (London: Pan, 2001), p 251.

order to increase awareness, if not acceptance, of the European Community as a political entity. As a result, the Commission has moved instead to introduce initiatives designed to increase mutual understanding among Europeans, such as the Socrates student exchange programme, which, it may be noted, also equips students to take advantage of the opportunities created by the internal market. Member State concerns over creeping 'Europeanization' may also explain the Community's failure, noted by Josh Holmes in Chapter 6, adequately to clarify its cultural objectives in the media field.

The blocking of Community initiatives at the governmental level does not, however, mean that further development in these areas is inevitably stalled. Yasemin Soysal has suggested that 'Europeanization' in fact occurs 'mainly outside intergovernmental structures and formal EU institutions, via informal institutional processes'.[6] Thus, in the field of education, the Community can still exert a degree of influence through facilitating, in coordination with other interested organizations such as the Council of Europe, the development of networks of specialists and interested bodies at the European level. It can also provide information and technical support. The creation and impact of such networks in the context of higher education is considered in Chapter 8 by Julian Lonbay.

The question of identity in an enlarging European Union is developed further in Part IV. Rachael Craufurd Smith considers the extent to which Article 151 can be used to foster a common European identity, while Theodora Kostakopoulou examines how Community law affects the civil status of those residing within the Member States; in particular, she suggests that recent Community initiatives in the field of asylum and immigration policy could ultimately affect deep-seated notions of nationality and identity.

It will be apparent from the foregoing that the European Union is not simply concerned with the removal of cultural barriers to the operation of the internal market; it has other political objectives which cross over into the cultural field. Moreover, the European Union has embedded within it certain values, such as respect for the rule of law and fundamental rights, which are widely regarded as cultural, though clearly not restricted to the European context. European Union law requires Member States to respect and implement these values, however much they conflict with established domestic practices. This is in stark contrast to the situation where Community law strikes down a national rule enforcing a domestic practice: in this latter instance, though the practice can no longer be required as a matter of domestic

[6] Soysal, Y N, 'Locating Europe', *European Societies*, 4(3) (2002), 265, at 272.

law, it is not precluded and may still survive as a result of individual consumer preferences.

Part V of this book considers the role played by culture in the European Union's external relations. It is tempting, when examining European Union cultural policy, to adopt an inward-looking perspective, focusing on the impact of European Union law on those living within the European Union. There is, however, an external dimension to European Union cultural policy which is expressly noted in the third paragraph of Article 151 of the EC Treaty. This states that the European Community and Member States are to 'foster cooperation with third countries and the competent international organisations in the sphere of culture, in particular the Council of Europe'. Given that many of the central questions relating to culture, the impact of globalization, for example, have relevance well beyond the borders of the European Union, international cooperation can offer many benefits. Relations with the Council of Europe are here particularly important, because the Council's membership embraces many of the most geographically proximate states to the European Union.

In Chapter 11, Joe McMahon considers how culture is deployed in the Community's development programmes and in its negotiations over world trade. Cultural concerns have led Member States to withhold their audio-visual sectors from the liberalization process established by the General Agreement on Trade in Services (GATS), and cultural arguments have been deployed by the Community in the context of agriculture, with landscape protection and animal welfare being employed, for example, in an attempt to justify the grant of agricultural subsidies. The feasibility of reaching political agreement to amend the World Trade Organization agreements on goods (GATT) and services to include a general cultural derogation is, however, virtually non-existent, and McMahon considers that the position of those countries wishing to subsidize particular cultural activities, or even restrict trade directly, could be strengthened by the adoption of a separate treaty on cultural diversity. There are currently a number of proposals for such a treaty, which is seen as a potential counterweight to GATT and GATS, and UNESCO has recently undertaken preliminary work with a view to presenting proposals for such a convention at its next general conference in autumn 2005. There remain, however, many important issues which have still to be fully addressed, most centrally, how such a treaty would relate to the existing World Trade Organization agreements. In Chapter 12, Olaf Weber considers in more detail the extent to which cultural considerations can be taken into account in the operation of GATT and GATS, and contrasts this with the operation of cultural derogations in European Community law.

When looking through the various chapters in this book one is struck not only by their diversity in terms of subject matter, but also by the recurrence of particular themes. Paul Kearns, in his conclusion, isolates a number of these cross-cutting issues, for example, the uncertainty surrounding the nature of the concept of culture, and the difficulty faced by the Community institutions when called to balance cultural and other competing policy considerations. Given their importance to an understanding of the relationship between European Union law and culture, it may also be helpful to consider one or two of these issues here at the very beginning, by way of a short introduction.

Perhaps one of the most central questions is whether the Community needs, and has in fact developed, a definition of culture. Although the European Community Treaty includes a title on 'culture', there is no attempt in Article 151 to define the term. Nor is there such a definition in Article 87 of the EC Treaty, which, in paragraph 3(d), authorizes the grant of state aid in order to 'promote culture and heritage conservation'. This, in itself, should not be considered particularly surprising. Although certain Treaty articles do define their subject matter—Title II on agriculture, for example, defines 'agricultural products' as 'the products of the soil, of stock-farming and of fisheries ...'—other titles, such as that on the environment, do not attempt such a definition, and instead set out specific objectives to be pursued in their particular area. Adoption of this latter approach in Article 151 serves, however, only to postpone, rather than avoid, controversy over the meaning of the word 'culture'. This is because the objectives in Article 151 are themselves framed in terms of support for culture, whether it be the 'culture of the Member States' or the 'common cultural heritage'.[7]

Raymond Williams's observation that 'culture' is one of the two or three most complex words in the English language has often been quoted, but within the European Union there is the added complication that the meaning of the term 'culture'—or *Kultur*, or *cultura* etc.—may shift subtly from one Member State to another.[8] Not only can the term have local peculiarities, it also displays a marked capacity for evolution over time, reflecting the particular preoccupations of the day. It has, for example, been variously used to indicate that which is civilized or cultivated; the everyday practices of a given society; or artistic and intellectual work of agreed value.[9] Its use is thus at

[7] Article 151(1), EC Treaty.

[8] Williams, R, *Keywords* (London: Fontana, 1983) and, for discussion of differing national conceptions of the term, see Eagleton, T, *The Idea of Culture* (Oxford: Blackwell, 2000), pp 9–13, and Paul Kearns, in Chapter 13 of this volume, at text following n 20. See also text accompanying n 30 below.

[9] For wide-ranging and lucid discussion, see Eagleton, above n 8, ch 1.

times normative, marking out what is thought to be good or valuable in society; at others merely descriptive, embracing even practices, for example criminal, that are dangerous or harmful. Culture can include the most esoteric of belief systems and the most mundane of traditions; it encompasses and gives meaning to social relations; it can form the basis of identity. For Niklas Luhmann it constitutes the memory of society, a memory which is inherently selective.[10]

Culture, used as a legal term of art, thus begins to appear rather unsatisfactory, in that not only is its meaning contested but it is also capable of embracing virtually all forms of human and, as Paul Kearns notes, possibly also animal interaction.[11] Niklas Luhmann has consequently suggested that, rather than attempt to link the term to particular, concrete social manifestations, we should instead consider it a concept with which to explore the meaning of difference.[12] When we refer to culture we do so in order to distinguish one group from another, one practice from another, and these distinctions are drawn for a variety of social and political purposes. The introduction of the culture title in the European Community Treaty is indeed a manifestation of a growing pre-occupation with difference and its consequences within an expanding European Union. Article 151 requires policy makers at the European level to consider what weight and importance should be ascribed to these differences and whether steps at the European, as opposed to national, level should be taken in response to them.

The culture title focuses our attention not only on the differences that exist *between* Member States, but also on the potential tensions caused by the growing cultural diversity *within* Member States, diversity which is itself a product, at least in part, of Community law. But to discuss difference also requires one to have an idea of what is similar, in that the concept of difference has meaning only where the various objects or practices under consideration are comparable. The culture title thus leads us to consider not only differences but also similarities at the European level, and creates a forum in which to discuss their implications for European integration. This, ultimately, feeds into the wider debate about European identity and may lead to the drawing of further distinctions, this time between 'Europe' and the rest of the world.

[10] On this aspect of culture, see Luhmann, N, *Die Gesellschaft der Gesellschaft* (Suhrkamp, Frankfurt a. M, 1997), ch 3, XIII '*Gedächtnis*', pp 576–94.

[11] Philip Allott, in his book *Eunomia: New Order for a New World* (Oxford: OUP, 1990), para 18.1, p 376, suggests that the culture of a society 'is the society seen as a whole, all that it has made of itself as actuality, all that it has conceived of itself as possibility'. On animal culture, see Paul Kearns, Chapter 13 of this volume, at n 26.

[12] Luhmann, n 10 above.

The potentially open-ended nature of the word 'culture' consequently necessitates careful examination of those differences which are considered relevant in legal discourse and the reasons for their identification. An abstract analysis of what culture *can* mean serves only to set the boundaries for such an examination, and it is interesting to note that the Commission itself has stated that it is unwilling to engage in '*academic argument* over the definition, purpose and substance of culture'.[13] Similarly, the Commission, in its 1996 *First Report on the Consideration of Cultural Aspects in European Community Action*, having discussed various possible definitions of 'culture', went on to conclude that it was 'not for an institution to define the content of the concept of culture' and that it intended to adopt a 'pragmatic approach'.[14] This, of course, does not absolve the Commission, or any other Community institution, from the responsibility of forming and articulating clearly its own view as to the 'nature, purpose and substance of culture' when applying or developing Community law in specific areas. There are indications that in certain contexts, for instance when applying derogations to fundamental Community law principles, the term 'culture' is given a narrower meaning than in others.[15] Ultimate authority for determining the meaning of Treaty provisions, including Article 151, rests with the Court of Justice.

It may thus be helpful to consider how the term 'culture' is used in Community law, and it is possible to identify a number of quite different functions. First, and perhaps most obviously, culture is deployed, primarily by the Member States, but also in some instances by legal persons, in an attempt to rein back and restrict the application of Community law. 'Culture' here lays bare the bundle of anxieties that surround European integration and its impact on national identity and established traditions. Its use is reactive, to preserve existing differences and prevent cross-cultural 'contamination'. The ability to rely on cultural arguments to restrain the reach of Community law stems both from judicial recognition, as in the *Cinéthèque* case, where the Court of Justice accepted that France could restrict the free movement of videocassettes in order to protect cinema distribution, and from direct recognition in the Treaty itself, as with the derogation for national treasures in Article 30 and the cultural exemption from the state aid rules in Article 87(3)(d).[16]

[13] European Commission, *Communication on Stronger Community Action in the Cultural Sector*, (1982) 15 Bull. EC, supp. 6/82, para 4 (emphasis added).

[14] European Commission, *First Report on the Consideration of Cultural Aspects in European Community Action*, COM(96) 160 final, at p 3.

[15] See text accompanying n 151 in Chapter 2.

[16] Cases 60 and 61/84, *Cinéthèque SA v Fédération Nationale des Cinémas Français* [1985] ECR 2605.

The onus in these situations is on the body or person seeking to rely on the derogation to establish that their cultural concerns are legitimate and compelling. One result of Community intervention in the cultural field is consequently to require Member States to articulate more clearly the basis for their own cultural policies. This is particularly apparent when one considers the way in which the Commission has used the Treaty state aid rules to push Member States into clarifying their reasons for funding public service broadcasting.[17] The Court of Justice or Commission is not, in such circumstances, required to elaborate a general theory of culture and, when accepting cultural arguments, may do little more than acknowledge that the body concerned has, or has not, made out a convincing case.

Given that it will often be difficult for a Member State to establish that legal intervention is necessary to protect a particular cultural practice, other justifications, potentially less inimical to the integration process, are frequently put forward. Many of the food quality cases, although at least in part about culture, are consequently framed in terms of consumer protection. Reliance on cultural arguments may also seem a risky strategy given that their weight, relative to other interests, within the Community legal system is far from clear. Article 151(4) merely calls for cultural considerations 'to be taken into account' when applying other Treaty articles, and there is nothing comparable to Article 95(3), which requires the Community, when introducing harmonizing legislation, to adopt a *high level* of protection for health, safety, and environmental and consumer protection. Culture is thus something of a joker in the pack, whose value is not pre-determined. This may lead to a suspicion that cultural arguments will tend to lose out when confronted with economic interests central to the European Community from its inception. Moreover, as it is usually possible to identify an economic rationale for domestic rules operating in the cultural domain, Member States run the risk that their legislation, though culturally motivated, will be considered to be primarily protectionist, and therefore unlawful.[18]

This does not, however, seem to be an inevitable result, and there are a number of cases in which the European Court of Justice has been willing to accept cultural over economic considerations.[19] Indeed, the uncertainty surrounding the scope and meaning of culture, coupled with its emotional pull, can lead to a possibly rather more surprising result, namely, undue deference

[17] For further details, see Josh Holmes, Chapter 6 of this volume.

[18] See text accompanying n 62, in Chapter 2, and the examination of the meaning of protectionism by Niamh Nic Shuibhne in Chapter 3 of this volume.

[19] See text accompanying n 53 in Chapter 2.

on the part of the Community institutions to socio-cultural claims. Culture here creates something of an analytical block. This is illustrated by the Community's treatment of sport, discussed by Stephen Weatherill in Chapter 4. Weatherill argues that although the Community institutions recognize that sport, as an activity, has special characteristics which necessitate some modification to the usual application of the Community competition and free movement rules, they do not always adequately analyse what is distinctive in socio-cultural terms about sport. Thus, concessions are made not only to rules which clearly have a legitimate sporting justification, for example, rules that prevent the last-minute transfer of players during a tournament in order to ensure fair competition between teams, but also to rules which do not, such as the football transfer rules.[20] Although the case law of the Court of Justice has undoubtedly led to significant modifications in the scope of the transfer rules, certain restrictions that prevent players from contracting freely, as in other professions, with their preferred employer appear to have been accepted by the Commission.[21] Cultural arguments *may* thus give additional weight, possibly quite considerable weight, to what are at least in part commercially motivated claims, and uncertainties over the nature of culture can work in favour of, as well as against, those who call it in aid in legal argument.

The increasing prominence of culture as a Community concern is not, however, solely the result of Member States' or regulatory bodies' deployment of cultural arguments in order to restrict the reach of Community law. Its prominence is also simply a reflection of its current economic importance. In EU countries such as the United Kingdom, agriculture plays a considerably reduced role in the domestic economy, traditional manufacturing industries such as coal and steel have long been in decline, and wealth increasingly stems from the provision of cultural goods and services, such as tourism, the media, and fashion. Europe's citizens have more money and time than ever before to expend on leisure activities, and industries that originally were regarded as marginal are now central to the economic success of the European Union.[22]

[20] See Cases C-176/96, *Jyri Lehtonen, Castors Canada Dry Namur-Braine ASBL v FRBSB* [2000] ECR I-2681 and C-415/93, *Union Royal Belge des Sociétés de Football Association ASBL and others v Jean-Marc Bosman* [1995] ECR I-4921. Certain sporting rules may help to preserve diversity in the way a game is played from one state to another, e.g., a rule restricting the number of non-national (EU) players who can be fielded in any given match, yet they would be unlawful as discriminatory under Community law, on which see the ruling in *Bosman*, above.

[21] For details of the reform of the FIFA rules governing international transfers, see [2001] 4 CMLR Antitrust Reports 940.

[22] Tourism currently employs 9 million people in Europe and accounts for 5.5% of GDP: 2003 figures provided by the Commission at http://europa.eu.int/comm/regional_policy/themes/cultur_en.htm.

Certain established industries are attempting to reposition themselves in the light of these developments. The farming community, for example, now seeks financial support in order to preserve, if not recreate, a particular form of man-made landscape, one which offers new possibilities as a recreational resource. The combination of economic and cultural concerns renders such claims particularly potent, and it is consequently important to maintain a clear distinction between economic and cultural arguments. Cultural arguments, as noted above in the context of sport, may be used to add superficial weight to an unattractive commercial initiative, while commercial initiatives, though possibly quite beneficial from a cultural perspective, may result in irreparable cultural damage if exploited inappropriately. Uncontrolled tourism, for example, can degrade, or even destroy, the very culture on which it is based.

The Community consequently recognizes the economic potential of culture, warranting its support and intervention. This support takes a number of different forms. On the one hand, the Community can seek to establish a favourable regulatory environment for cultural creation; on the other, it can provide funding for cultural industries or initiatives which are likely to be profitable and lead to new employment opportunities. Intervention of the first type, which imposes limited costs on the Community itself, may be illustrated by the various Community directives relating to copyright and neighbouring rights, designed to offer a high level of protection for Europe's creative community.[23] One might equally note here the establishment by the Community, against bitter opposition from the UK which feared for its established art market, of a resale right for artists.[24] In this instance the economic interests of artists were pitted against the economic interests of the major European art trading companies. Though there is clearly a risk here that trade might in future be diverted to third countries, the Community is mindful of the need to protect Europe's cultural industries from adverse external competition, to the extent permitted by its international obligations.[25] A familiar, if controversial, example is the 'requirement', established in the 1989 Television Without Frontiers Directive, that television broadcasters, located within the EU, allocate a majority of their broadcasting time to European works.[26] The

[23] See, e.g., Council Directive 93/98/EEC Harmonizing the Term of Protection of Copyright and Certain Related Rights, OJ [1993] L 290/9.

[24] European Parliament and Council Directive 2001/84/EC on the Retail Right for the Benefit of the Author of an Original Work of Art, OJ [2001] L 272/32.

[25] These concerns are reflected in Article 8 of the artists' resale right directive, above n 24, which allows for staggered implementation over a considerable period of time.

[26] Council Directive (89/552/EEC) on the Coordination of Certain Provisions Laid Down by Law, Regulation or Administrative Action in Member States Concerning the Pursuit of Television

quota, dubiously based on the right to free movement of services, was intended to protect European producers from American and Japanese competition, though, as Olaf Weber notes, it is equally capable of deterring the importation of independent Asian, African, and South-American movies.[27]

Intervention of the second type is illustrated by the three MEDIA programmes, designed to support television and film production and distribution, as well as by the various structural funds that finance a wide range of projects with a cultural dimension.[28] It must be emphasized that these funds support cultural initiatives only to the extent that they further the Community's industrial and economic objectives, on which these measures are directly based. By contrast, the Community's flagship cultural programme, Culture 2000, is founded explicitly on Article 151 with the remit to: enhance knowledge of the history and culture of European peoples; encourage cultural creativity and innovation; ensure the widest possible dissemination of knowledge and good practice in the conservation field; promote greater access to, and participation of, citizens in cultural activities; and, lastly, foster inter-cultural dialogue between the EU and the outside world.[29] As a result, assistance can be provided under the Culture 2000 programme specifically for cultural ends, regardless of whether the project is likely to have any economic or industrial benefits.

The preceding discussion has highlighted three key roles that culture currently performs within the Community legal system. First, a constraint on Community action, where domestic customs and practices appear to be threatened. Secondly, a basis for market intervention, whether in the form of regulation or through financial subsidies, on economic or industrial grounds. Thirdly, a basis for Community action in its own right under Article 151. It will also be apparent from the quotation from Commissioner Reding, noted at the start of this introduction, that certain influential members of the Community continue to see a central role for Community cultural policy in the process of European integration.[30] Not only are important values, such as

Broadcasting Activities, OJ [1989] L 298/23, as amended by European Parliament and Council Directive 97/36/EC, OJ [1997] L 202/60, Articles 4 and 6.

[27] See text following n 95 in Chapter 12 of this volume.

[28] See, e.g., Council Decision No 2000/821/EC on the Implementation of a Programme to Encourage the Development, Distribution and Promotion of European Audiovisual Works, OJ [2001] L 13/34. The Decision establishes the most recent MEDIA plus programme and is based on Article 157(3).

[29] European Parliament and Council Decision No 508/2000/EC Establishing the Culture 2000 Programme, OJ [2000] L 63/1.

[30] See also the speech by Romano Prodi, entitled 'Enlargement of the Union and European identity', given at the European University Institute, Florence, on 20 January 2003, available at http://europa.eu.int/comm/commissioners/prodi/sp . . . /firenze_en.ht.

tolerance and respect for diversity, considered to be culturally rooted, but culture is regarded as a useful tool in the drive to create a sense of solidarity and belonging among Europeans, particularly in the light of the Union's impending eastward extension. Such a task is compounded by the fact that perceptions of culture vary considerably between west and central/east European countries, because of their divergent histories. In those countries previously subject to Communist regimes, government deployment of culture for propaganda purposes has not been forgotten and citizens remain particularly sensitive to questions of nationality and language use.[31]

It is, moreover, questionable whether the commitment to draw out and emphasize those cultural aspects which Europeans share and hold in common, sits quite as easily as the Commission suggests alongside its other objective to help preserve, and increase popular understanding of, cultural diversity among and within the Member States. Member States are inevitably suspicious of any attempt to underline the existence of a common culture, in that they see its potential to bring into question existing (national) allegiances and frames of reference. Thus, Romano Prodi has suggested that 'European identity is inextricably linked to a new type of citizenship based on multiple forms of allegiance, ranging from the local town to the Union. The single national identity would be replaced by complementary identities.'[32] National histories will inevitably be relativized in such a process, with regional and transnational concerns receiving new emphasis. Tensions of this type help to explain why the operation of Article 151 has been so carefully circumscribed, in particular through lack of funds and the requirement that any implementing measures receive unanimous support in Council. If a new constitution for the European Union is ultimately adopted along the lines proposed by the Convention in July 2003 then matters falling within the scope of what is now Article 151 will instead be determined by majority voting in the Council, though unanimity is likely to be retained for international trade negotiations concerning culture and audio-visual services. Moreover, the July 2003 text continues to mark out culture as an area where Community action is largely subsidiary to that of the Member States. Even if one accepts that the subsidiarity principle leaves the Community considerable room for manoeuvre, and that qualified majority voting, if adopted, would make it easier for the Council to agree additional funding for cultural projects, the present economic climate renders it extremely unlikely that the Community will significantly increase its funding

[31] Stadler, B, *'Eastward Expansion' in the Cultural Sector. Reports from Central and East European Members of Cultural Networks*, study commissioned for Kulturkontakt and IG Kultur Österreich, Vienna, 1998, and available at http://www.eipcp.net/.

[32] Prodi, above n 30, p 2.

for cultural activities in the near future. Absent such additional finance, action under Article 151 is likely to remain at best marginal.[33]

If Member States have been careful to keep a lid on the operation of Article 151 for political or financial reasons, or both, it must be remembered that cultural issues can surface in almost any area of European Union law, from external relations to the free movement of goods. Article 151 is consequently merely the visible tip of a much larger iceberg. This book attempts to describe certain of the configurations of that iceberg, both above and below the waterline, but there remain numerous crags and interstices still to be explored.

[33] An indication of how the Member States intend to apply the subsidiarity principle in the cultural sphere may be obtained from the Council Resolution of 19 December 2002 Implementing the Work Plan on European Cooperation in the Field of Culture: European Added Value and Mobility of Persons and Circulation of Works in the Cultural Sector, OJ [2003] C 13/5, para 9.

Part I

The Development of Cultural Policy by the European Community

2

Community Intervention in the Cultural Field: Continuity or Change?

*Rachael Craufurd Smith**

'Homogenization' and 'convergence' are hallowed in western Europe like hard-to-please deities, to whom member peoples of the European community have to sacrifice peculiar traditions and tastes.[1]

. . . proximity can adulterate identity, but it can also refine it; for all human groups define themselves by means of self-differentiation from their neighbours. Immersion in multicultural states, which will continue to be a typical experience for increasing members of communities in the next century, may protect distinctive traditions, mentalities, and values from erosion at long range in the global village.[2]

There was little in the European Economic Treaty, as originally drafted in 1957, to indicate that Community competence could extend to cultural affairs. Only two Articles overtly suggested that the Community might be active in the cultural field: Article 36 EEC (now 30 EC), which allows Member States to restrict imports and exports in order to protect 'national treasures possessing artistic, historic or archaeological value', and Article 131 EEC (now 182 EC), which concerns Community association with third countries in order, *inter alia*, to assist their 'cultural development'. Thirty-five years were to elapse before the EEC Treaty was amended by the 1992 Treaty on European Union to include among the Community's activities 'a contribution . . . to the flowering of the cultures of the Member States'.[3] This commitment was further developed in a new Treaty Article specifically concerned with culture, now Article 151, and an additional discretionary exemption in the field of state aids for aid that promotes culture and heritage conservation, now Article 87(3)(d). The preamble to the Treaty on European Union notes

* Europa Institute, University of Edinburgh. I would like to thank Bruno de Witte, Niamh Nic Shuibhne, and Sean Smith for their helpful suggestions on earlier drafts of this chapter.

[1] Fernández-Armesto, F, *Millenium, A History of the Last Thousand Years* (New York, London: Scribner, 1995), p 729.

[2] Ibid.

[3] Article 3q.

the desire of the contracting parties to 'deepen the solidarity between their peoples while respecting their history, their culture and their traditions'. Most recently, the Charter of Fundamental Rights, approved in Nice in December 2000, provides in Article 22 that the 'Union shall respect cultural, religious and linguistic diversity'.

Despite there being, until 1993 when the Treaty on European Union came into force, no specific basis for Community action in the cultural field, the Community nevertheless profoundly affected, through its free movement, competition law, and fiscal provisions, national traditions and ways of life. This chapter examines whether, during the period prior to the adoption of Article 151, it is possible to discern any particular approach on the part of the Community institutions when faced with issues of cultural policy. It then considers the reasons underlying the adoption of Article 151 and whether this Article establishes clear foundations on which Community cultural policy can be constructed in the future.

1. Community intervention in the cultural domain: rhetoric and reality

Support for Community intervention in the cultural field was furnished fairly early on in a number of high-profile reports on the future of Europe.[4] These reports tended to take an essentially instrumental view of Community action in the cultural domain, as designed to further distinct political and social objectives. The success of the Community as a political institution was thought to require a cultural frame of reference, on which an enduring sense of allegiance could be based. This is particularly marked in the 1975 *Report on European Union* prepared by Leo Tindemans, Belgian Prime Minister, at the request of the European Council.[5] Noting that public support for European integration had initially stemmed from horror at the devastation of the Second World War and that memories of the war were beginning to fade, he looked for a new foundation on which popular commitment to the Community could be based. For this, he argued that the Community needed to be seen to play a positive role in everyday life, including cultural matters. The European Union, he concluded, had to 'make itself felt in education and culture, news

[4] Tindemans, L, *Report on European Union*, (1976) 9 Bull. EC, supp. 1/76, and Adonnino, P, *Second Report on a People's Europe*, (1985) 18 Bull. EC, supp. 7/85, at p 17.

[5] Tindemans, above n 4.

and communications, it must be manifest in the youth of our countries and in leisure time activities'.[6] Similar sentiments were expressed in the second Adonnino *Report on a People's Europe*, which noted that its proposals concerning citizenship rights, education, culture, communication, and the image of the Community would be 'meaningful to the citizen in various aspects of his daily life' and would make a 'substantial contribution to the realization of an ever closer union among the peoples of Europe'.[7]

The expression of such sentiments undoubtedly expanded the parameters of the debate over the future of European integration but had no direct impact on Community competence in the cultural field. In order to understand how the Community was able to introduce concrete cultural initiatives it is necessary instead to consider the activities of the various Community institutions. The approaches taken by these institutions have at times seemed distinctly paradoxical. The absence, for example, of an express basis for cultural action in the EEC Treaty led the Commission to stress its limited competence in cultural affairs. Nevertheless, official statements of caution belie the fact that the Commission, from the late 1970s onwards, was actively promoting a number of cultural measures. By contrast, the Member States were keen to emphasize at their European summit meetings the cultural and social aspects of European integration. Public support, it was felt, could not be assured on the basis of economic gains alone. When, however, representatives of the Member States in the Council came to consider concrete projects with a cultural dimension, concerns over Community competence in the cultural field, the appropriateness of the cultural objectives being pursued, or their financial implications frequently surfaced to impede or block agreement.[8]

The caution expressed by the Commission over action in this area was consequently not simply a response to the lack of an appropriate Treaty article. The Commission would also have been aware that any Community measure primarily motivated by cultural concerns would be problematic for certain Member States. This was undoubtedly so for Germany, where competence for cultural matters rests with the *Länder*; for countries such as Denmark, ever vigilant to prevent Community law encroaching further into the national domain; and for the UK, particularly keen during the Prime Ministership of Mrs Thatcher to contain Community expenditure. It was also recognized that

[6] Ibid., p 12. [7] Adonnino, above n 4, at p 18.

[8] For detailed discussion of the development of Community cultural policy, see Loman, J M E, Mortelmans, K J M, Post, H H G, and Watson, J S, *Culture and Community Law Before and After Maastricht* (Deventer: Kluwer, 1992), and, more recently, Nic Shuibhne, N, *Minority Language Policy: Culture, Citizenship and Fundamental Rights* (The Hague: Kluwer, 2002).

Community cultural initiatives could cause friction with international organizations already established in the field, notably the Council of Europe.

These concerns are reflected in the restraint apparent in the Commission's 1977 and 1982 communications on culture. The 1977 paper entitled *Community Action in the Cultural Sector* distinguished the 'cultural sector' from 'culture' and argued that Community support for the cultural sector could not be said to constitute a 'cultural policy'.[9] In its 1982 paper, *Stronger Community Action in the Cultural Sector*, the Commission argued that its intervention in the cultural field had to be based on similar economic and social arguments deployed in other areas of activity.[10] Its task was primarily to facilitate free trade in cultural goods and to improve the living and working conditions of those in the cultural sector. It was not the role of the Community to become involved in 'academic argument over the definition, purpose and substance of culture or to arrogate any executive powers or even the slightest guiding function'.[11] Nor was its role to coordinate the Member States' cultural policies: this was a matter properly left to the Council of Europe. Well into the 1980s, therefore, the Commission was of the view that although it was legitimate for the Community to apply well-established free movement and competition law principles to the cultural sector, it had no jurisdiction to develop distinct cultural policies.

Early forays into the cultural field consequently tended to be cautious and largely symbolic, such as the setting up of the European Community Youth Orchestra, the European sculpture competition, and the European City of Culture programme.[12] Intervention was also eclectic, ranging from support for architectural preservation to the translation of books. The Treaty free movement Articles, coupled with specific provisions relating to industrial policy and education, nevertheless afforded the Commission scope to develop significant initiatives in particular fields and, during the course of the 1980s, it proposed a number of important measures relating to education and the audio-visual sector.[13] By the end of the decade the tenor of the Commission's

[9] Commission of the European Communities (hereafter 'European Commission'), *Communication on Community Action in the Cultural Sector*, (1977) II Bull. EC, supp. 6/77, introduction at para 3. The growing awareness of the importance of cultural issues was reflected in the creation of a 'cultural problems' division within the Commission in the mid-1970s.

[10] European Commission, *Communication on Stronger Community Action in the Cultural Sector*, (1982) 15 Bull. EC, supp. 6/82.

[11] Ibid., introduction, at para 4.

[12] For details see Forrest, A, 'La dimension culturelle de la Communauté Européenne', *Revue du Marché Commun*, (1987) 307, at 326.

[13] See, e.g., European Commission, *Green Paper on the Establishment of the Common Market for Broadcasting, especially by Satellite and Cable*, COM(84) 300 final, and, for discussion of initiatives in the education field, Theiler, T, 'The European Union and the "European Dimension" in Schools: Theory and Evidence', *European Integration*, 21 (1992) 307.

documents had changed dramatically, in response both to waning popular support for European integration and the growing economic value of cultural goods and services. In its 1987 communication entitled *A Fresh Boost for Culture in the European Community*, it concluded that increased Community activity in the cultural sector was 'a political and economic necessity given the twin goals of completing the internal market by 1992 and progressing from a People's Europe to European Union'.[14] The document is notable for its emphasis on the need for a cultural dimension to European integration in order to create a sense of solidarity and secure popular support.

Though the Commission was initially reticent about the appropriateness of developing Community cultural policies, other institutions expressed considerable support for the idea that the Community should have a cultural dimension. As we have noted, the Heads of State or Government emphasized that the Community was more than simply an economic union. The final communiqué of the Hague Summit of 1969, for example, noted that Europe was an 'exceptional seat of development, culture and progress', which it was imperative to preserve.[15] Similar sentiments may be found in the final declaration of the 1972 Paris Summit, which stated that economic expansion was not an end in itself; rather, it was valuable only to the extent that it improved the quality of life and living standards of Member State citizens, with particular attention needing to be paid to intangible values.[16] The 1984 Fontainebleau Summit concluded that it was necessary for the Community to adopt measures 'to strengthen and promote its identity and its image both for its citizens and for the rest of the world'.[17] It was this latter summit that set up the Adonnino Committee with a mandate to put forward suggestions concerning Community symbols, such as a flag and anthem, the formation of European sports teams, the minting of a European coinage, and the twinning of children's classes.[18]

Despite Member State recognition that European integration required more than simply the removal of economic barriers to trade, adoption of a specific culture Article was not high enough on the agenda at the 1985 intergovernmental conference to result in a Treaty amendment. The proposal was consequently dropped in the horse-trading that led to agreement of the

[14] European Commission, *A Fresh Boost for Culture in the European Community*, (1987) 20 Bull. EC, supp. 4/87, p 6.

[15] (1970) I Bull. EC, ch 1, point 4 of the Communiqué.

[16] (1972) I Bull. EC, ch 1, point 3 of the Declaration. See also the 1973 Copenhagen Summit *Declaration on European Identity*. This recognized that it was the 'diversity of cultures within the framework of common European civilization, the attachment to common values and principles' as well as 'the increasing convergence of attitudes to life' which gave 'the European Identity its originality and its own dynamism': (1973) Bull. EC 12/73 at 2501, para 3.

[17] European Council meeting at Fontainebleau, *Conclusions of the presidency*, (1985) 18 Bull. EC, supp. 7/85, at p 5.

[18] Ibid.

Single European Act.[19] It was to be a further six years before sufficient support for such an amendment could be mustered at Maastricht. Even then, the UK was opposed to the new Article 128 (now 151) and, though it did not block its introduction, it nevertheless sought to ensure that the Article was drafted in such a way that its impact would be limited.[20]

Nor were the representatives of the Member States in the Council consistently supportive of Commission proposals that displayed a marked cultural element. Proposals in particular fields brought to the surface domestic preoccupations with national identity and sovereignty, so that their passage was often difficult, if not impossible. The Commission's early initiatives in the field of education, for example, were actively opposed by both Denmark and France on competence grounds,[21] while the 1989 Television Without Frontiers Directive, which laid the foundations for an internal market in television broadcasting, was passed in the Council but with both Denmark and Belgium voting against it.[22] Member States have in the past used state education and public broadcasting systems to create or shore up a sense of national identity; it is therefore little wonder that they were wary of attempts by the Commission to introduce a European dimension into the state curriculum and national broadcasting.[23]

The development of individual allegiance to political institutions may have been regarded by the Member States as a zero-sum game: increasing identification with 'Europe' as a political entity through initiatives in the educational and media fields could only be achieved at the cost of a reduction in individual allegiance to the nation state. Such concerns undoubtedly underpinned the Amsterdam Treaty amendment to Article 17, introduced to overcome Danish

[19] De Zwaan, J W, 'The Single European Act: Conclusion of a Unique Document', CMLRev, 23 (1986), 747, at pp 755 and 759.

[20] Collins, R, *Broadcasting and Audio-visual Policy in the European Single Market* (London: John Libbey, 1994), p 24, n 1.

[21] See discussion by Theiler, above n 13.

[22] *Council Directive on the coordination of certain provisions laid down by law, regulation or administrative action in Member States concerning the pursuit of television broadcasting activities* (the 'Television Without Frontiers Directive') OJ [1989] L 298/23. The passage of the Directive is discussed by Collins, above n 20, at p 71, and a brief overview of its content is provided by Olaf Weber in Chapter 12 of this volume. For more general discussion of Community audio-visual policy, see Theiler, T, 'Why the European Union failed to Europeanize its Audiovisual Policy', in Cederman, L-E (ed), *Constructing Europe's Identity, The External Dimension* (London: Lynne Rienner, 2001), at p 125. The Commission has also experienced internal divisions given that the various Directorates-General may approach cultural issues from quite different perspectives.

[23] Gellner, E, in *Nations and Nationalism* (Oxford: Blackwell, 1983), p 34, argues that '[a]t the base of the modern social order stands not the executioner but the professor . . . The monopoly of legitimate education is now more important, more central, than the monopoly of legitimate violence'.

resistance, which provides that 'citizenship of the Union shall complement and not replace national citizenship'. It is, of course, questionable whether the capital of allegiance is limited in this way. Identification with Britain as a political unit does not, for example, appear to have diminished the Scots' sense of being Scottish, or the Welsh sense of being Welsh. On the contrary, national and sub-national sentiment may flourish within large state units, in that '[i]f history has a lesson, it is that whenever a big state is nested, smaller scale identities and political aspirations incubate under its shell until eventually they poke their beaks through the cracks and take flight'.[24]

Despite Council scepticism, if not outright opposition, towards Commission and European Parliament attempts to foster a 'European identity', other cultural initiatives were regarded as desirable, or at least as not worthy of significant opposition. The picture is consequently far from simple, and there was certainly support for targeted Community initiatives from those countries burdened with the heavy cost of maintaining major cultural sites and institutions. The Greek presidency of 1983, for example, was keen to emphasize the importance of protecting and promoting Europe's cultural heritage, and the Acropolis in Athens, along with a number of other important archaeological and architectural sites, has benefited from Community support. Even in the sensitive audio-visual field, some states, such as France, favoured selective Community intervention to protect their national film and television industry from American and Japanese competition, leading to the introduction of European television quotas in the 1989 Television Without Frontiers Directive.[25] But strategic consideration of cultural affairs requires institutional support and coordination. This was facilitated by the ministers responsible for culture meeting, at first informally, in 1983, and then formally from 1984, within the Council. A special committee to advise the Council on cultural affairs was established in 1988.[26]

The approach of the European Parliament was much less ambivalent, a staunch supporter of Community cultural action from the 1970s onwards. Not only did the Parliament call, in a number of resolutions, for the adoption of essentially cultural measures, it also successfully employed its budgetary powers to push through significant increases in the sums allocated for cultural purposes during the 1970s and 1980s.[27] Thus, in 1976, Community expenditure

[24] Fernández-Armesto, above n 1, at p 731. [25] See above n 22.

[26] Council of the Ministers Responsible for Cultural Affairs meeting within the Council, *Resolution of 27 May 1988 on the Future Organization of their Work*, OJ [1988] C 197/01, mirroring the European Commission's proposal to set up a Permanent Committee on Culture in its 1987 document, *A Fresh Boost for Culture in the European Community*, above n 14.

[27] European Parliament, *Resolution on Measures to Protect the European Cultural Heritage*, OJ [1974] C 62/5. This called for a wide range of initiatives relating, *inter alia*, to education,

in the field was fixed at only 20,700 ecus, while by 1986 it had risen to 3,500,000 ecus.[28] Brief mention might also be made at this point of the Committee of the Regions, which has recently taken a keen interest in cultural matters. The Committee of the Regions was, however, established only in 1992 by the Treaty on European Union, and it consequently played no part in the early stages of the development of Community cultural policy. It is made up of representatives of local and regional bodies and, given that its powers are purely advisory, its influence is limited.

The concrete activities of the Commission, Council, and European Parliament suggest that it is important to look behind the rhetoric to the reality of Community intervention, and such inspection reveals that the Community had little choice but to be involved in cultural affairs. As the Member States began to recover from the deprivations of the Second World War, individual leisure time and disposable incomes increased. This in turn stimulated the development of cultural industries and the wider consumption of cultural goods and services.[29] Culture and commerce are not mutually exclusive, and concerns over the commodification of culture date back to the writings of the Frankfurt School in the 1930s and beyond. Where this expanding trade in cultural goods and services extended across the borders of the various Member States, it fell within the scope of the EEC Treaty.

Gradually, therefore, producers, traders, and workers in the cultural field began to look to Community law to gain access to markets and employment in other Member States. Community guarantees of free movement were used to challenge domestic rules that protected distinct cultural practices, whether national, regional, or local, from outside competition. Such practices were not necessarily associated with the state itself, but were located within the nation state and thus considered to be in some way indigenous. Fiscal advantages for domestic goods and services could be challenged under Articles 12 and 95 of the EEC Treaty (now Articles 25 and 90), and state aid under Article 92 (now Article 87). Lastly, competition law could be used to strike down collusive or abusive practices by private undertakings operating in the cultural field.

The question of the balance to be struck between specific Treaty objectives and cultural concerns consequently arose in a number of distinct contexts.

exchange of cultural works, free movement of cultural workers, harmonization of taxes on cultural goods and services, and the provision of funds for restoration work and the training of professionals.

[28] Forrest, above n 12.

[29] These trends were discussed in the 1987 Florence Conference on Culture and its Relation with Technology and the Economy, documented in (1987) 20 Bull. EC 3/87, at points 1.1.2–1.1.4.

First, in proceedings, whether judicial or administrative, designed to enforce Community law. The Treaty provisions guaranteeing free movement for goods, services, and persons create individual rights that can be relied on directly in domestic courts to challenge national restrictions. In certain circumstances national courts may, and in some instances must, refer questions of Community law to the Court of Justice under the preliminary reference procedure set out in Article 234. The Commission or another Member State can also question the legitimacy of national measures before the Court of Justice under Articles 226 and 227.

The Commission's power to raise a potential infringement of Community law by a Member State under Article 226 can prove a useful tactical tool. Prior to the passage of the 1989 Television Without Frontiers Directive, for example, the Commission referred domestic Dutch and Belgian media laws to the Court in an attempt to weaken Member State opposition to its proposals.[30] The Commission is required before making a referral to enter into a formal exchange of opinions with the Member State concerning the legality of the national measure. There is consequently scope at this initial stage for the Commission to explore with the Member State how its cultural concerns can be accommodated, if at all, within the Community legal system. When enforcing the Community competition and state aid rules, the Commission has also been asked to take into account cultural considerations, though there is limited scope for this on the wording of Articles 81 and 82.[31]

Secondly, cultural considerations may also be important when the Community legislates. Where, for example, domestic barriers to trade are found to be legitimate on cultural grounds, the Commission has the power to propose draft legislation to approximate or coordinate the national rules under, for example, Article 95. The Council and European Parliament will then explore the weight to be afforded competing free trade and cultural concerns when deciding whether to adopt the measure as drafted, or to amend it.

In order to assess the impact of Community law on cultural practices and domestic traditions it is thus necessary to consider the distinct roles played by the judicial and legislative organs of the Community. With only the most marginal reference to cultural concerns in the EEC Treaty, there was clearly a risk that the cultural impact of Community policies would be sidelined, or even ignored. The following section consequently explores the weight afforded to

[30] Collins, above n 20, at p 68.

[31] See, e.g., Joint Cases T-528/93, T-542/93, and T-546/93, *Métropole Télévision SA, Reti Televisive Italiane, Gestevisión Telecinco SA and Antena 3 de Televisión v Commission* [1996] 5 CMLR 386 and the more general discussion of this issue in Loman et al., above n 8, ch 3.

cultural considerations by the various institutions prior to the introduction of Article 151, and whether it is possible to identify, even at this stage, distinct Community, as opposed to Member State, objectives in the cultural field.

2. The accommodation of cultural concerns in European Community law prior to the Treaty on European Union: a hidden cultural agenda?

(a) Culture and the Court of Justice

Owing to traders' willingness to use Community law to gain access to foreign markets, the Court of Justice was, from an early stage, required to assess national regulations designed to preserve indigenous practices and traditions. In addition, the Commission, as we have noted, was not averse to using its power to refer national regulations to the Court under Article 226. The Court responded to these complaints by emphasizing that cultural goods and services were not automatically excluded from the scope of the Treaty. In *Commission v Italy*, the Italian Government argued that art works could not be assimilated to ordinary 'consumer goods and articles of general use'.[32] The idea that there was a general cultural exemption was firmly rejected by the Court of Justice, which held that it was sufficient for the application of the Treaty that the art works could be valued in money and form the subject of commercial transactions.

Though the Treaty provisions have been given a broad scope by the Court, Member States have also been afforded considerable latitude when seeking to justify domestic regulations. The sole indication in the EEC Treaty that Member States might be able to derogate from its provisions on cultural grounds was contained in Article 36 (now Article 30) with its reference to measures designed to protect national treasures. Nevertheless, the Court's jurisprudence on mandatory requirements and general interest objectives has enabled Member States to justify restrictions on foreign goods or services on a wide range of social and cultural grounds. Such restrictions must, however, be both non-discriminatory and proportionate. Thus, domestic regulations designed to promote knowledge of a country's cultural patrimony,[33] diversity

[32] Case 7/68, *Commission v Italy* [1968] ECR 423.

[33] Case 220/83, *Commission v France* [1986] ECR 3663.

in the media,[34] the provision of quality television services,[35] a non-commercial Sunday,[36] and a competitive balance among sports clubs,[37] have all been held to pursue legitimate objectives under Community law, as have measures designed to protect national languages[38] and the film industry.[39]

Though Community law is in principle able to accommodate Member State policies in the cultural field, in practice many domestic regulations of this type have been found to be either disproportionate or discriminatory.[40] State regulations designed to protect traditional foods and indigenous broadcasting services have fared particularly badly. The Court has not, however, adopted a similarly rigorous approach in all instances, and it is worth considering the reasons for this variation. It is, of course, possible to point to the financial importance of the markets in food and audio-visual services, as well as the very direct impact of the restrictions on foreign trade, to explain the strict scrutiny exercised by the Court.[41]

In the food quality cases there were also indications that the Court considered it inappropriate in the context of the internal market for Member States to attempt to maintain particular traditions through excluding foreign alternatives. Where the foreign goods at issue were not intrinsically harmful, just different from their indigenous counterparts, the Court sought to open up markets and introduce a new dynamic of consumer choice. The Court's readiness to strike down Dutch restrictions on foreign television services may also have been motivated by a belief in the advantages of exposure to alternative cultures and individual selection, though there is no express statement to this effect in its judgments. Indeed, the rulings are striking for the absence of any detailed consideration given to the cultural arguments put forward by the Netherlands, or the potential ramifications of the decisions themselves for the Dutch broadcasting system.

An initial point to note is that Community law requires Member States to articulate the reasons for domestic regulations that restrict the free movement

[34] Case C-353/89, *Commission v Netherlands* [1991] ECR I-4069. [35] Ibid.

[36] Case 145/88, *Torfaen BC v B & Q plc* [1989] ECR 3851.

[37] Case C-415/93, *Union Royale Belge des Sociétés de Football Association ASBL v Jean-Marc Bosman* [1995] ECR I-4921.

[38] Case 379/87, *Groener v Minister for Education* [1989] ECR 3967.

[39] Cases 60 and 61/84, *Cinéthèque SA v Fédération Nationale des Cinémas Français* [1985] ECR 2605.

[40] Lane, R, 'New Competences Under the Maastricht Treaty', CMLRev, 30 (1993), 939, at pp 952 *et seq*.

[41] Elias Steyger suggests that the Court may have been more willing to intervene in areas where it was expected from the start that Community law would have a major effect, as in the field of foodstuffs: Steyger, E, *National Traditions and European Community Law* (Aldershot: Dartmouth, 1997), at pp 235–6.

of goods or services. Once a restriction on trade is established, the burden of establishing a convincing rationale rests with the state. Yet particular customs may be important not because of their intrinsic value, but because they order our lives and create a sense of familiarity and belonging. Indeed, the reasons behind many cultural practices have become lost over time, or are no longer particularly relevant.[42] The German rules relating to the composition of beer, discussed below, were, for example, initially introduced to prevent wheat being used for brewing rather than bread making, clearly not a current concern. Nevertheless, the chances of a Member State justifying its support for a particular tradition that restricts trade simply on the basis of custom, that this is 'the way things are done here', appear somewhat slim. Such rules threaten the very basis of the internal market, in which not only goods but also workers with different cultural expectations are guaranteed free movement from one Member State to another. For this reason Member States rarely support their measures directly on the basis of custom or tradition alone, and instead point to other rationales such as public health or consumer protection.

Perhaps the best known of the food quality cases are *Commission v Germany* and *Drei Glocken and Kritzinger v USL Centro-Sud and Bolzano*.[43] In *Commission v Germany*, foreign importers challenged the German *Reinheitsgebot*, or beer purity law, which dates back to the sixteenth century. This restricts the raw ingredients of beer to malted barley, hops, yeast, and water. In consequence, imported beers containing additives could not be sold in Germany under the designation 'Bier'. When challenged by the Commission, the German Government sought to justify these restrictions on both public health and consumer protection grounds. In particular, it argued that Germans had become accustomed to a particular quality of beer and would be misled by foreign products, designated 'Bier', which did not conform to that standard. In *Drei Glocken*, Italian rules restricting the sale in Italy of non-durum wheat pasta were contested. Similar consumer protection arguments to those raised in *Commission v Germany* were put forward by Italy, and found considerable support from Advocate General Mancini, who emphasized Italian expectations that pasta would be firm and *al dente* after cooking, a result attributed only to durum wheat.[44]

In both cases the Court concluded that the national measures were disproportionate: consumers could be protected by adequate labelling, indicating

[42] For a discussion of tradition and its relation to identity, see Glenn, H P, *Legal Traditions of the World* (Oxford: OUP, 2000), chs 1 and 2.

[43] Case 178/84, *Commission v Germany* [1987] ECR 1227 and Case 407/85, *Drei Glocken and Kritzinger v USL Centro-Sud and Bolzano* [1988] ECR 4233.

[44] Case 407/85, *Drei Glocken*, above n 43, at p 4253.

the nature of the ingredients.[45] This conclusion was facilitated by the fact that the two countries had argued that their measures were necessary to protect consumers from confusion rather than simply to maintain established standards. The Court recognized in the German beer case that consumer expectations might vary from one Member State to another, but it also emphasized that such expectations had the capacity to evolve over time within states. Repeating a phrase it had previously employed when examining UK excise duties, the Court held that Member States were not permitted to 'crystallize consumer habits' so as to consolidate any advantage enjoyed by the national industry.[46] Only when targeting their own producers do Member States retain the capacity to mandate, through legislation, traditional forms of production.[47]

In neither instance did the Court approve or disapprove of any particular cultural tradition; rather it questioned the legitimacy of Member State attempts to insulate domestic traditions from exposure to foreign alternatives through legislative fiat. The Court was not here mandating change, only an openness to change. Italians remain free to buy durum wheat pasta in line with their culinary traditions, and Germans can still indulge a preference for domestic beer, brewed in the traditional way. It is important to note, however, that the Court's emphasis on the pre-eminence of the market and rational consumer choice, though apparently culturally agnostic, has significant cultural ramifications. Where consumers buy products out of choice rather than tradition an important cultural change has taken place. It is a change that enhances the role of marketing and product branding as individuals are encouraged, through their selection of goods and services, to create for themselves particular lifestyles.

These rulings caused consternation among the Member States and further consideration was given as to how specialist producers could protect their products from poor quality imitations or false indications of origin. The answer lay in the field of commercial property rights. As early as 1975, in a case concerning German rules relating to wines and spirits, the Court accepted that designations of origin could constitute valuable forms of industrial or commercial property within Article 30 (previously Article 36).[48] As a result, national regulations providing for the authentication and enforcement

[45] Case 178/84, *Commission v Germany*, above n 43, at para 35, in the case of the restriction on additives this was held to be too overarching; Case 40/85, *Drei Glocken*, above n 43, at para 16.

[46] Case 178/84, *Commission v Germany*, above n 43, at para 32, referring to Case 170/78, *Commission v United Kingdom* [1980] ECR 417.

[47] Case 237/82, *Jongeneel Kaas v Netherlands* [1984] ECR 483.

[48] Case 12/74, *Commission v Germany* [1975] ECR 181.

of such designations could in principle be maintained, even though they restricted trade within the European Community. The Court nevertheless held that, as a derogation to the normal free market principles, such regulations would be closely scrutinized to ensure that they were both effective and proportionate. Thus, designations or indications of origin would be legitimate only where the product possessed qualities or characteristics which stemmed directly from its origination in a specific area. It was also necessary that the specified territory be carefully limited to that which related to the particular product. This latter requirement serves to prevent Member States from using designations of origin in a crude way to protect domestic production. It was consequently unlawful for Germany to permit a particular designation '*Sekt*' to be applied to sparkling wines produced throughout Germany, where geographic conditions varied significantly, as well as to wines produced in any other country where German was the official language. A similarly rigorous approach on the part of the Court may be detected in the first '*Rioja* case', decided in 1992.[49]

Though Article 30 was initially applied in a strict way by the Court of Justice, Member States have nevertheless continued to rely on designations or indications of origin in order to protect traditional products from external competition. Moreover, subsequent cases have not always been so exacting. Thus, in the 1992 *Exportur* case, which concerned Spanish restrictions on use of the designations '*Turrón de Jijona*' and '*Turrón de Alicante*' for nougat, the Court accepted that indications of provenance could relate to products which were not specially or intrinsically linked to a particular geographic area; it was enough that they had been traditionally produced there.[50] This broadens the scope of protection considerably, to goods which could equally well be produced outside a given geographic area but which happen historically to have originated in, and be positively associated with, that area. The Court of Justice has not, therefore, left the preservation of traditional products entirely to the forces of the market, but it is property rights, as opposed to culture, which act as the countervailing force. Indeed, the case law focuses on the prevention of unfair competition and wrongful exploitation of another product's reputation, not on the preservation of traditional goods as a cultural objective in its own right.

As with the early food quality cases, it is possible to detect a rigorous application of the proportionality test when assessing attempts by the Netherlands to regulate the inflow of commercial television channels broadcast from other

[49] Case C-47/90, *Delhaize v Promalvin* [1992] ECR I-3669.

[50] Case C-3/91, *Exportur v LOR SA and Confiserie du Tech* [1992] ECR I-5529.

Member States, notably Luxembourg.[51] The resultant dissipation of advertising revenues to foreign cable and satellite services threatened to undermine the viability of the Netherlands' domestic 'pillarized' broadcasting system. According to this system, air-time was allocated to representative social, cultural, and religious groups in order to reflect the make-up of Dutch society. After initial legislation targeting foreign television services was found to be discriminatory by the Court of Justice, new regulations were introduced that prohibited cable companies from relaying foreign channels unless they complied with requirements broadly similar to those applied to Dutch broadcasters. The new broadcasting law, or Mediawet, restricted not only the timing and amount of advertising on non-domestic channels, but also the structure and organization of the foreign broadcasting companies.

Though the Court of Justice recognized the legitimacy in principle of national measures designed to ensure a plural broadcasting system and the provision of quality programming, in the *Gouda* and *Commission v Netherlands* cases all the contested regulations were found to contravene Community law on the basis that they were either protectionist or disproportionate.[52] The restrictions on foreign advertisements aimed at the Dutch public were held to be protectionist, designed to insulate the Dutch advertising agency STER from competition, rather than motivated by cultural goals. Though the regulations clearly limited the amount of advertising revenue that foreign broadcasting companies could recoup, this might have been considered merely an inevitable consequence of the cultural policies pursued by the Netherlands. A prohibition on Sunday advertising will be of limited effect if foreign broadcasters can fill their Sunday schedules with advertisements. Similarly, an attempt to contain the pervasive nature of commercial advertising is unlikely to be successful if advertising limits apply solely to domestic operators. Rather than consider the regulations to be primarily cultural in object, with inevitable economic consequences, the Court instead considered the legislation to be motivated by a desire to shore up the economic health of the domestic broadcasting system and to be consequently unlawful.

The Court's unwillingness to accept the cultural rationale put forward by the Netherlands' Government is striking, given its plausible connection to the regulations at issue. Indeed, it seems to have been sufficient that the Mediawet had the effect of protecting the interests of the Dutch advertising

[51] In particular, Case C 352/89, *Bond van Adverteerders v Netherlands* [1988] ECR 2085; Case C-288/89, *Collectieve Antennevoorziening Gouda and Others v Commissariaat voor de Media* [1991] ECR I-4007; and Case C-353/89, *Commission v Netherlands* [1991] I-4069.

[52] Cases C-288/89, *Gouda*, and C-353/89, *Commission v Netherlands*, above n 51.

agency STER, there being no discussion of evidence indicating that the Netherlands was wholly or partly motivated by economic concerns. What does seem probable is that the Court was influenced by the fact that the Netherlands had previously introduced legislation, the Kabelregeling, designed to protect the Dutch broadcasting system from *all* foreign competition for advertising revenues. This legislation had been held by the Court to be unlawful.[53] But one cannot conclude from the fact that the Kabelregeling was unlawful that the Mediawet that replaced it, and which merely extended domestic regulations to foreign broadcasters, was similarly protectionist. The rulings also run counter to the prior *Debauve* case, which held that advertising restrictions applicable to all broadcasters, regardless of their place of establishment or nationality, would be legitimate under EC law pending the introduction of harmonizing legislation.[54]

The Court does note, however, that the Mediawet applied solely to advertising aimed at the Dutch public, namely, advertising contained in programmes in Dutch or with Dutch subtitles, and not to advertisements included in other foreign services relayed over the Dutch cable networks. Frustratingly, it draws no direct conclusions from this observation. On the one hand, it is arguable that the fact that the regulations did not apply to all foreign channels brought into question the genuineness of the cultural objectives said to underpin them. Only those services likely to be attractive to Dutch advertisers were targeted. But it must be remembered that the Netherlands was seeking to maintain the distinct nature of its domestic services, and for this it was sufficient to target foreign services specifically aimed at a Dutch audience. By limiting the regulations in this way many foreign services would remain unrestricted by domestic regulations and could thus continue to meet the interests of specific sections of the Dutch public, for example, those whose first language was not Dutch. Restrictions on freedom of expression have a greater chance of being found to be legally acceptable when they are framed as narrowly as possible, but here the under-inclusive nature of the regulations appears to have been considered indicative of protectionism.

The Court also concluded that there was 'no necessary connection' between the Netherlands cultural policy, which sought to contain the influence of advertisers over programming, and the requirements imposed on foreign broadcasters.[55] These specified that advertisements had to be produced

[53] Case C 352/85, *Bond van Adverteerders v Netherlands*, above n 51.

[54] Case 52/79, *Procureur du Roi v Marc JVC Debauve and Others* [1980] ECR 833.

[55] Case C-288/89, *Gouda*, at para 42, and Case C-353/89, *Commission v Netherlands*, at para 24, both detailed above, n 51.

by a legal entity separate from the producer of the programmes, that broadcasters were not to enable third parties to make a profit, and that advertising revenues should be used solely for the production of programmes. The Court held that it was not indispensable in order to achieve the required degree of pluralism to constrain foreign broadcasters to conform to the Dutch model. Rather, in order to secure such pluralism the Netherlands Government might 'very well confine itself to formulating the statutes of its own bodies in an appropriate manner'.[56]

Once again the Court offered no explanation for concluding that the Netherlands had misjudged the concrete implications of its cultural policy. It is apparent, however, that the Court considered it unacceptable for the Netherlands to attempt to shape the nature of all television services directed at its population. In this it may have been influenced by the recent passage of the Television Without Frontiers Directive, which was designed to facilitate cross-border broadcasting in Europe.[57] In the Commission's initial proposals for the Directive it had noted that distinct cultural and social benefits could be gained from Member States opening their borders to foreign television stations.[58] The focus of the Dutch regulations was, however, essentially inward looking: to ensure that Dutch television continued to reflect the diversity of *Netherlands* society. Though the Netherlands might legitimately pursue this objective by regulating domestic broadcasters, a matter largely outwith the scope of Community law, it could not seek to do so through restricting foreign broadcasts, thereby reducing exposure to programming reflecting other Member States. In reaching its conclusion the Court may consequently have been mindful of the distinct Community interest in cross-border cultural exchange.

Subsequent broadcasting cases have displayed rather more sensitivity to the domestic concerns evident in these decisions. Indeed, the European Commission, when reviewing the Court's case law in the cultural field, has noted that these early cases 'appear *a priori* very strict' and that they were handed down before the coming into effect of the specific culture Article.[59] Given the time it takes for a preliminary reference to work through the system,

[56] Ibid. That the Netherlands remained competent to regulate what were regarded as its own domestic broadcasters may explain two subsequent cases in which the Government was successful, namely, Case C-148/91, *Veronica Omroep Organisatie v Commissariat voor de Media* [1993] ECR I-487 and Case 23/93, *TV10 SA* [1994] ECR I-4795.

[57] Television Without Frontiers Directive, above n 22.

[58] European Commission, above n 13.

[59] European Commission, *First Report on the Consideration of Cultural Aspects in European Community Action*, COM(96) 160 final, part I, p 26.

one would expect to see Article 151 having a direct impact on the Court's rulings only towards the end of 1995. Even prior to this, however, one can point to cases, such as the 1994 *TV10* case, which clearly engaged with the Dutch concerns. In *TV10*, the Court held that where a broadcaster deliberately establishes itself in a third state in order to evade domestic regulations which would otherwise be applicable, the state of reception is entitled to regulate that service as a domestic service.[60] *TV10* had established itself in Luxembourg but broadcast to the Netherlands, tailoring its channel, its programmes, actors, and actresses, for the Dutch market. In such circumstances the Court held that *TV10* could be required to conform to the Netherlands' media regulations.

The Dutch broadcasting cases illustrate the willingness of the Court to assess not only the genuineness of national measures introduced on the basis of domestic cultural policy, but also their necessity and effectiveness. Absent the formal recognition subsequently afforded to cultural concerns by Article 151 of the Treaty, there was clearly a risk that cultural considerations would be discounted when economic considerations were at play, particularly where there was any hint of protectionism. By definition, however, those domestic regulations referred to the Court of Justice on free movement grounds will have negative economic consequences for foreign traders or individuals. The Dutch broadcasting cases C-288/89 and C-352/89 nevertheless indicated that where a cultural policy has economic consequences for foreign operators, this may be sufficient for the Court to conclude that domestic measures are protectionist and therefore unlawful, even when they apply equally to domestic operators. Determining the primary motivation for legislation is unlikely to be easy, yet the Court did not explain why it found the Netherlands' stated objectives to be unconvincing. In the context of preliminary rulings it is, at least in theory, for the national court to establish the facts and apply the legal principles established by the Court of Justice to the case at hand. There may consequently be insufficient evidence for the Court to conclude that a Member State has in fact been acting in a protectionist way, or that its cultural policy is disproportionate; in such cases the matter should clearly be referred back to the national court.[61] In both the food quality and broadcasting cases

[60] Case 23/93, *TV10 SA*, above n 56. The scope of the principle established in *TV10* is not entirely clear, on which see Hansen, L H, 'The Development of the Circumvention Principle in the Area of Broadcasting', *Legal Issues of European Integration*, 2 (1998), p 111; Craufurd Smith, R, 'The Establishment of Companies in European Community Law: Choice of Law or Abuse of Rights?', *European Current Law*, (1999), p *xi*.

[61] It may be noted that the two cases under discussion involved both a preliminary reference and a direct action brought by the Commission. The procedure adopted in preliminary references differs from that in direct actions before the Court of First Instance or Court of Justice.

the Court nevertheless sent a clear message to Member States that it would scrutinize extremely carefully any attempt to protect indigenous practices by excluding or limiting foreign competition.

In other areas the Court of Justice was considerably more deferential to Member State social and cultural concerns, particularly where sensitive moral or religious questions were at stake. In such circumstances, the Court tended to avoid conflict with the Member States by adopting a non-intensive form of proportionality review, or devolving the issue entirely to the domestic court. Restrictions on Sunday trading, gambling, and the sale of pornography thus escaped strict scrutiny by the Court of Justice.[62] In the *Schindler* case, which concerned a United Kingdom prohibition on large-scale lotteries, the Court held that Member States should be afforded 'a sufficient degree of latitude' in assessing not only whether to restrict the operation of lotteries, but also whether they should be prohibited altogether.[63] This latitude contrasts with the rigour adopted in the Dutch media cases, in that the UK had at the time of the case already set in motion procedures for the introduction of a national lottery. The only significant check on state action in such contexts is designed to ensure that there has been no discrimination, and those regulations which have been struck down have generally been tainted by discrimination.[64]

It might be possible to distinguish cases of this type from the food quality and broadcasting cases discussed above on the basis that the foreign goods and services at issue were considered by the Member State to be socially harmful, a value judgment that the Court is not well placed to override.[65] By contrast,

In the former instance, given the division of competence between the domestic and European courts, the European Court of Justice does not call witnesses of its own motion or seek expert reports, nor is it possible for interested natural or legal persons to intervene, though the Member States and Community institutions may make observations. For discussion of the potential evidential limitations in the context of preliminary references, see Canor, I, 'Harmonizing the European Community's Standard of Judicial Review', *European Public Law*, 8 (2002), p 135.

[62] Case 145/88, *Torfaen Borough Council v B & Q plc* [1989] ECR 3851; Case C-275/92, *HM Customs and Excise v Schindler* [1994] ECR I-1039, which related to a reference raised prior to the coming into force of the TEU; and Case 34/79, *Henn and Darby* [1979] ECR 3795. Divergent national views as to the acceptability of abortion may also explain the Court's readiness to conclude that there was no Community element in Case C-159/90, *Society for the Protection of the Unborn Child v S Grogan* [1991] ECR I-4733. For discussion of these and related cases, see Steyger, above n 41, chs 3 and 4.

[63] Case C-275/92, *HM Customs and Excise v Schindler*, above n 62, para 61.

[64] e.g., Cases 121/85, *Conegate Ltd v Commissioners of Customs & Excise* [1986] ECR 1007 and 115–116/81, *Adoui and Cornuaille v Belgium* [1982] ECR 1665.

[65] On one view, however, media pluralism, a concern expressed by the Netherlands in the broadcasting cases discussed above, is essential for the operation of democratic government and the well-being of society. It may be noted that in the *Debauve* case, above n 54, the Court was not

in the food quality/broadcasting cases, the Member States sought to exclude foreign goods and services that were not intrinsically harmful to individual consumers but which, if allowed into the country, posed a competitive threat to indigenous products or well-established services.[66] In such circumstances the Court applied an exacting form of proportionality review, displaying a willingness to leave the evolution of the market largely in consumers' hands.

Interestingly, where national regulations concerned the way in which goods were to be marketed, as opposed to their content, the Court seemed in any event to take a non-interventionist approach, on occasion holding that the national measure fell outside the scope of Community law altogether. In *Blesgen*, for example, a Belgian prohibition on the sale of high alcohol drinks in public places was simply considered not to be caught by Article 30 EEC (now Article 28 EC).[67] The case law in this area was, however, far from consistent, and in *Keck and Mithourd* an attempt was made to clarify the position.[68] The Court drew the now familiar distinction between rules that relate to the characteristics of a product and those that concern selling arrangements. Rules of the latter type were to be regarded as falling outside the scope of Article 28 EC, provided there was no element of discrimination.

It was apparent from *Keck* that the Court's hands-off approach to selling arrangements stemmed less from respect for national sensitivities about marketing techniques and more from a concern to control its own burgeoning case load.[69] More importantly, the Court was of the view that rules relating to selling arrangements were not such as to prevent foreign goods from gaining access to domestic markets, though it accepted that they might affect the volume of goods sold, nor did they require the foreign goods to be substantively modified. From a cultural perspective this distinction is not, however, entirely coherent. As we have seen, the internal market promotes a culture of consumer choice, and increasingly this choice is built around branding and the lifestyle associated with a particular product. If Member States can regulate

prepared to judge the appropriateness of domestic advertising restrictions, given the very different views adopted by the Member States regarding advertising's social and political implications.

[66] In Case 178/84, *Commission v Germany*, above n 43, the arguments that additives in beer could pose a risk to human health were dismissed by the Court relatively easily, on the basis that Germany permitted the same additives to be used in other beverages.

[67] Case 75/81, *Belgium v Blesgen* [1982] ECR 1211.

[68] Cases 267–268/91, *Keck and Mithouard (Criminal Proceedings Against)* [1993] ECR I-6097. Decided after the Treaty on Union came into force, the case related to domestic proceedings dating back to 1991.

[69] For a discussion of the motivations behind *Keck*, see Weiler, J H H, 'The Constitution of the Common Market Place: Text and Context in the Evolution of the Free Movement of Goods', in Craig, P and De Búrca, G (eds), *The Evolution of EU Law* (Oxford: OUP, 1999), ch 10.

marketing so that it is tailored to domestic cultural traditions then the very consumer choice promoted by the Court in the beer and pasta cases could be undermined.[70]

It is possible that there is a further category of cases in which the Court held back from applying the free movement principles with their full rigour, even in the absence of moral or religious considerations. This is where the cultural practice was regarded as in some way foundational to a particular society. Thus, in *Groener* the Court upheld a requirement of proficiency in Irish for appointment to a full-time teaching post, even though knowledge of the Irish language was not needed to teach the art course concerned.[71] Although the Court applied a test of proportionality, it was not exacting in its examination and failed to consider whether other, less restrictive measures, for example, an obligation to obtain familiarity with the Irish language while in post, could have been adopted.[72] A similar sensitivity may also explain the Court's deference to certain sporting rules, such as those relating to the composition of national teams.[73] If such boundaries are being drawn then they will inevitably prove contentious. Should, for example, Member State attempts to preserve indigenous broadcasting services or culinary traditions be treated with similar deference to their attempts to preserve indigenous languages or the credibility of international sporting events? However appropriate the distinctions being drawn, the Court does appear to modify its approach depending on the type of cultural practice at issue.

Given the various lines of reasoning adopted by the Court where cultural considerations were at play, any conclusions drawn from the case law prior to the introduction of Article 151 must be tentative. The preceding discussion does, however, suggest that in at least two situations the Court was prepared to take a deferential attitude to Member State cultural concerns. First, where the foreign good or service was considered by the state of reception to be intrinsically socially harmful, for example pornography, and, secondly, where the domestic practice was regarded as in some way constitutive of national

[70] For traders one solution to this problem could be to challenge the marketing restriction as a distinct prohibition on the freedom to provide services, rather than as a constraint on the ability to sell the product itself.

[71] Case 379/87, *Groener v Minister for Education and the City of Dublin Vocational Education Committee* [1989] ECR 3967.

[72] Loman et al., above n 8, at p 58.

[73] Cases C-36/74, *Walrave & Koch v Union Cycliste Internationale* [1974] ECR 1405 and 13/76, *Donà v Mantero* [1976] ECR 1333, though sport may clearly fall within the scope of Community law as the seminal *Bosman* ruling, Case C-415/93, [1995] ECR I-4921, spectacularly confirmed. The Court's explanation of its deference to certain rules is that these are of purely sporting interest and of no economic import, though it is arguable that economic implications can usually be identified.

identity or of fundamental cultural importance, for example, national language. In other circumstances, with the exception of rules relating to the marketing of goods, measures that simply shielded domestic consumers from alternative foreign goods or services were assessed for protectionism and subjected to a rigorous proportionality review.

(b) Culture and the Community legislature

Cultural considerations were also influential in the legislative sphere prior to the introduction of Article 151 EC. When the Commission formulates draft legislation to approximate or coordinate Member State laws, it must, following extensive consultation, determine which, if any, of the national provisions should be reflected in the Community norm, and whether the Community norm should set a minimum or more exacting standard. In so doing, the Commission will have to strike a balance between the Community interests set out in the Treaty and other relevant policy considerations that, depending on the context, may be cultural. The Council and European Parliament undertake a similar assessment when scrutinizing draft legislation proposed by the Commission with a view to its adoption, amendment, or rejection. Though there was no scope under the EEC Treaty for legislation to be put forward directly on cultural grounds, cultural considerations could thus influence significantly the ultimate shape and content of particular measures.

This is illustrated by Community intervention in the audio-visual and educational sectors. During the late 1970s and early 1980s, the development of cable and satellite facilities rendered cross-border television services commercially feasible. This was, however, greatly complicated by the diversity of Member State broadcasting regulations. Though a number of domestic restrictions on foreign broadcasts were found by the Court of Justice to be unlawful, as the Dutch cases discussed above illustrate, certain regulations had been upheld on the basis that they pursued legitimate policy objectives.[74] Given the continuing existence of barriers to cross-border broadcasting, the Commission proposed that domestic rules in this area should be coordinated. An initial examination of the need for such a measure was contained in the Commission's 1984 *Green Paper on the Establishment of the Common Market for Broadcasting, especially by Satellite and Cable*.[75] The document is striking for the

[74] Case 52/79, *Debauve*, above n 54.

[75] European Commission, above n 13. The Television Without Frontiers Directive was ultimately agreed in 1989, above n 22. Paul Beaumont and Gordon Moir note that the Directive 'has an inescapably cultural backdrop': *The European Communities (Amendment) Act 1993 with the Treaty of Rome (As Amended), Text and Commentary*, (London: Sweet & Maxwell, 1994) p 142.

degree of attention paid to the cultural and social aspects of broadcasting. Cross-border broadcasts were held to further not only freedom of information, essential for a functioning democracy, but also cultural exchange, considered to be a source of cultural enrichment and creativity.[76] The Commission knew that its proposals would be highly controversial for certain Member States and sought to reassure them that social and cultural, as well as economic, considerations were being taken into account.

On closer inspection, however, the social and cultural objectives discussed in the Green Paper appear to have more of a Community than national orientation. As noted, Member States have traditionally used the mass media and domestic education systems to create or reinforce a sense of national identity and cohesion. Given long-standing concern at the level of popular support for European integration, evidenced in the 1975 Tindemans Report, it is not surprising that both the Commission and European Parliament began to consider how these important cultural vectors might be used to forge a sense of European, as opposed to national, identity. In 1974, for example, the Commission introduced an action programme entitled *Education in the European Community*, which called for the development of European studies in the school curriculum.[77] Similar preoccupations may be detected in the Commission's 1984 Broadcasting Green Paper, which included a separate section headed 'The New Technologies in the Service of European Integration'. This examined the 'significant contribution to European unification' which cross-border broadcasting was capable of making: not only would it be welcomed by those who moved to work in another Member State, affording them an opportunity to keep in touch with their state of origin, it could also 'help the peoples of Europe . . . recognize the common destiny they share in many areas' and stimulate interest in Community affairs.[78] Coordination of national laws consequently afforded the Commission an opportunity to develop a distinct *Community* cultural agenda.

In general, however, Community coordination or harmonization of Member State laws proved difficult. In particular, Article 100 (now Article 94) required that any directive introduced to approximate national laws be agreed unanimously in the Council. As a result, Member States could veto any measure

[76] European Commission, above n 13, at p 30.

[77] European Commission, *Education in the European Community*, (1974) II Bull. EC, supp. 3/74. The Commission was, however, less successful with this project than its attempt to regulate the broadcast sector. Member States were opposed to Community involvement in curricula matters and did not implement the various recommendations in this area, on which see Theiler, above n 13.

[78] European Commission, above n 13, at Part Two, 'Cultural and Social Aspects'.

that they felt conflicted with traditional standards and expectations. The position was eased somewhat from 1987 when a new Article 100a (now Article 95) came into operation, which authorizes the passage of harmonizing measures relating to the internal market on the basis of qualified majority voting in the Council. The difficulty inherent in formulating harmonizing measures able to command wide Member State support meant that relatively few such directives were agreed.

The approach adopted by the Court of Justice in the *Cassis de Dijon* case,[79] endorsing a system of mutual recognition by states of each other's product standards, but with ultimate safeguards for the protection of important general interests, resonated with the legislature and led to the adoption in 1985 of what is often referred to as the 'new approach'.[80] This evidenced a move away from attempts to harmonize in detail national rules relating to specific goods and services and a preference for establishing only essential safety and general interest requirements, to be fleshed out by various accredited standardization organisations. As a result, Community attempts to approximate national laws became much more focused and limited in their ambition, leaving Member States largely free to maintain domestic regulations, rooted in tradition, in relation to domestic producers. Most importantly, the preferred system of mutual recognition absolved the Community legislature from making contentious choices among regulations which sought to maintain distinct products and services.

This development is particularly marked in the field of food quality regulations, where, post-1985, the Commission indicated it would no longer attempt to establish the required composition of particular products.[81] Instead, it has moved to adopt general legislation setting out consumer protection and fair trading standards to be applied across whole sectors. Community regulations regarding the content of honey and chocolate are consequently likely to remain isolated examples of Community standardization in the food context.[82] The long-running chocolate saga illustrates not only how strongly Member States will fight to protect their established industries, but also how cultural preferences can become a serious issue in the development of Community law. Initial legislation had been passed in 1973, but final resolution

[79] Case 120/78, *Rewe Zentrale v Budesmonopolverwaltung für Branntwein* [1979] ECR 649.

[80] See, e.g., *Council Resolution of 7 May 1985 on a new approach to technical harmonization and standards*, OJ [1985] C 136/1.

[81] O'Rourke, R, *European Food Law* (Bembridge, Isle of Wight: Palladian Law Publishing, 1999), pp 56 and 76.

[82] Directive (EEC) No 74/409 (honey), OJ [1974] L 221/10, and Directive (EEC) No 73/241 (chocolate), OJ [1973] L 228/23, repealed by Directive (EC) No 2000/36; see below n 83.

of the vexed question whether chocolate with a certain percentage of vegetable fat rather than cocoa butter, of a type familiar in the UK, could be marketed as 'chocolate' throughout the EU was reached only in June 2000.[83]

Owing to the absence of a clear Treaty basis for considering cultural matters, it is not surprising that the cultural ramifications of Community policies received only patchy attention in legislation prior to the coming into force of Article 151. Moreover, pressure to take into account cultural concerns gained ground only gradually as the public and politicians became aware of the impact on established traditions and man-made environments of increasing industrialization and mechanization. In the context of agriculture, for example, Article 33 is framed in broad enough terms for social and environmental aspects, which arguably have considerable cultural ramifications, to be taken into account. Thus, Article 33(2) requires the Community to take into account 'the particular nature of agricultural activity, which results from the social structure of agriculture and from structural and natural disparities between the various agricultural regions'. Nevertheless, the Commission tended to direct its focus on markets and price controls, and it was only from the 1970s onwards that gradual steps were taken to integrate social and environmental concerns into the development of the Common Agricultural Policy (CAP).[84] This ultimately led to the establishment of a rural development policy which is now seen as CAP's 'second pillar'. Regulation 2078/92, for example, passed in 1992, paved the way for subventions from the European Agricultural Guidance and Guarantee Fund to be directed, *inter alia*, to the upkeep of the farmed landscape and preservation of the countryside.[85]

Agriculture is of interest for present purposes not only because of its etymological link with the word 'culture', but also because it was in the context of the agriculture title that the Community responded to Member State and industry concerns over the preservation of indigenous and specialty foods. As noted, the Court of Justice recognized early on that designations of origin might be justified under Article 30, even though they could impede intra-Community trade. The legislator built on this foundation to pass two directives in 1992, establishing a Community-wide system for protecting product names. These now form the basis of what the Community refers to as its

[83] European Parliament and Council Directive (EC) No 2000/36 Relating to Cocoa and Chocolate Products Intended for Human Consumption, OJ [2000] L 197/19.

[84] See McMahon, J A, *Law of the Common Agricultural Policy* (London: Longman, 2000), and Usher, J, *European Community Agricultural Law* (Oxford: OUP, 2001).

[85] Council Regulation (EEC) No 2078/92 on agricultural production methods compatible with the requirements of the protection of the environment and the maintenance of the countryside, OJ [1992] L 215/85.

'quality policy'. Regulation (EEC) No 2081/92, sets up a system for registering product names that are linked to a special region or geographic area, for example, the French cheese *Comté*.[86] Regulation (EEC) No 2082/92 introduces a system for protecting the use of names designating traditional foodstuffs.[87] This was supplemented by a further measure, establishing a special Community mark that guarantees the authenticity of the traditional products to which it is attached.[88] Regulation 2082/92 has been relied on most notably in the context of beer, for example, to authenticate the Belgian cherry beer *Kriek*, but also for cheeses such as Italian *mozzarella*, specialty meats, and pastries. The system of registration established by these regulations devolves the role of assessment principally to the Member States, with only a secondary control vested in the Commission. It is tempting to conclude that this not only recognizes the greater knowledge of local conditions held by Member States, but also their considerable sensitivity to any Community intervention in this area.

In retrospect, 1992 appears a significant year for the passage of Community legislation with a cultural dimension. Apart from initiatives in the field of rural development and food quality, 1992 was also the year in which the Community introduced measures to prevent national treasures which had been illegally exported from one Member State to another, being then exported outside the European Community altogether.[89] Further measures were taken the following year to facilitate the return of such objects to the Member State from which they had initially been unlawfully exported.[90]

From a cultural perspective, some of the most important legislative measures introduced prior to the introduction of Article 151 were those that established either general or specific funds capable of being used to support cultural events and initiatives. Both the European Social Fund and the European Regional Development Fund provided finance for cultural initiatives, though the latter on a more restricted scale than is currently the case.[91] The European

[86] Council Regulation (EEC) No 2081/92 on the protection of geographical indications and designations of origin for agricultural products and foodstuffs, OJ [1992] L 208/1. See also the previous sectoral Council Regulation (EEC) No 823/87 laying down special provisions relating to the quality of wines produced in specified areas, OJ [1987] L 84/59.

[87] Council Regulation (EEC) No 2082/92 on certificates of special character for agricultural products and foodstuffs, OJ [1992] L 208/9.

[88] Council Regulation (EC) No 2515/94, OJ [1994] L 275/1.

[89] Council Regulation (EEC) No 3911/92 on the export of cultural goods, OJ [1992] L 395/1. This, together with the subsequent Council Directive No 93/7, is discussed in detail in Chapter 5 by Andrea Biondi in this volume.

[90] Council Directive (EEC) No 93/7 on the return of unlawfully removed cultural objects, OJ [1993] L 74/74.

[91] See discussion by Loman et al, above n 8, at pp 159 and 162.

Agricultural Guidance and Guarantee Fund, increasingly relied on to assist in rural development, has already been mentioned.[92] Apart from these general funds the Community also set up a variety of schemes which related more directly to cultural issues or cultural industries. Thus, programmes were introduced to support minority languages, and language teaching more generally (LINGUA), and to assist the European film and broadcasting industries (MEDIA).[93]

Even prior to the Treaty on European Union, therefore, Community measures were being passed with a considerable cultural dimension. Intervention was, however, patchy, and its focus and orientation depended on its legal base. In certain areas, such as education, the Member States were not prepared to take forward initiatives which could challenge national allegiances. The 'new approach' re-oriented the Community away from harmonizing initiatives, thus leaving considerable scope for national diversity. This diversity was supported by measures establishing Community-wide systems to protect specific designations for traditional or specialty food and drink. Increasingly, too, significant funding was being directed towards initiatives with a notable cultural aspect. The inability to found measures directly on a cultural basis in the Treaty had, however, an inevitable impact on their focus and general direction. Funding for the media industries and for rural development was, for example, largely premised on industrial and employment concerns, though cultural considerations were not insignificant in the audio-visual context. Even the Community's food quality policy was primarily designed to protect small and specialist industries as well as consumers, rather than to ensure the survival of distinct culinary traditions. Whether or not these measures reflect a heightened sensitivity within the Community institutions to the impact of Community law on culture, they certainly suggest growing awareness of the economic value of the culture industries and the use to which culture can be put in social development.

(c) The existence of distinct Community values

The suggestion that there was no scope prior to the Treaty on European Union for the Community to develop its own cultural policies may also be questioned on the basis that particular social values were embedded in the

[92] See text above accompanying n 85.

[93] For more detailed discussion of these and other Community schemes, see Loman et al, above n 8, at pp159–68. The LINGUA programme was established by Council Decision (EEC) No 89/489, OJ [1989] L 239/24 and the MEDIA programme by Council Decision (EEC) No 90/685, OJ [1990] L 380/37.

EEC Treaty from the start. For example, the prohibition on discrimination on grounds of nationality and the requirement that women and men should receive equal pay for equal work have had an impact not only on social organization but also on the way in which individuals see themselves and others.[94] It is arguable that these values were introduced primarily for economic reasons, to protect French industry, already subject to equal pay legislation, from being undercut by products imported from other Member States free from such constraint and thus potentially more competitive. Indeed, from an economic perspective such provisions can be seen as an attempt to *remove* culture from the workplace: individuals are to be considered factors of production, paid for their labour regardless of sex or nationality.

Parallels can here be drawn with Community intervention to create an internal market. As we have seen, for individual choice to drive the development of the market in goods and services, the cultural biases in domestic legislation have to be removed. For individual choice to operate in the context of the labour market, the cultural biases in employment practices will equally have to be addressed, though this admittedly restricts the options available to individual employers.[95] The two contexts are not, of course, unrelated, in that removal of discrimination in the labour market enables women as well as men to exercise economic power and make choices as consumers.

But even if the principle of non-discrimination was introduced largely for economic reasons, its cultural significance cannot be denied. As the Court noted in *Defrenne v Sabena*, the equal pay provision 'forms part of the social objectives of the Community, which is not merely an economic union, but is at the same time intended, by common action, to ensure social progress and seek the constant improvement of the living and working conditions of their peoples, as is emphasized by the Preamble to the Treaty'.[96] The scope of the non-discrimination principle has been further developed in secondary legislation and the case law of the Court of Justice. When asked to go beyond a literal interpretation of the relevant Treaty Article or directive in order to give the principle of equality an expansive scope, the Court has tended to be cautious—in

[94] Articles 7 and 119 EEC (now 12 and 141 EC) respectively. There is an extensive literature on gender and the European Community, among which the recent articles by Jo Shaw and Catherine Barnard offer valuable insights: Shaw, J, 'Gender and the Court of Justice', in De Búrca, G and Weiler, J H H, *The European Court of Justice* (Oxford: OUP, 2002) at p 87; Barnard, C, 'Gender Equality and the EU: A Balance Sheet', in Alston, P (ed), *The EU and Human Rights* (Oxford: OUP, 1999), ch 8.

[95] The removal of explicit discriminatory practices does not, of course, guarantee substantive equality, given that ingrained social practices and prejudices may lead to continued exclusion.

[96] Case 43/75, *Defrenne v Sabena* [1976] ECR 455, at para 10.

the eyes of some, reactionary.[97] This has particularly been so when domestic traditions have been diverse and any change contentious. Thus, the Court has been unwilling to equate marriage with other long-term relationships, whether heterosexual or same-sex.[98] In other instances, however, the Court appears to have been more progressive, showing no hesitation in requiring that discriminatory practices, however ancient or firmly established, be abrogated or amended. In *Commission v France*, for example, it held that provisions designed to help women work and bring up a family, which included a reduction in working hours, leave to care for sick children, additional holidays, and time off for Mother's Day, were discriminatory because they were not available to working fathers.[99]

(d) Conclusion

What, then, is it possible to conclude from this analysis of the situation prior to the entry into force of the Treaty on European Union? First, that the Community judicial and legislative organs were, from the start, inevitably involved in questions of cultural policy. For the Court, these questions tended to arise not only in disputes as to the legitimacy of domestic cultural policies capable of impeding trade between Member States, but also when the Court was called to enforce the social values established in the EEC Treaty. Its rulings in the internal market and social policy fields can be seen to have fundamentally affected the culture not only of consumption but also of production, with wide-ranging implications for the structure of society in the home as

[97] For trenchant criticism of the Court's case law, see McGlynn, C, 'Ideologies of Motherhood in European Community Sex Equality Law', ELJ, 6 (2000), 29, and, in relation to recent developments, 'Pregnancy, parenthood and the Court of Justice in *Abdoulaye*', ELR, 25 (2000), 654. Shaw, above n 94, argues that certain of the Court's rulings in this area suggest a preoccupation with inter-institutional politics, in particular the relationship between the Court of Justice and domestic courts, rather than a genuine attempt to articulate what the equality provisions substantively require. For discussion of a similar point, see Canor, above n 61.

[98] Case 59/85, *Netherlands v Reed* [1986] ECR 1283. Caution can also be detected in recent rulings such as those in Cases C-122/99P and C-125/99P, *D v Council*, of 31 May 2001, available at http://curia.eu.int. For a refusal to extend the scope of the sex discrimination provisions to cover discrimination on the basis of sexual orientation, see Case C-249/96, *Grant v South West Trains* [1998] ECR I-621.

[99] Case 312/86, *Commission v France* [1988] ECR 6315. Such an approach can also be detected in recent rulings, thus the French system of pension credits for working mothers was struck down on a similar basis in Case C-366/99, *Joseph Griesmar v Ministre de l'Economie, des Finances et de l'Industrie, Ministre de la Fonction publique, de la Réforme de l'Etat et de la Décentralisation*, judgment of 29 November 2001, http://curia.eu.int. Such rulings do not, however, mandate the continuation of such facilities, though political realities might make their withdrawal from both men and women improbable.

well as in the workplace. At the legislative level one can equally see, alongside recognition of domestic cultural concerns, the articulation of distinct Community cultural interests.

Secondly, this situation was clearly unsatisfactory. Though the Community institutions were certainly not blind to the cultural ramifications of their actions, there was always the risk that, without specific recognition in the Treaty, cultural concerns would be afforded little weight, or even ignored. Culture may have been taken into account in the development of the Community's audio-visual policy, and proved a significant consideration in the context of the Structural Funds,[100] but policy in these areas was still largely a response to economic and industrial pressures.[101] Although Member States have considerable influence over the development of Community legislation, this influence was noticeably weakened with the extension of qualified majority voting in the Single European Act. With the loss of the Member State's legislative veto in significant areas, the Commission's willingness to develop cultural policies tailored to Community rather than domestic needs, would, from the Member States' point of view, have taken on a more troubling dimension.

In the judicial context, of course, Member States have no control, and arguably limited influence, over the ultimate outcome of a case.[102] The food quality and broadcasting cases would have brought home to Member States the economic forces unleashed by the Treaty, capable not only of creating new opportunities for domestic industry, but also of undermining indigenous traditions and established ways of life. Pauline Kurzer, in her book *Markets and Moral Regulation, Cultural Change in the European Union*, offers a fascinating account of how the Community free movement principles can alter national self-perceptions and established regulatory practices.[103] Kurzer argues, on the basis of a detailed analysis of domestic alcohol, drug, and abortion controls, that change has resulted more from growing individual awareness of regulatory regimes in other European countries and enhanced opportunities for European travel than from direct Community intervention. Indeed, the sensitive

[100] For detailed consideration see the European Commission's *First Report on the Consideration of Cultural Aspects in European Community Action*, above n 59, section II, chs 1 and 2.

[101] See above, section 2.*(b)*.

[102] Concerns expressed by national courts and Member States may influence the Court in certain instances. Elias Steyger suggests that it was concerted opposition on the part of the Member States to Community oversight of domestic gambling policies that led the Court to take such a deferential approach in the *Schindler* case, discussed above at text accompanying n 63. Steyger, E, above n 41, at p 95.

[103] Kurzer, P, *Markets and Moral Regulation, Cultural Change in the European Union* (Cambridge: Cambridge University Press, 2001).

nature of regulation in these areas has, for the most part, discouraged the Community from directly questioning established domestic restrictions.[104]

For the Commission, too, the situation was far from satisfactory. Any measure it proposed that had cultural ramifications ran the risk of being challenged for lack of a Treaty basis. Community intervention in the cultural field was consequently at best fragmented, at worst inconsistent or distorted.[105] It is, for example, questionable whether the European programme quotas in Article 4 of the Television Without Frontiers Directive were really designed to facilitate the free movement of television services within Europe.[106] Though undoubtedly intended to shore up programme production in the Member States, the quotas also curb transmission of American programmes and the cultural values reflected therein. As the Commission noted in its 1988 paper entitled *A Fresh Boost for Culture*, '[t]here is a general awareness that the invasion of American and Japanese programmes represents a threat to Europe's cultural independence'.[107] The concern of some Member States that Community law was inappropriately undermining domestic cultural policy was thus matched by the view that the Community should take on a more active role in protecting the diversity of European culture from external as well as internal threats. By 1992 there was consequently a sufficient alignment of Member State and Community interests to make a Treaty amendment possible. Indeed, given the extensive reach of Community law into the cultural domain, one is tempted to ask not why a new Treaty Article on culture was added in 1992, but why one was not introduced earlier.

3. Was Article 151 intended merely to constrain Community action in the cultural field?

Given Community law's capacity to disturb long-standing cultural practices, it is plausible to see Article 151 as an attempt on the part of the Member

[104] Though see discussion, below, of the *Gourmet International Products* case at text accompanying n 122.

[105] This lack of coherence was noted in the European Commission's *Communication on New Prospects for Community Cultural Action*, COM(92) 149 final, at Annex A, p 4, and underpinned its proposals for a framework for future intervention in the cultural field in its paper *A Fresh Boost for Culture in the European Community*, above n 14.

[106] On which see De Witte, B, 'The European Content Requirement in the EC Television Directive—Five Years After', in Barendt, E M (ed), *The Yearbook of Media and Entertainment Law* (Oxford: OUP, 1995), p 101.

[107] European Commission, *A Fresh Boost for Culture in the European Community*, above n 14, p 13.

States to rein the Community back from further intervention.[108] In their book *The Mad Officials*, Christopher Booker and Richard North explore the extent to which Community regulations are gradually eroding 'Britain's distinctive way of life': in Wales, for example, they point to restrictions on the use in thatching of the traditional 'seed aquila' reed because it is not an EEC approved variety; how Morecambe Bay shrimps must now be boiled in fresh water rather than sea water, thereby losing their traditional salty flavour; and how Cornish fishermen have been prevented from packing pilchards in wooden boxes lined with hessian, even though plastic containers render the fish more perishable in transit.[109] Such examples paint a picture of unique traditions being lost to future generations, though the authors also note that many of the restrictions they examined were ultimately found to be the result of over-zealous UK implementation, rather than the Community provisions themselves.[110]

Certain provisions in Article 151 were clearly designed to respond to domestic concerns of this type. Paragraph 1 states that the Community 'shall contribute to the flowering of the cultures of the Member States', but emphasizes that any such action must respect 'national and regional diversity'. Paragraph 4, as amended by the Treaty of Amsterdam, requires the Community to 'take cultural aspects into account in its action under other provisions of this Treaty, *in particular in order to respect and to promote the diversity of its cultures*' (emphasis added). Both provisions indicate that cultural variations should be taken seriously and given due weight, a concern also reflected in Article 6 of the Treaty on European Union, which states '[t]he Union shall respect the national identities of its Member States'.

The second paragraph of Article 151 underlines the subsidiary nature of the Community's role, namely, to encourage cooperation between the Member States and, where necessary, to support and supplement *their* action in specified areas. This would seem to exclude autonomous Community initiatives that are not integrated into a wider programme of Member State action. The paragraph might also be understood as limiting Community involvement to the four activities specified therein, namely: the 'dissemination of the culture and history of the European peoples'; 'conservation . . . of

[108] Detailed analysis of Article 151 is given by Niamh Nic Shuibhne, above n 8. At p 119 she notes that Article 151 may indeed appear 'more concerned with setting down boundaries, with establishing what the Community cannot do in this domain' than with creating scope for future Community initiatives in the field. On which point see also Steyger, above n 41, pp 87 and 244–6.

[109] Booker, C and North, R, *The Mad Officials* (London: Constable, 1994), at pp 15, 16, and 38.

[110] Ibid., at p 16.

cultural heritage of European significance'; 'non-commercial cultural exchanges'; and 'artistic and literary creation, including in the audio-visual sector'. It must be noted, however, that these activities are expressed in broad, open-ended terms, and are capable of encompassing a wide range of cultural initiatives.[111] The most constraining aspect of this list could ultimately prove to lie in the emphasis in the first and second categories on a European dimension, discussed in more detail in Chapter 9 below.

An alternative reading would regard the second paragraph of Article 151 as having been designed to highlight the advantages of Community and Member State coordination in the cultural field and to identify particular areas where such coordination could prove beneficial. On this view, the paragraph provides direction and focus, rather than formal constraint. There is, after all, no express statement that paragraph 2 establishes the outer limits to Community competence under paragraph 1, or that the list of activities in paragraph 2 should be regarded as exhaustive.

Lastly, the fifth paragraph of Article 151 severely restricts the legislative tools available to the Community when developing cultural policy. Although legal measures are to be adopted under the co-decision procedure, in which the European Parliament and Council are co-legislators, with the added requirement that the Committee of the Regions be consulted, such measures are to be 'incentive' measures and must not harmonize national laws.[112] The fifth paragraph of Article 151 also requires that all measures be approved unanimously in the Council, and thus affords each Member State a veto over any proposed measure, even non-binding recommendations. As Paul Beaumont and Gordon Moir point out, 'the culture provisions are by far the most restrictive of Community action', a point that lends weight to the argument that Article 151 was ultimately designed to constrain Community intervention and return control to the Member States.[113]

But to see Article 151 merely as an attempt by the Member States to reassert control over the cultural field is to focus on just one aspect of a complex

[111] Loman et al., above n 8, observe at p 194 that there is no mention of the media generally, only the audio-visual sector. Arguably the print media, which would therefore seem to be excluded, could be covered by the term 'artistic and literary creation'.

[112] Case C-376/98, *Germany v European Parliament and Council of the European Union* [2000] ECR I-8419, indicates that the prohibition on harmonization under Article 151 does not prevent harmonization taking place under other Treaty provisions, notably Article 100a, even where the measure is motivated by cultural considerations. In such circumstances harmonization will be legitimate, provided that there is a genuine basis for using the alternative Treaty Article, rather than a desire simply to avoid the constraints in Article 151. The type of initiatives envisaged in Article 151(2) would not in any event appear to lend themselves easily to harmonization.

[113] Beaumont and Moir, above n 75, at pp 32–141.

provision. Indeed, Article 151 has all the hallmarks of an uneasy compromise, pulled between a number of competing interests. On the one hand, the Treaty on European Union was undoubtedly used by the Member States to establish specific Community exclusion zones. Article 149, for example, calls on the Community to respect 'the responsibility of the Member States for the content of teaching and the organization of education systems and their cultural and linguistic diversity'. Article 151 can be seen to fit into this wider picture, deterring Community intervention that could undermine cultural diversity at the domestic level and precluding direct attempts at harmonization. On the other hand, one cannot ignore the fact that Article 151 explicitly establishes for the first time Community competence in the cultural field.

As noted, Member States may have had good reasons for regarding the development of cultural initiatives at the *Community* level to be desirable. At its most basic, certain countries would have hoped to gain financial assistance to help preserve, or revitalize, their indigenous cultures. Though the sums earmarked for the various culture programmes have been relatively limited, the funding allocated to cultural projects via the Structural Funds has been considerable.[114] Member States may also have seen Article 151 as a potential basis for Community action to redress any negative consequences of market liberalization. As the Dutch media cases discussed above indicate, exposure to market forces can undermine domestic cultural policies, yet it is the precise aim of the Community to open up markets to foreign, or perhaps one should say European, competition. In such circumstances one might expect some form of compensating Community action, such as the various MEDIA programmes, which, since 1986, have provided financial assistance for European audio-visual production and distribution.[115]

Additionally, Member States may have hoped that Article 151 would lead the Community institutions, judicial as well as legislative, to afford cultural issues greater weight when balancing cultural and commercial interests. Ultimately, some Member States may also have been willing to support Community cultural initiatives on the basis that these would illustrate to a sceptical populace the positive benefits of European integration. By requiring

[114] Delgado Moreira, J M, 'Cohesion and Citizenship in EU Cultural Policy', *Journal of Common Market Studies*, 38 (2000), p 449.

[115] Introduced initially under Article 235, the most recent programme was based on the industry title, Article 157(3): Council Decision 2000/821/EC on the implementation of a programme to encourage the development, distribution and promotion of European audiovisual works, OJ [2001] L 13/35. In reality, the quotas may do more to shore up the position of the major European programme producers in the face of foreign competition than assist the preservation of struggling domestic broadcasting industries.

unanimity for any Community measures in this area, Member States could rest assured that they would be able to veto any proposals that, in their view, threatened to undermine national identity or sensitive domestic policies. The attraction, therefore, of Article 151 for the Member States was that it not only steered the Community away from measures considered to be inherently damaging, it also facilitated action which could be positively beneficial.

4. Article 151: a new agenda for Community action in the cultural field?

It will be apparent from the foregoing section that Article 151 was designed both to influence the application of existing Treaty provisions and to lay the foundations for the development of distinct cultural policies in the future. This section examines the impact of Article 151 in each of these areas, and seeks to identify potential constraints on the meaningful application of the Article. One of the most problematic aspects of Article 151 is the language used: even a cursory examination reveals that many of the terms are vague or open-ended. Moreover, it is possible to point to potential tensions within the provisions themselves, something that is unsurprising given the very diverse motivations of those who framed and approved Article 151. Clearest of these is the tension between, on the one hand, the desire to preserve established cultures and national traditions, and, on the other, the desire to promote cultural exchange and innovation. This lack of clarity provides considerable latitude for the development of Community policies, but it also obscures difficult and contentious questions concerning Community objectives and priorities in the cultural field. It could equally undermine the effectiveness of certain provisions, leading to their application becoming little more than tokenism.

Some of these problems are apparent when one considers paragraph 4, which reflects Member State concerns over the impact of Community law on their indigenous cultures. Paragraph 4 requires 'the Community' to 'take cultural aspects into account' when acting under *other* Treaty provisions. The Community in this context may be taken to mean the Court of Justice, which derives its authority to act from the Treaty, as well as the Commission and Community legislative institutions. When interpreting and applying Community law, national courts may also have to consider the impact of paragraph 4, though in cases of uncertainty they may, and if a court of final instance must, seek guidance from the Court of Justice under Article 234.

The impact of paragraph 4 is problematic on two counts: first, the term 'cultural aspects' is very vague and offers no indication as to the purpose to be served by such consideration; and, secondly, the term 'take into account' imposes only a very limited obligation, potentially met by even the most superficial examination of cultural issues. It is interesting to compare paragraph 4 in this respect with Article 95(3) of the EC Treaty, which requires the Community, when introducing harmonizing legislation, to take as its base a *high level* of protection for health, safety, and environmental and consumer protection.

With regard to the lack of guidance as to which cultural considerations should be taken into account when applying paragraph 4, it is arguable that direction can be sought from paragraph 1, though this itself refers to a number of potentially divergent cultural objectives. In 1997 the Amsterdam Treaty amended paragraph 4 to require that consideration of cultural issues should 'in particular' be directed to ensuring respect for the diversity of the Community's cultures. This suggests that cultural diversity, and with it Member State concerns to protect their own traditions, should be prioritized but does not exclude other objectives. Cultural and commercial values cannot, however, be played off against each other according to some simple arithmetical formula, they are not commensurable, and there is no indication in paragraph 4 as to the weight to be afforded cultural and commercial considerations respectively.

For paragraph 4 to become a meaningful provision the Community institutions must not only make consistent efforts to identify the cultural aspects of any projected initiative at an early stage of its development, they must also consult widely with individuals and organizations (and not merely the more 'established' institutions) in order to make a serious assessment of its potential cultural impact. The Commission Directorate General responsible for Education and Culture can play a valuable coordinating role in this context, providing advice and drawing on its established contacts in the cultural field. It has also been suggested that the Community should introduce a specialist agency, linked to the Commission, to advise on cultural matters. Such an agency could evaluate Community proposals in the cultural field and monitor their implementation.[116] The effectiveness of paragraph 4 would equally be

[116] The Ruffolo Report for the European Parliament suggested the creation of such an agency and proposed that it should monitor the operation of Community funded cultural projects as well as the cultural policies and programmes of the Member States, with a view to ensuring the exchange of useful information. See European Parliament, Committee on Culture, Youth, Education, the Media and Sport (Rapporteur: Giorgio Ruffolo), A5–0281/2001, ***Report on cultural***

enhanced by a requirement that the Community, when adopting a measure, should explain the weight afforded to cultural considerations and the way in which they have been factored into the final provision.

The Council, in a resolution passed in January 2002, acknowledged that the implementation of paragraph 4 needed to be improved.[117] Certainly, it has not as yet had the same impact as the mainstreaming provision in the field of equality, introduced into the EC Treaty by the Treaty of Amsterdam.[118] This may in part be because in the field of sex equality there is an established and effective 'women's lobby' that operates at both the national and European levels. The ability of this lobby to feed into the EC agenda is assisted by the fact that it has a fairly clearly defined remit and set of objectives—as indeed does Article 3(2) of the EC Treaty, the mainstreaming provision. This is absent in the cultural field, which encompasses a wide range of cultural organizations, representing frequently divergent interests, for example, those of performers and artists, broadcasters and producers, art traders, museums and heritage conservation bodies.

If one turns to consider the impact of paragraph 4 in the judicial sphere, it is difficult to detect a significant change in approach. This is not, perhaps, surprising, given that the Court of Justice, prior to the Treaty on European Union, had already moved to afford cultural concerns specific recognition, beyond that expressly indicated in the Treaty. It is consequently possible that the judges of the European Court consider paragraph 4 to add little, if anything, to their previous jurisprudence. Some support for this view may be obtained from the seminal *Bosman* ruling, in which Germany argued that sport was akin to culture and that the first paragraph of Article 151 (then 128) required the Community to respect the cultural diversity of its Member States. The Court of Justice, however, rejected the relevance of paragraph 1, to which the national court had also referred in its reference, on the basis that the case turned instead on the application of the Treaty free movement principles.[119] The Court did not refer to the fourth paragraph of Article 151, nor

cooperation in the European Union, available at http://www.europarl.eu.int/meetdocs_all/committees/committeeslist.htm. The Committee of the Regions could also play a valuable role here, on which see text below accompanying n 184.

[117] Council Resolution of 21 January 2002 on the Role of Culture in the Development of the European Union, OJ [2002] C 32/2, at para B.

[118] Article 3(2), EC Treaty. For further consideration, see European Commission, *Communication on Incorporating Equal Opportunities for Women and Men into all Community Policies and Activities*, COM(96) 67 final, and *Communication Towards a Community Framework Strategy on Gender Equality (2001–2005)*, COM(2000) 335 final.

[119] Case 415/93, above n 37, at para 78.

draw any connection between the first and fourth paragraphs of that article. Instead, it proceeded to consider socio-cultural factors along established lines, as interests capable of justifying the imposition of restrictions on Community freedoms—though such a justification was held not to have been made out on the facts of the case.[120]

In relation to the free movement of goods, the Court in developing its case law under *Keck* has acknowledged that cultural factors may have a significant influence on consumer decisions.[121] In *Gourmet International Products (GIP)*, the Court held that a Swedish restriction on advertising, in this case one relating to alcoholic drinks, could affect the sale of foreign products more than domestic products precisely because domestic consumers were influenced by 'traditional social practices' and 'local habits and customs'.[122] Foreign producers were prevented from relying on advertising in order to break into the domestic market and change culturally determined preferences. The Court held that restrictions which disadvantage foreign goods in this way have to be assessed in relation both to any possible justifications and to proportionality. It accepted that health concerns, linked to a perceived culture of alcohol consumption in Sweden, could justify restrictions on advertising, but referred the question of proportionality back to the domestic court. Though the Court was here sensitive to the social context of the Swedish rules, it was also clearly unwilling to remove, *a priori*, from the ambit of judicial scrutiny domestic measures which shielded established preferences or lifestyles from foreign alternatives.

Where the Community has itself decided to protect distinctive domestic products from competition the Court of Justice, despite concerns that such protection might be abused by the Member States, has recently shown itself willing to accept a very extensive level of protection. In the *Ravil* and *Consorzio del Prosciutto di Parma* cases the Court went against the advice of Advocate General Alber, who concluded that the designation of Grana Padano cheese and Parma Ham under Regulation 2081/92 could not be used to prevent the grating or slicing of those products respectively by companies operating outside the designated areas of origin.[123] Consumer protection interests could in

[120] For consideration of whether sport, particularly professional sport, should be regarded as a cultural activity, see Chapter 4 by Stephen Weatherill in this volume.

[121] See above text accompanying n 58.

[122] Case C-405/98, *Konsumentombudsmannen (KO) and Gourmet International Products AB (GIP)* [2001] ECR I-1795, at para 21. For further consideration of the impact of Community law on northern drinking cultures, see Kurzer, above n 103.

[123] Joined Cases C-469/00 and C-108/01, *Ravil SARL v Bellon Import SARL and Biraghi SpA; Consorzio del Prosciutto di Parma and Salumificio S Rita SpA v Asda Stores Ltd and Hygrade Foods Ltd*,

his view be met by appropriate labelling or inspections. The Court disagreed, holding that unless protection extended beyond initial production to such processes as slicing or grating, the quality and authenticity of the cheese or ham could be compromised. The ability to control these processes helped to guarantee consumers the consistent quality which they expected of such products. It may be noted that the system of designation at issue in these cases did not exclude the sale of alternative products, or prevent potential customers finding out about such products, as in the *GIP* case above.

As before, it is possible to point to decisions in the context of free movement of goods and services that afford considerable deference to social and cultural concerns. In the field of gambling, for example, the Court in *Läärä* and *Zenatti* maintained a very limited form of review,[124] as it has when reviewing sporting rules that primarily seek to maintain the competitive nature of a given sport rather than regulate access to it.[125] As always, however, there are limits to the Court's deference, and in its recent *Gambelli* opinion the Court held that a Member State could not call in aid social and cultural concerns to justify restricting the foreign provision of gaming services when it was at the same time actively encouraging its public to participate in domestic state-licensed games of chance.[126] In relation to derogations relating to consumer protection the Court has also been willing to recognize the importance of local factors, moving away from the concept of a uniform 'Euro-consumer'. In *Estée Lauder Cosmetics*, for example, it confirmed that national courts, when

decided on 20 May 2003 and available at the Court website at http://curia.eu.int/en/content/juris/index.htm. A similarly strict approach can be detected in the Court's 'Feta' cases: Cases C-289/96, C-293/96, and C-299/96, *Denmark, Germany and France v Commission* [1999] ECR I-1541. The second '*Rioja*' case, Case C-388/95, *Belgium v Spain* [2000] ECR I-3123, seems rather less exacting, though here the Court noted that the designation was supported by extensive background information, which may distinguish it from the earlier *Delhaize* ruling discussed above at text accompanying n 49.

[124] Case C-124/97, *Läärä and Others v Jyväskylä and Finland* [1999] I-6067, and Case C-67/98, *Questore di Verona v Zenatti* [2001] 1 CMLR 201. In the latter case the Court referred the matter of proportionality back to the domestic court for final determination.

[125] Case 176/96, *Jyri Lehtonen, Castors Canada Dry Namur-Braine ASBL v Fédération Royale Belge des Sociétés de Basket-ball ASBL* [2000] ECR I-2681, and Joined Cases C-51/96 and C-191/97, *Christelle Deliège v Ligue Francophone de Judo et Disciplines Associées ASBL, Ligue Belge de Judo ASBL and Union Européene de Judo/François Pacquée* [2000] ECR I-2549, both of which emphasized the social importance of sport. It is, however, difficult to establish clear principles on which the cases can be distinguished and, for general discussion on this point, see Beloff, M, 'The Sporting Exception in EC Competition Law', *European Current Law*, (1999) p *lvi*.

[126] In *Gambelli* the Court, in indicating the double standards being applied by Italy, left the domestic court little room but to find the Italian rules contrary to Community law: Case C-243/01, *Penal Proceedings against Pergiorgio Gambelli e.a.* (n.y.r.), available at http://europa.eu.int/cj/en/content/juris/index.htm.

asking how a reasonably observant and circumspect consumer would respond to a particular marketing practice, could take into account the social, cultural, and linguistic factors that affect consumers in that state.[127] Overall, however, it is difficult to distinguish any significant shift in the approach of the Court to prioritize cultural concerns over and above its previous level of recognition.

Turning to the legislative field, we have noted that cultural concerns were taken into account in certain sectors, such as broadcasting, prior to the introduction of Article 151, but that this consideration was inevitably erratic. Paragraph 4 is consequently important, in that it calls for a more systematic approach to cultural issues, precipitating the Commission's initial 1996 Report on Consideration of Cultural Aspects in the European Community.[128] The Report provides, however, little more than an admittedly useful audit, and at the time of writing there had been no published follow-up. In January 2002, the Council requested the Member States to cooperate with the Commission to enable an update to be completed, and in May 2003 it called on the Commission to report specifically on the cultural dimension of the Structural Funds.[129] These reports, once published, should provide helpful information as to the concrete impact of paragraph 4.

As with the judicial field, there is little to suggest that the fourth paragraph of Article 151 has significantly altered the nature of Community legislation or its implementation. Even before the Maastricht Treaty the Community had taken steps to create a regulatory environment favourable to the creation and exploitation of cultural goods and services, in particular through removing barriers to cross-border trade. In 1985, for example, prior to its more general measures regarding educational qualifications, it had introduced a directive to ensure mutual recognition of diplomas and formal qualifications in the field of architecture,[130] while cases such as *Coditel* in the early 1980s spurred on the

[127] Case C-220/98, *Estée Lauder Cosmetics v Lancaster Group* [2000] ECR I-117. Consumer protection issues are discussed in more detail by Niamh Nic Shuibhne in Chapter 3 of this volume.

[128] European Commission, *First Report on the Consideration of Cultural Aspects in European Community Action*, above n 59. The European Parliament in its *Resolution on Cultural Cooperation in the European Union*, 2000/2323(INI), called for the creation of a European observatory to monitor cultural cooperation, 'with the aim of promoting the exchange of information and coordination between the cultural policies of the Member States and Community cultural policy': para 10.

[129] Council Resolution on the Role of Culture in the Development of the European Union, OJ [2002] C 32/2, paras A and B, and Council Resolution on the Horizontal Aspects of Culture: Increasing Synergies with other Sectors and Community Actions and Exchanging Good Practices in Relation to the Social and Economic Dimensions of Culture, OJ [2003] C 136/1, para 10.

[130] Council Directive 85/384/EEC on the Mutual Recognition of Diplomas, Certificates and Other Evidence of Formal Qualifications in Architecture, Including Measures to Facilitate the Effective Exercise of the Right of Establishment and Freedom to Provide Services, OJ [1985] L 223/15.

Community to consider regulating copyright and related rights at the European level.[131] The first intellectual property directive, which concerned computer programmes, was passed in 1991 and subsequent directives have harmonized, *inter alia*, the term of protection of copyright (at 70 years from the death of the author) and established a uniform artists' resale right for the EU area.[132]

These directives highlight the often difficult task that the Community faces in the cultural field, in that harmonization inevitably favours certain interests over others. The artists' resale right, for example, which obviously benefits creative artists, is considered potentially damaging by those who work in the art trade, because of its potential to divert trade from established art centres in the European Union, such as London, to third countries. Similarly, although the extensive term of copyright protection benefits those who have created artistic works, it also prevents those works coming into the public domain for a considerable period of time and may thus inhibit future creativity.[133]

It is certainly possible to point to areas which, in the past, were approached by the Community largely from an economic perspective, but where cultural concerns have begun to exert a greater influence over policy. In the field of agriculture, for example, further moves have been taken to support rural development, the upkeep of the landscape, and 'historical features on agricultural land'.[134] Thus, assistance has been provided for the upkeep of local farm animal breeds, indigenous to a particular area, though the emphasis here

[131] Case 62/79, *SA Compagnie Générale pour la Diffusion de la Télévision, Coditel, and other v SA Ciné Vog Films and Others* [1980] ECR 881. The need for harmonization in this area was also considered in some detail by the Commission in its 1984 Green Paper, above n 13, at pp 300 *et seq.*

[132] Council Directive 93/98/EEC Harmonizing the Term of Protection of Copyright and Certain Related Rights, OJ [1993] L 290/9, and European Parliament and Council Directive 2001/84/EC on the Resale Right for the Benefit of the Author of an Original Work of Art, OJ [2001] L 272/32.

[133] Waelde, C, *Copyright and the Internet: Closing the Gates on the Public Domain*, PhD thesis, University of Edinburgh, 2003.

[134] As evidenced in Council Regulation (EC) No 1257/1999 on Support for Rural Development from the European Agricultural Guidance and Guarantee Fund and Amending Certain Regulations, OJ [1999] L 160/80, in particular Article 22. See also European Commission, *First Report on the Consideration of Cultural Aspects in European Community Action*, above n 59, and the Committee of the Regions' opinion of 16 January 1997 on this Report at CdR 206/1996. The Court of Justice has held that CAP does not exempt agricultural producers from national provisions intended to attain objectives other than those covered by the CAP, such as the protection and enhancement of the environment or the cultural heritage of the area concerned. This suggests that CAP is still seen as designed to meet the objectives set out in Article 33(1), which afford no real scope for consideration of cultural concerns: Case C-309/1996, *Annibaldi v Sindaco del Comune di Guidonia and Presidente Regione Lazio* [1997] ECR I-7493, at para 20.

is largely environmental, in that the breed must be shown to play a role in maintaining the environment of the area in which it exists.[135] The main resource for such initiatives is the European Agricultural Guidance and Guarantee Fund (EAGGF), one of four Community Structural Funds, designed to offer financial assistance for the alleviation of structural economic and social problems in the Member States. Cultural aspects are also beginning to play a part in external trade negotiations over agriculture, as Joseph McMahon discusses further in Chapter 11 in this volume.[136]

It would be difficult, however, to maintain that paragraph 4 of Article 151 has itself influenced this shift, given that moves in this direction were already underway well before the entry into force of Article 151. It is more probable that this trend is a result of the changing nature of western agriculture, with economic value increasingly being derived from the land's cultural potential in the form of tourism and recreation facilities. Similar observations may be made with regard to the other Structural Funds, whose support for culture equally reflects the growing importance of culture-related industries in providing employment. Culture is now regarded a useful tool in facilitating economic and social regeneration in depressed areas. Thus, the European Regional Development Fund, in coordination with the EAGGF, provides significant finance for initiatives in the field of culture and tourism,[137] with diverse regional projects ranging from improving the infrastructure and services of Greek museums, fostering better access to cultural sites in Portugal, and promoting regional identity in Cornwall and the Scilly Isles.[138]

Turning to consider whether the fourth paragraph of Article 151 has had any influence on the Commission in its application of Community competition law, it is noticeable that on an initial reading of Articles 81 and 82 there appears little, if any, scope for cultural concerns to be accommodated. The

[135] Commission Regulation (EC) No 1750/1999 Laying Down Detailed Rules for the Application of Council Regulation (EC) No 1257/1999 on Support for Rural Development from the EAGGF, OJ [1999] L 214/31.

[136] See also the Commission's discussion paper given at the International Conference on Non-Trade Concerns at Ullenswang, Norway, 2–4 July 2000, entitled 'Agriculture's Contribution to Environmentally and Culturally Related Non-Trade Concerns', available at http://europa.eu.int/comm/agriculture/external/wto/document/nor2_en.pdf.

[137] Council Regulation (EC) No 1783/1999 of the European Parliament and of the Council of 12 June 1999 on the European Regional Development Fund, OJ [1999] L 213/1, and Council Regulation (EC) No 1257/1999 on support for rural development from the EAGGF and amending and repealing certain regulations, OJ [1999] L 160/80. Community funding more generally is detailed in the European Commission's *First Report into the Consideration of Cultural Aspects*, above n 59.

[138] For details see http://www.europa.eu.int/comm/regional_policy/index_en.htm.

Article 151 requirement to take cultural considerations 'into account' arguably applies only where a reading of the relevant Treaty provision allows for this possibility. It may be relevant to note that Articles 81 and 82, which relate to collusive agreements and abuses by dominant firms respectively, were not amended in 1992, whereas a specific cultural derogation was added to the state aid provisions set out in Article 87. Despite this apparent constraint, the Commission has been prepared to consider the cultural and social impact of particular agreements when considering whether or not to grant a derogation under Article 81(3).[139] This is particularly evident in the field of sport, the Commission noting on a number of occasions its conviction that 'sport performs a very important social, integrating and cultural function' and its intention to 'interpret the EU competition rules in this context'.[140] It may be noted in relation both to sport and public service broadcasting, where questions have also been raised about market sharing agreements, that the Member States have exerted considerable pressure on the Commission to accommodate socio-cultural concerns. In particular, the Member States have been active in agreeing protocols and declarations appended to the EC Treaty, and passing resolutions.[141] One may conjecture that pressure of this kind is more likely to have an influence on the Commission than the vague requirements imposed by the fourth paragraph of Article 151.

[139] e.g., the Commission approved the Eurovision system of joint purchasing of television rights under Article 81(3) on the basis, *inter alia*, that it enabled the participating public service broadcasters to 'show more and higher quality, sports programmes, both popular sports and minority sports, to European television viewers': Commission Decision 2000/400/EC of 10 May 2000 Relating to a Proceeding Pursuant to Article 81 of the EC Treaty, OJ [2000] L 151/18, at para 91. The decision was annulled by the Court of First Instance on 8 October 2002 because of the unduly restrictive nature of the sub-licensing rules: Joined Cases T-185/00, T-216/00, and T-300/00, *Métropole télévision SA (M6) et al v Commission*, available on the Court website at: http:// europa.eu.int/cj/en/content/juris/index.htm.

[140] Monti, M, 'Competition and Sport, the Rules of the Game', speech given at a conference on *Governance in Sport* held in Brussels, 26 February 2001, and available at http://europa.eu.int/comm/competition/speeches/index_2001.html. See also Commission press release of 5 June 2002 on 'The Application of the EU's Competition Rules to Sport', MEMO/02/127, available at http://europa.eu.int/rapid/start/cgi/guesten.ksh?qry. For critical evaluation of Commission intervention in this area, see Chapter 4 by Stephen Weatherill in this volume.

[141] In the field of public service broadcasting, see the Protocol on the System of Public Broadcasting in the Member States, appended to the EC Treaty by the Treaty of Amsterdam. In the field of sport, see the Amsterdam Treaty Declaration on Sport, and the Declaration on the specific characteristics of sport and its social function in Europe, adopted at the European Council in Nice. Of interest also is the joint statement of 10 September 2000 by Chancellor Gerhard Schröder and Prime Minister Tony Blair on professional soccer at: http://eng.budesregierung.de/dokumente/Pressemi . . ./ ix_17866.ht.

The Commission has recently made clear, however, that cultural considerations will be taken into account only where they can be repackaged as an aspect of one or other of the conditions explicitly set out in Article 81(3). This means that the cultural benefit must be linked to improvements in the production or distribution of goods, or technical or economic progress.[142] In areas other than sport the Commission has been markedly less receptive to arguments that market restrictions should be maintained for cultural reasons. Thus, the acceptability under Article 81(3) of agreements between publishers and booksellers designed to fix book prices has been repeatedly rejected by the Commission.[143] The publishing industry has not been able to convince the Commission that the disadvantages caused to consumers by such agreements, which prevent competition on price, are sufficiently counterbalanced by other potential benefits. The latter include the provision of a wide selection of titles, in that publishers and booksellers can use profits from sales of the most popular books, for example, the latest Harry Potter story, to cross-subsidize other titles and thereby maintain their range. Only where an agreement has virtually no impact on cross-border sales, and thus falls outside the scope of Article 81 altogether, does the Commission appear willing to accept price fixing arrangements.[144] Not only is the Commission clearly unconvinced by the economic arguments put forward to support such agreements, it

[142] See discussion by Stephen Weatherill in this volume at text accompanying n 50 in Chapter 4. The Commission in its October 2003 Communication, *Draft Notice, Guidelines on the Application of Article 81(3) of the Treaty*, expressly stated at para 38 that '[i]t is not . . . the role of Article 81 and the authorities enforcing this Treaty provision to allow undertakings to restrict competition in pursuit of general interest aims': http://europa.eu.int/comm/competition/antitrust/legislation/.

[143] *BVB/VBVB*, OJ [1982] L 54/36. For a useful overview of the history of Community intervention in this area, see Jean-François Pons, 'L'économie du livre dans l'espace européen', speech given on 30 September 2000, available at http://europa.eu.int/comm/competition/speeches/text/sp2000_018_fr.pdf. The paper also discusses the parallel line of cases, commencing with Case 229/83, *Leclerc v au blé vert* [1985] ECR 1, which concern the compatibility of national legislation on book prices with what is now Article 28 of the EC Treaty. Though not excluding such legislation in principle, the Court in *Leclerc* refused to countenance reliance on cultural arguments not specified in what is now Article 30 in circumstances where the rules were discriminatory. For more recent consideration of this issue, see Chapter 3 by Niamh Nic Shuibhne in this volume.

[144] See, e.g., the Commission's acceptance of certain undertakings regarding the operation of the German fixed price system, detailed in Commission press release IP/02/461 of 22 March 2002. Although Commissioner Monti indicated in the press release that the Commission had 'taken account of the national interest in maintaining these systems which are aimed at preserving cultural and linguistic diversity in Europe', it is not clear how this consideration actually influenced the outcome of the investigation, in that the German agreement was only likely to affect cross-border sales in circumstances where there was a clear and deliberate attempt to evade the fixed book arrangements.

is also concerned to ensure that new marketing developments, for example, international Internet sales pioneered by companies such as Amazon, are not stifled by collusive agreements or national regulations. Not all Member States accept the Commission's general approach in this matter and national price controls remain in several countries. The Council has also indicated that the impact of new forms of delivery on more traditional outlets should be monitored, in that each provides the reading public with a quite different type of service.[145]

In the state aid field an explicit derogation for 'aid to promote culture' was, as noted above, added to the Treaty in the form of Article 87(3)(d) in 1992. Derogations to fundamental principles of Community law are generally construed strictly, and there are indications that the Commission intends to keep careful control over the scope of Article 87(3)(d) with its open-ended reference to 'culture'. This approach is not apparently precluded by Article 151(4), which merely requires the Commission to take cultural issues 'into account'. Thus, in its *Kinderkanal* and *Phoenix* decision the Commission refused to consider television broadcasting in general to be a cultural activity and, as a result, concluded that aid for television stations broadcasting educational and current affairs programmes could not benefit from the exception in Article 87(3)(d).[146] This ruling suggests a rather narrow conception of culture, possibly one linked to the fine arts. A similar bias can be detected in the Commission's earlier *CELF* ruling, in which it approved French aid for small book orders on the basis that this would further French culture and language within Article 87(3)(d).[147] The Commission noted that small orders would probably relate to 'specialized' books or 'works of literature such as poetry, novels, essays and art books' and would not cover educational textbooks, usually bought in bulk.[148] Wider concerns, such as support for the production of films of national interest, reflecting the history and social practices of a particular country, can, however, be detected in other decisions regarding aid for film production.[149] The

[145] Council Resolution of 12 February 2001 on the Application of National Fixed Book-Price Systems, OJ [2001] C 73/5.

[146] Case NN-70/98, OJ [1999] C 238/3, at para 43.

[147] See, e.g., Commission Decision of 10 June 1998 Concerning State Aid in Favour of CELF, OJ [1999] L 44/37.

[148] Ibid., p 52.

[149] Case N 237/2000, *Ireland: Extension of Aid Schemes to Film and TV Production*, SG(2000) D/107013. Note also Council Resolution of 12 February 2001 on National Aid to the Film and Audiovisual Industries, OJ [2001] C 73/3. A wide approach was equally taken in Case NN 11/2002, *UK: Individual Cases of Application Based on the National Heritage Memorial Fund*, in which aid for projects of a scenic, historic, archaeological, aesthetic, architectural, engineering, artistic, or scientific nature (relating also to plants and animals) was held to be covered by Article 87(3)(d), available at http://europa.eu.int/comm/competition/state_aid/register/ii/by_primary_obj_aid_to_culture.html.

Commission's restrictive interpretation of Article 87(3)(d) in the context of television broadcasting has, moreoever, had limited impact on the Member States' ability to finance their public broadcasting systems. This is because the Commission was willing, prior to the ECJ's decision in *Altmark*, to exempt a number of national funding schemes on the alternative basis of Article 86(2) relating to services of general economic interest, and in so doing afforded Member States considerable discretion in this area.[150]

The restrictive approach evident in the Commission's interpretation of Article 87(3)(d) in the *Kinderkanal* and *Phoenix* decision may be contrasted with its readiness to adopt a more expansive interpretation of culture when applying Article 151.[151] This highlights the fact that 'culture' in Community law may mean different things in different contexts: when delimiting, for example, national derogations or the scope of Community competence. These variations in interpretation may also be a consequence of the vertically fragmented nature of the Commission administration: the lead Directorate-General in the context of Articles 81 to 89, for example, is the Directorate-General for competition, whose outlook and priorities may well differ from those of the Directorate-General directly responsible for education and culture.

The impact of the fourth paragraph of Article 151 consequently appears to have been rather patchy, with evidence of its operation in certain areas of competition law, but rather less evidence to suggest that it has affected pre-existing approaches in the judicial or legislative contexts. In contrast, paragraphs 1, 2, 3, and 5 of Article 151 represent an important break with the past, in that they enable the Community to establish new initiatives specifically to support culture. Many measures with a distinct cultural remit will, however, continue to be adopted under other Treaty Articles. There are two reasons for this: first, it appears that the Member States are reluctant to allocate significant funds to projects under Article 151; and, secondly, there are, as noted, major constraints on the type of measures that can be adopted under this Article and on the process of adoption itself. Thus, the Article envisages the

[150] Though Member States are required to clarify their objectives and establish that any funding provided does not exceed what is necessary to provide the services in question. For more detailed explanation of this area, see Chapter 6 by Josh Holmes in this volume and, for previous commentary, Craufurd Smith, R, 'State Support for Public Service Broadcasting: The Position under European Community Law', *Legal Issues of Economic Integration*, 28 (2001), p 3. Given the recent ruling of the Court of Justice in Case C-280/00, *Altmark Trans GmbH and Regierungspräsidium Magdeburg v Nahverkehrsgesellschaft Altmark GmbH*, available at http://curia.eu.int/en/content/juris/index.htm, state funding for public service broadcasting will in many instances fall outside the scope of the Treaty state aid provisions, on the basis that it constitutes payment for a service and does not advantage the recipient within the meaning of Article 87(1).

[151] See discussion below at text accompanying n 158.

passing of 'incentive' measures only and excludes harmonization, while unanimous voting is required in the Council. These limitations may in part explain why the MEDIA plus programme, introduced at the end of 2000, was based solely on the third paragraph of Article 157, the industry Article, even though the decision refers to the importance of ensuring that WTO negotiations do not threaten Member States' cultural and audio-visual policies, and expressly includes among its objectives 'respect for and promotion of linguistic and cultural diversity in Europe'.[152] Though the MEDIA programme does not attempt to harmonize national laws, and could potentially have been introduced under Article 151, Article 157(3) has the attraction of not requiring Council unanimity. The Commission may consequently prefer to rely on an Article other than Article 151 when proposing measures with a cultural dimension, in that this may allow the objections of particular Member States in relation, for example, to the financial implications of a project to be overridden.

The temptation to introduce what are essentially cultural measures on grounds other than Article 151 could consequently be quite significant, but the Community legislature, by taking such action, runs the risk of proceedings for annulment being brought on the basis that it has acted outwith its powers.[153] In order to defend itself, the legislature would have to show that there were genuine grounds, other than cultural, for the measure, even though cultural considerations were also at play.[154] The overlap that often exists between cultural, industrial, and free movement concerns may nevertheless render it relatively easy to justify the use of a Treaty base other than Article 151 in such circumstances.

Since Article 151 was introduced significant steps have been taken to determine the main lines of Community cultural policy. Between 1996 and 1999 the Community initiated three major action programmes: Kaleidoscope (total budget for 1996–1998, €26.5 million), Ariane (total budget for 1997–1999, €11.1 million), and Raphaël (total budget for 1997–2000, €30 million).[155] Kaleidosope aimed at promoting cultural creation and supporting projects with a European dimension, understood as involving partnerships between organizations from at least three Member States. Ariane offered support for books and reading, in particular for translation. Lastly, Raphaël offered

[152] Council Decision (EC) No 2000/821 on the Implementation of a Programme to Encourage the Development, Distribution and Promotion of European Audiovisual Works, OJ [2001] L 13/35, at recital 14 and Article 2.

[153] Case C-376/98, *Germany v European Parliament and Council* [2000] ECR I-8419.

[154] Ibid., para 88.

[155] Council Decisions (EC) Nos 719/96, OJ [1996] L 99/20; 2085/97, OJ [1997] L 291/26; and 2228/97, OJ [1997] L 305/31, respectively.

assistance to Member States to help preserve cultural heritage of European significance. The limited finance available for these programmes meant, however, that many applicants for funds were unsuccessful and the results tended to be fragmented. In January 2000 they were replaced by the Culture 2000 programme, which draws together the existing strands of Community support for culture under one financial framework.[156] As one would expect, the main lines of action of Culture 2000, which is set to run to the end of 2004, closely map the contours of Article 151. The focus is thus on initiatives designed to increase awareness of European cultures and European values; to highlight cultural diversity and promote innovation; to conserve and safeguard cultural heritage of European significance; to facilitate access to culture; and to establish an effective external cultural policy.

As previously noted, the conception of culture employed by the Commission in its application of the Culture 2000 programme appears wider than that used in other contexts, such as the control of state aid. The Commission was criticized over its management of the programmes that preceded Culture 2000, both for its failure, on occasion, to discuss the definition of culture at all and for adopting an unduly narrow definition, one which was considered to favour high culture and material objects, such as buildings and art treasures, over the symbolic or spiritual dimensions of culture.[157] A rather more expansive approach is evident in the Commission's *Communication on the First European Community Framework Programme in Support of Culture*, in which it noted that 'culture is no longer restricted to "highbrow" culture (fine arts, music, dance, theatre, literature). Today, the concept also covers popular culture, mass-produced culture, everyday culture.'[158] In establishing Community initiatives under Article 151 the Commission has therefore kept its options open and maintained a potentially broad sphere of operations.

This expansiveness has ultimately caused problems for the operation of the Culture 2000 programme. The Commission itself is of the view that 'the very wide variety of themes and the low visibility of Community support undertaken' has made it impossible to conclude 'that the goals of ensuring access and participation by the largest number of citizens in cultural activities and

[156] European Parliament and Council Decision No 508/2000/EC Establishing the Culture 2000 Programme, OJ [2000] L 63/1.

[157] Committee of the Regions, *Opinion on Culture and Cultural Differences and their Significance for the Future of Europe*, Opinion of 13 March 1998, COM 7/004, at para 2.1.3, discussing its earlier comments on the Raphaël programme.

[158] European Commission, *Communication on the First European Community Framework Programme in Support of Culture* (2000–2004), COM(1998) 266 final, p 3.

reinforcing the citizen's feeling of belonging' have been met.[159] In a recent report on the implementation of Culture 2000, the European Parliament noted that the programme's objectives had fluctuated from one year to the next and that this, coupled with an unduly bureaucratic approach and administrative delays, had led to confusion among potential applicants.[160] Concern was also voiced at the fact that the experts, appointed to make an initial determination as to eligibility for grants, were required to apply a range of extremely open-ended criteria. The Parliament concluded that there was a need for greater focus and continuity in the operation of the programme. It also called for reassessment of the composition and operation of the committee of experts, and the provision of greater feedback to those applicants who fail to win funding.

Most importantly, Community action targeted specifically at the cultural field has been circumscribed by the limited funds made available for this purpose. Though Culture 2000 was framed in extremely ambitious terms, with regard to both ambit and objectives, it was allocated a budget of just €167 million. This represents only a fraction of the sums earmarked for the MEDIA programme (€400 million for the period 2001–2005) and is dwarfed by the sums allocated to the Structural Funds (€195 billion for the period 2000–2006). The Media and Structural Funds do, however, indicate the existence of other important sources of Community funding for cultural projects which are not founded on Article 151. Delgado Moreira has calculated that support for cultural projects from the Structural Funds between 1994 and 1999 amounted to around 12.8 billion ecus.[161] Overall, therefore, Community assistance for culture far exceeds that allocated to the Culture 2000 programme. This indicates that there is a greater readiness on the part of the Member States to support cultural projects that pursue established economic or developmental goals, where the return on their investment may be considered rather more tangible.[162] It may also be relevant that cohesion policy is an area where Member States continue to exert considerable influence over the national projects which receive Community funding.[163] The fact that culture

[159] European Commission, preparatory documentation for the Second Forum on Cultural Cooperation in Europe, paper entitled *Rethinking the Future of Cultural Cooperation in Europe*, p 4.

[160] European Parliament, *Report on the implementation of the 'Culture 2000' programme*, A5–0018/2002 final.

[161] Delgado Moreira, above n 114, at p 459.

[162] It may be noted that Structural Fund support is also conditional on national funding, the 'additionality' principle.

[163] The respective influence of the Commission, European Parliament, Member States, and sub-state actors is discussed in Peterson, J and Bomberg, E, *Decision-Making in the European Union* (London: Macmillan Press, 1999), at pp 156–70.

is not itself the primary object of such funds inevitably influences, however, the type of projects which receive grants. Thus, support for cultural initiatives by the Regional Development Fund is conditional on the funded activity creating sustainable jobs.[164]

The above analysis suggests that the impact of Article 151 has been extremely variable. Without an appropriate framework for the consistent application of the fourth paragraph of Article 151, and with only limited official data concerning its operation, it is difficult to draw firm conclusions as to the influence of this provision. There is, however, very little to indicate that it has affected to any significant degree the activities of the Court of Justice or Community legislature, though it may have influenced the Commission in certain areas when applying the Treaty competition provisions. Cultural concerns were recognized prior to 1992 within the Community legal system, and the growing awareness of cultural issues that we now see in certain sectors, such as agriculture or the operation of the Structural Funds, probably has more to do with changes to society and effective lobbying than Article 151 itself. Paragraph 4 has consequently still to realize its full (arguably far from insignificant) potential.

By contrast, paragraphs 1 to 3 of Article 151 have already had a tangible impact, enabling the Community to start to develop distinct cultural policies. Important steps have been taken to identify key objectives, and many valuable projects and networks have received Community support. But, as we have also noted, this aspect of Article 151 has equally encountered difficulties. Uncertainty has been created by the very open-ended nature of certain Community initiatives and the administration of the Culture 2000 programme has been far from satisfactory. Perhaps most importantly, limited funding and the procedural restrictions contained in Article 151(5) have significantly constrained the development of Community cultural initiatives.

5. Concluding observations

It would seem appropriate at the end of this essentially backward-looking chapter to consider how Community activities in the cultural field might develop in the future. One can conclude from the text of the Draft Treaty for a Constitution for Europe, agreed in July 2003, that if a new Constitution is ultimately adopted there will be relatively few changes to Community

[164] Council Regulation (EC) No 1783/1999 on the European Regional Development Fund, above n 137, at Article 2(2)(d).

competence in this area.[165] The Draft Constitution incorporates the text of Article 151 almost verbatim, although it does introduce one important amendment, in that the requirement of Council unanimity is replaced with majority voting.[166] With 10 new members joining the Union in 2004, this change would seem essential if cultural initiatives are to have any chance of being agreed. Although Member States may consequently find themselves outvoted on cultural issues, the prohibition on introducing harmonizing measures has been maintained, and it is harmonization which Member States are likely to consider the most threatening form of action in this context. Without the ability to fall back on their 'veto' in the Council, Member States may instead place greater reliance on the principle of subsidiarity. The importance ascribed to subsidiarity in this context is underlined by the decision to position the culture Article in the Draft Constitution within a new category of what are termed 'supporting, coordinating or complementary' actions. In future Member States could well employ subsidiarity not only to deter measures at any early stage of their development, but also, if the Constitution is agreed in its present form, to challenge measures after their adoption.[167]

It may be noted that although the Convention members were prepared to move to majority voting in the context of the proposed new culture Article, they were not prepared to do the same with regard to international trade negotiations. Article III-217(4) of the Draft Constitution maintains Council unanimity for trade negotiations in relation to 'cultural and audiovisual services where these risk prejudicing the Union's cultural and linguistic diversity'.

With regard to the Culture 2000 programme, it is expected that this will be extended for a further two years until the end of 2006, with the same objectives and roughly the same financial allocation, despite the inevitable impact of the forthcoming enlargement.[168] A new programme will then take its place, and the Commission has embarked on a public consultation exercise to determine its objectives and mode of operation.[169] The foregoing analysis of

[165] CONV 850/03, Draft Treaty establishing a Constitution for Europe, available at http://european-convention.eu.int/docs/Treaty/cv00850.en03.pdf.

[166] The provision relating to culture in the Draft Treaty is currently Article III-176.

[167] Therese Kaufmann and Gerald Raunig, at p 12 of their 2002 study, *Anticipating European Cultural Policies*, available at the website of the European Institute for Progressive Cultural Policies at http://www.eipcp.net/, note that 'a too narrow application of the subsidiarity principle in connection with the requirement of [Council] unanimity . . . has slowed the processing of cultural programmes considerably'.

[168] Commission press release IP/03/549, 'Culture 2000 and MEDIA programmes up to 2006', available at the Europa website at http://europa.eu.int/rapid/start/cgi/guesten.ksh.

[169] European Commission, *Designing the Future Programme of Cultural Cooperation for the European Union after 2006, Public Consultation Programme*, April 2003, at http://europa.eu.int/comm/culture/eac/consult_en_fin.pdf.

Article 151 has highlighted a number of issues, three of which are considered in more detail below, which must be addressed if a successful replacement to the Culture 2000 programme is to be introduced. It may be noted that there are important overlaps between these issues, which concern the Community's priorities in the cultural field; the impact of the principle of subsidiarity in this area; and the appropriate level of public or institutional participation in the framing and implementation of Community cultural initiatives. Nor, it should be added, is there one 'right answer' to the questions asked.

(a) What priorities should the Community have in the cultural field?

The vague and potentially all-embracing nature of the word 'culture' encourages the framing of over-general and ambitious cultural policies. One of the criticisms levelled at the Culture 2000 programme by the many organizations that attended the Community's 2001 Forum on Cultural Cooperation was that the programme was 'too general and over-reaching' and that its broad scope was ultimately unproductive.[170] As a result, funds have been spread too thinly and potential applicants for assistance have sometimes found it difficult to ascertain the exact criteria on which their projects have been accepted or rejected. Member States are unwilling to allocate significant finance for the development of policies under Article 151 and, without there being any apparent prospect of a change in this situation, the Community will have to be realistic as to what it can achieve under this head. This is not to conclude that the general objectives identified in the Culture 2000 programme, such as facilitating access to culture or assisting with conservation, should inevitably be cut back, but it may not be possible to pursue all of these objectives at the same time, and clear priorities need to be established for any area which is actively pursued. The financial problems are likely to be exacerbated with the entry of new Community members in 2004, many of whom have extremely limited funds for cultural projects and who will consequently look to the EU for assistance.[171]

[170] Commission report on the debates held during the Forum on Cultural Cooperation in Europe, which took place in Brussels on 21 and 22 November 2001, available at http://europa.eu.int/comm/culture/eac/pdf_word/synthese.pdf, in particular at pp 4 and 8.

[171] Many cultural organizations operating in central and eastern Europe are experiencing severe financial problems. Even participation in Europe-wide networks has proved difficult, particularly given the inability of the accession countries during the early stages of the Culture 2000 programme to recoup their costs from Community sources, on which see the study by Raimund Minichbauer and Elke Mitterdorfer, 'European Cultural Networks and Networking in Central and Eastern Europe', published in 2000 and available at the website of the European Institute for Progressive Cultural Policies, at http://www.eipcp.net/.

It has been noted that there are significant resources available for cultural initiatives outside the ambit of Article 151, in particular from the Structural Funds. Community action under Article 151 could thus be increasingly coordinated with, or even replaced by, initiatives under other Treaty Articles. Such coordination is not without its dangers, however, given the economic objectives that underpin the majority of these funds, and care will have to be taken that the cultural aspects of a given project are not compromised. This will require effective cooperation and dialogue among the various Directorates-General concerned, with initiatives being taken forward in partnership. Culture should not be superficially 'taken into account' once the main lines of a project have already been determined. The Council has recently called on the Commission to compile a report on the cultural dimension of the EU Structural Funds for the period 1994–1999, and this may help to clarify the considerable synergies that are possible in this area.[172]

It may also be observed that not all Community actions require major financial input. An important dimension to the Culture 2000 programme, for example, has been the provision of support for networks among those involved in the cultural field in order to stimulate innovation, increase awareness of other cultures, and lead to the exchange of useful information and skills. The development of specific websites can also be an effective way of making culture more widely accessible. Expenditure need not always be significant, therefore, to have an appreciable impact.

There are clearly many potential answers to the question 'which cultural activities should be prioritized at Community level'. Certain activities are likely to prove contentious because of the operation of the subsidiarity principle, considered below, but even if we exclude these from consideration, extensive possibilities remain. Should, for example, the Community restrict itself to working 'upstream' to encourage artistic training and 'downstream' to support the distribution of culture, thereby cutting out aid for creation itself, which may well be contentious. Alternatively, should the Community provide sectoral funding on a rotating basis, supporting, for example, performing arts one year and cultural heritage the next, as it has done to some extent with the Culture 2000 programme? The participants at the 2001 Forum on Cultural Cooperation in Europe, although unable to agree a specific list of objectives, identified the following as important: promoting cultural dialogue both

[172] Council Resolution of 26 May 2003 on the Horizontal Aspects of Culture: Increasing Synergies with other Sectors and Community Actions and Exchanging Good Practices in Relation to the Social and Economic Dimensions of Culture, OJ [2003] C 136/1, in particular at para 10.

beyond the boundaries of Europe and within Europe; facilitating the mobility of artists and their works; encouraging innovation; assisting networks and enhancing synergies among projects or networks.[173] It is interesting that this list does not include facilitating access to cultural works, promoting cultural and artistic events, or encouraging awareness of culture or history, which were considered to be unduly ambitious.[174]

The Council has itself taken steps to identify what it considers to be the priority areas for Community intervention in the cultural field. Some of the objectives, which are held to be indicative only, are clearly designed to set parameters to Community intervention in this area and ensure effective administration, thus there is a reference to the need to identify what constitutes 'added European value', to ensure synergies among the various Community activities that affect culture, and to enhance cooperation among the Member States with regard to cultural statistics and cultural goods. Other elements closely match the objectives identified by the Forum participants, such as the promotion of dialogue among different cultures, international cooperation, facilitating mobility for those in the cultural sector, and analysing the means of encouraging the development of the creative industries in the Community. The Council list diverges in flagging up the importance of culture for social inclusion and the need for initiatives to improve 'access to, and visibility of, cultural action of the Community'. This latter objective points to the strategic use of cultural policy in order to enhance public support for the European Union, with the possible implication that funding will not be available for cultural activities which offer a more critical perspective on European integration. To the extent that this objective merely seeks to ensure the visibility of Community cultural initiatives in order to enhance access it is unobjectionable, but if intended for more instrumental purposes it should be rejected.

In a similar vein, Therese Kaufmann and Gerald Raunig, in a recent study, argue against Community funding for emblematic or symbolic projects. They instead call on the Community to foster the development of critical public spheres in which the role of culture in society can be debated and culture used to enhance the political process.[175] Public participation in the cultural field is emphasized, particularly in relation to the new information technologies, and the authors adopt a multilateral and outward-looking perspective, entailing

[173] See record of the 2001 Forum detailed at text referred to above at n 170, pp 8–9.

[174] Ibid.

[175] Kaufmann, T and Raunig, G, 'Anticipating European Cultural Policies', November 2002 position paper, available at http://www.eipcp.net/.

enhanced cooperation among individuals and organizations located not only in Europe but worldwide.

It is equally important that Community cultural programmes engage with contemporary issues and problems. For this, the Community will need to reflect on the major motors of change in modern European societies, since only then will it be in a position to engage in debate as to whether Community intervention is desirable, or even possible, in order to influence these developments. Pursuing this approach might lead the Community to focus, for example, on a cluster of projects designed to further cultural understanding and reduce tensions in multicultural societies; to identify those aspects of the rural and urban landscape which enhance the quality of citizens' lives, and to consider how these aspects might be promoted or protected; or to explore how cultural institutions and public spaces can remain accessible to, and meaningful for, the public in the light of technological change and the freezing, or cutting back, of traditional sources of revenue. Apart from financial support for particular projects, the Community can here perform an extremely useful role in supporting research and acting as a forum for the development and exchange of ideas. The Community has in fact engaged in a number of projects along these lines, but for the most part outside the scope of Article 151. Given the variety of interests at play, projects of this type require close cooperation among the various Directorates-General concerned, along the lines indicated above.

Though any list of priorities will inevitably prove contentious given the range of interests at stake, there is likely to be greater acceptance of the ultimate outcome if the general public and specialized organizations have had adequate opportunities to comment on proposals and express their points of view, an issue discussed in more detail at point *(c)* below. Legitimacy may be derived from the open nature of the consultation process, the clarity with which policy objectives are identified, and the existence of mechanisms through which institutions can be made accountable for the implementation of those objectives.

(b) What are the implications of subsidiarity for Community cultural action?

It has been suggested that a move to majority voting in the Council for cultural measures could result in Member States making greater use of the principle of subsidiarity in order to block measures. Certain states appear unconvinced of the desirability of ascribing to the Community competence in the cultural field at all, and would prefer cultural issues to be determined at the national level. Thus, the Dutch representative at the convention established to draft a European Constitution, Frans Timmermans, is reported as having stated that '[m]any in the Convention feel that culture should be given back to the national level and that there is a disadvantage with economies of scale'.[176] It is consequently important to clarify the operation of the subsidiarity principle so as to prevent its improper deployment as a mechanism merely to slow down or block new cultural initiatives.

The Council included in its June 2002 work plan the objective of clarifying what constitutes 'European added value',[177] and in December of that year it set out a list of cumulative factors which it considered to be indicative of European added value.[178] Though this latter phrase may not be entirely on all fours with the term 'subsidiarity' in Article 5 of the Treaty, it is probable that the Member States consider them to be closely linked.[179] The factors identified by the Council include the multilateral nature of a given project; the fact that it encourages cooperation among Member States; the fact that it addresses, reaches, and benefits primarily citizens in Europe and enhances mutual knowledge of cultures; and, lastly, that the project aims at broad visibility, accessibility, and sustainability. The value of this list is, however, undermined by the lack of explanatory reasoning, and certain of the factors appear questionable. The requirement that projects should primarily benefit citizens in Europe, for example, could clearly restrict international initiatives, while it is arguable that a multilateral element, though a good basis for Community intervention, should not always be required. Thus, there may be a case for Community assistance to help preserve a particular heritage site, where the Member State in which it is located does not have the resources to accomplish the restoration. It will usually, however, be relatively easy to incorporate a multilateral element by ensuring the participation of experts from different countries. The criterion of 'visibility' is also of doubtful relevance, a point previously made in section *(a)* above. The Council's list is consequently not

[176] European Policy Centre, Communication to Members S24/03, 3 April 2003, *Education and Culture in the Consitututional Treaty*, at http://europa.eu.int/futurum/documents/other/oth080403_en.pdf, p 3.

[177] Council Resolution of 25 June 2002 on a New Work Plan on European Cooperation in the Field of Culture, OJ [2002] C 162/05, Annex.

[178] Council Resolution of 19 December 2002 Implementing the Work Plan on European Cooperation in the Field of Culture: European Added Value and Mobility of Persons and Circulation of Works in the Cultural Sector, OJ [2003] C 13/5, para 9.

[179] For there to be compliance with Article 5 it must be shown that the cultural action could 'not be sufficiently achieved by the Member States', and that by reason of its 'scale or effects' it would be better achieved by the Community.

the last word on this subject and further consideration is needed as to the criteria to be employed when determining whether cultural objectives are to be pursued at the international, Community, national, or sub-national levels.

(c) How to ensure adequate participation in the formulation, agreement, and implementation of Community cultural programmes

Do the procedures used to determine cultural policy, and to implement it, allow sufficient input from interested parties? As the previous discussion will have illustrated, different individuals, groups, and institutions have very different agendas with regard to cultural policy, so that dialogue between them can be extremely beneficial, causing parties to develop or reconsider their positions. It is thus important for cultural issues to be identified at an early stage of policy formation to enable all interested parties to play a role in the consultation process. The participants at the 2001 Forum on Cultural Cooperation in Europe noted that although the Commission had generally instituted effective consultation procedures when developing policies in the field of research, the environment, and development, this had not always been so in the cultural field.[180] One way to enhance participation would be to establish a permanent advisory body, a possible 'Cultural Observatory', linked to the Commission.[181] The various networks of actors operating in the cultural field which the Commission has helped to develop may also constitute a useful reference point in this context.

But dialogue can also take place within, as well as between, institutions, and this is particularly so in the context of the European Community. For example, when incentive measures are proposed under Article 151, the lead Directorate-General in the Commission will be the Directorate-General for Culture and Education, but the process of inter-service consultation requires that all other interested Directorates-General be consulted. Similarly, where cultural issues are raised outside the immediate confines of Article 151, in the field of the internal market or competition policy, for example, the Directorate-General for Culture and Education will have to be consulted. The lead Directorate-General is not, however, required to adapt its proposals in the light of comments received and may prefer to argue for its position at Cabinet or College of Commissioner levels. Given that paragraph 4 of Article 151 merely requires cultural issues to be 'taken into account' outside the confines of the title on culture, the Directorate-General for Culture and Education

[180] See report of the proceedings of the 2001 Forum detailed above at n 170, at p 7.
[181] Ibid., and text accompanying n 116 above.

may find that it has relatively little influence when faced with one of its more established, heavyweight counterparts.

More serious concerns may be expressed regarding the role of the European Parliament in the legislative process. The use of the co-decision procedure in Article 151 undoubtedly enhances its input, affording it an ultimate power of veto, though the current requirement of unanimity in the Council also curtails what can realistically be achieved under this Article. The Parliament is not required, however, to be consulted on Council recommendations under Article 151 and, in other areas where cultural issues may arise, its role in the legislative process is limited. It has, for example, merely a right to be consulted on any increase in the rights of European citizens (Article 22), on actions to combat discrimination based, *inter alia*, on sex, racial or ethnic origin, religion or belief (Article 13), on the Common Agricultural Policy (Article 37), on the liberalization of services in the single market (Article 52), and on measures regarding state aids (Article 89). Such influence that the Parliament has in the field of cohesion policy stems largely from its budgetary competence.[182] It has no input at all in the setting of the common customs tariff, the common commercial policy, or in formulating recommendations in the fields of employment or education. Given that it is precisely in these areas that difficult balances may have to be struck between commercial and cultural interests, for example in the context of World Trade Organization negotiations, greater input from the democratically elected Parliament is clearly required.[183]

From the point of view of the Committee of the Regions the position is even less satisfactory: it is not a fully-fledged Community institution and its role is purely of an advisory nature. Though it has developed a number of thoughtful opinions on the Community's cultural policy, these have been of limited influence. The Committee must currently be consulted on Community proposals in 10 areas, one of which is, of course, incentive measures (though not recommendations) under Article 151, but there are contexts in which cultural issues could arise where the Committee will have no input at all. Thus, where a cultural issue is raised in the context of an internal market, competition or Common Agricultural Policy measure, there is no obligation on the

[182] Peterson and Bomberg, above n 163, pp 158–9.

[183] The Draft Treaty establishing a Constitution for Europe, above n 165, if agreed along the lines of the July 2003 draft would improve the position of the European Parliament in certain respects. The Parliament would, e.g., be a co-legislator in those areas of discrimination currently enumerated in Article 13 and in relation to citizens' rights and the procedures governing European Parliament elections: Articles III 8–10. In these areas the draft does, however, require unanimity in the Council.

Council or Commission to consult the Committee. To date, the Committee appears to have had most influence on the Commission. Cooperation with the European Parliament has to some extent been undermined by rivalry over claims to regional representation, while the attitude of the Council to the Committee has been characterized simply as one of 'benign indifference'.[184]

Despite the enhancement of the Committee's democratic credentials by the Nice Treaty, which requires its members to be elected representatives of regional or local bodies, or politically accountable to an elected assembly, it is open to debate whether its role should extend beyond the purely advisory.[185] But even at the consultative level, it is clear that improvements could be made. Spurred on by the debate surrounding the Commission's White Paper on *European Governance*, the Committee argued for greater involvement in the early stages of policy formation, with an organizational capacity to prepare exploratory reports, as well as a role in reviewing the impact of Community measures at the local and regional levels.[186] A case can also be made for some input at the conciliation stage of the co-decision procedure in those instances where prior consultation is mandatory. It is apparent that the Committee could offer particularly valuable advice on the operation and implementation of the Community's cultural programmes. The Committee has also called for the right to bring annulment actions under Article 230 in order, among other things, to ensure respect for the principle of subsidiarity, and it is arguable that the Committee could play a similar role in monitoring the application of paragraph 4 of Article 151.

Once a measure has been agreed the Community will generally rely on expert assistance to implement it, and it is important that this is sufficiently representative. There has recently been some interest in the creation of decentralized bodies, linking partners from different European countries, to implement Community policy in the cultural field.[187] But alongside the experts there should also be scope for the public to play an active role in the implementation of cultural programmes which directly affect them. An example of a forward-looking measure that emphasizes public involvement is the Council of Europe European Landscape Convention, which seeks to protect

[184] Jeffery, C, 'Social and Regional Interests: ESC and Committee of the Regions', in Peterson, J and Shackleton, M, *The Institutions of the European Union* (Oxford: OUP, 2002), at pp 341–2.

[185] Jeffery, ibid., discusses the German Länders' early support for a distinct legislative role.

[186] Committee of the Regions' opinions on *European Governance*, COR/02/03662, and the *Division of powers in the European Union*, COR/02/03658. European Commission, *European Governance White Paper*, COM (2001) 428 final.

[187] See report of the proceedings of the 2001 Forum, detailed above at n 170, at p 12.

European landscapes through a mix of national initiatives and European cooperation.[188] The Convention is premised on the understanding that landscape is of considerable cultural importance and plays a significant role in shaping identity. In terms of operation, the Convention requires a high level of public consultation and participation, both when valuable landscapes, and the forces operating upon them, are identified and when landscape quality objectives are set.

(d) Conclusion

Ten years after its introduction, it is apparent that the title on culture in the European Community Treaty remains as Delphic and controversial as ever. One must not forget, however, that the open-ended nature of the provisions in Article 151 affords considerable scope for the articulation of fundamental values and the development of policies designed to enhance creativity and cross-cultural understanding. Such understanding is particularly important given the present climate of social uncertainty and rising xenophobia. The very vagueness of the terms used in Article 151 can form the basis for fruitful dialogue within an enlarged Community and with the wider world. From this perspective, Article 151 provides only a point of departure, as opposed to a definitive route map, for those seeking to establish a set of coherent and meaningful cultural policies for the European Union.

[188] Council of Europe, European Landscape Convention, ETS No 176, available at http://conventions.coe.int/. See, in particular, Article 5c.

Part II

Trading Cultures: Culture and Commerce in the European Union

3

Labels, Locals, and the Free Movement of Goods

*Niamh Nic Shuibhne**

1. Introduction

The very idea of free movement of goods throughout the European Community raises questions of compatibility, and thus potential clashes, with national or regional production requirements and localized consumer tastes: essentially, how can a balance be struck between what the market *can* provide and what producers and consumers *already* know and practise? This concern is nothing new; the Community institutions have long grappled with the implications of this dynamic, and the Court of Justice (ECJ) in particular has generated some of the classic principles of internal market law in the process.[1] The approach of the Court and of the EC legislative actors does warrant substantive debate, but it is a debate already well underway. In the bulk of EC case law and legislation, 'local' interest is entangled typically with the objective of consumer protection; and, in particular, the Court's faith in both the value of market breadth and the omnipotence of appropriate product labelling in this context is well documented.[2]

* School of Law, University of Edinburgh. Thanks to Robert Lane, Victor Tadros, and John Usher, and to Rachael Craufurd Smith and the participants in the Edinburgh workshop.

[1] Many of these issues will be raised throughout the paper, but some of the key judgments in this context include Case 120/78, *Rewe-Zentrale AG v Bundesmonopolverwaltung für Branntwein (Cassis de Dijon)* [1979] ECR 649 and, in application, Case 178/84, *Commission v Germany* [1987] ECR 1227 (*German Beer Purity*) and Case 407/85, *Drei Glocken v USL Centro-Sud* [1988] ECR 4233 (*Durum Wheat Pasta*); more recently, see Case C-405/98, *Konsumentombudsmannen (KO) v Gourmet International Products AB (GIP)* [2001] ECR I-1795, Case C-123/00, *Bellamy v English Shop Wholesale SA* [2001] ECR I-2795, and Case C-416/00, *Morellato*, judgment of 18 September 2003, not yet reported.

[2] Again, these points will be developed in the course of this paper, but see generally, Weatherill, S, *EC Consumer Law and Policy* (London: Longman, 1997), Steyger, E, *National Traditions and European Community Law: Margarine and Marriage* (Aldershot: Dartmouth, 1997), and von Heydebrand ud Lasa, H-C, 'Free Movement of Foodstuffs, Consumer Protection and Food

In order to look afresh at the internal/local market tension, the key objective of this paper is to bring cultural diversity itself more to centre stage, asking, essentially, if cultural diversity can (or should) take greater prominence in respect of the free movement of goods, above and beyond its status as an offshoot of consumer protection. Through this lens, we see culture infusing everyday consumer and trade practices; we see further that language choice infuses culture. The methodological focus of the paper is thus rooted in Articles 28 and 30 EC, in the domain of quantitative restrictions on imports and measures having equivalent effect, in discrimination and market access, in the principle of proportionality, and in the potential for justification. But the underlying threads invoke a broad and inclusive conception of culture, looking to the diversity inherent in locality and whether this merits specific protection in the EC trade paradigm, or not.

In summary, Article 28 states curtly that '[q]uantitative restrictions on imports and all measures having equivalent effect shall be prohibited between Member States'. The meaning of 'equivalent effect' was established (enduringly) by the Court of Justice in *Dassonville*, to encompass '[a]ll trading rules enacted by Member States which are capable of hindering, directly or indirectly, actually or potentially, intra-Community trade'.[3] The full implications of this definition became all the more apparent in *Cassis de Dijon*, where the Court confirmed that even 'indistinctly applicable' measures (that is, national rules applying to both national and imported products) could fall foul of Article 28, where the impact of the rule was likely in fact/effect to hinder trade between Member States—thus generating indirect discrimination. In this way, the scope of Article 28 was steered beyond the need to establish a protectionist intent.[4] The Court later attempted to contain the expansionist potential it had created, however, when it distinguished in *Keck and Mithouard* between rules relating inherently to the product itself (still potentially caught by Article 28 EC) and what it termed 'certain selling arrangements' that applied equally to all products, both in law and in fact/effect, and were thus outwith the scope of the provision.[5] Lastly, in terms of justification of measures found *prima facie* to breach Article 28, distinctly applicable measures can be saved only by Member State recourse to Article 30 EC, a provision that

Standards in the European Community: Has the Court of Justice got it Wrong?', *ELRev*, 16 (1991), 391–415.

[3] Case 8/74, *Procureur du Roi v Dassonville* [1974] ECR 837, para 5; see also Article 2 of (the now redundant) Directive 70/50, OJ [1970] L 13/29.

[4] See Bernard, N, 'Discrimination and Free Movement in EC Law', *ICLQ*, 45 (1996), 82–108, at 91.

[5] Case C-267–268/91, *Criminal Proceedings against Keck and Mithouard* [1993] ECR I-6097, especially at paras 11–18.

codifies an exhaustive list of grounds (including the protection of health and life of humans, and the protection of national treasures possessing artistic, historic, or archaeological value, but excluding consumer protection), subject to the overriding principle of proportionality (a concept fleshed out below). Article 30 EC also marks the first point of argument for the justification of indistinctly applicable rules;[6] but here, Member States may seek also to establish objective justification in terms of 'mandatory (or imperative) requirements', an open-ended category first established by the Court in *Cassis de Dijon* but subject, once again, to proportionality.[7]

Against this general background, and more definitively to site the specific role of culture in the free movement of goods, the parameters of this paper will first be marked in a substantive sense by introducing the 'labels and locals' regimes referred to in the title (see section 2.). To this end, the Community rules on product labelling and on the registration of protected product names will be outlined; emphasis will be placed primarily on the rules relating to foodstuffs, in an attempt to look at a manageable sector and so that the rules on labelling and product origin can more readily be compared. The core proposition of adopting culture/cultural diversity as an exception to the free movement of goods will then be explored (see section 3.)—in other words, to what extent can the protection of culture be used to justify a measure which amounts otherwise to a breach of Article 28 EC? The different ways in which Article 28 EC can be breached will need to be borne in mind here, given the different justificatory regimes that apply to the different forms or types of discrimination acknowledged in EC law. Lastly, although the scope of the paper is necessarily limited by its concentration on culture and the specific rules on product labelling and registration, it is nevertheless hoped that the conclusions developed in this context (see section 4.) reverberate across the spectrum of free movement more generally.

2. Labels and locals: outlining the EC protection regime

It was stated at the outset that the reconciliation of free movement ideology with local production and local market variables is something which has

[6] This point is discussed more fully in section 3. below.

[7] The simplistic manner in which the quantitative restriction framework is condensed above belies the uncertainties and confusions underlying some of its key concepts. Notwithstanding voluminous case law, legislation, and academic commentary on the free movement of goods, there is considerable divergence in terms of the use of relevant terminology, and its intended meaning and effect. The descriptive framework for the free movement of goods understood and intended here is drawn from Nic Shuibhne, N, 'The Free Movement of Goods and Article 28 EC: An Evolving Framework', *ELRev*, 27/4 (2002), 408–25.

always (unsurprisingly) had to concern the Community institutions. This section outlines two sets of rules relevant in this context (concentrating mainly, as noted, on foodstuffs): first, the rules developed—both legislative and judicial—in respect of product labelling; and, secondly, the more recently codified rules on product origin. To some extent, both frameworks are linked, though the impulse that drives the latter, and which would seek to maintain geographically localized markets, arguably succumbs to the widespread promotion of labelling more generally. In this sense, somewhat disparate (even opposing) motivations seem, initially at least, to lie behind the evolution of both regimes; moreover, a degree of judicial and legislative inconsistency can also be discerned. The extent to which the protection of cultural diversity features as a consideration will be presented where possible, thus setting the scene for more substantive discussion of this question in section 3. To this end, the linguistic aspects of the labelling regime are considered separately and in particular detail.

(a) Community rules on product labelling: ECJ jurisprudence and Directive 2000/13[8]

The basic rationale behind the Community rules on labelling stems from the landmark decision in *Cassis de Dijon*, the ethos of which was summarized above. To secure the free movement of goods throughout the Member States—and taking, as a base, a principle of mutual recognition rather than requiring all-out Community harmonization—it is preferred that product characteristics should (at least, up to a point) be communicated to the consumer by the appropriate use of labelling, rather than by demanding nationally responsive variations in the composition of the products themselves. Essentially, this means that locally formed consumer habits and various other product traditions will not usually defeat the goal of the common market, implying a hierarchy of information over expectation. It is a logic applied consistently and firmly by the Court of Justice,[9] and it does acknowledge the value of consumer protection. But this holds true only when read against a specific conception of consumer protection and of proportionality. As Weatherill has noted, this '[i]n part . . . depends on perceptions of the capacity of the consumer to look after him- or herself in the market',[10] a point, or characteristic, developed further below.

[8] OJ [2000] L 109/29; this Directive—on the approximation of the laws of the Member States relating to the labelling, presentation, and advertising of foodstuffs—consolidates in a single text the much-amended and now redundant Directive 79/112 (OJ [1979] L 33/1).

[9] See the citations in n 1 above and, generally, see Steyger, n 2 above, ch 2.

[10] Weatherill, n 2 above, p 47.

In addition to the judicial rules (which are of general application), national measures relating more specifically to the labelling, presentation, and advertising of foodstuffs (for sale to consumers) have been partially harmonized for over 20 years by Directive 79/112 (now 2000/13).[11] And, over and above this general legislative framework, a number of supplementary directives have been enacted for specific product categories.[12] The requirements imposed by Directive 2000/13 will not be scrutinized here, the detail of which may be ascertained simply by reading the Directive itself. Rather, in keeping with the overall aims of the paper, attention is directed to a more general consumer protection question which emerges (with the particular issues thrown up by the language of labelling discussed separately below). As stated expressly in its preamble (at recital 6), and confirmed consistently by the Court of Justice, Directive 2000/13 is grounded in consumer information and protection. In the main text, a number of general rules are set out in respect of what must appear on food labels—essentially, these concern the product name and certain 'particulars' (Article 3, with further elaboration in subsequent provisions of specific terms used therein—see, for example, Article 6 in respect of 'ingredients').[13] Critically, and notwithstanding the general principle that labelling is sufficient to bring differences in product characteristics to the attention of consumers, the Court has acknowledged that there *are* some situations 'in which product differences are so substantial as to permit national authorities to require separate product names'.[14]

Outwith the scope of this (and any other relevant) Directive—in other words, in the absence of harmonization—Member States are notionally free to regulate labelling matters themselves, via the adoption of national measures to codify national standards. But there exists still an overriding obligation

[11] See n 8 above. On harmonization of market rules and the notion of pre-emption, see Weatherill, n 2 above, pp 14–17.

[12] See Lister, C, 'The naming of foods: The European Community's rules for non-brand food products', *ELRev*, 18 (1993), 179–201, at 183. On the relationship between general and specific legislative provisions in this context, see Case C-136/96, *Scotch Whisky Association v Compagnie financière européenne de prises de participation and others* [1998] ECR-I 4571, paras 44–48.

[13] See Lister, n 12 above, pp 184–91, who identifies key trends within the ECJ judgments dealing with food names.

[14] Ibid., p 190, citing, e.g., Case 298/87, *Smanor SA* [1988] ECR 4489 (frozen yoghurt) and Case 286/86, *Ministère Public v Deserbais* [1988] ECR 4907 (Edam cheese); see, in the interim, the continued wrangling which led to Case C-317/97P, *Smanor and Ségaud v Commission* [1998] ECR I-4269 and, more recently, Case C-448/98, *Criminal Proceedings against Guimont* [2000] ECR I-10663, para 30, and Case C-366/98, *Geffroy v Casino France SNC* [2000] ECR I-6579, para 22. Advocate General Saggio has discussed what is now Article 5(1) of Directive 2000/13 as effectively codifying the Court's case law in this context (see para 18 of his Opinion in *Guimont*).

to comply with Article 28 EC and with the Court's *Cassis de Dijon* jurisprudence on mutual recognition: thus, Member States may be required to justify their national labelling requirements *and* to demonstrate that they are proportionate to the objective they seek to achieve. There exists, therefore, something of a dual or parallel system of rules on labelling—both legislative and judicial, with the latter applicable even where the former might not be. Moreover, the judicial rules, of course, apply generally and not just to foodstuffs, while the legislative schemes are more likely to match specific rules to specific categories of product.[15] The important point is that the Court's jurisprudence on labelling follows essentially the same rationale irrespective of whether a Community or national measure is being assessed—that similar considerations will apply to product categories covered by EC legislative provisions *and* to those which are not. And again, almost exclusively in this context, the underlying precept is that of consumer protection.

On one view, it would be necessary to consider, then, how successfully the EC labelling rules strike a balance between the competing interests of the internal market and the locally-attached consumer. The Court's view is, however, a bit different; it prefers to let the consumer loose in the Community market, a privilege which is deemed to take precedence over protection of localized habits and customs, and in which the integrity of consumer choice and the autonomy of consumer decision-making are adequately protected by the provision of information (legitimately, in the vast majority of cases, via labels). In this vein, Weatherill discusses some of the Court's case law in which the interests of consumer information and consumer protection vie for precedence, identifying instances where national rules on consumer protection were upheld (usually including a fusion with protection from unfair commercial practices).[16] These cases aside, though, what emerges more strongly is the Court's 'typical assumption of a "reasonably circumspect" consumer'.[17] This can be translated, for present purposes, into the consumer who actually reads, and understands, product labels and can make informed choices in consequence. But attention is often drawn also to the shortcomings of the labelling panacea.[18] Most prominently, perhaps, von Heydebrand ud Lasa's arguments

[15] See Steyger, n 2 above, p 50.

[16] See Weatherill, n 2 above, pp 52–7, referring to Case 286/81, *Oosthoek* [1982] ECR 4575 and Case 328/87, *Buet v Ministère Public* [1989] ECR 1235.

[17] Ibid., p 58, referring *inter alia* to Case C-315/92, *Verband Sozialer Wettbewerb v Clinique Laboratoires and Estée Lauder* [1994] ECR I-397. See also the discussion in Steyger, n 2 above, pp 35–7, on Case 174/82, *Sandoz BV* [1983] ECR 2445.

[18] See especially, von Heydebrand ud Lasa, n 2 above, p 401 *et seq*. Von Heydebrand ud Lasa does set out advantages of the labelling solution (pp 406–07), including its promotion of the free

converge basically towards his observation that consumers 'expect a certain amount of paternalism'.[19] But the reality is that the 'circumspect consumer' criterion has become all the more firmly entrenched; in *Gut Springenheide*, for example, the ECJ refers to 'the presumed expectations of an average consumer who is reasonably well informed and reasonably observant and circumspect'.[20] It is also likely that most national courts now take this interpretation for granted.[21]

Thus, we can perhaps now point to the 'euro-consumer', a creature not so much 'of Europe' but 'of the European Court'. There seems also to be a sliding scale of risk; in *Gut Springenheide*, for example, the circumspect consumer test was deemed to apply given that 'a mistake as to the product's characteristics cannot pose any risk to public health'.[22] The Court did not elaborate, however, on an alternative test for precisely such cases. Overall, the guiding requirement is seen to be that of proportionality; this means that any impingement on the free movement of goods—even one that is accepted as protecting consumers—must go only so far as is truly necessary to protect that interest.

But, significantly, there is also emerging more than a hint of subsidiarity. In the 'lifting cream' case, for example, in the context of misleading advertising/labels, the Court noted that social, cultural, and linguistic factors must be borne in mind in the application of the 'circumspect consumer' test; moreover, the national court could, if it considered this to be necessary, commission an expert opinion or survey to determine whether or not the particular promotional statement being challenged was, in fact, misleading for consumers in *that* Member State.[23] This results in an ostensibly objective test, but with an undeniably subjective slant attached. In this way, and leading to an arguably paradoxical result, the consumer is viewed ultimately through something of a local lens—so far as this is compatible with general assumptions

movement of goods and lower per unit costs for exporters, not to mention the reduction in the Commission's administrative load because of the resultant reduction in the need for harmonization of legislation; his sketch of the disadvantages, however (pp 408–12) is consumer-driven, suggesting overall a reduced level of consumer protection.

[19] Ibid., p 402.

[20] Case C-210/96, *Gut Springenheide and Tusky* [1998] ECR I-4657, para 31; see also Case C-303/97, *Sektkellerei Kessler* [1999] ECR I-513, paras 33 and 36.

[21] See, e.g., the observations of the German referring court in Case C-220/98, *Estée Lauder v Lancaster* [2000] ECR I-117, which noted that the ECJ 'presupposes a certain measure of alertness and discrimination on the part of the consumer' (reproduced at para 17).

[22] *Gut Springenheide*, n 20 above, para 28.

[23] *Estée Lauder*, n 21 above, paras 29 and 31; the directive approach of the Court here contrasts strongly with the more stridently prescriptive tone in *Verband Sozialer Wettbewerb*, n 17 above.

made regarding his or her circumspection and powers of observation, but with a significant degree of localness none the less. Is the ECJ euro-consumer something, then, of a misnomer? Because it would appear that an objective facet of his or her character—expressed through legislative and judicial faith in the market-widening potential of labelling and devised precisely to promote the free movement of goods over and above local prejudices—is *itself* subject, in the final analysis, to those very same (local) 'social, cultural, and linguistic' criteria. In common-sense terms, how could these criteria be ignored? But in internal market terms, how far can they be allowed into the equation? Originally, not very far, thinking of the *German Beer Purity* or *Durum Wheat Pasta* cases. But the no-win situation in which the Community institutions find themselves seems to have come further to the fore in more recent case law. There is a discernible sense of the Court handing the market 'back'. And this quandary is revealed even more acutely in the following section, which looks at one of the most potent channels of culture and localism—language.

(b) Labelling and language: easily understood?

Framing culturally local (or locally cultural) questions in consumer protection terms is, as evidenced by the sheer weight of jurisprudence, a perfectly valid approach; it is sometimes, however, a fairly subtle one, in that it is not always self-evident that cultural influences are in fact at play, or that consumer interests can protect those which are. And, as discussed later below, the rules on product origin have now taken root to protect precisely the situations in which localized criteria are clearly not subtle at all—or, more correctly, at least where this can be shown to fit within the framework of the relevant EC framework. Staying for now within the sphere of labelling rules, however, there is one strong manifestation of local and cultural difference that cannot really be avoided—given the importance that labels have assumed as a tool for facilitating the free movement of goods while catering for the interest of consumer protection, one of the most basic questions to be addressed, then, is the language(s) in which product labels must actually be written. Even within a single state, the competing concerns of different language groups may need to be taken into account; the task of setting language rules for a harmonized cross-border market—in which the consumers speak a multitude of languages—is altogether more complex. And EU enlargement has increased even the 'official' EU languages from 11 to 20.

As a starting point, the Court of Justice has treated specific linguistic requirements vis-à-vis labelling rules as measures having equivalent effect to a quantitative restriction (MEQRs), thus potentially breaching Article 28 EC, notwithstanding the close link between language and culture/identity (and, therefore, national and regional sensitivities).[24] On this view, if every Member State had specific linguistic requirements for all product labelling, the freedom of the EC market would clearly be impeded, just as it has been held to be where there existed specific rules on the ingredients of pasta or the purity of beer. Linguistic labelling rules are indistinctly applicable—in other words, they apply to both national and imported products—but they generate indirect discrimination, given that national producers will already satisfy national requirements and thus enjoy a competitive advantage within the domestic market. And so, if the rules setting national labelling standards are to be saved, objective justification in terms of mandatory or imperative requirements must come into play. To date, arguments made in this context have been grounded in the interest of consumer protection. Translating this into practical terms, we encounter at all turns the idea that product labels must be in a language 'easily understood' by the consumer, an attempt to avoid a plethora of state-specific rules yet still satisfying the basic need effectively to transmit information to the EC consumer. The 'easily understood' solution is codified in Article 16(1) of Directive 2000/13—formerly Article 14 of Directive 79/112[25]—unless 'the consumer is informed by means of other measures'.[26] Lastly, Article 16(3) provides for the possibility that labelling particulars may be indicated in several languages.[27]

The criterion of 'easily understood' was taken on board judicially as well as legislatively, obviously in cases involving interpretation of the Directive itself but also, significantly, even where labelling of the products in question fell outwith harmonized Community rules.[28] And crucially, a language 'easily understood' by consumers has been held not always to coincide with a state's national, official, and/or regional language(s)—contrary to what seems to have been assumed by the Member States and leading Steyger to note surprise that disputes on this aspect of the Directive did not arise before

[24] This was confirmed by the Court in Case C-169/99, *Hans Schwarzkopf GmbH & Co KG v Zentrale zur Bekämpfung unlauteren Wettbewerbs eV* [2001] ECR I-5901, para 39.

[25] Key amendments to this basic language rule—found now in Article 16(2) of Directive 2000/13—are discussed in detail below.

[26] The transmission of information by 'other measures' is understood typically to refer to 'the use of pictogrammes or signs other than words' (*Schwarzkopf*, n 24 above, para 40; see also, in relation to foodstuffs, Case C-33/97, *Colim v Bigg's* [1999] ECR I-3975, para 29).

[27] On multilingual labelling, see the decision in *Schwarzkopf*, n 24 above (relating to Directive 76/768 (OJ [1976] L 262/169) as amended by Directive 93/95 (OJ [1993] L 151/32), on, *inter alia*, the labelling of cosmetic products); the reasoning of the Court seems almost contradictory, however—cf. in particular, paras 34 and 35.

[28] *Colim*, n 26 above.

Piageme I.[29] The Court has since developed its reasoning through, most notably, *Meyhui*,[30] *Piageme II*,[31] *Colim*, and *Goerres*.[32] The judgment in *Colim* consolidated previous case law to a large extent, since it set down the principles to be applied for situations both within and outwith (what was then) Directive 79/112. Reflecting the exercise of shared Community/Member State competence, the Court dealt with the power to set language requirements as follows:

> [F]or certain categories of product, Community directives require the national language or languages to be used in order to enhance consumer or public health protection. When those directives fully harmonise the language requirements applicable for a given product, the Member States cannot impose additional language requirements. By contrast, where there is only partial Community harmonisation or none at all, the Member States in principle retain the power to impose additional language requirements.[33]

The competence of a Member State to impose additional language requirements is, however, limited by the fact that rules of this nature can constitute a barrier to intra-Community trade 'in so far as products coming from other Member States have to be given different labelling involving additional packaging costs'.[34] Such restrictions are directly at odds with the free movement of goods and are prohibited by Article 28 EC; they can be saved only where their application can be justified by recourse to the mandatory requirements—in other words, to a public interest objective taking precedence over the free movement of goods.[35] Additionally, they must apply without distinction to all national and imported products, and must be proportionate to the objective pursued. As ever, the public interest objective usually raised here is that of consumer protection, based on the premise that product information is of no practical value unless it is presented in a language that the consumer understands. As seen already in respect of assessing whether labelling particulars might be misleading, the task of ascertaining when a language might or might not be understood by consumers falls, in reality, to the national court, with only limited guidance from the Court of Justice.[36] As already noted, this may

[29] Steyger, n 2 above, p 40; Case C-369/89, *Piageme and others v BVBA Peeters* [1991] ECR I-2971.

[30] Case C-51/93, *Meyhui v Schott Zwiesel Glaswerke* [1994] ECR I-3879.

[31] Case C-85/94, *Piageme and others v BVBA Peeters* [1995] ECR I-2955.

[32] Case C-385/96, *Goerres* [1998] ECR I-4431.

[33] *Colim*, n 26 above, paras 33–35.

[34] Ibid., para 36.

[35] Case C-33/97, *Colim*, n. 26 above, para 38, referring to *Meyhui* (para 10). See also Case C-315/92, *Verband Sozialer Wettbewerb*, n 17 above, para 13.

[36] See *Piageme II*, n 31 above, paras 29–30; confirmed in, e.g., *Goerres*, n 32 above, para 20. The ECJ has indicated factors which may be 'relevant, though not decisive in themselves', including 'the possible similarity of words in different languages, the widespread knowledge concerned of

or may not coincide with the language(s) of the area in which the goods are being sold; this question is broached again below, however, in the context of asking who exactly the consumer might be in different situations.

In her case note on *Colim*, Terryn argued that the judgment allowed a Member State to require the language of a particular area to be used 'without allowing, as an alternative, the use of another language easily understood by consumers . . . [representing] a victory for consumer protection and an implicit acknowledgement of the legitimate interest on the part of Member States to protect and promote their national languages'.[37] But while the relevant passage in *Colim* is arguably ambiguous,[38] the judgment of the Court in *Goerres* militates against Terryn's interpretation; here, the Court confirmed that Article 14 of Directive 79/112 did not preclude national legislation prescribing the use of a specific language for the labelling of foodstuffs *so long as* that legislation—following on from *Piageme I*[39]—also permits the use of another language, as an alternative, that is easily understood by consumers.[40] It is unlikely, then, that the Court in *Colim* intended to depart from its earlier case law; indeed, there is every indication in the judgment of consolidation rather than rejection.

This interpretative knot cannot be left aside, however, in light of subsequent amendments to Directive 79/112 which remain 'live' in Directive 2000/13—and which arguably codify Terryn's (mis)interpretation of the case law. Directive 97/4,[41] amending Directive 79/112, repealed what was Article 14(2) and inserted a new Article 13a, still requiring foodstuffs to be labelled in

more than one language, or the existence of special circumstances such as a wide-ranging advertising campaign or widespread distribution of the product' (*Piageme II*, para 30).

[37] Evelyn Terryn, case note on *Colim v Bigg's*, *Columbia Journal of European Law*, 6/2 (2000), 231, at 240.

[38] At para 44, the judgment provides that: '. . . in the absence of full harmonisation of language requirements applicable to information appearing on imported products, the Member States may adopt national measures requiring such information to be given in the language of the area in which the products are sold or in another language which may be readily understood by consumers in that area, provided that those national measures apply without distinction to all national and imported products and are proportionate to the objective of consumer protection which they pursue.' Terryn interprets 'or' in the middle of this paragraph to imply that one or the other *exclusively* may be used (which amounts, in effect, to an overruling of *Piageme I*), whereas it is clearer from reading the judgment in *Goerres* that *both* possibilities must be provided for to pass the *Piageme* test (see n. 40 below, and accompanying text).

[39] *Piageme I*, n 29 above, at paras 14–17.

[40] *Goerres*, n 32 above, at, in particular, paras 16–21; confirmed in *Geffroy*, n 14 above, at para 28. Ironically, in *Goerres*, the products at issue were labelled in French, Italian, or English and *not* in German (contrary to the German labelling regulations being challenged).

[41] OJ [1997] L43/21.

a language easily understood by the consumer but, as summarized by the Court of Justice, 'permitting Member States to stipulate, in accordance with the rules of the Treaty, that the labelling particulars required by Directive 79/112 are to be given in at least one or more official languages of the Community'.[42] But the degree to which this allows a Member State to stipulate, in effect, that only one of its own national or official languages must be used for labelling foodstuffs marketed within its territory is perhaps clearer if the provision—now Article 16(2) of Directive 2000/13—is quoted directly:

> Within its own territory, the Member State in which the product is marketed may, in accordance with the rules of the Treaty, stipulate that those labelling particulars shall be given in one or more languages which it shall determine from among the official languages of the Community.

There is no '*at least* one' proviso in reality. In other words, exclusive stipulation of a local language—which is precisely what was rejected judicially in *Piageme*, *Colim*, and *Goerres*—has now been sanctioned legislatively; notably, in *Geffroy*, the Court alluded to the fact that it could not consider (what was then) Article 13a, as it had not entered into force at the material time.[43] Significantly, the Article 16(2) approach, obviously favoured by the Member States themselves, is also evident in other areas of the free movement of goods.[44]

It would seem, then, that the Member States do not trust the Court of Justice successfully to manage local linguistic affairs.[45] It is a concern shared by the European Parliament, which had sought to include in Directive 79/112 a straightforward imposition, in respect of labelling particulars, of the official language of the Member State in which the product was sold.[46] Interestingly, the Commission felt that this would '[go] beyond what is provided for in the Treaty'.[47] It suggested instead that 'in response to the concerns expressed by Parliament and the Member States . . . it would be expedient to add a provision

[42] See *Geffroy*, n 14 above, para 6.

[43] Ibid., para 16.

[44] See in particular, Article 6(4) of Directive 1999/44 on certain aspects of the sale of consumer goods and associated guarantees (OJ [1999] L 171/12), which provides, once again, that '[w]ithin its own territory, the Member State in which the consumer goods are marketed may, in accordance with the rules of the Treaty, provide that the guarantee be drafted in one or more languages which it shall determine from among the official languages of the Community.' Article 6(4) did not make an appearance in preliminary Commission documents (COM (95) 520 and COM (98) 217), or in the opinion of the European Parliament (OJ [1998] C 104/30), but was inserted by the Member States acting via the Council (see OJ [1998] C 333/46).

[45] In this vein, see also the contribution to this volume by Bruno de Witte (Chapter 7), especially at n 76 and n 77 and accompanying text.

[46] See COM (94) 24 final, p 4.

[47] Ibid.

to Article 14 stipulating that Member States may define the concept of easily understood language(s) in accordance with the rules of the Treaty'.[48] It is difficult, however, to see the material difference in effect here. In reality, allowing a Member State to determine which of the official Community languages should be used for products marketed within its territory will amount almost certainly to the imposition of its official language (thinking of 'official' here in Community terms only, since, for example, minority languages which are not recognized by the Treaty are excluded,[49] a point returned to in another context below). Is this simply a more realistic restatement of the 'easily understood' logic, given that the majority of consumers in any state will 'easily understand' that state's official (for Community purposes) language, or is it a more chauvinistic attempt to derail the less nationally rigid approach of the Court?

Before this question is addressed in a substantive sense, however, the phrase which threads through the reworked legislative formula—'in accordance with the rules of the Treaty'—must be considered. It is assumed here that this implies, in effect, the *acquis communautaire*, broader than, but including, the narrower implications of *provisions* of the Treaty (as denoted, for example, in Article 14 EC). Because herein lies the paradox—how can what amounts in effect to the imposition of (potentially) one language, which is determined by the Member States individually, conform to Article 28 EC and Community law on MEQRs more generally? It is probable that the Member States, acting via the Council, wished to codify a (not necessarily correct) presumption that a state's official language(s) will inevitably pass the 'easily understood' test; and that they have done so by removing the alternative possibility of using some non-determined language 'easily understood'—an option so carefully preserved over time by the Court of Justice. A legislative erosion of the case law is not problematic *per se*, except where that legislative reversal is *itself* unlawful. Because it is not at all clear how the new Article 16(2) fits with our entrenched understanding of Article 28; even on a purely factual analysis, creating and imposing a rigid language rule for each Member State still generates an obstacle to the free movement of goods—it still generates an advantage for the home producer and, in consequence, still generates an MEQR. So it is hard to avoid thinking that something which must ostensibly accord with

[48] Ibid.

[49] As discussed by De Witte in Chapter 7 of this volume, there are 20 official Community languages, representing at least one official language for all of the 25 Member States; additional languages may well be official in national (constitutional and/or legislative) terms but this has no bearing on their (non) status within the Community languages regime.

'the rules of the Treaty' cannot, in fact, do so. Moreover, '[i]t is settled law that the prohibition of quantitative restrictions and of all measures having equivalent effect applies not only to national measures but also to measures adopted by the Community institutions'.[50] So the judicial rules on labels and languages, for now, still apply in the absence of express harmonization to the contrary in EC legislation; they must also be deemed to apply even where labelling legislation exists but remains silent as to language requirements (or where the codification of 'easily understood' has not been disturbed). This state of things thus slices open the formerly (at least relatively) neat legal framework on labelling rules.

If the formulation in Article 16(2) is challenged, the Court may declare the provision unlawful having regard to the 'rules of the Treaty'. Or, more interestingly still, it may choose instead to provide a safety net, accepting arguments grounded in a public interest objective taking precedence over the free movement of goods. Looking at existing case law, it is fair to presume that the interest put forward is likely to be that of consumer protection—but how will the Court save Article 16(2) on grounds of consumer protection when it has advocated for years that that very same interest can *only* be catered for effectively by always allowing for an alternative language 'easily understood' to be used? The extent of the dilemma is heightened still further when proportionality enters the equation. And there are a number of consumer-oriented arguments that have not yet been discussed by the Court but which must surely defeat the exclusivity of Article 16(2)—the fact, for example, that not all consumers in a multilingual state will necessarily understand the official language determined, for Community purposes, by their own Member State (thinking in particular of speakers of minority languages), or the bias in favour of home consumers rather than those from other Member States (tourists, for example) which the formulation cements by freezing an analysis of the market in purely national terms.[51]

The loose ends, the interpretative and practical complexities engendered by the application of consumer justifications, seem thus to create as many difficulties as they address; and so alternate grounds for justification—based on linguistic and cultural protection *per se* rather than as an offshoot of consumer interests—must be contemplated, since they give, at least, a more rounded view of the real concerns at play here and could, to some extent, validate the

[50] Advocate General Fennelly in *Estée Lauder*, n 21 above, para 22, referring to the Court of Justice in Case C-39/90, *Denkavit Futtermittel v Land Baden-Württemberg* [1991] ECR I-3069, at para 15, as confirmed in language-specific cases including *Meyhui*, n 30 above, para 11, and *Schwarzkopf*, n 24 above, para 37.

[51] I am grateful to John Usher for raising the latter point.

underlying cultural insecurities of the Member States much more comprehensively than a consumer interest justification can. Steyger has argued that language policy was, in reality if not in the judgments, a key aspect of the *Piageme* jurisprudence;[52] Terryn has also pointed out that consideration of linguistic justification would accord with case law on the free movement of workers.[53] Section 3. below details more substantive consideration of a cultural/linguistic justification vis-à-vis Article 28; for now, the preliminary conclusion put forward earlier seems reinforced—that consumer protection as grounds for justification is just not enough and, moreover, throws up Byzantine inconsistencies when attempting to separate 'consumer' from 'local'. Before this idea is developed still further, it is first necessary to look at an aspect of EC law which openly and intentionally accommodates the reality of localism—the rules on product origin.

(c) Bringing it all back home? The product-name origin rules

Lister has observed that the product-name origin rules 'reflect different priorities'.[54] In striking contrast to the ethos of mutual recognition, rules relating to product origin seek instead to conserve local traditions and/or methods, thus standing askew from the more typical promotion of market integration which characterizes the labelling rules. Given the prolonged efforts of Community institutions to open up the EC market, it is not really surprising that the implementation of rules leading firmly in the other direction is relatively recent. Again, it is not the intention of this section comprehensively to detail the product origin rules; aspects of the relevant framework will be outlined, but the task here is to establish and develop the philosophy behind its incarnation. The key provision is Regulation 2081/92,[55] the purpose of which—for agricultural products intended for human consumption and foodstuffs (but

[52] Steyger, n 2 above, p 40.

[53] Terryn, n 37 above, p 241, drawing a parallel between *Colim* and Case 379/87, *Anita Groener v Minister for Education and the Dublin Vocational Education Committee* [1989] ECR 3967, in which the attachment of an Irish language competence requirement to a teaching vacancy was accepted by the Court of Justice because of Ireland's policy of promoting the Irish language—the constitutionally protected national and first official language of the state. The status of Irish as a *de facto* minority language was not discussed by the Court although it was arguably influential: see Nic Shuibhne, N, *EC Law and Minority Language Policy: Culture, Citizenship and Fundamental Rights* (The Hague: Kluwer, 2002), pp 80–105. Discussion of language policy in terms of public interest objectives has since taken place in cases dealing expressly with minority languages: see in particular Case C-274/96, *Criminal Proceedings against Bickel and Franz* [1998] ECR I-7637.

[54] Lister, n 12 above, p 181.

[55] OJ [1992] L 208/1 (as amended). A related measure, Regulation 2082/92 (OJ [1992] L 208/9), deals with issuing certificates of specific character for agricultural products and foodstuffs.

excepting wine and spirits)—is 'to ensure uniform protection within the Community of geographical names which comply with . . . the rules specifically laid down [therein]'.[56] This is achieved in practice via registration procedures established in the main body of the Regulation. Article 2 sets down the defining criteria for both designations of origin and geographical indications. Designations of origin denote the quality or characteristics of a product which 'are essentially or exclusively due to a particular geographical environment with its inherent natural and human factors, and the production, processing and preparation of which take place in the defined geographical area' (Article 2(2)(a)). According to Article 2(2)(b), the Regulation is relevant to 'geographical indications in respect of which there is a direct link between both a specific quality, reputation or other characteristic of the product and its specific geographical origin'.[57] In other words, registration is not possible in the case of 'simple geographical indications of source [where] there is no link between the characteristics of the product and its geographical provenance'.[58] The Court made it clear that Member States are still free to protect 'simple' indications of source via national measures,[59] but it should be remembered that such measures would still have to comply with Article 28 rules on MEQRs where imports might be affected.[60]

Article 3(1) of the Regulation provides fairly bluntly that product-names which 'have become generic may not be registered'; guidance is then given in order to establish whether this is the case or not for particular product-names. To this end, Article 3(3) required the Commission initially to draw up—in consultation with the Member States—a (non-exhaustive) list of names regarded as generic in the context of agricultural products and foodstuffs. Article 13(1)(b) stipulates that any 'misuse, imitation or evocation' of registered names is protected against. The Court has described an 'evocation' as '[covering] a situation where the term used to designate a product incorporates part of a protected designation, so that when the consumer is confronted with the name of the product, the image triggered in his mind is that of the product whose designation is protected'.[61] Article 13(2) deals with the

[56] Case C-129, 130/97, *Criminal Proceedings against Chiciak and Fol* [1998] ECR I-3315, para 25.

[57] Case C-312/98, *Schutzverband gegen Unwesen in der Wirtschaft eV v Warsteiner Brauerei Haus Cramer GmbH & Co KG* [2000] ECR I-9087, para 43, referring to Joined Cases C-321–24/94, *Criminal Proceedings against Pistre, Barthes, Milhau and Oberti* [1997] ECR I-2343, para 35.

[58] *Warsteiner Brauerei*, n 57 above, para 44.

[59] Ibid., para 45.

[60] On this point, see the Opinion of Advocate General Jacobs in *Warsteiner Brauerei*, n 57 above, paras 43–48.

[61] Case C-87/97, *Consorzio per la tutela del formaggio Gorgonzola* [1999] ECR I-1301, para 25; but see also the Court's comment, at para 26, that 'it is possible . . . for a protected designation to

(limited) continued use of designations and indications in respect of products which pre-date registration; Article 14(2) provides for continued use of earlier trade marks, on two conditions: first, the trade mark must have been registered in good faith before the application for registration of the designation of origin was lodged; secondly, continued use of the trade mark must comply with the relevant parts of Directive 89/104 (the trade marks Directive).[62] In respect of compound product-names, constituent parts of the registered name are *not* protected in an individual sense via registration of the whole product name.[63] It has recently been confirmed, however, that protection of product specifications may extend to aspects such as slicing and packaging.[64]

Registration of a designation of origin is exhaustive in terms of Member State competence, since a Member State may not, for example, alter the designation via national law after it has been registered under Regulation 2081/92.[65] The decision in the *Feta Cheese* case illustrates, however, the extent to which Member States retain power to challenge classifications made by the Commission.[66] But in the overall scheme of the Regulation, perhaps there is a

be evoked where there is no likelihood of confusion between the products concerned and even where no Community protection extends to the parts of that designation which are echoed in the term or terms at issue'. The name 'cambozola' was considered to be an evocation of 'gorgonzola' in the present case, on the grounds that both products were *inter alia* soft blue cheeses, similar in appearance, and with names ending in the same two syllables.

[62] *Gorgonzola*, n 61 above, paras 31 and 37; Directive 89/104 (OJ [1989] L 40/1) relates essentially to avoiding deception of the consumer as regards the nature, quality, and origin of the goods.

[63] *Chiciak and Fol*, n 56 above, paras 34–39, contrary to the submission of the Commission (see para 35; the Commission had argued that protection applied to each of the terms and not just to the name as a whole, provided that a generic or common term was not involved).

[64] Case C-108/01, *Consorzio del Prosciutto di Parma, Salumificio S Rita SpA v Asda Stores Ltd and Hygrade Foods Ltd* [2003] ECR I-5121. The Court also discussed the fact that such requirements, while constituting measures equivalent to a quantitative restriction on exports and thus falling foul of Article 29 EC, were nonetheless justified and therefore compatible with that provision, but accepted that the requirements might not be relied upon against economic actors on the grounds of legal certainty.

[65] *Chiciak and Fol*, n 56 above, para 33. Member States do have some provisional powers in respect of protecting a particular product name while waiting for a decision from the Commission on registration (but these limited interim powers are themselves derived from the Regulation and are usurped as soon as the Commission decision takes effect)—see paras 31–33 and note, in particular, Regulation 535/97, OJ [1997] L 83/3 (amending Regulation 2081/92). This aspect of *Chiciak* was confirmed in *Gorgonzola*, n 61 above, at para 18.

[66] Joined Cases C-289, 293 and 299/96, *Denmark v Commission; France v Commission; Germany v Commission* [1999] ECR I-1541; the Commission had decided that 'feta' was not a generic product name, given that it 'continues to connote Greek origin for most of those who know it' (para 38), but the Court, annulling the Commission measure, held that the Commission had not taken due account of products from other Member States already (legally) on the market.

certain retention of security for the Commission, bearing in mind the control it exercises at key points of the registration procedure—yes, the value of localism is allowed to persist, but only, in reality, where the Commission agrees that this is valuable. Nonetheless, codification of product-name rules does display a certain degree of institutional confidence in the market, given the fossilization of localized interests here in contrast to the more typical view of such 'parochialism' as anathema in the context of market integration.[67]

(d) Conclusion: goods 'versus' culture

Lister characterizes EC labelling rules as essentially pro-market, pro-integration, pro-free movement of goods, pro-product innovation, and pro-market entry; by contrast, the product-name origin rules are 'more candidly protective'.[68] This assertion certainly holds true in general terms. But analysis in the preceding sections leads to a slightly less certain, and perhaps more real, view of the labelling rules, which does not render them quite so distinct from the localized interests protected via product origin. A key feature of the labelling rules regime is its attachment to a particular construction of consumer protection; the Court has animated the sketch lurking in what was Directive 79/112 and the earlier case law on MEQRs, bringing to life the circumspect euro-consumer, all the more to transcend any lingering local market biases. But the dissociation of 'consumer' from 'local' is not altogether straightforward—or successful—because the Court of Justice expressly, and increasingly, urges national courts to take on board the idiosyncrasies of national markets—their 'social, cultural, and linguistic' characteristics—when second-guessing the behaviour of the (supposed) euro-consumer. The mottled textures of this reasoning become all the more evident when the specific context of language is considered, the recent legislative amendments in this regard straining openly against the very 'rules of the Treaty' they purport to respect. It is not that consumer protection is an inadequate consideration in itself; rather, it is more that it is inadequate in relation to the multiple disparities it has been invoked to cure. In his critique of the Community preference for foodstuff labelling, von Heydebrand ud Lasa goes beyond protection of the consumer in a formalist sense, arguing that 'diverse food standards are also a mirror of the diverse cultures, traditions, values and consumer habits in Europe. A legal premise which tends to isolate from those factors can hardly be regarded as

[67] For further recent guidance on protected designations of origin under the Regulation, see Case C-66/00, *Dante Bigi v Consorzio del Formaggio Parmigiano Reggiano* [2002] ECR I-5197.

[68] Lister, n 12 above, pp 200–1.

good law'.[69] He asks further why 'the creation of a common market should require the strong disregard of those needs'.[70] The following section seeks precisely to explore this question, asking whether it might be more appropriate expressly and more consistently to take on board a local/cultural justification for breaches of Article 28.

3. Making exceptions: the justification hierarchy

This section addresses the extent to which arguments grounded in culture should be (or already are) accepted to justify national (and institutional) measures which amount to *prima facie* breaches of Article 28 EC. The elasticity of consumer protection has been over-estimated and over-emphasized, to the extent that different strands of ECJ case law almost close in on themselves. The Community legislature has attempted to carve something of an out-clause, as seen most clearly in the context of the language rules. But it is an arguably unlawful attempt, given that the present legal backdrop remains dominated (even if not altogether overwhelmed) by Article 28 and the might of the harmonization crusade more generally. Would refocusing in a cultural direction save provisions like Article 16(2)? Or more properly, should it?

(a) Justification and Article 28 EC: the sliding scale

Looking at the free movement of goods in terms of discrimination,[71] the justification hierarchy is determined by the 'type' of breach of Article 28 EC found to exist in any given situation. Prohibition of instances of direct discrimination (or discrimination in law) stems clearly from Article 28 of the Treaty and, likewise, justification of directly discriminatory quantitative restrictions can only be sought by relying on Article 30. The scope of indirect discrimination is fuzzier. Although certainly hinted at in Article 28—'measures having equivalent *effect*'—it was not until the Court's decisions in *Dassonville* and *Cassis de Dijon* that the potential for indistinctly applicable measures which generate indirect discrimination (or discrimination in effect) to fall foul of Article 28 was made fully explicit. And tellingly, justification in

[69] Von Heydebrand ud Lasa, n 2 above, p 413. [70] Ibid., p 414.

[71] A stance arguably encouraged by the decisions in *Gourmet International Products AB (GIP)*, n 1 above, and Case C-254/98 *Schutzverband gegen unlauteren Wettbewerb v TK-Heimdienst Sass GmbH* [2000] ECR I-151, and again, most recently, in Case C-416/00 *Morellato*, judgment of 18 September 2003, not yet reported.

this context fell correspondingly to be designed by the Court; to this end, the employment of mandatory or imperative requirements accords with the use of objective justification phraseology for other Treaty freedoms.[72] It should be remembered, however, that (in contrast to the rules on workers, services, and establishment) instances of non-discrimination have largely, to date, been ruled outwith the scope of Article 28 EC, thus rendering justification irrelevant in that context.[73]

For present purposes—since most of the case law discussed above concerns indistinctly applicable measures—the application of the mandatory requirements system is relatively straightforward. While Article 30 is typically looked to in the first instance,[74] the introduction of other grounds for justification where Article 30 cannot assist—putting forward, in effect, a 'new' mandatory requirement—is perfectly legitimate, established in *Cassis de Dijon* and reinforced consistently since.[75] The interest of consumer protection has predominated in the labelling case law but, somewhat ironically, it is an approach that almost inevitably causes the balance to be struck in favour of the market. This is complicated, and especially in recent decisions, by the fact that the Court shows some sympathy to localized interests in its own engineering of the euro-consumer. But crucially, in this context of indirect discrimination, there is no *legal* obstacle preventing the submission of alternative arguments grounded in cultural or linguistic diversity. It is a policy choice. Determination of the mandatory requirements rests primarily on whether or not the interest being considered is 'consistent with specific objectives or interests of the Community Treaties'.[76] And there are a number of Treaty provisions that

[72] Terminology differs somewhat across the freedoms, but the underlying rationale of objective justification is comparable. See, e.g., the decision of the ECJ in Case C-237/94, *O'Flynn v Adjudication Officer* [1996] ECR I-2617, where it confirmed that measures which discriminate in fact if not in law, and thus breach Article 39 EC, may be justified by 'objective considerations independent of the nationality concerned' (para 19). See also Case C-19/92, *Dieter Kraus v Land Baden-Württemberg* [1993] ECR I-1663 (on freedom of establishment, 'imperative requirements in the general interest') and Case 33/74, *Van Binsbergen v Bestuur van de Bedrijfsvereniging voor de Metaalnijverheid* [1974] ECR 1299 (on freedom to provide services, 'overriding rules relating to the public interest'). In all cases, including Article 28, justification arguments are subject to an overriding test of proportionality.

[73] For more discussion of this point, see Nic Shuibhne, n 7 above, especially at pp 416–7.

[74] See, e.g., Joined Cases C-1 and 176/90, *Aragonesa de Publicidad Exterior and Publivia v Departamento de Sanidad y Seguridad Social de Cataluña* [1991] ECR I-4151, para 13.

[75] Classic examples of mandatory requirements found to be legitimate (subject to proportionality) include Case 302/86, *Commission v Denmark* [1988] ECR 4607 (environmental protection) and Case C-368/95, *Vereinigte Familia Press v Heinrich Bauer Verlag* [1997] ECR I-3689 (press diversity).

[76] Advocate General van Gerven in Cases C-306/88, 304/90, and 169/91, *Stoke-on-Trent and Norwich City Councils v B&Q plc* [1992] ECR I-6457, para 23 of his Opinion.

could be drawn from in the cultural context, most notably Article 151 EC (in particular, paragraph 4, which, as part of the family of integration clauses found in the Treaty, commits the Community 'to take cultural aspects into account in its action under other provisions of this Treaty, *in particular in order to respect and to promote the diversity of its cultures*').[77]

It is astounding that arguments in this vein are *not* typically put forward by the Member States given, as seen above, their deliberate legislative efforts to this end. It might be fair to reiterate that Member States do not trust the Court of Justice to get the balance right (or, less charitably, to provide the result they would prefer)—a point returned to again below—but it becomes less convincing to accept this before the ECJ is given the chance to mould an interpretative response in the first place; moreover, it does not take into account fairly encouraging signs in other evolving domains of the case law, again discussed further below. In the context of goods, justification of national measures on cultural grounds has really just been flirted with. The decision in *Cinéthèque*[78]—relating to promotion of the cinematographic industry—is perhaps the closest example in this context, the socio-cultural aspects of the Sunday trading litigation having become enmeshed in the aftermath of *Keck*.[79] That more open discussion of the value of culture in its localized context has not taken place before the Court is surprising; that it should take place in respect of the free movement of workers but not the free movement of goods is fairly anomalous.[80] What is more surprising still, however, is that most of the discussion on broadening the justification spectrum has instead taken place in the context of *direct* discrimination.

(b) Article 30 EC: an emerging erosion

The rule that directly discriminatory breaches of Article 28 EC can be saved only by arguments rooted in Article 30 is one consistently reaffirmed by the Court of Justice; moreover, the Court has stated expressly that the protection

[77] Emphasis added; for more detailed discussion on Article 151(4) EC, see Nic Shuibhne, n 53 above, pp 141–6.

[78] Cases 60–61/84, *Cinéthèque v Fédération Nationale des Cinémas Français* [1985] ECR 2605.

[79] See in particular, the decisions in Case C-145/88, *Torfaen BC v B&Q* [1989] ECR 3851 and *Stoke-on-Trent and Norwich City Councils*, n 76 above. In the latter case, Advocate General van Gerven pondered the existence of a 'general, less specific category of grounds of justification—that is to say . . . those which reflect certain political and economic choices . . . [in accordance] with national or regional socio-cultural characteristics' (at para 23 of his Opinion); this point is picked up again below.

[80] See again, the decisions of the Court in *Groener* and *Bickel and Franz*, both at n 53 above, and Case C-281/98, *Angonese v Cassa di Risparmio di Bolzano SpA* [2000] ECR I-4139.

of 'creativity and cultural diversity' in the realm of publishing is *not* enumerated in that provision.[81] It would seem pointless, then, to investigate justification on cultural grounds to match instances of directly discriminatory national measures, aside from the very particular scope of protecting 'national treasures possessing artistic, historic or archaeological value' (bearing in mind the reluctance of the Court to manipulate the 'public policy' derogation beyond what is strictly necessary[82]). This could not cover the linguistic aspect of food labels, for example; nor does it offer a channel for cultural/local consumer arguments more generally.[83] The first question to ask, then, is whether the text of Article 30 EC should be amended to include a broader statement on cultural justification. Two concerns may be flagged here: first, should the grounds for justifying direct discrimination be extended at all, given the particular gravity attached to this category of breaches to date; and, second, would inclusion of a cultural justification serve to undo the very idea of a common market, built up over the years precisely by piercing local protectionism disguised as culture? These questions are considered more substantively in section 3.*(c)* below; here, a stealthily emerging 'unwritten' addition to Article 30 is first explored.

Following on from the Sunday trading litigation, Advocate General van Gerven continued to contemplate the idea of an implied cultural justification, arguably even beyond instances of indirect discrimination, in *Fedicine*.[84] The case involved a dispute over the circulation of films in Spain; legislation imposed certain conditions on film distributors in respect of dubbing licences, which meant effectively that films in the official languages of Spain, as opposed to those of other countries, were required to be favoured. The applicants claimed that this infringed their freedom to provide services under Community law. Advocate General van Gerven confirmed initially that '[t]he Court has consistently held that national rules involving discriminatory treatment as regards provision of services from another Member State can be compatible with Community law only if they can be brought within the scope of an express derogation of the Treaty.'[85] He then considered whether Spain could avail itself of the public policy derogation in Article 66 EEC (now 55 EC). Having concluded that this provision did *not* vindicate the Spanish legislation,

[81] See Case 229/83, *Leclerc v Au Blé Vert* [1985] ECR 1, at para 30.

[82] See, e.g., Case 231/83, *Cullet v Centre Leclerc* [1985] ECR 305.

[83] Weatherill, n 2 above, at p 42, has noted that while there is no explicit reference to the consumer in Article 30 EC, 'the notion of the protection of the health and life of humans is capable of covering [his or her] physical integrity'.

[84] Case C-17/92, *Federacíon de Distribuidores Cinematográficos (Fedicine) v Spanish State* [1993] ECR I-2239.

[85] Ibid., para 15 of the Opinion.

the Advocate General went on to deliberate 'whether . . . it is not possible to find in Community law some other ground of justification than public policy, in particular reference to an overriding reason of general importance connected with the protection of the cultural heritage'.[86] At first glance, this approach contrasts directly with the rule that only express, Treaty-based derogations can be considered; the discrimination complained of in the instant case was, however, of an indirect and not overt nature. The Advocate General was clearly influenced by the increasing importance attached to cultural heritage via the Treaty on European Union (TEU), by then adopted but not yet in force. He quoted from Article 128 (now 151) EC, in respect of the Community's expected contribution to the 'flowering of the cultures of the Member States', and referred to the new Article 92(3)(d) (now 87(3)(d)) EC on state aid in the cultural domain. He then observed that, even before the TEU was ratified, '[m]any judgments show that the Court too is not insensitive to [cultural] diversity and the specific requirements of policy which the effort to preserve cultural individuality involves'.[87] In support of this claim, he listed a number of cases—including, in the context of goods, *Cinéthèque* and the Sunday trading cases[88]—where national cultural policy was deemed to constitute an overriding requirement of general interest that justified the restriction of Community freedoms once the general tests of proportionality and non-discrimination were satisfied.[89]

What is not altogether clear from the Opinion, however, is whether the Advocate General intended that the implied 'cultural heritage' derogation should be restricted to indirect discrimination only, or whether it might apply also even to directly discriminatory measures[90]—a controversial proposition, though one which seems to be gaining some (implied) credence in other strands of recent case law. In *Bosman*, for example, in the context of workers, the Court of Justice considered arguments based on cultural and national identity not only in respect of the non-discriminatory transfer fee system, but

86 Ibid., para 22.

87 Ibid., para 23. In Case C-415/93, *Union Royale Belge des Sociétés de Football Association ASBL v Jean-Marc Bosman* [1995] ECR I-4921, the ECJ held that Article 151 EC cannot itself—in a substantive sense—be used to limit the scope of a fundamental Community freedom such as freedom of movement for workers: para 78. This is not the same thing as arguments grounded in cultural concerns constituting a derogation from Community freedoms, which is what is being discussed here; nor does it take into consideration the particular mandate codified in Article 151(4).

88 *Fedicine*, n 84 above, para 25 of the Opinion.

89 Advocate General van Gerven did not, however, agree that this overriding requirement applied in the present case, 'since it has not been shown that the contested [legislation] seeks in the first place to preserve and promote Spain's own culture' (ibid., para 28).

90 *Fedicine*, n 84 above, para 27.

equally when dealing with the directly discriminatory nationality clauses in respect of foreign players.[91] Arnull has suggested that this aspect of *Bosman* might be considered within the specificity of case law on sport, to certain aspects of which the Treaty rules on freedom of movement do not apply.[92] It is difficult to see how this reasoning holds up, however, given that the Court had actually decided that Article 39 and the prohibition on nationality discrimination therein expressly *did* apply to the nationality clause rules. We are left, then, in a position of some uncertainty vis-à-vis the presumed cast-iron decree that justification for directly discriminatory measures can be drawn only from Treaty provisions. And, moreover, jurisprudence on the free movement of goods has not been immune from this trend.

It is fair to note that cases in which the mandatory requirements logic appears to have been applied to directly discriminatory breaches of Article 28 are not numerous; but they *do* exist, and it is the inconsistency which results that is especially problematic. The example raised most often in this context is the decision in the *Walloon Waste* case.[93] Advocate General Jacobs had classified the measure being challenged quite clearly as distinctly applicable—directly discriminatory—meaning that justification based on environmental arguments, however well-intended, simply could not be heard. Despite his having demonstrated this 'beyond argument',[94] the Court went on to find that the measure was not discriminatory, thus allowing invocation of the environmental justification. To achieve this, the Court drew heavily on the dubiously conclusive 'particular nature of waste'.[95] Can this creative approach really be preferred? What the Court really wanted to say is that environmental issues matter; but however worthy this may be, it does not conform to the established rules on invoking mandatory requirements. Similarly, in *Decker*,[96] the national scheme at issue (relating to reimbursement of the cost of medical products) distinguished between products bought on the home market and those bought in other Member States, in terms of prior authorization being a requirement in the latter case but not in the former—thus amounting to a

[91] Bosman, n 87 above, paras 115–137; this anomaly is even more striking in the Opinion of Advocate General Lenz, who had remarked that '[n]o deep cognition is required to reach the conclusion that the rules on foreign players are of a discriminatory nature. They represent an absolutely classic case of discrimination on grounds of nationality' (at para 135 of his Opinion).

[92] Arnull, A, *The European Union and its Court of Justice* (Oxford: OUP, 1999), p 310, citing Case 13/76, *Donà v Mantero* [1976] ECR 1333, para 14.

[93] Case C-2/90, *Commission v Belgium (Walloon Waste)* [1992] ECR I-4431.

[94] Arnull, n 92 above, p 272.

[95] *Walloon Waste*, n 93 above, para 34, drawing from what is now Article 174(2) EC.

[96] Case C-120/95, *Decker v Caisse de Maladie des Employés Privés* [1998] ECR I-1831.

clear example of discrimination in law. Nonetheless, the Court went on to discuss the fact that '[while] aims of a purely economic nature cannot justify a barrier to the fundamental principle of the free movement of goods . . . it cannot be excluded that the risk of seriously undermining the financial balance of the social security system may constitute an overriding reason in the general interest capable of justifying a barrier of that kind.'[97] The Court did not find that the challenged measure *was* justifiable, but even the possibility should not have been entertained; for this very reason, *Wyatt and Dashwood* have criticized the Court in *Decker* as being simply 'wrong'.[98] Moreover, in *Walloon Waste*, the Court made some attempt to categorize the measure as indistinctly applicable; there is silence on the same point in *Decker*.

In contrast, the Court of Justice gave something of a contemporary reading to 'protection of the health and life of humans, animals and plants' in *Bluhme*, including within its scope the 'maintenance of biodiversity'.[99] The measure at issue in *Bluhme* was directly discriminatory, but an imaginative reading of Article 30 was preferred here over the less orthodox approach taken in *Walloon Waste* and *Decker*. Then, in *Échirolles*, the Court confirmed that its earlier decision in *Leclerc* still stands, since 'Articles [28 and 30] have not been amended'.[100] So, what's going on? Awareness, at least, of the inconsistencies is evident in a remarkable recent opinion from Advocate General Jacobs; in *PreussenElektra*, he discussed whether the (directly) discriminatory measure challenged could be justified on grounds of environmental protection.[101] On the same reasoning as he had employed in *Walloon Waste*, he found, once again, that justification was precluded since 'it was *until recently* well-established case law that imperative requirements could not be relied on to justify national measures which were not applicable to domestic products and imported products without distinction'.[102] In an attempt further to expand a questionable distinction, the Commission had sought to rely on the decision in *Walloon Waste*. Advocate General Jacobs responded as follows:

In my view, the reasoning in *Walloon Waste* is flawed and should not be relied on in the present case. The question whether or not a measure applies without distinction to

[97] Ibid., para 39.

[98] Arnull, A, Dashwood, A, Ross, M, and Wyatt, D, *Wyatt and Dashwood's European Union Law*, 4th edn, (London: Sweet & Maxwell, 2000), p 356.

[99] Case C-67/97, *Criminal Proceedings against Bluhme* (the Danish beekeeping case) [1998] ECR I-8033.

[100] Case C-9/99, *Échirolles Distribution SA v Association du Dauphiné and Others* [2000] ECR I-8207, para 24.

[101] Case C-379/98, *PreussenElektra AG v Schleswag AG* [2001] ECR I-2099.

[102] Ibid., para 220 of the Opinion (emphasis added).

domestic and imported products is from a logical point of view a preliminary and neutral one. Its only function under the Court's case law is to determine which grounds of justification are available. I consider therefore that in assessing whether a measure is directly discriminatory regard cannot be had to whether the measure is appropriate.

But the judgment in *Walloon Waste* also shows something else, namely that it is desirable that even directly discriminatory measures can sometimes be justified on grounds of environmental protection.[103]

The Advocate General went on to cite more recent case law in which the Court has been fairly ambiguous as to the type of discrimination at issue while nonetheless relying on the imperative requirement of environmental protection.[104] He concluded that 'on the one hand, it cannot be ruled out that the relevance of the distinction between Article 30 . . . interests and rule of reason exceptions is on the decline. On the other hand the Court has not formally abandoned the rule that imperative requirements cannot be invoked in connection with directly discriminatory measures.'[105] He then recommended that the Court should 'clarify its position in order to provide the necessary legal certainty'.[106] But the Court did not take up the gauntlet in *PreussenElektra*; nor has it done so since. Advocate General Jacobs argued that a more flexible approach to environmental protection might well be merited, bearing in mind, *inter alia*, Treaty amendments showing 'a heightened concern for the environment even though Article [30] itself was not amended'.[107] Again, however worthy, such an extension is surely *ultra vires* the Court at present. But the argument that Article 30 might no longer reflect adequately concerns and interests heightened elsewhere in the Treaty could surely be applied also to justification on grounds of culture. What is clear is that Community rules on justification are in a state of flux; what remains more fully to be considered is the place of culture in this evolving debate.

(c) Conclusion: 'objectively' cultural?

A number of general questions arise from the preceding sections. Should Article 30 be amended, so that the grounds for justification therein might be

[103] Ibid., paras 225–226.

[104] In addition to *Decker*, n 96 above, Joined Cases C-34–36/95, *KO v De Agostini and TV-Shop* [1997] ECR I-3843 (paras 44 and 45), Case C-158/96, *Kohll v Union des Caisses de Maladies* [1998] ECR I-1931 (paras 35 and 41), Case C-203/96, *Dusseldorp and others v Minister van Volkshuisvesting, Ruimtelijke Ordening en Mileubeheer* [1998] ECR I-4075 (paras 44 and 49), and Case C-389/96, *Aher-Waggon v Germany* [1998] ECR I-4473 (para 19) were cited.

[105] *PreussenElektra*, n 101 above, para 228 of the Opinion.

[106] Ibid., para 229.

[107] Ibid., para 230.

extended? Maintaining a closed list of grounds for justification can be looked at as a value-judgment—in the cultural context, the inclusion of national treasures but not other cultural possibilities, renders the protection of a painting or sculpture, for example, more valuable than protection of a language or traditional method of food production (not to mention, more important than consumer protection, the environment, and so on). Is this appropriate, or should there be a generic 'objective justification' test irrespective of the type of breach of Article 28 involved, rendering Article 30 effectively redundant?[108] The main advantage of a generic objective justification test is that cases could be considered on their individual merit, uninhibited by rigid, predetermined value-judgments. In either case—amendment of Article 30 or its abandonment altogether—would justification on cultural grounds merit consideration?

At present, the distinction in the justification hierarchy is entirely judge-made. The whole concept of an open-ended list of imperative requirements (or, in respect of the other freedoms, objective justification) is arguably already contrary to the provisions of the Treaty, which do not distinguish between direct and indirect discrimination at all, or at least not in terms of justification. It was noted above that Article 28 *could* be read to refer both to directly and indirectly discriminatory measures; but there is no similar division in Article 30. The logic of *Cassis de Dijon* is simply accepted, with the result that its legality is rarely questioned. But it does amount to a value-judgment, confirming inversely that some forms of discriminatory treatment are worse, and thus more difficult to justify, than others. Again, this is a judicial statement, not a constitutional one—and not a legislative one. Arnull discusses one aspect of the case law, which views directly discriminatory measures as coming within the scope of Article 28 but which may be justified, while indirectly discriminatory measures—where successfully coupled with a mandatory requirement—are actually outside its scope.[109] He concedes the 'artificiality' of this division himself, however, citing Advocate General van Gerven in *Aragonesa*, who had credited the distinction with 'little if any practical import, since the conditions governing the applicability of the *Cassis de Dijon* doctrine and of Article [30] are the same (absence of harmonisation, examination of the criteria of necessity and proportionality, prohibition of arbitrary discrimination or disguised restriction on trade).'[110] Arnull concludes that

[108] On this question, see Arnull, n 92 above, pp 273–4.

[109] Arnull, n 92 above, pp 266–7, citing Case 113/80, *Commission v Ireland* [1981] ECR 1625 and Case 177/83, *Kohl v Ringelhan* [1984] ECR 3651 in support of this view.

[110] Arnull, ibid., citing Advocate General van Gerven in *Aragonesa*. The logic of the distinction crumbles further when *Keck* is brought into the equation. And in a language-specific context, see

indirectly discriminatory measures 'benefit from an extended category of derogations [which] is of course incompatible with the view that Article 30 . . . is to be strictly construed, but to seek to conceal that incompatibility by denying that mandatory requirements are derogations amounts to little more than sophistry'.[111]

Since it cannot be grounded in the Treaty, then, the view that some forms of discrimination are seen to be worse than others must instead be considered in a moral rather than legal context. On this point, Bernard draws in brief from legal theory and, in particular, from the work of John Gardner.[112] Gardner frames direct discrimination in terms of an element of culpability, a finding of intention.[113] But 'intention' here 'depends on the wrongdoer's decision and not upon his motives'.[114] This fits well with the EC notion of discrimination; but it potentially covers both direct *and* indirect actions, given the established emphasis in Community law—across the spectrum of discrimination—on effect, not on intention *or* on motivation. On the other hand, Gardner argues that 'indirect discrimination does not, in the absence of intention, involve the nexus of wrongdoing involved in direct discrimination'.[115] Drawing further from Gardner's work, in the more specific field of criminal law theory, the upshot of this distinction is that indirect discrimination generates fairly automatic recourse to open-ended possibilities for justification, while directly discriminatory acts can only be justified having recourse to 'cancelling permissions' set down strictly by law.[116]

Applying both of these strands of thought—on definition and on justification—to Community law, we find something of an awkward mix in philosophical terms. The emphasis placed on effect by the Court of Justice gravitates towards Gardner's conception of direct discrimination; but his hypothesis is broader, less literally tied to what the national measure might say explicitly, in that it covers also some instances of what constitutes *in*direct discrimination in EC law—in the main, where the behaviour of the Member

para 38 of *Colim*, n 28 above, in which the Court speaks plainly of prohibitions needing to be *justified* in the context of Article 28 and indirect discrimination.

[111] Arnull, n 92 above, p 269.

[112] Bernard, n 4 above, p 93 (n 40), referring to John Gardner, 'Liberals and Unlawful Discrimination', *Oxford Journal of Legal Studies*, 9/1 (1989), 1–22. See also, Gardner, J, 'Justifications and Reasons', in A P Simester and A T H Smith (eds), *Harm and Culpability* (Oxford: Clarendon, 1996), 103–29.

[113] Gardner (1989), n 112 above, p 4.

[114] Ibid. As Tadros has observed, 'legal prohibition would not get very far if it were to be dependent on the agent recognising, or even having recognised at the time of the offence, the wrongfulness of his actions': Tadros, V, 'Practical Reasoning and Intentional Action', *Legal Studies*, 20/1 (2000), 104–23, at 105.

[115] Gardner (1989), n 112 above, p 5.

[116] Gardner (1996), n 112 above, p 116.

States leans strongly and obviously in the direction of protectionism. Analogous to criminal law theory, however, a difference in terms of degrees of harm *is* portrayed to some extent in Community law, in that (recalling the Article 30/ imperative requirements distinction) the same breadth of opportunity for justification simply does not exist for measures that discriminate directly. Given the somewhat unorthodox moral basis for this, vis-à-vis the difference in EC law on classification of discrimination *per se*, it becomes harder to apply legal theory arguments either for or against continuation of the justification hierarchy. Gardner explores a justification model based on the coincidence of 'guiding' and 'explanatory' reasons.[117] Translating this approach to the Community context would move further into the subjective domain of intention than has traditionally been the case. In terms of scope, it would probably still catch both direct and indirect discrimination as we currently understand their Community meaning; and Gardner's effects-oriented notion of 'intention'—which is not hinged on motivation—is especially significant here.[118] But the key difficulty lies in the requirement of coincidence for guiding and explanatory reasons—is it feasible, or even possible, to measure whether a Member State has *actually* acted for the reasons it claims? This is, again, a subjective and probing approach which, in the Community context, may not be particularly quantifiable or politically wise. The degree of neutrality, in terms both of intention and motivation, which the EC effects-based approach confers on Member States might seem morally questionable at times, but it may well be the reason why the Community market continues actually to function.

In summary, Gardner postulates a philosophical difference between discriminating directly and indirectly, in terms both of consequence *and* definition. Community law has adopted a fairly skewed version of this distinction, but there exists some distinction nonetheless. It is not the purpose of this paper to solve the dilemmas sketched here; but the moral questions highlighted need to be borne in mind in deciding whether Article 30 should be amended or whether a generic objective justification test should take its place; and while the nature and consequences of the acts themselves are not always readily comparable, recourse to criminal law theory on harm and justification could certainly provoke a useful debate in the future.

[117] Ibid., p 105, where Gardner writes that '[n]o action of belief is justified unless it is true both that there was an applicable (guiding) reason for so acting or so believing and that this corresponded with the (explanatory) reason why the action was performed and the belief held'.

[118] Tadros, n 114 above, at p 122, has noted in this context that '[a] mere belief that a particular consequence will come about is not sufficient for that consequence to be intended as that concept is ordinarily used. But as far as the attribution of culpability is concerned, it appears that a belief that consequences will come about is sufficient'.

The final undertaking here, then, is to ask whether justification on cultural grounds would have a place at either table. The role that a cultural justification could play within the free movement of goods has been flagged throughout this chapter, notably in light of the limitations of consumer interest arguments. Difficulties arise, however, when seeking to translate cultural justification into practice. One of the key issues, obviously, is attempting to define what might/might not come within the scope of 'culture' itself. The basic premise that protection of cultural diversity is a good thing (and an objective promoted by the EC Treaty) does not really help much when trying to set some parameters and boundaries. It is generally preferable that 'culture' be read broadly where possible, in order not to exclude less traditional or less aesthetic aspects of the concept;[119] other contributors to this volume grapple with this question, not always concluding in the same vein.

In the specific context of the free movement of goods, however, a fairly delicate balance is required to be struck—while certain local practices and traditions are indeed 'cultural', recognition of this fact in all cases will serve to unpick the very fabric of the internal market so carefully constructed for almost 50 years. From this perspective, the addition to Article 30 of an environmental justification is probably more straightforward; significantly, both the natural and working environment were tacked onto the already-present Article 30 grounds when Article 95(4) EC was inserted by the Single European Act.

For cultural matters, perhaps the generic objective justification test—which allows for assessment on a case-by-case basis—is more appropriate, especially when combined with the overriding requirement of proportionality. The main difficulty here is more or less a matter of trust. There has always been a hands-off assumption in respect of sensitive policy issues closely connected with the identities and 'cultures' of the Member States; the volume of intense analysis generated by the Court's decision in *Grogan* is a clear example of this.[120] In the cultural context, the Court of Justice has gained a degree of confidence in

[119] See Nic Shuibhne, n 7 above, pp 107–14. The anomalous results generated by an overly narrow or literal interpretation of culture are evident throughout the decision in Case C-42/97, *European Parliament v Council of the European Union* [1999] ECR I-869 (see the discussion in Nic Shuibhne, pp 143–6).

[120] Case C-159/90, *SPUC v Grogan* [1991] ECR I-4685; see Phelan, D R, 'Right to Life of the Unborn v. Promotion of Trade in Services: The ECJ and the Normative Shaping of the European Union', *Modern Law Review*, 55/5 (1992), 670, and de Búrca, G, 'Fundamental Rights and the Reach of EC Law', *Oxford Journal of Legal Studies*, 13 (1993), 283. See also Coppel, J and O'Neill, A, 'The European Court of Justice: Taking Rights Seriously?', *Common Market Law Review*, 29 (1992), 669–92, at 685–9, and Weiler, J H H and Lockhart, N J S, '"Taking Rights Seriously" Seriously: The European Court of Justice and its Fundamental Rights Jurisprudence', *Common Market Law Review*, 32/1 and 32/2 (1995), 51–94 and 579–627 respectively, at 597–605.

its more recent case law; the extent to which a Member State's language policy was actively assessed in *Bickel and Franz*, for example, contrasts with the reticence of the Court more stringently to discuss discrimination and proportionality in *Groener*. While this may reflect a growing sense of conviction in Luxembourg, it will hardly quell Member State reservations that national and/or regional interests are best left to them. This tension runs much more broadly than Article 28, however, reflecting the ongoing jarring of EC and Member State competence boundaries. Thus, while it must be borne in mind, it is not enough to defeat arguments in favour of some sort of cultural justification that could be grappled with, where appropriate, by the Court of Justice.

4. Conclusion: a place for culture and culture in its place?

This paper originated with a fairly innocent mandate, to investigate Community rules on labels, locals, and languages against the backdrop of Article 28 EC. While the increasing inconsistencies found both in case law and legislation have implications far beyond culture, they do impinge acutely in this context, since the acceptability of cultural justification where Article 28 is *prima facie* breached is tied inherently to the decisions of wider implication that demand to be made. When looking at the case law on labels and locals, it becomes clear that the traditional tactic here—raising consumer protection—is not, on its own, sufficient to force legitimate questions to be addressed by the Court of Justice. And yet recent case law on the euro-consumer seems to slide further back into localism. The longer the uncertainty persists, the more the Member States will attempt to deal with such matters on a more nationally-sensitive—and arguably, then, less Community-oriented—basis. Even if cultural diversity wins out here in the short term, there are other significant, and worrying, consequences. The friction between the Member States and the Community on competence division more generally will clearly be exacerbated. The security of the internal market ethos more generally is also made vulnerable to a fragmentary trend; in particular, the preserve of Articles 28 and 30 is already strained. A more open discussion of cultural justification should provide more of a valve of release here than consumer protection on its own. But legitimate questions of cultural diversity vis-à-vis trade in goods could remain at the fringes of the Community agenda unless their broader import is highlighted. What needs to be worked out is the very content of the

Community orientation in cultural matters. The balance requiring to be struck here—respecting cultural diversity and yet preserving the fundamental tenets of the internal market—is undoubtedly complex. But the task must be confronted. It involves, in a sense, handing over a multitude of distinct cultural interpretations and hoping that some sense can be made of them without undermining either their integrity *or* that of the EC market order. Perhaps it will prove an impossible task for the Community institutions. But they should, at least, be given the chance.

4

Sport as Culture in EC Law

*Stephen Weatherill**

1. Introduction

Capital burns off the nuance in a culture. Foreign investment, global markets, corporate acquisitions, the flow of information through transnational media . . . not that people want the same things, necessarily, but they want the same range of choices. (Don DeLillo, *Underworld*, New York: Simon and Schuster 1997, p 785)

My approach in this paper will be to inquire into aspects of the business of sport that are treated as different from 'normal' businesses; to inquire what legal devices reflect these special characteristics; and then to consider whether the distinct treatment is justified, which will involve not only consideration of the peculiar economic context of organized sport but also some assessment of the perceived 'cultural quality' of sport. Are sport's cultural properties being burned off by commercial growth?

I am particularly concerned to identify precisely what is at stake. It is commonplace to hear statements which assert that professional sport is a business but that it is 'special' in some respects. I accept this, but will endeavour to elucidate what this involves. It will be my submission that there is a general tendency to exaggerate the differences of professional sport from 'normal' commercial activity, and a consequent propensity to introduce or maintain distinctive self-regulatory and/ or legal rules which may not be justified on close inspection. At the very least I argue that professional sport's perceived special status is frequently asserted and commonly accepted without adequate intellectual articulation of the true underlying issues. I propose to investigate this by looking at two distinct aspects in sport: first, circumstances in which sport claims immunities or exemptions from normal assumptions of legal control; and, secondly, circumstances in which sport is subjected to requirements

* Somerville College, Oxford.

that would not normally be imposed on other commercial activities. The first issue, where sport enjoys a benefit, will be illustrated with reference to two topics, those of player transfer fees and the collective selling of broadcasting rights. The second issue, where sport carries a burden, will be illustrated with reference to the so-called 'protected events' legislation, under which rights to broadcast some sport competitions may not be disposed of as freely as other such property rights.

I approach these questions fully aware of the allegation of bias that is frequently aimed at the institutions of the European Community—principally the Court and the Commission—by representatives of sports federations. The Community lacks legislative competence in the field of sport. Indeed, even today, the word 'sport' is absent from the EC Treaty itself. But in so far as sport generates practices of economic significance, they are in principle subject to the control of EC law, most prominently the Treaty rules governing free movement and competition, as confirmed by the European Court in *Walrave and Koch v Union Cycliste Internationale* in 1974[1] and *Donà v Mantero* in 1976.[2] This approach was famously confirmed by the European Court in *Bosman*.[3] Sport, like other sectors such as education, environmental policy, and consumer protection, demonstrates how the law of the EC may exercise a wider influence than a formal inspection of the text of the Treaty may lead one to expect, primarily because of the extended reach of the rules governing the building of an integrated, competitive market. The alleged bias manifests itself in an application of EC trade law to sport which reflects the market-making imperatives of the Treaty while failing to pay adequate respect to the economic peculiarities of sport. In particular, it is objected that EC law neglects sport's distinctive cultural context in society and its contribution to the realization of social and cultural objectives that are broader than economic gain alone. So, it is said, EC law does not understand sport. I am conscious of the strength of this feeling within sport. It is, among other things, the stimulus to periodic campaigns in favour of Treaty revision designed to have sport placed partly, or even wholly, outwith the ambit of EC law. And I intend to take seriously the anxiety that the EC institutions, applying the EC Treaty to sport, are hampered by constitutional limitations associated with the EC's limited competence in the field when invited to investigate the richness of its cultural contribution. But my task is to explore what these fine ambitions

[1] Case 36/74, *Walrave and Koch v Union Cycliste Internationale* [1974] ECR 1405.

[2] Case 13/76, *Donà v Mantero* [1976] ECR 1333.

[3] Case C-415/93, *Union Royale Belge des Sociétés de Football Association ASBL v Jean-Marc Bosman* [1995] ECR I-4921.

really mean, and how they are and should be reflected in the application of EC law to the systems of regulation found in sport. I entertain a suspicion that appeals to culture are being used in the sports sector as a cover for economic protectionism by business interests to the detriment of employees and consumers. I wonder too about the utility of treating 'sport' as a single phenomenon. I am particularly sceptical that high-minded sporting values and anxieties to promote a healthy lifestyle, tolerance, and respect for others have much to do with modern professional sport.

2. Concessions made to the distinctive nature of sporting competition

In *Bosman* the European Court found two distinct existing practices in professional football to be incompatible with the Treaty provision governing the free movement of workers, Article 39 (ex 48) EC. The system governing the transfer of players between clubs and the rules requiring discrimination on the basis of nationality in European club football competitions were both found to violate that provision. Adjustments have been made to the transfer system, while the nationality rules have been abandoned in so far as they apply to EU nationals.

The vital point for present purposes is that the Court did not deny that football in particular, or sport in general, possesses unusual characteristics that distinguish it from 'normal' commercial sectors. Rather, the Court insisted only that the economic significance of sport secured its subjection to EC law and that those unusual characteristics should then be taken into account in shaping the application of the law. There is, then, room for acknowledging that 'sport is special', but that room exists within the jurisdiction of the institutions of the EC.

The exact nature of the Court's concession in *Bosman* requires examination. In paragraph 106 of the ruling it remarked that:

> In view of the considerable social importance of sporting activities and in particular football in the Community, the aims of maintaining a balance between clubs by preserving a certain degree of equality and uncertainty as to results and of encouraging the recruitment and training of young players must be accepted as legitimate.

The practices challenged in the case did not adequately contribute to these aims and they were judged to fall foul of Article 39 (ex 48) EC. But the Court's recognition in *Bosman* that sport has 'considerable social importance' and that it has two distinct legitimate aims set the scene for subsequent inquiry into exactly what type of practice might permissibly be pursued by governing bodies in sport in conformity with Community law in circumstances where 'normal' commercial actors would expect to be condemned for violation of the Treaty. Both the European Court and the Commission have been challenged to refine the contours of the acceptance that 'sport is—to some extent—special', and to elaborate the implications of this nuanced legal test in its application to particular sporting practices. I choose the player transfer system and the collective sale of rights to broadcast matches to illustrate the pattern of the intriguing evolving debate, but first I question the Court's wisdom in its 'twin-track' concession to the distinctive aims of professional sport. In fact, far from having failed to appreciate the unusual character of sport, of which it so often stands accused, the Court has, in my submission, adopted an inflated view of the distinct nature of sport as an economic activity.

In short, I agree with the Court that the aim 'of maintaining a balance between clubs by preserving a certain degree of equality and uncertainty as to results' is a matter that is peculiar to sport. I do not agree that the aim of 'encouraging the recruitment and training of young players' is distinctive to sport.

The legitimate aim of 'maintaining a balance between clubs by preserving a certain degree of equality and uncertainty as to results' reflects the unusual economic structure of sports leagues. In 'normal' industries one would not identify any economic basis for such mutual interdependence. The commercial undertaking covets its rival's market share with ferocity. It does not wish to sustain its rival's well-being. Monopoly power is a rational goal, for it brings potentially rich economic gains as a result of freedom from competition. This, of course, is precisely why market economies deploy legal controls to obstruct the acquisition of monopoly power and to supervise the conduct of actors that come to possess such economic might. But in football a single club is economically useless. It needs rivals to play against. And not just rivals who are routinely thrashed. The industry depends on the existence of credible competition in order to attract consumers, which encompasses the need for strong rivals so that results are not a foregone conclusion and the need to eliminate any whiff of suspicion about match-fixing or any other interference with the genuine nature of competition. Clubs in sports leagues enjoy a relationship of mutual interdependence which is not the norm in other spheres of commercial activity. So, for example, one would expect this economic rational notion of 'solidarity' to generate a degree of wealth distribution from strong to weak within the sport. Doubtless a difficult balance has to be struck between rewarding the successful and strengthening the unsuccessful.[4] North American sport, dominated by 'closed Leagues', is characterized by much more interventionism than European sport. But the key point for present purposes is that, by contrast, incentives to devise such a strategy are completely absent from a typical manufacturing or service industry. The interesting questions in sport then surround the issue of how this peculiar economic status should be reflected in the legal regulation of practices that are presented as necessary to secure equality between clubs and uncertainty as to results. I consider this below in connection with player transfer systems and collective selling of broadcasting rights.[5]

The aim of 'of encouraging the recruitment and training of young players' must also be accepted as legitimate, according to the European Court in *Bosman*, but I do not think this is correctly regarded as an issue that is in any way special to the nature of sport. In fact, I consider the Court is here over-generous to the claims of sporting associations. Naturally, clubs protest that they would abandon youth training were they not allowed to maintain some system which compensates them for costs incurred when the employee moves on, but the question is whether this is in any way convincing. Surely a club that chose to neglect youth training would simply perform poorly in comparison with more far-sighted rivals? A transfer system doubtless encourages a higher level of investment in training than would otherwise occur, but what is missing from the ruling in *Bosman* and the Commission's subsequent approach to the matter is any supplementary explanation why sports clubs should be treated as a special case on this point. Supermarkets and universities train young employees even though they might subsequently quit the company, and expect no transfer fee as an incentive: so why is football different?

[4] For economic analysis, see, e.g., Cairns, P, Jennett, T, and Sloane, P, 'The Economics of Professional Team Sports: A Survey of Theory and Evidence', *Journal of Economic Studies*, 13 (1986), 3; Quirk, J and Fort, R, *Pay Dirt: the Business of Professional Team Sports* (Oxford and New York: Princeton University Press, 1997); Dobson, S and Goddard, J, *The Economics of Football* (Cambridge: Cambridge UP, 2001); Rosen S and Sanderson, A, 'Labour Markets in Professional Sports', *The Economic Journal*, 111 (2001), F47; Buzzacchi, L, Szymanski, S, and Valletti, T, 'Equality of Opportunity and Equality of Outcome: Open Leagues, Closed Leagues and Competitive Balance', *Journal of Industry, Competition and Trade*, 3 (2003), 167. The home page of Stefan Szymanski is a rich mine: http://www.ms.ic.ac.uk/stefan.

[5] On rules precluding multiple ownership of clubs, see the decision based on EC and Swiss law of the Court for Arbitration in Sport (CAS), an arbitral body established by the industry and based in Lausanne, in CAS 98/200, *AEK Athens and Slavia Prague v UEFA*, 20 August 1999. The Commission subsequently chose to treat this as a rule that interfered with commerce yet which, given its contribution to honesty in sports practice, fell outside the scope of the Treaty competition rules provided it was applied in a non-discriminatory manner: COMP/37.806, *ENIC/ UEFA*, IP/02/942, 27 June 2002.

I do not exclude the possibility that economic rationales may exist.[6] The ability of football players is immediately visible on the pitch, so clubs that invest in training quickly lose the advantage they enjoy in having more information than predator employers about an employee's developed skills. Perhaps that generates an unusually strong unwillingness to invest in training, although a similar rationale would apply to musicians or actors who are not currently subjected to a transfer system. But no such analysis has ever been conducted in the context of EU policy-making. The EU institutions since *Bosman* have proceeded on the unexplained assumption that sport is 'special' in its need to protect and promote youth training. Until this argument is supported by convincing evidence, football should be required to follow normal commercial practice, in which the method for retaining the services of valued employees is to offer them an attractive contract and keep them happy while they perform it. Admittedly, at a detailed level, contractual arrangements in football tend to take the shape of fixed-term deals, rather than contracts of indefinite duration with a notice period capable of exercise by either party, but this is not a difference which defeats the basic submission that the importance of recruiting and training young workers is a matter which in principle applies to all industries equally, and that it is not one which should be taken as justifying abnormal regulation within the sports industry.

I conclude that the economics of football are special when it comes to preserving competitive equality between clubs, but that the economics of football are not special when it comes to encouraging the training of young players. This conditions the analysis below of the proper legal approach to the transfer system and to the collective selling of broadcasting rights.

3. Benefits claimed because of the distinctive nature of sporting competition: the player transfer system

The transfer system in football, damaged but not eliminated by the ruling in *Bosman*, has mutated over the last century and may be found in different guises in different jurisdictions at different times.[7] However, its essence is

[6] See, e.g., Feess, E and Muehleusser, G, 'Economic Consequences of Transfer Fee Regulations in European Football', *European Journal of Law and Economics*, 13 (2002), 221.

[7] Advocate General Lenz's Opinion in *Bosman* contains an extensive and detailed examination, see n 3 above. For a useful collection of materials and some analysis, see Blanpain, R and Inston, R, *The Bosman Case: The End of the Transfer System?* (Leuven: Peeters, 1996); also Beloff, M, Kerr, T, and Demetriou, M, *Sports Law* (Oxford: Hart Publishing, 1999), ch 4; Greenfield, S, 'The Ties

simply described. Players are unable simply to move freely between clubs in the exercise of their contractual freedom. Employment as a footballer is different from employment as a plumber or professor. A club was—and is—able to field a player in an official match only once it has secured the player's registration, held by the previous employer. That registration will be released only when the previous club is satisfied with the terms offered by the new club, which typically has involved payment of a fee. A club which chose simply to field a player without complying with the requirements of the transfer system would find itself subject to heavy and immediate penalties imposed by national and transnational governing bodies.

(a) The transfer system before and after Bosman

Bosman had fallen foul of the transfer system when he found himself prevented from joining a French club because the Belgian club which held his registration refused to release it, even though Bosman's contract of employment with the Belgian club had come to an end. The Court, having acknowledged sport's 'considerable social importance' and embraced as legitimate 'the aims of maintaining a balance between clubs by preserving a certain degree of equality and uncertainty as to results and of encouraging the recruitment and training of young players', nonetheless came to the conclusion that the transfer system in professional football constituted a violation of Article 39 (ex 48). It is well established in EC trade law that both the ends pursued and the means employed by a restrictive measure must be justified. The Court regarded the means employed in the football industry as inapt to achieve ends which might be capable of justification in principle. The Court did not consider that the transfer system acted as an adequate method of maintaining balance between clubs. The rules neither precluded richer clubs buying the best players, nor prevented the 'availability of financial resources from being a decisive factor in competitive sport thus considerably altering the balance between clubs'. Moreover, the Court observed that because only a handful of young players will repay the investment by making the professional grade, it is impossible to predict the fees that will be obtained. In any event such fees will be unrelated to the actual cost of training all players. The system was hit-and-miss, rather than a carefully constructed distributive mechanism. The Court

that Bind: Charting Contemporary Sporting Contractual Relations', in Greenfield, S and Osborn, G, *Law and Sport in Contemporary Society* (London, Portland: Frank Cass, 2000), ch 8; Dubey, J-P, *La libre circulation des sportifs en Europe* (Berne: Staempfli Editions SA, 2000), pp 272–317, 569–83.

concluded that 'the same aims can be achieved at least as efficiently by other means which do not impede freedom of movement for workers'.[8]

The judgment therefore required alterations to be made to the transfer system as it applied to players in Bosman's position, whose contracts of employment had expired and who wished to exercise their right to migrate between Member States of the EU. But it is readily arguable that the transfer system rested on even shakier foundations than the *Bosman* ruling itself suggested.[9] The Court declined to consider the matter from the perspective of the competition rules in the EC Treaty, but it seems highly probable that, had it addressed that matter, it would have condemned the practices as unlawful restrictions on trade imposed 'horizontally' between employers, involving also governing authorities in sport. This was clearly the view expressed in the case by Advocate General Lenz. It is important to appreciate that the competition rules are lurking in the background, for they could readily be employed to strike at persisting remnants of the transfer system that would not be imperilled by the invocation of Article 39 (ex 48) EC. This is particularly relevant to challenges to restrictions imposed on non-EU nationals and to impediments applying to transfers which are purely internal to a single Member State (which would include one between England and Scotland). Moreover, seeking to exploit EC law still further beyond the fact pattern in *Bosman*, it is submitted that a violation of EC law may also be established where transfers of players are blocked where those players have unilaterally terminated their contracts and fulfilled relevant obligations under local employment law. This would further slice into the persisting viability of what remains of the transfer system post-*Bosman*. It may even be argued that individual mobility would be unlawfully restricted by collective arrangements in the game even where local rules governing discharge of the employment relationship are not satisfied (that is, where the player is in breach of contract, in English law terms), and

[8] Para 110 of the judgment at n 3 above; and see more fully the Opinion of Advocate General Lenz.

[9] For exploration, see, e.g., Thill, M, 'L'arrêt Bosman et ses implications pour la libre circulation des sportifs a l'interieur de l'U.E. dans des contextes factuels differents de ceux de l'affaire Bosman', *Revue du Marché Unique Européen*, [1996] 89; Weatherill, S, Annotation of the *Bosman* ruling, CMLRev, 33 (1996), 991; Morris, P, Morrow, S, and Spink, P, 'EC Law and Professional Football: *Bosman* and its Implications', MLR, 59 (1996), 893; O'Keeffe, D and Osborne, P, 'The European Court Scores a Goal', *International Journal of Comparative Labour Law and Industrial Relations*, [1996], 111; Seche, J-C, 'Quand les Juges tirent au but', CDE, 32 (1996), 355; Hilf, M, 'Das Bosman-Urteil des EuGH', NJW, [1996], 1169; Weatherill, S, 'European Football Law', in *Collected Courses of the 7th Session of the Academy of European Law* (The Hague, London and Boston: Kluwer Law International, 1999), pp 339–82; Spink, P, 'Blowing the Whistle on Football's Domestic Transfer Fee', *Juridical Review*, [1999], 73.

that the consequences of such action should belong under national private law alone, not least because different jurisdictions in the EU adopt very different approaches to such employee freedom, ranging from liberal to restrictive. On this view, the law of free movement forbids collectively-imposed sanctions on players wishing to escape agreed contractual obligations and pushes the consequences of such 'player power' into the realms of national private law, privileging astute contract negotiation with top-quality performers by an employer. This is normal in most industries, and in my submission the essence of the Court's approach in *Bosman* is that the football labour market should be organized in much the same way as any other labour market.

(b) The 2001 agreement on the transfer system

Bosman has prompted significant change in the practice of clubs in their dealings with players,[10] and some of the potential wider implications argued for above (though by no means all of them) have also been instrumental in inducing the shaping of a revised system. But the transfer system lives on, albeit in modified and scaled-down fashion. In March 2001 it was announced that, after extended and sometimes acrimonious discussion, an agreement had been reached between the Commission and football's governing bodies for the world, FIFA, and for Europe, UEFA. The Commission went so far as to announce that the deal of March 2001 had been 'formalised' through an exchange of letters recorded in a Commission Press Release[11] between Mr Monti and the President of FIFA, Mr Sepp Blatter. In the aftermath of this legally ambiguous 'compromise' the International Federation of Professional Footballers' Associations, FIFPro, which had been heavily involved in the negotiation until at a late stage it walked away in dissatisfaction at what was being proposed and ultimately agreed in March 2001, seemed a likely source of legal challenge to this deal. However, FIFPro's anxieties were addressed,[12]

[10] Cf. Gardiner, S and Welch, R, 'Show Me the Money: Regulation of the Migration of Professional Sportsmen in *Post-Bosman* Europe', in Caiger, A and Gardiner, S (eds), *Professional Sport in the EU: Regulation and Re-Regulation* (The Hague: TMC Asser Press, 2000), pp 107–26; Antinioni, P and Cubbin, J, 'The Bosman Ruling and the Emergence of a Single Market in Soccer Talent', *European Journal of Law and Economics*, 9 (2000), 157.

[11] IP/01/314, 'Outcome of discussions between the Commission and FIFA/UEFA on FIFA Regulations on international football transfers', 5 March 2001; 'formalisées' in French, 'formell besiegelt' in German, phrases which, like the English version, lack precise meaning under EC law. Cf. Egger, A and Stix-Hackl, C, 'Sports and Competition Law: a Never-Ending Story?', *European Competition Law Review*, [2002], 81, 90–91.

[12] On discontinued proceedings before the Belgian courts, see Bennett, M, 'They think it's all over, . . . it is now!—How Extra Time was Required to Finally Settle Football's Transfer Saga',

and in August 2001 FIFA and FIFPro were able to strike an agreement about FIFPro's participation in the implementation of the new rules, which entered into force on 1 September 2001.[13] Eventually, in June 2002, the Commission closed its investigation, declaring 'the end of the Commission's involvement in disputes between players, clubs and football organisations'.[14] Commissioner Monti stated that '[t]he new rules find a balance between the players' fundamental right to free movement and stability of contracts together with the legitimate objective of integrity of the sport and the stability of championships'.[15]

The key features of this system that the Commission is prepared to treat as compatible with EC competition law and the law of free movement provide:

- that in the case of players aged under 23, a system of training compensation should be in place to encourage and reward the training effort of clubs, in particular small clubs;
- that there should be the creation of solidarity mechanisms that would redistribute a significant proportion of income to clubs involved in the training and education of a player, including amateur clubs;
- that international transfers of players aged under 18 are to be allowed subject to agreed conditions;
- that there shall be created one transfer period per season, and a further limited mid-season window, with a limit of one transfer per player per season;
- that there shall be minimum and maximum duration of contracts of respectively one and five years;
- that contracts are to be protected for a period of three years up to age 28 and for two years thereafter;
- that the system of sanctions to be introduced should preserve the regularity and proper functioning of sporting competition so that unilateral breaches of contract are possible only at the end of a season;
- that financial compensation can be paid if a contract is breached unilaterally, whether by the player or the club;

Sport and the Law Journal, 9 (2001), 180. At EC level, a players' union brought an application claiming illegal failure to act on a complaint about the transfer system in Case T-42/01, *SETCA-FGTB v Commission*, but the case was removed from the Court's register on 24 January 2002, and the complaint (COMP/36.583) was rejected on 30 May 2002 as part of the Commission's closure of the investigation. Relevant documentation is collected at http://europa.eu.int/comm/sport/key_files/circ/a_circ_en.html.

[13] On how European law stimulates trans-national trade unionism, see Dabscheck, B, 'International Unionism's Competitive Edge', *Relations Industrielles/Industrial Relations*, 58 (2003), 85.

[14] IP/02/824, 'Commission closes investigations into FIFA regulations on international football transfers', 5 June 2002. The Commission does not propose to take the matter on to a formal plane.

[15] Noted ibid.

- that proportionate sporting sanctions may be applied to players, clubs, or agents in the case of unilateral breaches of contract without just cause, in the protected period;
- that there shall be created an effective, quick, and objective arbitration body, with members chosen in equal numbers by players and clubs and with an independent chairman; and
- that arbitration is voluntary and does not prevent recourse to national courts.

Collectively agreed and enforced restrictions on player mobility and associated sanctions imposed on contract-breakers are plainly to be reduced compared with past practice, but football will still be allowed to maintain arrangements that would not be tolerated in other industries. Is this lawful? It requires testing against the demands of EC competition law and the law governing free movement.

(c) Outstanding legal questions

The Court has accepted that in some circumstances collective bargains designed to regulate conditions of employment may escape the scope of application of Article 81(1).[16] Neither the method of its production nor its content brings the 2001 agreement on transfers within the sanctuary recognized by the Court. The level of collective involvement was inconsistent and fragmented; the effect is not to improve players' working conditions. I do not believe the relevant criteria for this concession are met by the new transfer deal. Nor should the criteria be stretched to confer autonomy upon it.

Assuming the arrangements are in principle subject to control pursuant to Articles 81 and 39 EC, the key issue surrounds the scope of justification. It is probable that the mode of justification runs roughly, and perhaps precisely, in parallel whether one examines the matter under the competition rules or the free movement rules in the Treaty.[17] The primary stated justification for this system is to be found in the Court's ruling in *Bosman*. It is encouraging the recruiting and training of young players. I have argued above that this represents a mistaken concession to the perceived special characteristics of professional sport and I take the view that the idea that this is a sport-specific issue would

[16] e.g., Case C-67/96, *Albany International v Stichting Bedrijfspensioenfonds Textielindustrie* [1999] ECR I-5751; Case C-219/97, *Maatschappij Drijvende Bokken BV v Stichting Pensioenfonds* [1999] ECR I-6121.

[17] For much fuller investigation and defence of this thesis, see Mortelmans, K, 'Towards Convergence in the Application of the Rules on Free Movement and on Competition', *CMLRev*, 38 (2001) 613. Cf. Weatherill, S, '"Fair Play Please!": Recent Developments in the Application of EC Law to Sport', *CMLRev*, 40 (2003), 51, at 80–86.

and should be demolished were it to be revisited by the European Court. However, even were one to accept at face value this aspect of the judgment in *Bosman*, it is difficult to defend the view that arrangements within the industry that envisage persisting collectively-enforced restrictions on player mobility, of a type absent from other industries, are compatible with EC law. That is to say, I do not think any transfer system of this nature can survive. The key paragraph of Mr Lenz's Opinion is paragraph 239, in which he suggests that an adjusted transfer system could be justified if, first, fees were limited to the costs incurred in training the player by the previous club (or previous clubs) and, secondly, provided the fee was payable only in the case of a first change of clubs where the previous club had trained the player. This would exclude the multi-million euro deal. But even Mr Lenz cautiously concedes that such a system might not be sustainable in the light of the counter-argument that its objectives 'could also be attained by a system of redistribution of a proportion of income, without the players' right to freedom of movement having to be restricted for that purpose'. The football associations, he noted, had not submitted anything to refute that objection. Nothing in the Court's judgment seems to support Mr Lenz's tentative embrace of a revamped transfer system. Paragraph 114 of the ruling seems to exclude it. It states firmly that Article 39 (ex 48) of the EC Treaty 'precludes the application of rules laid down by sporting associations, under which a professional footballer who is a national of one Member State may not, on the expiry of his contract with a club, be employed by a club of another Member State unless the latter club has paid to the former club a transfer, training or development fee'. This strikes directly at attempts to impose restrictions on the ability of (particularly younger) players to contract with their preferred employer which feature in the 'compromise'. I would also be sceptical of the lawfulness of aspects which require a player to abide by a contract for at least three years or else suffer a suspension imposed by the governing authorities of football. The case of the unilateral contract-breaker is not covered directly by *Bosman*, but, as articulated above, I maintain that the EC rules are in principle equally applicable to restrictions imposed in this instance. This is collective action designed to encourage observance of an individual contract rather than simply leaving the matter to applicable national law. It is submitted that this contribution to stabilizing club squads goes beyond the space allowed to football by the Court in *Bosman*.

I therefore take the view that the compromise deal struck on transfers is incompatible with EC law.[18] In economic terms my submission is that the

[18] It may also be vulnerable to attack under national law, though this will vary state by state.

transfer system simply does not do what is claimed for it, as already exposed by the Court in *Bosman*. It is haphazard in its distribution of gains, and far from promoting competitive balance it instead strengthens the hand of clubs with deep pockets and tempts clubs to embark on financially imprudent adventures. In legal terms, the insistence on individual economic freedoms that is driven by Article 39 EC, supplemented by, and in some factual situations extended by, Articles 81 and 82 EC, fatally damages attempts to resuscitate a transfer system claimed to serve the collective interests of the game. The 'compromise' system would have been vulnerable to challenge by a private litigant relying on the directly effective right contained in Article 39 (ex 48) even had the Commission gone so far as to grant the revised arrangements an exemption under Article 81(3), a step which it has not taken. The Commission has been surprisingly triumphant in announcing that the deal had been successfully brokered. In closing the Commission's investigation in June 2002, Commissioner Monti, declaring 'the end of the Commission's involvement in disputes between players, clubs and football organisations', added that it 'is understood that EU law is able to take into account the specificity of sport, and in particular to recognise that sport performs a very important social, integrating and cultural function'.[19] This claim has no convincing connection with the transfer system, and the Commission's deal may yet be shown up as no more shrewd or enduring than its readiness to acquiesce in nationality-based discrimination in club football under the 'Bangemann compromise' of 1991, a cosy arrangement the basis of which was exploded by the Court in *Bosman*.[20]

I would not exclude the possibility that it could be regarded as legally permissible for football to devise an internal taxation system to transfer money into the hands of nursery clubs, as part of a scheme for sustaining a larger number of clubs than would survive in 'pure' market conditions and to diminish gaps in economic strength between clubs. Nor would I exclude the permissibility of 'transfer windows', which typically prevent players being acquired and immediately fielded by a new club in the later stages of a competition, or rules that forbid a player appearing for more than one club during a particular competition. These are a feature of the compromise agreement. Such rules doubtless dampen the market and exert an incidental effect on patterns of player mobility, but, by restricting the ability of rich clubs to poach

[19] IP/02/824, n 14 above.

[20] See paras 126 and 136 of the *Bosman* ruling, n 3 above. Cf. Will, M (ed), *Sportrecht in Europa*, (Heidelberg: C F Mueller, 1993); Weatherill, S, 'Discrimination on Grounds of Nationality in Sport', *Yearbook of European Law*, 9 (1989), 55.

their rivals' star players at the sharp end of the season, they serve the legitimate purpose of ensuring the competition remains credible.[21] By contrast, the transfer system does no such thing. In conclusion, it is my submission that the wider mission to maintain a degree of competitive equality and a form of organizational solidarity within the sport may justify unusual forms of intervention by governing bodies, but that, in line with the Court's strong assertion of free movement rights in its *Bosman* ruling, any such systems must be wholly disassociated from any collective attempt to impose residual restrictions on the ability of players to contract with their preferred employer.[22] The case against even the revised transfer system is all the stronger if one accepts the view that the Court in *Bosman* was wrong to treat the interest in encouraging the training and recruitment of young players as peculiar to sport. Football may be different; footballers should not be.

4. Benefits claimed because of the distinctive nature of sporting competition: collective selling of rights to broadcast matches

The transfer system is defended largely and, in my view, unpersuasively on the basis of its claimed contribution to inducing the training and recruitment of young players. By contrast the issue of collective selling of rights to broadcast matches engages the first and, in my submission, more convincing limb of the Court's identification in *Bosman* of 'what is special about sport', the anxiety to sustain a degree of competitive equality between participant clubs. As explained above, I do not take issue with this distinctive feature of organized sport as a matter of principle. What is intriguing in the case of collective selling is the extent to which this desire to sustain the internal strength of the industry permits sport to pursue practices that impose costs on third parties.

(a) Collective selling—the problems

One would expect the peculiar economic interdependence of clubs to be reflected in rules which secure a certain equality between clubs designed to

[21] Cf. Case C-176/96, *Jyri Lehtonen, Castors Canada Dry Namur-Braine ASBL v Fédération Royale Belge des Sociétés de Basket-ball ASBL* [2000] ECR I-2681, albeit that the system of 'windows' at stake in that case was tainted by unacceptable discrimination.

[22] Cf. Foster, K, 'Transfer Fees: Still (il)legal After All These Years?', Singer & Friedlander Football Review 2000–01, *http://www.le.ac.uk/crss/sf-review/00-01/contents01.html*; Blanpain, R, *The Legal Status of Sportsmen and Sportswomen under International, European and Belgian National and Regional Law* (Dordrecht, Boston, New York: Kluwer, 2003), esp. at p 60.

keep alive healthy competition. Systems of internal wealth distribution would not exist in 'normal' industries, but in sport they are indispensable, though, of course, fixing the desirable ambit of such intervention requires refined calculation.[23] One would suppose that the establishment of a 'solidarity fund' within a sport, to which wealthier clubs are required to contribute from the proceeds of, *inter alia*, the sale of broadcasting rights and ticket income, and on which poorer clubs may draw for financial support, would escape supervision under EC competition law. It would not restrict competition within the meaning of Article 81(1); rather, it is an arrangement that is inherent to the business of professional sport. And there are other matters that are agreed collectively between participants in a sports competition which are, loosely, the rules of the game, rather than restrictions on competition. Examples include fixing the numbers of players per team[24] and the scheduling of fixtures. Such arrangements do not fall within the scope of Article 81 at all.[25]

Collective selling of broadcasting rights is different. If rights are available only on a collective basis—so that a purchaser can buy only the output of the whole League—then a market for acquisition of rights belonging to individual clubs (comprising access to their home games) has been suppressed. Broadcasters are forced to compete for one package and are unable to deal with individual clubs, among whom there would otherwise be competition in selling.[26] It is admittedly plain that clubs would have nothing to sell unless other clubs agreed to play against them. Fixtures cannot be arranged unilaterally—this is the nature of sport. But once clubs agree to play against each other, the subsequent decision to sell rights to broadcast matches on a

[23] Cf. n 4 above.

[24] Cf. Joined Cases C-51/96 and C-191/97, *Christelle Deliège v Ligue Francophone de Judo et Disciplines Associées ASBL, Ligue Belge de Judo ASBL and Union Européene de Judo/François Pacquée* [2000] ECR I-2549.

[25] Cf. summary in Roth, P (ed), *Bellamy and Child's European Community Law of Competition*, 5th edn (London: Sweet & Maxwell, 2000), para 4-150; also Pons, J-F, 'Sports and European Competition Policy', speech given on 14 October 1999, available at http://europa.eu.int/comm/competition/speeches/index_theme_24.html, and Weatherill, S, 'Sports under EC Competition Law and US Antitrust Law', in Hawk B (ed), *International Antitrust Law and Policy: Annual Proceedings of the Fordham Corporate Law Institute for 1999* (Yonkers, NY: Juris Publishing Inc., 2000), ch 6, pp 75–92, and ch 8, pp 113–26, respectively. For recent statements of practice by Commission officials (including the above-mentioned Pons), consult http://europa.eu.int/comm/sport/index_en.html. Cf. also Mortelmans, n 17 above, esp at 628; Weatherill, n 17 above.

[26] The collectively sold package may be (and increasingly is) broken down into constituent units—live matches, recorded highlights, etc.—but this does not affect the basic issue, which is the suppression of sales by individual clubs. Moreover, rights may be, but need not be, sold exclusively—exclusivity is a matter that is distinct from collectivity. See, on exclusivity, Fleming, H, 'Exclusive Rights to Broadcast Sporting Events in Europe', *European Competition Law Review*, [1999], 143.

collective basis is restrictive of competition.[27] And whereas it may well be convenient for sports leagues, and perhaps even for (some) broadcasters too, to arrange the sale of rights on a collective basis, it is by no means necessary to do so to make the league viable.[28] So collective selling restricts competition within the meaning of Article 81(1) EC, in so far as it has an effect on inter-State trade. It is unlawful unless it is justified.

As far as football is concerned, the principal justification is plain, and it is rooted in the notion of organizational solidarity which the European Court recognized as a legitimate concern of sport in *Bosman*. Resources raised from collective selling can be distributed within the game in a fashion which reflects not only relative success and popularity but also the need to sustain lively competition. So the stronger clubs—judged by on-field performance and off-field popularity—will receive more than the weaker clubs, but the league will devise a mechanism that ensures the gap will be less wide than it would be were the clubs to go to market on an individual basis. Moreover, in accordance with orthodox economic logic, the fact that the collective system of selling has restricted supply will ensure that the price paid by buyers will be higher than the (aggregate) price that would have been paid for rights sold on an individual basis by clubs. So collective selling allows proceeds to be shared between clubs on a more equitable basis than would prevail in the absence of such a system; but moreover, it ensures that the pie that is to be sliced up is larger than it otherwise would be.

The objection to this lies in the impact on third parties—the purchasing broadcasters. The restriction on competition caused by the collective agreement between clubs causes a diminution in choice and an increase in price. And although the system may indeed allow clubs to raise more revenue than would otherwise be possible, and may also permit them to make administratively convenient arrangements to distribute that income among clubs, the fundamental question is just why the sports industry should be permitted to improve its position at the expense of third parties, a category here covering

[27] The precise nature of this 'right' is dictated by national law; cf. Beloff et al., n 7 above, pp 134–6, also pp 153–6; Brinckman D and Vollebregt, E, 'The Marketing of Sport and its Relation to EC Competition Law', *European Competition Law Review*, [1998], 281; Nitsche, I, 'Collective Marketing of Broadcasting Rights in Europe', *European Competition Law Review*, [2000], 208. See also paras 118–124 of Decision 2003/778 *Champions League*, OJ [2003] L 291/25, considered more fully below. For comments on the position under English law by the Restrictive Practices Court, see para 219 of *Re the supply of services facilitating the broadcasting on television of Premier League football matches* [1999] UKCLR 258, considered in more depth below.

[28] Cf. Cave, M and Crandall, R W, 'Sports Rights and the Broadcast Industry', *The Economic Journal*, 111 (2001), F4, esp at F18. See also Decision 2003/778 *Champions League*, n 27 above, considered more fully below.

both existing broadcasters and potential broadcasters kept out of the market by the restrictions imposed on supply. It is submitted that the orthodox approach under Article 81 would be to condemn collective selling as an unlawful restriction on competition between clubs and broadcasters, and to expect clubs to sell rights on an individual basis. Only then, once this has occurred, would the issue of sport's need for internal organizational solidarity be properly invoked. It would be permissible for participant clubs to work together to distribute proceeds from these individual sales in a manner which reflects the collective need to sustain healthy competition. So popular, successful clubs would, in effect, be 'taxed'—according to the internal arrangements planned by the participants in the sporting competition—in order to assist clubs able to raise much lower sums of money from sale of broadcasting rights. That is to say, the sports-specific anxiety to sustain an attractively competitive league would be reflected only after third party broadcasters have enjoyed the right to participate in a 'normal' competitive market for sale of rights. The question is whether there is any room for sport to argue that its special interests should prevail over those of broadcasters—that collective selling should be permitted, despite its detrimental impact on broadcasters, because sport is entitled to maximize its revenues and/or entitled to raise money collectively so as to facilitate its ready internal distribution.

(b) Collective selling—law and practice before Champions League

The matter is not the subject of an authoritative and final determination at EC level. It has, however, been the subject of inquiry at national level; and the issues have been approached increasingly actively at EC level.

Collective selling of rights has been the subject of examination *inter alios loci* in Germany and in England. Plainly a decision at national level does not in any way bind the institutions of the EC. But comparisons may illuminate both the law and the politics of the matter. In Germany, collective selling was condemned by the competition authorities but subsequently granted statutory approval.[29] This, of course, cannot displace the application of Article 81 in Germany. The matter was also examined at the some length by the UK's Restrictive Practices Court in its 1999 ruling which found in favour of the legality of collective selling arrangements practised within the English (football) Premier League.[30] Unfortunately, the decision of the Restrictive

[29] §31 Gesetz gegen Wettbewerbsbeschraenkungen, as amended with effect from 1 January 1999.

[30] *Re the supply of services facilitating the broadcasting on television of Premier League football matches* [1999] UKCLR 258.

Practices Court is flawed as a model. The judgment convincingly identifies the advantages that accrue to the Premier League in particular and to football at all levels more generally from the collective arrangements governing sale of broadcasting rights. The judgment concludes that, were the current arrangements to be struck down, their replacement by forms of less restrictive coordination between clubs aimed at income sharing is, at best, an uncertain prospect. So ruling against the challenged arrangements would risk causing significant damage to the healthy balance of the competition. The problem with this approach is that it pays insufficient regard to the question whether the 'good of the game' in this sense should prevail over the interests of third party purchasing broadcasters in having the restriction on competition removed, or at least reduced, so that there emerges competition between selling clubs. That would, one would suppose, diminish football's overall income, and perhaps also damage the effective distribution of wealth between clubs, but the broadcaster is entitled to the wry observation that the members of any dismantled cartel typically find that competition forces down the price their product can command. That is the point of cartel-busting. So why should parties outside the football industry be forced to subsidize internal peculiarities?

The problem is that the Restrictive Practices Court felt unable to explore the nuances of this matter. The decision was taken under the antiquated and subsequently repealed Restrictive Trade Practices Act. The court considered that the legislation confined it to choosing between the public interest in maintaining the current arrangements and in having no restrictions at all, and it preferred the former. The Court remarked on the difficulty it perceived in fashioning a reliable system of wealth distribution were the prevailing collective selling arrangements to be abrogated. But it did not—and felt it could not—assess the middle ground, in which a greater degree of competition could be injected into the market without adopting an entirely unconfined model of individual selling, for example by maintaining in existence a collectively-sold bloc of matches alongside which remaining matches could be made available on an individual basis.[31] The Restrictive Practices Court's failure to assess this type of method for meeting both the concerns of organizational solidarity in the sport and also the competitive nature of the market for broadcasting rights renders its analysis of the agreements unreliable, or—more charitably—of interest only to historians of the Restrictive Trade

[31] Cf. Szymanski, S, 'Hearts, Minds and the Restrictive Practices Court Case', in Hamil, S, Michie, J, Oughton, C, and Warby, S (eds), *Football in the Digital Age: Whose Game is it Anyway?* (Edinburgh: Mainstream Publishing, 2000), ch 23; also Spink, P and Morris, P, 'The Battle for TV Rights in Professional Football', in Caiger and Gardiner, n 10 above, pp 165–96.

Practices Act but not to those wishing to identify the correct way to apply Article 81 EC. The Commission duly intervened and asked that the participants notify the agreements to it. Both the English and the German arrangements are now under investigation in the light of the anxiety that they lead to unlawful foreclosure of competing broadcasters.[32]

This is the key to the Commission's preoccupation with sport. It seeks to shape a policy appropriate to the rapidly changing needs of the broadcasting industry. Acquisition of rights to show popular sports events is a central strategy in the acquisition and retention of high market shares. Careful and cautious scrutiny is therefore inevitable. Of particular pertinence to this paper is the appreciation that the Commission is visibly conscious of the perception that the application of orthodox trade law may undervalue the distinct cultural and social contribution of sport. The core of the problem is how to judge whether this perception is reality; and, if it is, how, if at all, to shape the law accordingly.

A revealing example is provided by the Commission's Decision of April 2001 concerning a connected matter, UEFA's rules permitting national football associations to prohibit the broadcasting of football matches within their territory during a two-and-a-half hour period on a Saturday or Sunday corresponding to the normal time at which fixtures are scheduled in the relevant country. This, one would suppose, impedes the commercial freedom of broadcasters to conclude deals to show matches at designated 'blocked' times, but it serves the end of sustaining a lively atmosphere in stadia by encouraging spectators to attend matches 'live' rather than merely fester in front of a television set. The Commission concluded that the rules fall outwith the scope of application of Article 81. In the press release concerning this matter, Mr Monti is quoted as observing that the decision 'reflects the Commission's respect of the specific characteristics of sport and of its cultural and social function'.[33] However, the text of the formal Decision published by the Commission reveals a different, narrower story.[34] The Decision is in fact based on routine market analysis. The Commission finds that the UEFA rules do not appreciably restrict competition within the meaning of Article 81(1).[35] It explicitly states that it therefore need not assess the extent to which the televising of football exerts a negative impact on attendance at matches.[36] The Decision is, admittedly, built on appreciation of the specific nature of the

[32] England: IP/02/1951, 20 December 2002; Germany: IP/03/1106, 24 July 2003.

[33] IP/01/583, 20 April 2001.

[34] Comm. Dec. 2001/478, OJ [2001] L 171/12.

[35] Paras 49–61 of the Decision. The Commission will monitor change in market structure, particularly in the wake of the 'Internet revolution': para 56.

[36] Para 59, n 34 above.

market for rights to broadcast football matches, but it is to go too far to make Mr Monti's breezy claim that it reflects the Commission's respect for sport's 'cultural and social function'. Here one may suppose the Commission is seeking to build up credit for itself in the face of allegations that its application of EC trade law is liable to destroy the foundations of sport. And, while one may wonder whether the Commission may be storing up trouble for itself in making extravagant claims about its competence to cater for cultural and social matters, one may also sympathize with the Commission's anxieties, given the ill-informed ferocity of the attacks which it frequently faces from sports administrators and opportunistic national politicians.

(c) Champions League

The decision on UEFA's system of national 'blocked' periods is explicitly stated not to prejudice assessment of collective selling of broadcasting rights to football matches under Article 81(1).[37] In July 2001 the Commission sent a statement of objections to UEFA, European football's governing body, complaining that its arrangements for the sale of broadcasting rights to the Champions League, the principal European club football competition, infringe Article 81.[38] UEFA sells rights collectively on behalf of all participating clubs. It has preferred to sell to broadcasters on an exclusive basis, typically under arrangements covering a period of several years. The Commission is careful to observe that it does not object to collective selling of sports rights as such.[39] However, it states that it considers that UEFA's scheme constitutes a substantial restriction on competition, not least because of the foreclosure of the market to potential entrants into a sector capable of dynamic evolution, and that although it in principle recognizes the need for wealth distribution and solidarity within the sport, the UEFA arrangements go beyond what is necessary to achieve these legitimate ends.

The Champions League is a tournament that includes up to four entrants from each country that is a member of UEFA, and it represents a vastly inflated version of the 'European Cup' which it replaced some 10 years ago, to which only national champion clubs (and the winner of the previous season's competition, if not also national champion) gained access. There is a widespread assumption that UEFA expanded the competition under pressure from leading clubs eager for a higher number of more lucrative European matches and willing to break away from the governing body should their commercial

[37] Ibid., para 60. [38] IP/01/1043, 20 July 2001.
[39] 'Background Note', Memo 01/271, 20 July 2001.

ambitions be left unsatisfied.[40] It is notorious that the rise of the Champions League has coincided with a diminution in the percentage of revenue raised that is shared among clubs outside the game's elite. Moreover, the vast rewards on offer to the small pool of clubs able regularly to participate in the Champions League may conceivably have made a significant contribution to weakening the competitive health of national league championships. One may accordingly suspect that the Commission, in seeking to apply Article 81 to challenge collective selling in the face of the sports industry's objection that such arrangements are essential to sustain internal organizational solidarity, has cunningly picked out the softest target.

UEFA duly responded by proposing an amended system involving, in short, an 'unbundling' of the package of rights available for purchase. More operators, including Internet content providers as well as more traditional public and private broadcasters, will be able to acquire a degree of involvement in the coverage of the Champions League. The Commission expressed itself favourably disposed to this plan for competitive diversification which, it considered, would benefit football fans while also assisting the growth of new technology in the media sector.[41]

The Commission concluded its investigation by adopting a formal Decision in the *Champions League* case in July 2003.[42] It concluded that the collective selling arrangements restricted competition within the meaning of Article 81(1), but it exempted the deal pursuant to Article 81(3). The system created a single point of sale for defined 'packages' of matches, which the Commission considered generated efficiencies that were of a particularly significant magnitude as a result of the elimination of the need for broadcasters to deal with many different clubs subject to different ownership structures in different jurisdictions throughout Europe. Transaction costs were kept relatively low. Moreover, the joint selling scheme tightened UEFA's grip on the competition's organization and allowed the commercially advantageous 'branding' of the Champions League as an unfragmented European product. Media operators would share in the advantages and they would be duly transmitted to consumers. The restrictions on competition were judged indispensable to provide these economic gains and competition would not be eliminated in respect of a substantial part of the media rights in question. The Article 81(3) criteria for exemption were satisfied. This important Decision will doubtless

[40] See Bose, M, *Manchester Unlimited* (London: Orion Business Books, 1999), ch 2.

[41] IP/02/806, 3 June 2002; OJ [2002] C 196/3.

[42] Decision 2003/778, OJ [2003] L 291/25.

assume a high profile in future treatment of rights selling arrangements within national sports leagues under both EC and national competition law.

In pursuit of exemption UEFA also advanced an argument founded on *solidarity*.[43] It argued that raising revenue in this way enabled it to share income for the general benefit of the game. The Commission accepted the desirability of promoting a balance between clubs playing in a league. It also accepted the value in encouraging the supply of young players. These objectives may be realized by cross-subsidy from rich to poor. This, of course, loudly echoes *Bosman*. The Commission expressed itself in favour of the 'financial solidarity' principle, and referred to its endorsement in the Nice Declaration on Sport, examined further below. But—crucially—could such desiderata suffice to outweigh the restrictions on competition inherent in a system of collective selling? The Commission skipped clear of this point. It did not need to decide it. The criteria for exemption were already made out as a result of acceptance of the contribution of joint selling to delivering efficiencies, suppressing transaction costs, and improving the brand.

The issue avoided by the Commission is of great legal and political delicacy. It is one to which the Commission has been gently and cautiously drawing attention for some time. In its Helsinki Report on Sport, published in 1999,[44] the Commission sketched its view of the role of a 'European Sports Model'. This possesses a number of features, most prominently grouped around the contrasts drawn with North American sports practice.[45] For the Commission, European sport is characterized by, among other features, the notion of solidarity, stretching from the apex of the sport to the 'grass roots'. This has a direct connection with the question of the permissibility of collective selling of broadcasting rights. The Commission commented in the Helsinki Report that any possible exemption granted to collective selling arrangements would have to take account of the benefits for consumers and the proportionate nature of the restrictions in relation to the end in view. This is orthodox fare under Article 81(3) EC. It observed that it is therefore appropriate 'to examine the extent to which a link can be established between the joint sale of rights and financial solidarity between professional and amateur sport, the objectives of the training of young sportsmen and women and those of promoting sporting

[43] Paras 164–167 of the Decision.

[44] COM (1999) 644 and/2. For comment, see Weatherill, S, 'The Helsinki Report on Sport', *ELRev*, 25 (2000) 282.

[45] Cf. Weatherill, S, 'Resisting the Pressures of Americanization: the influence of European Community Law on the "European Sport Model"', in Greenfield and Osborn, n 7 above, pp 155–81.

activities among the population'. In similar vein Commissioner Monti has cautiously suggested that 'financial solidarity between clubs or between professional and amateur sport' could be a relevant factor in assessing whether to grant an exemption to collective selling.[46] This is strikingly less orthodox as an articulation of the matters that are properly taken into account under Article 81(3). This line of thinking hints intriguingly at use of the power to exempt restrictive practices as a method for insisting that fostering the social and educational function of sport is a condition for giving a green light to collective selling. The cartel is permissible provided its proceeds are shared throughout the sport for the sake of its general health.[47] This suggests that collective selling designed solely as a tool of wealth maximization for the participants alone would not be exempted. So a 'breakaway' league of the type lately mooted in European football,[48] may, by ridding itself of its roots in the wider organization of the sport, thereby lose one commercially attractive opportunity, that of collective sale of broadcasting rights.

But although on this point the Commission's thinking has close similarities to the anxiety over support for the game's grass roots to which the Restrictive Practices Court paid heed in the Premier League case in applying the UK's now abandoned restrictive practices regime,[49] the Commission may here have floated an idea that would exceed the proper scope of Article 81(3). By cautious contrast, *Champions League* explicitly avoids addressing the relevance of horizontal financial solidarity (mutual support within a league) and wholly ignores the issue of vertical financial solidarity (apex to 'grass roots' base). Moreover, the approach to be found in the Commission's October 2003 draft guidelines on the application of Article 81(3) is committed to preventing any stretching of the criteria for exemption beyond those found in Article 81(3).[50] This seems to reveal a preference to barricade Article 81's walls against incursion by what may loosely be termed 'non-efficiency' factors. On this reading, if a practice is incapable of exemption pursuant to Article 81(3) it cannot be saved by reference to horizontal Treaty provisions such as Article 151(4). And

[46] Speech delivered in Brussels at a Conference on *Governance in Sport*, 26 February 2001, available as Speech/01/84 via http://europa.eu.int/comm/sport/key_files/comp/a_comp_en.html.

[47] Support for this approach is expressed by the Committee of the Regions, Opinion on the European Model of Sport, OJ [1999] C 374/56, para 3.8.

[48] 'Project Gandalf', the European Football League, was notified to the Commission, OJ [1999] C 70/5, and though the breakaway has not (yet) been executed the threat was enough to generate changes by UEFA that benefited larger clubs. See, e.g., Van Den Brink, P, 'EC Competition Law and the Regulation of Football', *European Competition Law Review*, [2000], 359, esp 364–5. The 'G-14' group of leading clubs has its own website: http://www.g14.com/intro.htm.

[49] N 30 above.

[50] Available via http://europa.eu.int/comm/competition/antitrust/legislation. See esp para 38.

if it merits exemption under Article 81(3), it cannot be denied it for neglect of other interests. This implies that the promotion of cultural objectives which are not congruent with decision-making orthodoxy under Article 81 is possible only under other Treaty provisions. It cannot yet be stated with confidence that the Commission has got this right, although this line of reasoning does bear some resemblance to the Court's attitude to the relevance of the horizontal provisions of the Treaty in the exercise of the competence to harmonize under Article 95. The conditions for recourse to Article 95 must first be satisfied before any question of the impact of the horizontal provisions can arise.[51]

5. Burdens imposed because of the distinctive nature of sporting competition: 'protected' or 'listed' events

Legislation governing 'protected' or 'listed' events is popularly supposed to have been introduced in order to ensure that particularly high-profile sporting fixtures are available to the general public without the need to pay a subscription to the broadcaster, but, at least in its EC dimension, this is in fact a misleadingly inflated view of the degree of legal intervention that exists. The relevant legislation at EC level is a good deal less interventionist, and a good deal more ambiguous, than the common misperception holds.

(a) 'Listed events' under the 'Television Without Frontiers' Directive

The so-called 'Television Without Frontiers' Directive, Directive 89/552, was amended by Directive 97/36,[52] and it is the latter Directive that provides the source of the relevant provisions. The Directives are based on the Treaty provisions governing coordination of laws in the establishment and services sectors,[53] and are accordingly measures of market integration, operative in a sector technologically well suited to trans-frontier growth. Because several Member States have regimes which, in differing ways, involve some degree of intervention into the manner of broadcasting major sporting events, it was decided that some attempt should be made to supply an EC-level framework for resolving the collision between such regimes and the quest for an integrated European market. This, of course, is a classic example of the endemic

[51] Case C-376/98, *Germany v Parliament and Council* [2000] ECR I-8419 ('Tobacco Advertising').

[52] OJ [1989] L 298/23, OJ [1997] L 202/60 respectively. See generally on this regime, Jones, CA, 'Television without Frontiers', *Yearbook of European Law*, 19 (1999–2000), 299.

[53] Articles 47(2) and 55 (ex 57(2) and 66) EC.

tendency of a policy of trade integration to spill over into other sectors. Because states have taken a stance on patterns of intervention designed to limit market freedoms, the EC, devising a regulatory framework for a broader European market, must respond by making its own choices about the content of the regime that shall be adopted at European level. So coordination and harmonization is much more than a technical process of fixing a framework of common rules for a common market; instead it involves inevitable and sensitive selections of regulatory style and philosophy. So, in this instance, questions of sport and culture, in respect of which the EC lacks any general legislative competence, are nevertheless drawn on to its legislative agenda as a result of the wide-ranging functional impact of the programme of harmonization and coordination of laws. In this vein, recital 25 of Directive 97/36 observes that Article 128(4) EC (now Article 151(4)) 'requires the Community to take cultural aspects into account in its action under other provisions of the Treaty'. Harmonization is permissible only provided a sufficient contribution to market-building is demonstrated, but in shaping the content of the harmonized regime it is perfectly proper for cultural policy to be taken into account, just as consumer policy and public health policy affect the shaping of market-integrative rules at EC level.[54]

So, offering a fine illustration of these regulatory ripples, the opportunity was taken on the amendment effected by Directive 97/36 to include new provisions on 'protected events' in the EC regime.[55] But, as one may have anticipated, given the sensitivity of the issues at stake, there is no question of the matter being dealt with exhaustively at EC level. In fact, the EC rules governing protected events are a very strange beast indeed. Of particular relevance to the current paper, they illustrate the point that the 'cultural' aspects of sport are extraordinarily ill-defined, although here the outcome of the shaping of legal intervention is that sport is subjected to unusual burdens, in contrast with the matters explored elsewhere which concern sport's modestly successful search for unusual benefits and immunities.

The relevant provision is Article 1(4) of Directive 97/36, which among other things provides for the insertion of a new Article 3a into Directive 89/552. Article 3a provides that

Each Member State may take measures in accordance with Community law to ensure that broadcasters under its jurisdiction do not broadcast on an exclusive basis events

[54] Articles 153(2), 152(1) EC. Cf. Case C-376/98, n 51 above; for discussion of the impact of this case on cultural aspects of harmonized laws, see Katsirea, I, 'Why the European Broadcasting Quota should be Abolished', ELRev, 28 (2003), 190.

[55] See Craufurd Smith, R and Boettcher, B, 'Football and Fundamental Rights: Regulating Access to Major Sporting Events on Television', *European Public Law*, 8 (2002), 107.

which are regarded by that Member State as being of major importance for society in such a way as to deprive a substantial proportion of the public in that Member State of the possibility of following such events via live coverage or deferred coverage on free television.

The anxiety is plainly that broadcasters to whom a fee must be paid by viewers to secure access to transmissions will acquire exclusive rights to major events with the consequence that the general population will be deprived of the opportunity to view such events for free,[56] but the word 'may', the fourth word in this extract, is vital to grasping the nature of the regime. There is no obligation imposed on Member States. The Commission has properly emphasized that this is a 'voluntary provision'.[57] The issue is national choices, not EC requirements. Article 3a of Directive 89/552 does not define more precisely the circumstances in which the power conferred may or should be exercised. Having introduced the notion of events of 'major importance for society', the provision proceeds simply to require a Member State that chooses to exercise this power to draw up a list of events which it considers to fall into this category, and then to notify the Commission of measures taken or to be taken to protect them from falling into the hands of broadcasters who will act in such a way as to deprive a substantial proportion of the public in that Member State of the possibility of following such event on free television. These measures are to be scrutinized by the Commission and published in the *Official Journal*. A complementary transnational dimension is added by Article 3a(3) of Directive 89/552. This provides that Member States shall ensure that broadcasters under their jurisdiction do not exercise the exclusive rights purchased by those broadcasters in such a way that a substantial proportion of the public in another Member State is deprived of the possibility of following events which are designated by that other Member State as carrying major importance for society. This is, of course, necessarily a mandatory rather than voluntary provision as far as Member State authorities are concerned; were it otherwise, one state's choices would be readily undermined by another's lack of concern in so far as broadcasters established in the latter state had acquired rights 'listed' by the former state.

The event of 'major importance for society' is a category which is amplified in the Preamble,[58] but which is nevertheless inevitably subjectively defined.

[56] 'Free' television for these purposes means 'broadcasting on a channel, either public or commercial, of programmes which are accessible to the public without payment in addition to the modes of funding of broadcasting that are widely prevailing in each Member State (such as licence fee and/or the basic tier subscription fee to a cable network': recital 22).

[57] Third Report on the application of Directive 89/552, COM (2001) 9, p 8.

[58] They should be 'outstanding events which are of interest to the general public in the European Union or in a given Member State or in an important component part of a given member State':

As one would have readily predicted, state practice varies. The majority of states have designated no events as carrying major importance for society pursuant to Directive 89/552. Those that have exercised the available power have made very different choices.[59] It comes as no surprise that no Member State apart from the United Kingdom reckons the televising of test match cricket to fall within the preferred scope of protection; nor that Italy alone lists the San Remo music festival. But there is wide variation even in connection with events which one would suppose would be of more or less equally powerful interest state by state. The finals of Football's World Cup, staged every four years and won by a European country as often as not, are 'listed' in their entirety in the United Kingdom, whereas as far as Germany, Austria, and Ireland are concerned only the final, semi-finals, opening match, and matches of the respective national team are included on the list, while Italy lists only the final and matches of the Italian national team. Moreover, the lists change. Denmark notified the Commission of its list in 1999 but withdrew this with effect from the beginning of 2002, and it now operates no list of the type recognized by Directive 89/552.

Commercially this legislation has the potential to be very significant indeed. Technological growth and, in particular, the rise of privately-owned broadcasting companies, a sector that has flourished since deregulation became fashionable beginning in the late 1980s, have injected a great many more players on to the demand-side of the market[60] and, with supply of major sporting events incapable of parallel increase because of consumer attachment to the existing small pool of established major events,[61] the cost of acquiring rights to major sporting events has accordingly increased dramatically in recent years. Indeed, it is well known that broadcasters seeking to enter new markets regard acquisition of exclusive sports rights as the pre-eminent method for rapid acquisition of a viable market share. This characteristic has further contributed to the race upwards in pricing. Traditional 'free' public

recital 21; recital 18 refers non-exhaustively to the 'Olympic games, the football World Cup and European football championship'.

[59] The most recent consolidated list of measures may be found at OJ 2003 C183/03, and includes measures notified by Italy, Germany, Austria, Ireland, and the United Kingdom. For a full list, see http://europa.eu.int/comm/avpolicy/regul/twf/3bis/implement_en.htm.

[60] See generally Craufurd Smith, R, *Broadcasting Law and Fundamental Rights* (Oxford: Clarendon Press, 1997).

[61] On inelasticity of demand for major events, see Comm. Dec. 2000/400 *Eurovision* OJ [2000] L 151/18 (annulled, but not on the point of market definition, in Cases T-185/00 et al., *M6 and others v Commission* [2002] ECR II-3805); Comm. Dec. 2000/12 *1998 Football World Cup* OJ [2000] L 5/55.

broadcasters now find themselves operating in a much less cosy competitive climate than that which prevailed 20 years ago. In so far as this legislation governing 'protected events' involves a priority for such broadcasters it may be thought beneficial to consumers, for it improves the chances of popular events being available for free viewing. From the perspective of the sports industry, by contrast, direct or indirect interference with the right to sell to the highest bidder is commercially alarming, and may call into question the opportunity fully to exploit an extraordinarily lucrative market.

(b) Interpreting the Directive

Given this huge, commercially sensitive issue, it is astonishing that the provisions of the EC Directive are so imprecise, yet that imprecision is testimony to the awkward issues that arise when sport as commerce and sport as hot topic in society merge. Once a state draws up the list of events that it perceives as being of 'major importance for society', it is entitled to take measures to ensure that broadcasters do not broadcast those events on an exclusive basis 'in such a way as to deprive a substantial proportion of the public in that Member State of the possibility of following such events via live coverage or deferred coverage on free television'. That may be interpreted to cover intervention that requires coverage on free television. That would plainly severely reduce the price that any other broadcaster would be willing to pay; exclusivity is worth a large premium to the commercial broadcaster eager to increase its portfolio of subscribers and interested advertisers. This would also involve a profound interference with the exercise of the property rights of sporting bodies.[62] But is the Directive properly interpreted in this way? Might it be that the public broadcaster is guaranteed access only to the bidding process on a non-discriminatory and transparent basis, so that there is a 'possibility' for the general population to have the opportunity of viewing the event on free television, but that it has no legal basis for complaint if exclusive rights are ultimately awarded to a broadcaster with a smaller audience and access to the services of which is dependent on payment by viewers? That would not simply be a question of price, for a free broadcaster may be able to promise a larger audience, which may be more attractive to a sporting body aiming to enhance its long-term popularity and to satisfy its sponsors than the short-term profit represented by a higher fee paid by a broadcaster whose services are not available free of charge to the viewer. But, admittedly, according to

[62] Cf. Jones, n 52 above, 326–36.

this interpretation, economic gain, not access of the general population, would be the key factor in the awarding process.

There is no ruling of the European Court on this point. Litigation lawyers would lick their lips at these conundrums, and their appetite will be whetted further by inspection of the progress of litigation on the point before English courts. In *R v Independent Television Commission, ex parte TV Danmark 1 Ltd*,[63] the House of Lords took a fundamentally different approach to the interpretation of this regime from that preferred by the Court of Appeal. Of itself this confirms the ambiguous nature of the legal rules. The litigation arose against the background of Article 3a(3) of the Directive. The applicant, TV Danmark, a satellite television company newly established in England but targeting the Danish market, had acquired exclusive rights to broadcast World Cup football matches of the Danish national team, events that had been 'listed' under the Directive by Denmark.[64] TV Danmark had bought these rights on an exclusive basis after a bidding process in which they had, as part of a strategy to secure a presence in the market, beaten Danish public broadcasters who would have been able to broadcast the games to at least 90 per cent of the Danish population, the threshold laid down under Danish law and which TV Danmark would not be able to cross. This was, then, exactly the situation envisaged by Article 3a(3) of Directive 89/552, as amended by Directive 97/36. Under the UK's implementing legislation, in such circumstances the broadcaster was unable to screen the event without having secured the prior consent of the Independent Television Commission (ITC). The ITC, accepting that the rights had been bought by TV Danmark after a fair process and for a fair price, refused consent, taking the view that the Directive precluded it from granting consent in circumstances such as these, where the acquirer had refused to offer to free broadcasters the chance to share the rights on payment of a reasonable fee. An application for judicial review of the ITC decision failed at first instance but succeeded before the Court of Appeal, which held that the protection envisaged by the Directive was exhausted once a fair auction of the rights had taken place.[65] The House of Lords took a different view of the requirements imposed on the UK by the Directive. It found it necessary for the ITC to exercise its discretion so as to prevent the exercise by broadcasters of exclusive rights in such a way that a substantial proportion of the population in another Member State would be deprived of the possibility of watching a listed event on television. So their Lordships concluded, contrary to

[63] *R v Independent Television Commission, ex parte TV Danmark 1 Ltd* [2001] 1 WLR 1604.

[64] As mentioned above, Denmark has now abandoned its list.

[65] The Court of Appeal decision is reported at [2001] 1 WLR 74.

the view of the Court of Appeal, that it was not mandatory for the ITC to give consent to a broadcaster in TV Danmark's position, which had acquired the rights in a free and fair auction, and accordingly the ITC's original decision should stand.

The House of Lords decision, when contrasted with that of the Court of Appeal, plainly gives much greater respect to protection of the Danish choice about the importance of access to viewing the matches and correspondingly less to market forces and the interests of a non-Danish undertaking that had won a fair and open bidding process. Lord Hoffman, who gave the main speech, treated Article 3a(3) of the Directive as having carved out a defined circumstance in which market competition and unhampered enjoyment of contractual rights would not be permitted free rein. He rejected the Court of Appeal's view that the way in which the rights had been acquired was relevant. Instead he considered that Article 3a(3) of the Directive could not have been met if the general population could not watch the match when it was broadcast.

So, according to the interpretation of Directive 89/552 adopted by the House of Lords, the ITC does not have to grant consent to the holder of the exclusive rights even if the holder has won those rights in a free and fair competition. But would it ever be entitled to grant consent to a pay channel if free broadcasters do not have a share in the rights? Lord Hoffman seems to think not. He envisages that the exclusive right holder must always make an offer of a share—though plainly this will greatly affect the price which a channel in TV Danmark's position would be prepared to bid in the first place, for it is exclusivity which is the jewel. This seems to render the whole process commercially eccentric, even unviable, but it is, according to Lord Hoffman, exactly the interventionist model chosen by the EC legislature. But what price is expected of the free broadcaster? What if the free broadcaster offers a peppercorn for a share of the rights? Would the Directive then properly be interpreted to preclude a body in the position of the ITC from granting consent to the right-holder to broadcast the event on an exclusive basis to a small segment of the population of the listing Member State? This is to peer into a very awkward world of assessing 'fair' prices in a market already rigged by public intervention.[66] The European Court was not permitted the opportunity to explore this rocky terrain. The House of Lords, though a court of final instance and here overturning a contrary judgment of the court immediately below it in the judicial hierarchy, made no reference to Luxembourg under Article 234 EC. The Commission for its part has done no more than briefly

[66] Cf. Craufurd Smith and Boettcher, n 55 above, with particular reference to the controversial sale of rights to broadcast the World Cup Finals 2002 in the UK.

mention this case in its fourth report on the application of Directive 89/552 in the context of a broad comment that application of Article 3a in the period under review had been 'satisfactory',[67] an approval repeated in the Discussion Paper released in April 2003 as part of the Commission's consultation exercise on the Directive.[68]

(c) The purpose of the regime

Enough of the detail. Why does this regime even exist? Why are sports events treated in this manner, which has such profound (albeit, in detail, uncertain) commercial consequences? A troublingly unbalanced 1996 Resolution of the European Parliament considers 'it essential for all spectators to have a right of access to major sports events, just as they have a right to information' while paying no attention to the costs that right-holders incur as a result of the legal safeguarding of such a 'right'.[69] Recital 18 to Directive 97/36 refers to a 'right to information' and to ensuring 'wide access by the public to television coverage' of events of major importance to society. Article 10 of the European Convention for the Protection of Human Rights and Fundamental Freedoms (ECHR) provides that the right to freedom of expression shall include the right to 'receive and impart information without interference by public authorities and regardless of frontiers'. This formulation is now also to be found in Article 11 of the EU Charter of Fundamental Rights of the European Union, proclaimed at Nice in December 2000,[70] which is to be interpreted to conform with the Convention.[71] True, Article 10 of the ECHR adds that states are not to be prevented from requiring the licensing of broadcasting or television enterprises, a proviso absent from Article 11 of the EU Charter. But in any event this seems to bear no relevance to the specific issue of 'protected events'.

So is the citizen's 'right to information', albeit that it is a right contingent on his or her Member State choosing to activate the power conferred by Article 3a of Directive 89/552, the key to understanding this legislation? Lord Hoffman began his speech in the *TV Danmark* case by asserting that the case concerned 'the right of the European Citizen to watch his national football team on television'. One might here detect a touch of the absurd, and one may

[67] COM (2002) 778, p 10.

[68] Available via http://europa.eu.int/comm/avpolicy/regul/review-twf2003/consult_en.htm. As one might expect, the BBC response to the Commission is warmly supportive of the House of Lords ruling. See http://europa.eu.int/comm/avpolicy/regul/review-twf2003/contribution.htm.

[69] Resolution on the broadcasting of sports events, OJ [1996] C 166/109.

[70] OJ [2000] C 364/1.

[71] Article 52 EU Charter.

well suppose that Lord Hoffman fully intends to jolt his audience into thinking critically about just what (in his perception) the EC legislature has chosen to do under this Directive. Can one truly consider that the watching of doubtless exciting and interesting sports events properly engages the language of fundamental rights? Such a proposition exceeds what is currently recognized as the scope of the right to information under the law of the European Convention.[72] One may go so far as to condemn such an approach as apt to demean the quality and dignity of rights discourse. And, moreover, the card of fundamental rights is a trump, but not one held by only one player. The rights to freedom of expression of broadcasters are in no small measure damaged by these interventionist provisions, whereas both the EC legal order and that of the European Convention recognize that commercial parties fall within the personal scope of this regime, albeit that their rights are not absolute.[73]

It is a strenuous effort to devise an intellectually satisfying and rational basis for this legislation. The Commission's April 2003 Discussion Paper understandably attempts no such thing,[74] confining itself to seeking views on whether the procedures should be more tightly defined.[75] Several responses to the Discussion Paper advocated a clarification of the purpose of the system but most—again, understandably—exhibited a primary interest simply to defend their own interests. For example, both the BBC and ITV praised the regime, while by contrast UEFA criticized the legislative favouritism of one type of broadcaster over another.[76] In teasing out the intent of this legislation, the best guess is that some notion of a citizen's entitlement, albeit falling short of a constitutional right, to watch a national representative sporting team in action is at stake, although, admittedly, the events listed exceed this category. Perhaps part of the motivation for intervention is that national and international sports bodies, though typically in form creatures of private law, nonetheless in practice hold a form of general representative function, acting on behalf of the nation when a team is picked to play in international competition, and that accordingly a control over their commercial activities is justified

[72] Cf. more fully Craufurd Smith and Boettcher, n 55 above.

[73] e.g., Case C-260/89, *ERT v Dimotiki* [1991] ECR I-2925; Case C-368/95, *Vereinigte Familiapress Zeitungs- und vertriebs GmbH v Heinrich Bauer Verlag* [1997] ECR I-3689; *Informationsverein Lentia and others v Austria*, A No 276, (1993) 17 EHRR 93. See Wyatt, D, 'Freedom of Expression in the EU Legal Order and in EU Relations with Third Countries', in Beatson, J and Cripps, Y (eds), *Freedom of Information: Essays in Honour of DGT Williams* (Oxford: Clarendon Press, 2000); Craufurd Smith, n 60 above, esp ch 7.

[74] N 68 above.

[75] A perspective doubtless in part inspired by pending litigation on its proper role: Case T-33/01, *Infront WM v Commission*.

[76] N 68 above.

in the public interest. This is capable of being combined with some notion of social solidarity in the nation generated by such events in order to find a rationale of sorts for the decision to create the category of events of 'major importance of society'. Participation even as a television viewer in a football World Cup or an Olympic Games, both of which are staged only once every four years, could be taken to contribute to the construction of a shared sense of identity and of history, and as an indispensable basis for social communication.[77] One may optimistically hope that, in so far as minority sections of a nation's population enjoy a disproportionately high representation among the cream of a country's sporting performers, the sight of the team or individual athletes in action may promote tolerance and respect for diversity in society. This appealing vision may be illustrated by the successful exploits of the multi-ethnic French national football side of recent years. But in response to every example of sport as a force for cohesion, it is not hard to paint a less agreeable picture. In 2001, two friendly football matches between countries with a troubled recent shared history, France and Algeria, and Portugal and Angola, were abandoned without reaching their allotted duration of 90 minutes as a result of violence among players and/or supporters. And in the uniquely odious case of the English national football team it is regrettably easy to reflect that scenes of young white men who travel in aggressive celebration of a deeply intolerant culture do nothing to foster social cohesion. Patriotism is too often transformed from allegiance to one's own country into disrespect or even hatred of other countries, and national representative sport has no special claim to be able successfully to achieve or promote the benefits of intercultural dialogue without suffering the burdens of sustained or deepened division.

My conclusion is that the EC's legislation governing 'protected events' diminishes the commercial value of the rights to broadcast such events by interfering in the ability of the holder of the rights to extract the highest price the market would yield. The advantages generated by this intervention, and the rationales for legislating in this way, are remarkably under-explained. What is required is a balancing of the competing interests. If this has been done by the EC legislature then it has been kept very quiet. The impression is that, once more, sport is subjected to a 'special' regime without any sufficiently careful examination of what is and should be at stake.

[77] Cf. from the Australian perspective Fraser, D and McMahon, K, 'When Too Much Sport is Barely Enough: Broadcasting Regulation and National Identity', *Entertainment Law*, 1 (2002), 1.

6. Is there a broader cultural context?

In the Introduction to this paper, I observed that EC law is alleged to carry a bias which reflects the market-making imperatives of the Treaty while failing to pay adequate respect to the economic peculiarities of sport, and, moreover, that EC law suffers criticism for failure to pay due regard to the social and cultural contribution of sport. In fact, I consider that these are fundamentally different issues. The peculiar economic context of professional sport is distinct from the wider social and cultural place of sport in society, although both issues may find a home under the (perhaps unhelpfully broad) rubric of 'culture'.

The Declaration on Sport attached to the Amsterdam Treaty asserts that

> [t]he Conference emphasises the social significance of sport, in particular its role in forging identity and bringing people together. The Conference therefore calls on the bodies of the European Union to listen to sports associations when important questions affecting sport are at issue. In this connection, special consideration should be given to the particular characteristics of amateur sport.

At one level this is feeble. In particular, it is emphatically not subversive of the core of the *Bosman* ruling's firm application of the fundamental Treaty rules governing free movement law to sport. This was expressly acknowledged by the European Court in *Deliège* and in *Lehtonen*.[78] However, at a different level, the Amsterdam Declaration is rather bold. Whatever reservations one may entertain about the value of forging identity through sport, and however much one may wonder whether sport truly brings people together in any meaningful way, it is important that sport's 'social significance' is freely asserted precisely because the Treaty 'proper' allows no explicit room for account to be taken of such implications. So the Amsterdam Declaration is significant for peering beyond the limits imposed by the EC's attributed competence and appreciating a wider role for sport on society. And its reference to amateur sport is particularly illuminating, for it encourages us to make constructive strides towards re-thinking whether 'sport' makes sense as a single-issue definitional category.

The Commission's Helsinki Report on Sport was mentioned above in the specific context of collective selling of broadcasting rights.[79] It is of more general interest. The Report is directed at safeguarding current sports structures and at maintaining the social function of sport within the Community framework, which were areas on which the Commission had been invited to report

[78] Cases C-51/96 and 191/97, n 24 above, paras 41–42 of the judgment; Case C-176/96, n 21 above, paras 32–33 of the judgment.

[79] n 44 above.

by the Vienna European Council of December 1998. The Report begins with the ambitious assertion that it 'gives pointers for reconciling the economic dimension of sport with its popular, educational, social and cultural dimensions'. It maintains the Commission's identification of 'a European approach to sport based on common concepts and principles', which includes sport's role as 'an instrument of social cohesion and education'. It is suggested that tensions have emerged between this function and the economic motivations for sport which have increased in recent years. One example cited is

> the temptation for certain sporting operators and certain large clubs to leave the federations in order to derive the maximum benefit from the economic potential of sport for themselves alone. This tendency may jeopardise the principle of financial solidarity between professional and amateur sport and the system of promotion and relegation common to most federations.

The Commission asserts the value in preserving 'the social function of sport and therefore the current structures of the organisation of sport in Europe' while assimilating a changing legal and commercial environment.

More fully than in the Amsterdam Declaration, one may observe in the Helsinki Report the strain that is placed on describing 'sport' as a single phenomenon and on developing a policy that will comfortably fit all the ambitions of those involved in sporting activity. This encompasses the regulated, from the summit to the grass roots of the game, and also the regulator, since different perspectives among relevant Directorates-General within the Commission doubtless create further fault lines. From any standpoint, the tension between sport as an instrument of social cohesion and sport as a money-making enterprise is all too clear. In fact, a realistic depiction of sport as a pyramid, with the professional game at the apex, below which are slotted semi-professional sport, amateur sport, and, located at the base, purely recreational sport, is increasingly hard to sustain. Professional sport has little to do with the social function of sport mentioned in the Helsinki Report. Conversely, recreational sport has no economic motivation. The apex and the base remain linked by their subjection in principle to the same set of rules governing conduct on the field. And the notion of 'vertical solidarity', whereby revenue raised through lucrative deals struck in the professional game is used in part to sustain the grass roots, has not been abandoned entirely in Europe. But, as the Helsinki Report confesses, the growth in commercialism in the professional game poses real and imminent threats to this model. The Commission, of course, has limited competence to act. Its mooted readiness to exempt collective selling of broadcasting rights only on condition that the proceeds are shared around the sport more widely is truly intriguing,[80] but to Europe's leading football clubs, plotting new arrangements that would free them of the irritation of having to hand over even a small percentage of their revenue to their weaker brethren and to the grass roots, this is a relatively peripheral anxiety. The Commission's vision for the protection of the 'European Sport Model' involves consultation between interested levels of governance—sports governing bodies, Member States, European institutions. A partnership is presented as the way forward. But, at least in the case of professional football, it is not clear that the leading clubs are interested.

A Declaration on 'the specific characteristics of sport and its social function in Europe, of which account should be taken in implementing common policies', was annexed to the Conclusions of the Nice European Council held in December 2000. This concedes the absence of any direct Community powers in the area, but accepts that in action taken under the Treaty the institutions of the Community must 'take account of the social, educational and cultural functions inherent in sport and making it special, in order that the code of ethics and the solidarity essential to the preservation of its social role may be respected and nurtured'. The European Council calls also for the preservation of 'the cohesion and ties of solidarity binding the practice of sports at every level'. Under a sub-title 'Amateur sport and sport for all', it is proclaimed that 'Sport is a human activity resting on fundamental social, educational and cultural values. It is a factor making for integration, involvement in social life, tolerance, acceptance of differences and playing by the rules.' The Declaration acknowledges the central decision-making competence of sports federations, but insists on their 'special responsibilities' in the light of sport's social functions.

A process of dialogue endures. In October 2001 the 'European Sports Forum' was convened in Brussels in collaboration with the Belgian Presidency of the EU. The Forum included, among other things, a working group on the follow-up to the Nice Declaration.[81] In its published conclusions, the insistence on the value of a partnership between interested actors is sustained, alongside assertion of the social and educational function of sport, though the working group's most striking conclusion is its shamelessly opportunistic claim that 'In the light of current international events, it is more than ever before essential to spread the message of peace and respect for others conveyed by sport'. A separate working group, dealing with 'sport and the social economy', concluded that sport should remain faithful to the values of the social

[80] See section 4 of this paper for discussion of the status of this view.

[81] Documentation is available via http://europa.eu.int/comm/sport/info/events/forum2001_en.html.

economy, which 'is composed of people-centred organisations and enterprises based on democracy, solidarity and valorisation of social, cultural and environmental resources'. It identified these as 'civic values [that] transcend the logic of profit-seeking interest'. It is painfully difficult to avoid treating this as anything other than an exercise in self-parody, but through the haze of good intentions one can perceive once again the remarkably high-minded aspirations of sport—or at least the interest of sporting bodies in portraying themselves as equipped with a role that should be seen as more than merely commercially driven as an adept strategy designed to extract legal concessions.

The European Sports Forum was held in Copenhagen in 2002, at which Conclusions on *Taking Account of Sport in Community Policies and Measures* included a Portuguese proposal for a provision empowering action in the field of sport to be inserted into the Treaty. After years of periodic pleas to have sport partially or wholly excluded from the Treaty, it is intriguing that this nudge in the opposite direction was enough to provoke the Convention on the Future of Europe to include sport in the Draft Constitutional Treaty released in July 2003. It is proposed that the Union shall have a competence to act in support of its Member States in the field of sport.[82] It shall contribute to the promotion of European sporting issues, given the social and educational function of sport.[83] In November 2003 the latest annual European Sports Forum took place in Verona. It hosted three working groups: 'Sport as a factor for social integration'; 'The role of European sport in an international context'; and, most bewildering of all, 'Sport and media literacy'.

So what is 'sport' today? And what challenge(s) does it present to regulators?[84] The leading football clubs, and operators in some other lucrative sports such as motor racing, are commercially ambitious and powerful companies. How they fulfil, and why they would fulfil, a role as contributors to the promotion of social, educational, and cultural values is increasingly difficult to identify. In fact, the sharp increase in the economic motivation for their activities is precisely the reason why they should, in principle, be accordingly subjected to the orthodox rules of EC trade law. The list of formal and informal Commission interventions duly grows ever longer.[85] Certainly the application of such rules

[82] Article I-16. [83] Article III-182.

[84] For general discussion, see Foster, K, 'How can Sport be Regulated?', in Greenfield and Osborn, n 7 above, ch 14; Parrish, R, 'Reconciling Conflicting Approaches to Sport in the European Union', and Foster, K, 'Can Sport be Regulated by Europe? An Analysis of Alternative Models', both in Caiger and Gardiner, n 10 above, pp 21–42 and pp 43–64, respectively.

[85] Cf. Memo/02/127, 'The application of the EU's competition rules to sports', 5 June 2002, but the list has already lengthened, cf. nn 5, 31, and 41 above. For a survey, see Weatherill, n 17 above.

should pay due regard to the peculiar characteristic of mutual interdependence which marks the relationship between participants in a professional sports league. This is a sports-specific issue, but it is perfectly capable of forming part of appropriately nuanced economic and legal analysis. After all, the application of Article 81 is *always* conditioned by the particular context in which arrangements are struck. The Court's fundamentally important decision in *Wouters* increasingly serves as the starting point in determining whether an apparent restriction on competition is properly pulled within the grip of Article 81(1).[86] The Court stated that 'account must first of all be taken of the overall context in which the decision of the association of undertakings was taken or produces its effects. More particularly, account must be taken of its objectives. . . . It has then to be considered whether the consequential effects restrictive of competition are inherent in the pursuit of those objectives.' This observation was delivered in the context of rules prohibiting multi-disciplinary partnerships between members of the Bar and accountants, but it can readily be transplanted to underpin an argument that the overall context in which sports regulation occurs, built around pursuit of a broad objective of healthy equality of competitive opportunity, produces effects which though restrictive of competition are nonetheless inherent in the pursuit of those objectives.[87] Only if a restriction on competition within the meaning of Article 81(1) is at stake does the inquiry move to the possibility of exemption pursuant to Article 81(3).[88]

This is sports law and sports economics, and it is central to deciding how to control governing bodies whose regulation of sport has a spill-over impact on commercial activities. But in so far as professional sport claims virtue in making a broader contribution to culture, one should be sceptical of what it seeks. In so far as the 'culture' of sport is simply 'the way things have always been done', one should not regard defence of 'culture' as a sufficient reason to find justification for practices perpetuated in sport. The transfer system provides a good example. Rarely, if ever, has the industry engaged with the need to demonstrate a rational basis for such collective intervention in contractual freedom. Rather the assumption has been that the rules are 'part of the game'—and should remain so. That is legally and intellectually inadequate.

[86] Case C-309/99, *J C J Wouters, J W Savelbergh, Price Waterhouse Belastingadviseurs BV v Algemene Raad van de Nederlandse Orde van Advocaten* [2002] ECR I-1577. Cf. Case C-67/96, n 16 above. Strains of this approach are evident in Advocate General Lenz's Opinion in *Bosman*.

[87] The Commission's decision in *ENIC/ UEFA*, n 5 above, cites *Wouters*. For its invocation in relation to salary caps, see Hornsby, S, 'The Harder the Cap, the Softer the Law?', *Sport and the Law Journal*, 10 (2002), 142.

[88] As in *Champions League*, n 42 above.

The vigorous application of EC trade law to generate modification of indefensible practices that maltreat employees is entirely appropriate.

Outside the realms of the wealth cascading into professional football and motor racing, sport has a rather different function. Wealth maximization is not the dominant concern. As the Amsterdam and Nice Declarations and the Helsinki Report assert, sport has an important and valuable social, educational, and cultural role. This deserves protection and promotion. But constitutionally this is not the EC's concern. And economically it does not seem to be a significant concern of major clubs. These are matters for public authorities in the Member States and for governing bodies in sport. Some of the most intriguing tensions in the years to come are likely to centre on the attempts of governing bodies to satisfy the commercial aspirations of the most powerful participants while also maintaining vertical solidarity within the sport and preserving the broader integrity of the character of the event.

7. Conclusion

If religion is the opium of the people, tradition is an even more sinister analgesic, simply because it rarely appears sinister. If religion is a tight band, a throbbing vein and a needle, tradition is a far homelier concoction . . . the kind of thing your grandmother might have made. (Zadie Smith, *White Teeth*, Penguin 2000, p 193)

Professional football, in particular, has made much of the virtue of tradition, but in so far as it deploys its defence as a camouflage for the maintenance of inefficient or unfair practices in a world of increasing commercial exploitation of the sport's attractions, its subjection to EC trade law is entirely proper.

The transfer system provides an example of the imposition of burdens on players which, it is argued, is justified because of the sports-specific objective of inducing the recruitment and training of young players. I have argued that the EC rules of free movement are fatally damaging to any such system that involves persisting restrictions on player mobility and, furthermore, I have argued that in any event the notion that the need to encourage employers to recruit and train young players is peculiar to professional sport is misplaced. Sport is special in the need for internal organizational solidarity, and this provides an economic incentive to pursue, and a legal reason to authorize, the agreed distribution of wealth between participant clubs in a league. The issue of collective selling of broadcasting rights pitches this legitimate objective of sports clubs against the expectation of third party broadcasters that output shall not be restricted in this fashion. The Commission's apparent willingness, aired in its Helsinki Report, to link exemption of collective selling to wealth distribution throughout the sport, from top to bottom, represents a valiant attempt to offer inducements to sustain the pattern of vertical solidarity within a sport that it regards as characteristically European. However, its legal competence to insist on even this as a condition of exemption is far from clear and it has chosen cautiously to evade the issue in *Champions League*. More generally, the Community simply does not possess the regulatory competence to prevent professional sport in Europe mutating through breakaways from governing bodies, or through concessions extracted by large clubs by the threat of breakaway, towards the wealth-maximizing model typical of North American professional sport. In this vein, the EC regime governing protected or listed events may be regarded as a case of the biter bit. Sport, eager to extol its distinctive contribution in society when in pursuit of concessions from the application of orthodox legal regulation, here finds itself forced to suffer commercial detriment under a system which is driven by a wholly opaque notion of access to televised top-flight sport as a right of the citizen. This is a regime that urgently requires clarification, both with regard to its detailed application and, more fundamentally, its very purpose.

The EC in general and the Commission and the Court in particular possess limited competence in the field of sport. Elaboration of the social and cultural functions of sport belongs with the public authorities in the Member States and with sports federations. The Community's competence in these realms is lacking, but there is no compelling case for extending it. Below the professional level, EC action would add no evident value. In its economic manifestations, sport is subject to EC trade law. Given the burgeoning commercial significance of sport there is no convincing reason why this should not be so, provided that the peculiar economic interdependence of participants is taken into account—which it is, both by the Court and by the Commission. A wider 'cultural' aspect to professional sport is, however, hard to discern and such submissions by the industry deserve a sceptical hearing. 'Vertical solidarity' in European sport is under threat, but it is leading clubs, not the Court or the Commission, that are responsible. To end where this paper began, in so far as capital has burned off the nuance in sporting culture, it is professional sport that has embraced commercial growth and the institutions of the European Community have done no more than respond. And ultimately, sport in Europe today encompasses a great many different activities and motivations, to the point where pursuit of a 'Policy on Sport' may involve a misguided quest for uniformity.

5

The Gardener and other Stories: the Peregrinations of Cultural Artefacts within the European Union

*Andrea Biondi**

1. *The Gardener*'s curse

The tale of *The Gardener*, an oil measuring 61 cm × 50 cm painted by Vincent Van Gogh in 1889, certainly lives up to its creator's troubled life. The painting—which since 1954 has been declared a work of art of 'historical and artistic interest' under Italian law—was bought in 1977 by Mr Beyeler, a Swiss national, from Mr Verusio, an Italian art collector. In order to get a better deal, Mr Beyeler bought it through an intermediary, Mr Pierangeli, an antiques dealer in Rome. The price was fixed very low, at 600,000,000 Italian Lire.

The sale to Mr Pierangeli was reported to the Italian authorities and for years he appeared to be the lawful owner. After a failed attempt to export the painting to the UK, which strangely led to *The Gardener* being taken to Sicily, Mr Beyeler tried to sell the painting to the Guggenheim Museum in Venice. On this occasion he partially disclosed that he was the real owner and informed the Italian Ministry of Heritage of his intention to sell the painting. He also formally requested that the Ministry declare whether it intended to exercise its right of pre-emption, provided by Italian law. This right enables the Ministry to effect a compulsory purchase of a work of art that is considered to be of particular artistic and historical importance. By that time, in 1983, the requested price for the painting had rocketed to US$11,000,000. After several years of confused negotiations, during which *The Gardener* was temporarily stored in the Modern and Contemporary Art Gallery in Rome, the Ministry finally decided in 1988 to exercise its right of pre-emption.

* Centre of European Law, King's College London.

However, the Ministry recompensed only the price of the 1977 sale, arguing that it was in this sale that the painting's property rights were transferred. Moreover, the two-month limitation period within which the right of pre-emption had to be exercised was not applicable, the original notification not being valid as it did not correctly identify the real owner.

The knockdown bargain acquired by the Italian state did not at all please Mr Beyeler, who challenged (unsuccessfully) the decision of the Ministry before all instances of Italian courts. The case even went before the Italian Constitutional Court as Mr Beyeler argued that his right of property—guaranteed by Article 42 of the Italian Constitution—had been infringed.[1] In 1995 the Constitutional Court found instead that the exercise of the right of pre-emption was in the public interest and thus constituted a justifiable limitation of his property rights. In 1996 Mr Beyeler lodged a complaint against Italy with the European Commission of Human Rights for breach of his right of property. Meanwhile *The Gardener* remained in peace at the Rome Museum, that is until the night of 19 November 1998, when it was stolen in an armed robbery along with two other paintings. It was later found in rather mysterious circumstances by the Carabinieri on 6 July of the next year. In 1999 *The Gardener* was safely back in the Rome Museum. On 5 January 2000, the European Court of Human Rights ruled that Italy had indeed violated Article 1 of Protocol 1, which guarantees peaceful enjoyment of ownership rights.[2]

In conclusion, none of the characters involved in this story is found to be particularly endearing, with the exception being, of course, *The Gardener* himself. However, this sort of tale is all too common in an area of the law where emotions are as high as the financial interests involved. This area of the law is highly specialized, involving a limited number of players, all having conflicting interests. The owner's property rights, which include the right to sell and to export the work, can easily clash with a country's right to retain the work within its borders. The need to allow international exchange of cultural objects conflicts with the need for physical preservation. Moreover, the law in this field is often dependent on subjective judgement, and is influenced by scientific opinion that changes according to different cultural and social contexts.[3] The main problems are in fact well known and easily identified,

[1] Corte Costituzionale, Case No 269, 20–24 June 1995, *Gazzetta Ufficiale*, n 27, 28.6.1995, 36.

[2] *Beyeler v Italy* (App No 33202/96), 5 January 2000, ECHR Reports (2000–2001). For comment, see Seidhl-Hohenveldern, I, 'State Pre-emption of Foreign Owned Paintings and International Law', *International Journal of Cultural Property*, (2001), 70.

[3] See in general Merryman, J H, 'A Licit International Trade in Cultural Objects', *International Journal of Cultural Property*, (1995), 13.

revolving around the rules applicable to the international circulation of cultural objects. *The Gardener* story exhibits them all: strict national export rules, individual property rights, the definition of public interest, and the recovery of stolen works of art.

2. The Community and the free circulation of works of art

The international community has made many attempts to lay down common rules for the regulation of the circulation of works of art. The 1970 UNESCO Convention on the Means of Prohibiting and Preventing the Illicit Import, Export, and Transfer of Ownership of Cultural Property, and the UNIDROIT Convention on Stolen and Illegally Exported Cultural Goods are probably the most well known examples.[4] Much has been written about the shortcomings and failures of these international documents.[5] This article will focus mainly on the attempts made by the European Community. There is no doubt that the Community is entitled to legislate in this area. After all, this is an issue of free movement of goods, given that cultural artefacts have long been considered to fall within the scope of Article 28 and Article 29 of the EC Treaty. The Court of Justice back in 1968 ruled that 'whatever may be the characteristics which distinguish the articles in question from other types of merchandise, nevertheless they resemble the latter, inasmuch as they can be valued in money and so be the subject of commercial transactions'.[6]

Nevertheless, it has also been clear that this kind of merchandise, by definition, must be considered slightly special. The Treaty itself includes in Article 30 the *protection of national treasures possessing artistic, historic, and archaeological value* as one of the grounds that Member States can invoke to derogate from the principle of free movement. Although this particular justification has never been raised before the European Court of Justice (ECJ), the Court itself seems aware that these cultural objects are different. In a series of cases regarding the application of a tax reduction provision to cultural objects under the

4 Respectively UNESCO Doc 16C/17, Annex, 1970 and UNIDROIT Final Act, Rome 24 June 1995.

5 See, in general, Prott, L and O'Keeffe, P J, *Law and the Cultural Heritage* (London, 1989), vol III, chs 13 and 14; Palmer, N, 'Recovering Stolen Art', *Current Legal Problems*, (1994), 215; and Shier, R, 'International Art Trade and the Law, *Recueil des Cours*, 243 (1993), 74.

6 Case 7/68, *Commission v Italian Republic* [1968] ECR 423.

EC Common Custom Tariffs Code, the ECJ implicitly recognized that a differentiation in the tax regimes was fully justified.[7] In particular, in the *Giant Soft Fan* decision, a case concerning the customs classification of a work by the American artist Claes Oldenburg, the Court recognized that a wall relief made of cardboard and expanded polystyrene sprayed with black paint and oil and attached to a wooden panel by means of wire and synthetic resin is to be regarded as a work of art and exempted from certain customs tariffs.[8] Thus, even the rather controversial nature of this piece of art did not prevent the Luxembourg judges from recognizing the special status of cultural goods.

As for the necessity of legislating in this area, it was widely accepted that the sharp divergences in the regulation of the circulation of works of art between all Member States did constitute an impediment to full realization of the internal market. Other concerns, such as the fight against illegal traffic in stolen goods, were also common to all governments. Thus, after years of negotiations, the Community adopted two measures: Council Regulation No 3911/92 on the export of cultural goods to third countries[9] and Council Directive 93/7 on the return of unlawfully removed cultural objects.[10] It should immediately be noted that their purpose was that of integrating and not supplementing national legislation. Both measures specify that Member States retain the right to define their national heritage and to adopt such measures as they deem appropriate to protect it, provided that the limits of Article 30 EC are respected.[11] Thus, both measures apply only to those cultural objects listed in a specific Annex[12] and which are classified as national treasures under the terms of the legislation or administrative procedures of the Member States.

The belated adoption of these measures was generally welcomed with enthusiasm, which was also shared by the present author.[13] A few years down the line, however, it is time to question whether such optimism was fully justified.

[7] See Case 200/84, *Erika Daiber v Hauptzollamt Reutlingen* [1985] ECR 3363; Case 155/84, *Onnasch v Hauptzollamt Berlin-Packhof* [1985] ECR 1449; Case C-259/97, *Clees v Hauptzollamt Reutlingen* [1998] ECR I-8127.

[8] *Onnasch*, above n 7.

[9] OJ [1992] L 395/1.

[10] OJ [1993] L 74/74.

[11] See the 12th Recital of the Regulation and 2nd Recital of the Directive.

[12] Goods are stated to include: products of archaeological excavations; dismembered monuments; incunabula; archives; mosaics and drawings; engravings; photographs; maps; statuary; books; collections; means of transport; pictures. Council Regulation No 2469/96 (OJ [1996] L 335/9) and Directive 96/100 (OJ [1997] L 60/59) added watercolours, gouaches, and pastels. The measures of protection provided may apply to the goods listed only if a certain monetary threshold has been reached.

[13] See, in general: Byrne-Sutton, Q and Renold, M A (eds), *Les Objets d'art dans l'Union Européenne, Etudes en Droit de l'Art* (Geneva: Studies in Art Law, 1993); Chiti, E (ed), *Beni*

3. The content of the two measures

(a) Regulation No 3911/92 on export to third countries

The aim of Regulation No 3911/92 is essentially the harmonization of the export rules of Member States, but only as far as exports outside the Community are concerned. The main novelty was the introduction of a standard licence. In practice, any export—either definitive or temporary—of cultural goods listed in the Annex to the Regulation is subject to the presentation of a licence, issued by the competent authorities of the Member State. The state competent to issue such an export licence (thereafter valid in the whole Community) is the state in whose territory the object is located following 'either lawful and definitive dispatch from another Member State, or importation from a third country, or reimportation from a third country after lawful dispatch from a Member State to that country'. Therefore, the licence should always be granted, provided that the object in question was lawfully imported into the state's territory.[14] Another Regulation specifies what export licence form should be used, (there are at least three main forms), the formalities to be completed, and the documents required.[15]

(b) Regulation No 3911/92 on export to third countries: an assessment

Regulation 3911 was successful in its purpose of introducing standardized provisions for the export of cultural objects. For certain countries, such as the United Kingdom, this meant introducing new rules for the first time. However, as admitted by the European Commission in the first report on the implementation of the two measures, 'the effectiveness of customs control on the exports of cultural goods to a third country varies according to the Member States' attitude and behaviour as regards various aspects of culture

Culturali e Comunità Europea (Milan: Giuffre, 1994); Rigaux, F, 'Libre circulation des biens culturels et protection des trésors nationaux', ERPL, 2 (1994), 95; Voudouri, D, 'Circulation et protection des biens culturels dans l'Europe sans frontières', RDP, 2 (1994), 479; Mattera, A, 'La libre circulation des oeuvres d'art à l'interieur de la Communauté et la protection des trésors nationaux ayant une valeur artistique, historique ou archéologique', RDMUE, (1993), 9; Von Plehwe, T, 'European Union and the Free Movement of Cultural Goods', *European Law Review*, 20 (1995), 431; and Biondi, A, 'The Merchant, The Thief and the Citizen: The Free Circulation of Works of Art in the European Community', *Common Market Law Review*, 36 (1997), 1173.

[14] However, this would not be the case if the object is considered by the state to be a national treasure, or if the state decides to exercise its right of compulsory purchase.

[15] Commission Regulation No 752/93, OJ [1993] L 77/24, amended by Regulation No 1526/98, OJ [1998] L20l/47, which lays down rules on the drawing-up, issuing, and format of the licence.

and art'.[16] This seems to be a polite way of saying that Member States are generally doing whatever they want. The most controversial part is also the most important part of the Regulation. As stated above, the Regulation requires the Member State where the object is located not to issue a licence in the case of an object unlawfully removed from the state of origin. In practice this means that it would be incumbent on the state to carry out checks, or to request information and to consult with the state of origin. Again, as the Commission admitted, the Member States concerned have rarely done this: 'the authorities confine themselves to issuing the export licence, on the basis of the documentation which is incomplete or has no connection whatsoever with the object, and do not carry out detailed checks as to its provenence and legality'.[17]

However, looking on the bright side, it should be remarked that the United Kingdom export authorities in particular have been pretty active in requiring proof of legality of the cultural objects transferred. Moreover, several countries have also adopted specific provisions on the issue. In Italy, new organic legislation on the whole area of cultural property has been introduced. This new 'code' provides for a mechanism of prior consultation with the Member State concerned.[18]

Still, the effectiveness of the system is largely dependent on the willingness of national administrations to cooperate with one another. In this respect it is interesting to note that Article 5 of the Regulation provides that Member States may restrict the number of customs offices empowered to handle the formalities involved. Few countries have made use of such an option. France has in particular specifically created a customs office to deal exclusively with works of art.[19] This is an approach that should be welcomed: the creation of specialized administrations will favour collaboration, improve expertise, and in short will lead to better control on exports.

(c) Directive 93/7 on the return of cultural objects

The Directive, adopted on the basis of Article 95 EC, provides a mechanism for the physical return of cultural goods unlawfully removed from the territory of a Member State. The Directive applies only to specific objects: those which are classified as 'national treasures' (before or after the unlawful removal) and which also fall into one of the categories listed in an Annex to the Directive. The Directive confers on the Member State from whose territory

[16] COM (2000) 325 final (25.05.2000). [17] Ibid., p 8.

[18] Testo Unico, DLgs, 29 October 1999, in *Gazzetta Ufficiale*, n 229/L/1999.

[19] Loi No 95-877, 3/8/1995, *Recueil Dalloz Sirey*, 1995, 29e cahier, Législation, 400.

the object has been unlawfully removed, the right to bring an action for its return in the courts of the Member State where the item is traced. The competent court should limit itself to verifying that the object has been unlawfully removed and then to ordering the return of the object to its territory of origin. Every object removed in breach of the Member State's rules on the protection of national treasures, in breach of Regulation 3911/92, or when not returned at the end of a period of lawful temporary removal, is considered as 'unlawfully removed'.

This new action may be brought by states only and not by individuals. This, however, does not imply that it would be impossible for a private individual to bring a civil action, since the Directive is concerned only with the return of the object and not with the issue of ownership.

(d) Directive 93/7: an assessment

Great expectations were raised by the Directive, of seeing an efficient system for the return of unlawfully exported objects finally established, because, contrary to very similar instruments such as the UNIDROIT Convention on Stolen and Illegally Exported Cultural Goods, European law has teeth. Several specific provisions seem to guarantee a certain effectiveness of the procedure laid down in the Directive. *In primis*, Article 8, which provides that

> Where the return of the cultural object is ordered, the competent court in the requested State shall order the possessor (if genuinely bona fide) such compensation as it deems fair provided that it is satisfied that the possessor exercised due care and attention in acquiring the object.

Such a provision simply gets rid of one of the most acute problems in ensuring the restitution of works of art, which is that many European legal systems recognize the principle that ownership is acquired through possession in good faith.[20] Under the Directive the possessor is entitled to fair compensation, although he or she cannot prevent the restitution of the cultural object.

Secondly, the procedure provided for by the Directive requires the return of the cultural object once the court of the state in which the object had been found is satisfied that the object had been removed from the state of origin in breach of its rules on the circulation of works of art. In other words, the national court becomes an indirect enforcer of the other Member State's legislation. Once again all the possible exceptions based on the principle that foreign

[20] See Cooper, R, 'Good Faith Acquisition of Stolen Art' in *Art Antiquity and the Law*, II (1997), 55.

penal, revenue, and other public laws will not be enforced directly or indirectly by national courts are overcome.

Another important provision was introduced concerning the law governing property rights once the object is returned to the state of origin. Article 12 provides that ownership of a cultural object after return 'shall be governed by the law of the requesting Member State'. This implies a derogation from the *lex rei sitae* principle, according to which the validity of a transfer of movable property and its effect on property rights are governed by the law of the country where the movable property is located at the time of the transfer. This principle has a corollary: title acquired by applying the *lex rei sitae* will be recognized as valid in another country, should the movable property be removed from the country where it was situated at the time when such title was acquired. Such a provision is clearly aimed at simplifying the procedure and at ensuring the physical return of the cultural object to its state of origin.

Despite all these positive points, or perhaps because of them, it is noted that the procedure as laid down in the Directive has never been applied. The data contained in the European Commission report are clear: Member States have sent to the Commission 12 notifications of discovery of objects. Only one case has been brought on the basis of the Directive, by Finland before the High Court in London for the restitution of some ancient coins. The return was completed, however, before the Court had handed down the judgment, as an amicable settlement was reached between the Finnish Government and the possessor.

The reasons for such dispiriting results are several. First of all, the process of implementation has been long delayed. It is also true that certain provisions posed notable problems of adaptation for certain Member States. Article 8 was one such provision. A uniform definition of the position of the possessor proved to be elusive. For instance, national legislation such as that of Italy requires evidence of 'good faith' as a precondition for compensating the possessor, whilst the Directive requires due care only, thus creating very divergent standards. The good faith requirement puts the emphasis on property rights. The Directive seems to suggest instead that the enquiry about the possessor's intention should be related only to the circumstances by which the cultural object acquired had been reasonably thought of as lawfully circulating. Moreover, administrative machinery to support the restitution procedure has been difficult to establish and Member States have not been particularly active. Most Member States have failed to transpose the obligation to provide all information concerning such a restitution procedure, provided for by Article 6 of the Directive.

It is, however, still striking that despite a massive spin campaign promoting the Directive, not a single judicial proceeding has been brought to a conclusion. Two main reasons for this can be indicated: first, the mixture of public law and private law issues included in the Directive; and, secondly, the distrust of judicial enforcement in this kind of dispute.[21]

(e) Public v private law issues

Directive 93/7 attempts to solve, in a single measure, possible controversies arising from two very different areas of the law: the restitution of stolen cultural property, which is typically a question of private law (ownership right); and the illegal export of this kind of property, usually a matter of public law. This admirable effort to achieve uniformity does, however, result in a corresponding vagueness and uncertainty. The best example is provided in the concept of cultural goods.

Both the Directive and the Regulation, as indicated, apply to 'national treasures' only, irrespective of whether the object is stolen or unlawfully exported. As *The Gardener* litigation proves, the scope of such a concept is pretty wide. In the case before the European Court of Human Rights, the Italian Government justified its decision to consider the portrait a national treasure, and thus to exercise its right of pre-emption, on the ground that there were very few Van Gogh paintings in Italian galleries. Italy also contended that it wanted to prevent a later possible export. The Court accepted this argument in the main and held that Italy could exercise its right of pre-emption in the general interest of universal culture.[22] The Court sanctioned only 'how' such a right was exercised.

A 'universal culture' based definition may be too wide, especially in the context of the internal market. A more reasonable interpretation is to consider a

[21] It could also be argued that the prospect of having to reimburse bona fide third parties in another country is not especially appealing to states. It is Article 8 which prescribes where the burden of proof should lie and who is to pay the compensation should the return of a cultural object be ordered. The burden of proof is regulated by the legislation of the state where the return procedure takes place; and compensation is paid by the requesting state. Therefore, it may well be possible that a state is obliged to pay for an object which it had not previously owned. In the case of private property, though, national implementing legislation seems already to have dealt with this issue. For instance, French legislation requires the owner (if different from the bona fide possessor) to pay a sum equivalent to the compensation paid by the French Government (Sec.3, Art. 19, Loi No 95-877, n 19 above). The same provision is included in Article 81 of the Italian Law on the protection of cultural heritage (D.Lgs 29 October 1999, n 490, above n 18). Furthermore, both measures provide that if nobody claims the returned object, it should become the property of that state.

[22] *Beyeler*, above n 2, sec.113.

national treasure an object that has a genuine link with the state concerned. This is what the UNIDROIT Convention requires. Article 5 provides that a court will order the return of an unlawfully exported object only if the requesting state proves that the object is of 'significant importance' for the state.[23] Some other examples of national legislation also adopt such a stance. For instance, Austrian legislation defines as Austrian heritage:

1. all works by artists or writing emanating from or addressed to personalities born in Austria, or those having exercised their activities there or having died in Austria;
2. portraits or sculptures representing such persons;
3. Austrian topographic views;
4. cultural goods concerning Austrian personalities or events;
5. cultural objects produced in Austria;
6. cultural objects discovered in Austria;
7. cultural objects connected with Austria (for example, local costumes).[24]

Thus, only objects so closely associated with national identity 'that their absence from the national territory truly impairs the object-nation relationship' should be treated as 'culturally immoveable'.[25]

This qualification would also be appropriate for the internal market, where Community interests of ensuring respect for the principle of free movement, the obligations deriving from Article 30 EC, and the principle of proportionality all need to be taken on board. Moreover, as Professor Merryman persuasively argues, 'cultural nationalism' should be counterbalanced by an interest in 'the international distribution of cultural property'.[26] As the Preamble of the 1970 UNESCO Convention proclaims: 'The interchange of cultural property among nationals for scientific and educational purposes increases the knowledge of the civilization of Man enriches the cultural life of all peoples and ensures mutual respect and appreciation among nations'.[27] This same ethos should inspire the creation of the common European cultural heritage of which Article 152 EC speaks.

In the case of stolen goods, instead, it might be preferable to come up with a more flexible definition, as the fight against art looting is a common

[23] *Beyeler*, above n 2, sec. 113.

[24] Article 6, Bundesgesetzblatt, 1986 No 323. See, in general, Cordini, A, 'Il patrimonio culturale negli ordinamenti giuridici contemporanei', *Diritto e Gestione dell'Ambiente*, 1 (2001), 87.

[25] Merryman, above n 3, at 23. Another reason to prevent the export of cultural objects is when export may seriously threaten the physical integrity of the object.

[26] Ibid.

[27] Convention on the Means of Prohibiting and Preventing the Illicit Import, Export and Transfer of Ownership of Cultural Property 1970, above n 4.

concern. In this respect the UNIDROIT Convention simply provides that 'the possessor of a cultural object which has been stolen shall return it' (Article 3). In this case the notion of national treasure should automatically be wider so that no Member State can encourage trafficking in stolen goods. Introducing into the Directive a distinction between stolen and unlawfully exported goods may be one way of addressing the interests involved, especially when balancing ownership rights against the rights of the state requesting the return of a work of art.

(f) Judicial enforcement and other alternative dispute resolution methods

The Directive is firmly based on a public enforcement model procedure where having one's day in court is still central. However, it is becoming more and more accepted that in disputes involving works of art, such a model may not be completely appropriate. Many have argued in favour of increased use of arbitration and mediation in this kind of dispute.[28]

The Directive itself provides in Article 4(6) for the possibility of a state authority acting as an intermediary between the possessor and the requesting Member State. To this end, the competent authorities 'may facilitate the implementation of an arbitration procedure'. The advantages of adopting a model of arbitration (based either on pre-existing ones, or on a new one) are fairly clear:

- *Neutrality*: arbitration will have the advantage of 'de-nationalizing' a certain dispute. Parties are free to select arbitrators of any nationality, and may even exclude an arbitrator of a certain nationality. Such 'neutrality' may even extend to the use of a legal system from a country not connected with the dispute. As has been observed, not only does arbitration provide for a more impartial assessment, but it can also take into account the emotions of the parties. Arbitration is usually less formal than court proceedings and promotes a 'more self-liberating discussion' between the parties.[29] Arbitration may also be governed not by reference to a specific legal system, but to supra-national or 'deterritorialized' legal principles.[30] Although far from being accepted as prevailing practice, it can be argued that in the area of

[28] See Sidorsky, E, 'The 1995 UNIDROIT Convention on Stolen or Illegally Exported Cultural Objects: The Role of International Arbitration', *International Journal of Cultural Property*, (1996), 19.

[29] Byrne-Sutton and Renold, above n 13.

[30] The expression is borrowed from Palmer, N and Kaye, P, 'International dispute resolution: cross border loans and exhibitions', in Palmer, N (ed), *Art Loans*, (Dordrecht: Kluwer, 1997), 373, at 380.

cultural property, the use of certain 'denationalized' principles will be very helpful. A good example is 'the general and internationally recognised principles and standards upheld and applied by prudent and experienced museum trustees, directors curators and administrators', drawn from various codes of practice for dealers or museums, codes which are now very common.[31]

- *Expertise*: the selection of an arbitrator who is an established expert in the field has the clear advantage of providing very consistent and well-founded decisions. A related advantage is the clarification of contested concepts such as 'due diligence' or 'good faith', leading to the creation of uniform standards.
- *Efficiency*: arbitration may offer great advantages in terms of efficiency and costs, especially when a party involved is a state or another public body. A state will have a lot to gain from engaging in arbitration in cases where the object is located in a country whose courts do not easily apply the public laws of other Member States, or which, for other historical, political, and cultural reasons, may be less responsive to claims of restitution.
- *Inventiveness*: arbitration can be a creative instrument in merging conflicting interests. A famous example is often cited. A cultural foundation, the Norton Simon, acquired an Indian sculpture depicting Shiva, which the Indian Government requested be returned to it. After years of tug of war, the case was settled on the agreement that the Simon Foundation would return and give up any rights over the sculpture in exchange for the Foundation receiving from India a 10-year loan of the sculpture. Similarly, when Turkey claimed the restitution of a garland sarcophagus, lent to the Brooklyn Museum, the case was settled on the basis that the lender of the sarcophagus, a private collector, should donate the artefact to the American-Turkish Society. Later, the American-Turkish Society sent it back to Turkey, where it remains on loan indefinitely.[32]

These arguments have considerable persuasive force and the future may indeed lie in the creation of a specialized arbitration court for art-related disputes.[33] The recent establishment of the Venice Court of National and International Arbitration (VENCA), with a specific competence for cultural

[31] Ibid.

[32] Cases reported in Borodkin, J, 'The Economics of Antiquities Looting and a Proposed Legal Alternative', *Columbia Law Review*, 95 (1995), 377.

[33] Rigaux, F, 'The Protection of Cultural Heritage: Aspects of EC Law', (1994) MNVI 69.

property, is the first tangible example.[34] Recourse to arbitration, however, involves recognizing that mutual understanding and collaboration between Member States is still far from being achieved. Moreover, mediation and arbitration are forms of settlement in which public input is considerably diminished. After all, another reason for recourse to arbitration and mediation is the confidentiality of proceedings, allowing the dispute to be settled out of the public eye. It will be necessary to stress the importance of openness and public accountability, perhaps by insisting that Member States should systematically record any return order produced by an amicable settlement and communicate it to the Commission (as provided for in the Directive itself in Article 16).

4. Conclusions

The measures adopted by the Community are definitively a step in the right direction and their enactment contributed greatly to raising awareness about the protection of cultural heritage. Much, however, can still be done to improve the application of the two measures. In particular, enhanced collaboration and assistance between national authorities should be encouraged. The state of play at the moment seems to indicate that national authorities are not particularly concerned with contributing to the development of a common European cultural heritage endorsed in Article 152 EC.

In conclusion, to go back to our tale of Van Gogh's *The Gardener*, one of the most striking features of this portrait is the subject's sarcastic half-smile. Taking into account all the uncertainties surrounding the rules applicable to European works of art, one must conclude that he is taking it pretty well.

[34] The VENCA rules are reported in *The Journal of International Arbitration*, 16 (1999), 81.

Part III

Communicating Culture in the European Union: The Media, Language, and Education

6

European Community Law and the Cultural Aspects of Television

*Joshua Holmes**

1. Introduction

Television in Europe has always been treated differently even from other closely related sectors. Although the era of monopoly is now ended, the public broadcasters continue to receive substantial state subsidies, and private operators are intensively regulated. This exceptional treatment is frequently justified by reference to television's supposed 'cultural' role.[1] In part, television might be classed as culture in the sense of 'the works and practices of intellectual and especially artistic activity'.[2] As this meaning has expanded beyond high culture to encompass expressive activity more generally, television can plausibly claim to be the pre-eminent contemporary cultural medium, in view both of the resources devoted to its production and the time spent on its consumption. The defence of an expansive public involvement in television draws more heavily, however, on an alternative meaning of culture, as the shared practices and understandings constitutive of society.[3] As the

* Legal Secretary at the European Court of Justice, Lecturer in Law, University College London.

[1] See, e.g., the Commission's *Second Communication on Services of General Interest in Europe* (COM(2000) 580 final, p 35): 'The broadcast media play a central role in the functioning of modern democratic societies, in particular in the development and transmission of social values. Therefore, the broadcasting sector has, since its inception, been subject to specific regulation in the general interest.' See, in similar vein, the interpretative protocol on the system of public broadcasting in the Member States, annexed to the EC Treaty, which states that public broadcasting arrangements are 'directly related to the democratic, social and cultural needs of each society'.

[2] Raymond Williams offered this as 'now the most widespread usage' in his classic discussion of the meaning of culture in *Keywords* (Oxford: Oxford University Press, 1983), at 87–93, specifying it to include 'music, literature, painting and sculpture, theatre and film'.

[3] This sense of culture broadly corresponds with the alternative meaning of culture identified by Williams, n 2 above, as 'a particular way of life, whether of a people, a period, a group, or humanity in general'.

dominant instrument of mass communication, television is argued to play a significant role in the transmission and development of culture in this much wider sense. The power which it thereby possesses has until recently been highly concentrated owing to the small number of channels able to broadcast. At the same time, various market failures have been identified, undermining the case for deregulation. Therefore, television regulation has been organized around a cultural policy paradigm, in which the main objective of public involvement has been to shape the development of public culture in acceptable ways.

At the same time, television is also a major business, comprising multiple markets that are evolving rapidly with the deployment of new communications technologies. The range of services available has steadily grown over the last two decades, auguring the end of spectrum scarcity, and with it one plank in the cultural policy case for state involvement. Ideological change has also strengthened faith in markets, whilst various social trends have weakened confidence in the ability of the state to mark out a path for the development of public culture. Therefore, cultural policy has come under severe challenge as the central paradigm of national television regulation.

EC law and policy have become involved in a number of ways in the audio-visual sector as a result of the tendency of television markets and technologies to overspill national boundaries. First, the 'economic' rules contained in the EC Treaty have reshaped many aspects of national audio-visual policy. Secondly, harmonizing Community legislation has introduced a platform of common regulatory arrangements. Thirdly, various Community support programmes and subsidy schemes apply to promote television production. The aim of this piece is in part to determine whether these various interventions reveal an approach towards national cultural policies in the television sector which is at once coherent and sufficiently accommodating of national preoccupations. It also examines whether a distinctively European cultural policy has yet emerged, and whether more could or should be done in this regard.

It will be argued that there is underlying Community action in this area a relatively consistent dual-pronged policy towards national cultural policies. On the one hand, EC law has exercised a constraining influence, preventing states from pursuing strategies of cultural closure or national preference in advancing their cultural policy objectives. On the other hand, EC law has exercised a discursive influence over almost every other aspect of national cultural policy in the audio-visual sphere, requiring states to appraise, explain, and defend their arrangements. In its constraining aspect, the Community has required significant adjustments to national regulatory arrangements, but has left intact a serviceable array of policy mechanisms at the disposal of Member States. In its discursive aspect, it has been experienced as painful by the institutions of national cultural policy given the widespread uncertainty and scepticism about the purposes of television regulation. However, EC law and policy reveal rather than create these insecurities, and may actually strengthen national cultural policies by spurring them to arrive at a more forceful articulation of the underlying values at stake. Thus far, however, the Community has not developed much by way of a cultural policy of its own. The challenges confronting such a project are formidable, but in the long term it may be a necessary staging post on the thicker trajectories of European political integration.

2. Television, culture, and policy

(a) Television regulation as cultural policy

Before examining EC law and policy, it is first necessary to develop a fuller account of national audio-visual regulation in Europe. Historically, such regulation has been directed primarily towards the attainment of cultural policy goals. The idea of cultural policy can be best explained by reference to two convergent senses of culture. The first sense might be termed 'public culture':[4] it refers to a set of practices and understandings which are 'embodied in social practices and transmitted by habituation'.[5] Because of their complexity, they 'defy explicit learning or comprehensive articulation'.[6] Similarly, when we employ them, we do so in a partly unreflective manner, acting, as it were, automatically: 'the density of our activities, their multiplicity of dimensions and aspects make it impossible to consider and decide deliberately on all of them'.[7] This culture is public because its existence depends precisely upon its shared status within a group of people. If it were not shared, it could not be transmitted through habituation. Nor could it be used to social effect without conscious consideration or detailed explication.[8]

An individual may be exposed to various public cultures depending upon the groups of which he or she is a member. Even instrumentally and functionally

[4] This sense of culture is frequently evoked, but is often used in a very vague manner. The version offered here draws heavily on a brief but suggestive exploration undertaken by the philosopher Joseph Raz, in *Ethics in the Public Domain* (Oxford: Clarendon Press, 1995 (revised edn)), ch 8.

[5] Ibid., at 177. [6] Ibid. [7] Ibid., at 176.

[8] On the essentially public character of culture, see Geertz, C, *The Interpretation of Cultures* (New York: Basic Books, 1973), 8: 'Culture, this acted document, thus is public . . . Though ideational, it does not exist in someone's head; though unphysical is not an occult entity.'

defined organizations have some tendency to develop a culture in this sense.[9] However, the richest and most complex sources of public culture derive from our membership of groups exercising a pervasive and fundamental influence over our identity, in particular our national, ethnic, or religious affiliations, as when we speak of 'Dutch culture', 'Catalan culture', 'Jewish culture', and so on. The practices and understandings through which social interaction is facilitated, and our choices expressed, are not discrete but interlocking, drawing upon one another.[10] Thus, public culture is in large part developed through our membership of groups which bequeath to us a whole assemblage of practices and understandings, assimilated through long attachment, usually from childhood.

Cultural policy can be understood as an effort by the state to influence the transmission and development of this public culture. A narrow definition is needed, however, given that many public policies aim in one way or another to affect public culture. For instance, penal law may aim to alter practices and understandings not merely through an immediate deterrent effect, but by generating a stigmatic association in public culture. Similarly, the state's involvement in education is partly directed at influencing the development of future citizens, but education policy is usually considered at a remove from cultural policy, having its own related but distinct discourse. What marks out cultural policy is its deployment of culture in the narrower sense of expressive, creative, or communicative activity as the instrument of its ambitions. It takes a hand in the transmission and development of the public culture specifically via the domains of creation and communication.[11]

The cultural policies developed by European states since the Second World War have all been shaped, in one way or another, by important normative constraints upon the nature and extent of state intervention in both the public culture and culture as expressive activity. The lesson that was learnt in the post-war period in Europe from the appalling consequences of propaganda within the fascist states, was not that states should take no role in cultural

[9] Hence the frequent references in social scientific literature to organizational culture or corporate culture. See, e.g., Handy, C, *Understanding Organizations* (London: Penguin, 1993).

[10] See Raz, above n 4, at 177.

[11] For an analysis along similar lines, see de Witte, B, 'The Cultural Dimension of Community Law', in *Collected Courses of the Academy of European Law*, vol IV, book 1, 229, at 248–9. He suggests that within the 'large cluster' of influences upon culture in its broadest sense, it is possible to identify 'a number of social institutions, whose specific role is to represent and reproduce the value system characterizing that particular society, and which may be characterized as cultural institutions in the narrow sense . . . Among these cultural institutions are the educational system, the mass media, the arts and language.' It is in relation to these cultural institutions that cultural policy operates.

processes. Rather, cultural policy came to be regarded as essential to ensure the reconstruction of public culture in a form inhospitable to extremism. At the same time, that policy had to be carefully structured, and designed in such a way as to prevent its misuse.

It is unsurprising that audio-visual regulation should have been particularly susceptible to this cultural policy agenda. Television is the primary example of creativity and mass communication on an industrial scale, transforming expressive activity into a standardized commodity for mass consumption. It is widely perceived as occupying a position of unique power in modern societies, shaping peoples' implicit understanding of themselves and those around them. No other medium commands so much of peoples' time, reaches into the intimacy of their home, and has such visceral impact upon the senses. More than any other instrument of communication, television appears likely to make good a connection between public culture and culture as expressive activity.[12] Although television has been subjected to exceptional treatment in all European states, the cultural policies pursued have varied significantly from country to country in both their objectives and their methods. Nonetheless, certain recurrent features can be discerned, which may be explained by the long history of interchange and emulation which characterized audio-visual policy-making since the very inception of television broadcasting. At the level of objectives, it is possible to isolate two distinctive aspects of public culture at which efforts have been addressed through the regulation of television: national culture and political culture.

As regards national culture, television has been seen as a mechanism for creating a binding national identity. In some states, at certain stages in their recent history, the identity concerned was conceived of in unitary terms, and was imposed in the face of local difference.[13] In other states, and with increasing prevalence across Europe, emphasis has alternatively been placed upon

[12] See, e.g., the German Constitutional Court's 'Broadcasting (VAT)' Decision of 1971, BvergGE 31, 314, at 325: 'Not least due to the development of television technology, broadcasting has become one of the most powerful means of communication and mass media which, because of its wide-reaching effects and possibilities as well as the danger of misuse for one-sided influencing of public opinion, cannot be left to the free play of market forces . . . '

[13] This objective is often now incorporated only obliquely in the statutory framework, but its historical association with public service broadcasting is beyond doubt: see Barendt, E M, *Broadcasting Law—A Comparative Study* (Oxford: Clarendon Press, 1993), 53–4. The French Law relating to liberty of communication, Loi 86–1067 (as amended by Loi 2000–719), Article 43–11, para 2, contains an echo of it, by providing that public service broadcasters are to 'assure the promotion of the French language and bring out the cultural and linguistic heritage'. The Article then moderates the implication of unitary integration with reference to the 'local and regional diversity' of that heritage.

reflecting the plurality of socio-cultural currents comprising the nation by ensuring that all have air-time devoted to them, and sometimes also upon promoting understanding and solidarity across cultural divides.[14]

Television has also been presented as having an important role to play in the political processes of a democracy, helping to kindle and sustain a common political culture. This political culture may in part consist of a shared foundation of knowledge and awareness of the differing strands of opinion on a particular topic, which enables people to orient themselves in complex political debates, and which it is the role of television to disseminate as widely as possible. More ambitiously, it may be thought to entail a particular set of attitudes and argumentative conventions which unite otherwise diverse groups, and which allow them (or their representatives) to discuss issues in a deliberative manner.[15] Again, television may help to constitute such a deliberative political culture.

(b) The public broadcasters

As with the objectives of cultural policy so also with the practical arrangements for their advancement, European states have shown great variety but also important commonalities. For one, all states have employed an important institutional component in regulating television for reasons of cultural policy, by establishing a public broadcaster or broadcasters. Such institutions have typically been vertically integrated across all of the components of the industry. They have received part of their funding from the state by means of a universal licence fee, but have often also raised revenue through advertising. They usually have a non-commercial governance structure, designed to influence their editorial policy from public and private pressures alike, and often including an element of participation for representatives of users and of various socio-cultural groups.

[14] This sentiment is apparent, again in the French context, from Loi 86–1067 (n 13, above), Article 43–11, para 2, with its evocation of the role of broadcasting in promoting 'exchanges between the different parts of the population', and from the Constitutional Court's Decision 86–12, *Journal Officiel* of 19 September 1986, at 11294, with its reference to the constitutional importance, in the audio-visual sphere, of preserving 'the pluralist character of the sociocultural currents of expression'.

[15] Reference is often made, in this regard, to Juergen Habermas' work. In *Between Facts and Norms* (Oxford: Polity Press, 1996), at 362, he emphasizes that: '[t]he diffusion of information and points of view via effective broadcasting media is not the only thing that matters in public processes of communication, nor is it the most important . . . [T]he rules of a shared practice of communication are of greater significance for structuring public opinion. Agreement on issues and contributions *develops* only as the result of more or less exhaustive controversy in which proposals, information, and reasons can be more or less rationally dealt with.'

Their role in advancing national cultural policies derives from the public service mission with which they are typically charged. They are required to serve the whole of a given territory. They may also be expected to produce certain specified genres of content, such as children's programming, news coverage, or religious material. Lastly, and most importantly, they are entrusted with a broadly phrased duty to aspire to meet certain qualitative criteria. Underlying this last aspect of the public service mission is a belief that the cultural policy concerns at stake in the audio-visual sphere simply cannot be rendered as rules, imposed from the outside upon broadcasters, the performance of which is capable of straightforward measurement.[16] Rather, subtle and multi-faceted commitments comprising more ambitious projects of cultural construction can only be worked out and realized by means of a network of sustained relationships, which in turn requires an institutional setting. The public broadcasters are thus defended as a repository of values, transmitted by means of their own distinctive organizational culture or ethos. On this basis, cultural policy has traditionally been conducted at a remove from the state, by intermediate institutions acting under broadly termed mandates.

For much of the post-war period, European states pursued a strategy of *cultural closure* by granting to their public broadcasters a monopoly over all or many of the activities comprising the television industry. Rival broadcasters and production companies were prevented from establishing themselves within the borders of the state. Steps were also often taken against broadcasters operating outside the state but targeting an audience within it. This strategy of cultural closure aimed to guarantee a captive audience for the public broadcasters, ensuring that the influence of these institutions upon the construction of the national culture was not diluted by television from other sources.

In the last 20 years, European countries have all but abandoned cultural closure as an objective of national audio-visual policy. Public broadcasting monopolies have been revoked, commercial enterprises have begun broadcasting, and

[16] See, e.g., Graham, A and Davies, G, *Broadcasting, Society and Policy in the Multimedia Age* (Luton: University of Luton Press, 1997), 37: '[I]n the particular case of broadcasting, rules-based intervention is necessary but not sufficient . . . rules are insufficient [because] many of the issues concerning broadcasting are qualitative rather than quantitative in nature . . . These broad principles which should guide part of broadcasting could not be incorporated in any *precise* set or rules . . . Of course, it would still be possible for there to be a legislative framework containing these principles and for the *judgments* about the principles to be delegated to a broadcasting authority. However . . . the regulators, unable to appeal to a firm rule may give in to pressure from those they are regulating . . . Similarly, if producers are required to act in necessarily loosely defined ways and in ways that are *against* their commercial interests, it may be more efficient to establish a public [broadcaster] with explicitly non-commercial goals than to police a complex and imprecise set of regulations.'

television channels produced in other European countries are now widely available alongside domestic offerings. This opening up has, not, however, ended the pursuit of cultural policy objectives towards television. The public broadcasters remain a powerful presence in the audio-visual landscape. Their role as a vehicle of cultural policy has been downgraded from that of sole provider under the old strategy of cultural closure to the more modest one of standard-bearer. They continue to receive public funding, and are now claimed to further a strategy of *availability*, serving to ensure that the right kinds of content remain broadly accessible across the whole national territory.

(c) The regulatory component of audio-visual cultural policy

Nor have states been prepared to make the public broadcasters the only vehicles of their cultural policies, but have instead imposed regulatory obligations of various kinds upon new private entrants. Programmers must observe a variety of content-based obligations: a duty of political impartiality, for instance, or an obligation to carry a quota of particular programme genres, such as arts and documentaries, or children's programming. Similarly, television platforms providers (cable or satellite operators, for instance) may be subject to 'must carry' rules which oblige them to retransmit the public service channels. The introduction of these obligations has typically been accompanied by the establishment of specialist regulatory bodies whose task it is to monitor and enforce compliance. Thus, the institutional component of cultural policy in the field of television has been supplemented by an increasingly important regulatory component. Inevitably, the horizons of cultural policy pursued via this means are more limited. Effectiveness demands a more quantitative focus, in order to supply targets capable of measurement and enforcement.

This diversification of the instruments whereby national cultural policy is pursued has confronted countries with a new set of strategic choices. One option is to pursue, in place of cultural closure, a strategy of *cultural preference*, whereby domestic programmes or producers are granted various regulatory advantages over their out-of-state counterparts. All European countries have adopted at least some cultural preferences. They continue to subsidize the public broadcasters, potentially advantaging them over other undertakings, domestic or out-of-state. They give certain national producers exclusive access to terrestrial spectrum, which remains in most states the main distribution channel. They require platform providers to carry national producers, even when other services must thereby be dropped. Often, also, they impose obligations upon broadcasters to ensure that a certain percentage of their content is in the national language.

The alternative is for states to adopt a strategy of *uniformity*, imposing generally applicable standards upon all producers and services of a given type. This strategy does not rule out the widespread practice of *tiered* regulation, whereby different levels of obligation are imposed upon different classes of broadcaster (for example, national free-to-air, cable, satellite, etc.), provided that the rules are applied without distinction within a given class. Typical examples of uniformly applicable rules are those relating to the number of advertisements that may be carried, or to the impartiality of news coverage, or to the amount of time to be devoted to particular genres. It is possible to distinguish two variations on this type of strategy. More ambitiously, a state might pursue a global uniformity of output, by extending its regulatory obligations to all of the services which are available within its borders, whether internal or out-of-state in origin. More modestly, it might apply its rules exclusively to domestically produced services of a given category, thereby securing only a uniformity of internal service production.

(d) Other policies towards cultural production

Although public policy intervention in the context of television has traditionally been organized to pursue objectives of cultural policy, European states have also, to an increasing degree, pursued other policies which operate upon, or have effects in relation to, the creative and communications industries. Like cultural policy, these policies influence the patterns of cultural production, often in important ways. Unlike traditional cultural policy, however, their motivation is not to shape the public culture, although they may have an incidental effect upon it.

Some of the alternative policies towards cultural production are closely related to, and at times overlapping with, traditional cultural policy. For example, a perennial policy affecting audio-visual regulation, usually in the keeping of the judicial branch, is the protection of free expression.[17] In some times and places, this goal has been seen as a partial alternative to, and limitation upon, the pursuit of a cultural policy either by institutional or regulatory means. More typically in Europe, cultural policy has been seen to bear a close

[17] On the interaction between cultural policy in the shape of public service broadcasting and freedom of expression guarantees, see generally Craufurd Smith, R, *Broadcasting Law and Fundamental Rights* (Oxford: OUP, 1997).

relation to the goal of free expression, and even, on occasion, to be mandated by it.[18]

Another example of an objective which may be related to, but is distinct from, cultural policy in its traditional sense, is that of industrial policy, the objective of promoting the development of the audio-visual industry so as to boost the national economy. Industrial policy and cultural policy may go hand in hand: the production of domestic content may at once be promoted as a means of generating employment and in order to ensure that a significant proportion of audio-visual material reflects the domestic culture. Industrial policy may also, however, be deployed in a manner which undermines certain conceptions of cultural policy. Thus, in the 1980s, the ambitions of European governments to promote their telecommunications and satellite industries resulted in support for the development and deployment within Europe of technologies that rendered unsustainable the strategies of cultural closure which had previously characterized many national cultural policies.[19]

(e) The development of policies towards cultural policy

Sometimes, these various other policies towards cultural production are presented as a substitute for cultural policy. Thus, the liberalization of the sector is presented by some as a process whereby the market comes to determine the patterns of cultural production, leaving the public culture to develop 'autonomously', and the state to exercise a residual role in policing competition. More usually, however, policies towards cultural production have been conceived of as supplementary policy goals, to be set alongside the more traditional cultural policy agenda of the state. Given that tensions inevitably arise between the different types of policy, it has then been necessary to develop methods of choosing from amongst the rival proscriptions on offer. The result has been the development of meta-frameworks in order to supply a principled basis for advocating a particular prioritization on the part of the state. Such frameworks comprise what might be called *policies towards cultural*

[18] The clearest and strongest example of the conflation of cultural policy and freedom of expression is apparent in the German Constitutional Court's case law. For discussion, see Barendt, n 13 above, ch 3.

[19] See Noam, E, *Television in Europe* (New York: OUP, 1991), who notes that the deployment of both cable and satellite was hastened in Europe as a result of 'several major countries adopt[ing] a political agenda of technology development' (at 8): 'Such efforts led to a proliferation of video channels, not as part of media or cultural policy but as a result of economic and development policy in the electronics sector. One part of government promoted activities whose indirect impacts another part of government decried. In the end, economic policy, fanned by the increased globalization of competition, won out over cultural policy . . . '

policy, which fit cultural policy into the wider policy mosaic, recognizing its validity and importance but fixing external parameters for its operation.

3. EC law and the regulation of television

This schema for understanding the policies and strategies at work in national audio-visual regulation is of help in analysing the impact of EC law and policy in the sector. The motor for EC legal involvement has consistently been the primary trade and competition rules contained in the EC Treaty. By applying these norms to the cultural industries, thereby acknowledging their economic dimension, EC law clearly pursues a policy towards cultural production, aimed at creating a competitive common market in cultural output. EC law and policy do not, however, give absolute priority to this economic policy over the traditional preoccupations of national cultural policy. Both the Community courts and legislators have sought to arrive at an accommodation between Community economic policy and national cultural policies relating to television. The Community has therefore developed a policy towards cultural policy. Yet to emerge at the current stage of European integration is any independent cultural policy for Europe that seeks to foster a distinctively European public culture. This section examines three aspects of the EC's involvement in the audio-visual sphere: first, the application of the primary economic rules of the Treaty to national television regulation; secondly, the most important EC legislation in this field; and, thirdly, the various programmes which have been organized at the Community level for subsidizing production in the audio-visual sector. The aim is to work out in more detail the nature of Community policy towards national cultural policies.

(a) The application of the EC Treaty rules

The competition and free movement provisions contained in the Treaty, which aim to promote the common market project, are applicable in all domains of economic activity, and between them control the activities of private undertakings and Member States alike. Their potential application to television therefore depends upon its being conceptualized as an economic activity. The European Court of Justice early took the approach that activities do not fall outside the Treaty framework simply because they comprise a 'cultural' element, either because they possess an aesthetic, expressive, or communicative aspect, or because they are associated with the cultural identity of a particular people within Europe.[20] There were features of television, however, which still gave rise to doubts. It was universally conducted by one or a few broadcasters, who were either public or quasi-public in character. In the light of this very broad consensus amongst the Member States, when a challenge was brought under EC law to the Italian public broadcaster's monopoly in the case of *Sacchi*,[21] both the Italian and the German Governments were prepared to argue that television fell outside the competition and free movement provisions altogether. The Court of Justice, however, rejected this approach: at least some aspects of television broadcasting were potentially subject to the free movement rules, and were clearly therefore economic activities in the eyes of the Court. Such has since been the Court's consistent approach and, as a consequence, a number of the rules contained in the Treaty have come to exert an influence over national audio-visual regulation.

Of the free movement rules, the most influential has been Article 49 (ex 59), which prohibits 'restrictions on freedom to provide services within the Community . . . in respect of national of Member States who are established in a State of the Community other than that of the person for whom the services are intended.' In *Sacchi*, the European Court of Justice made clear that, if television broadcasting fell anywhere within the trade provisions, it was as a 'service' within the meaning of Article 49.[22] Also important have been the rights accorded to companies engaged in the supply of television services by Article 43 (ex 52), which prohibits 'restrictions on the freedom of establishment of nationals of a Member State in the territory of another Member State'.[23] These provisions have the potential to apply to many aspects of national audio-visual regulation which restrict the free circulation of television services and the companies which supply them.

As an economic activity, the competition rules are equally applicable to the television industry. Articles 81 and 82 (ex 85 and 86), because they are addressed to undertakings, are not directly applicable to state regulations, although public undertakings are subject to these provisions, allowing EC competition law to

[20] See de Witte, n 11 above, at 249: 'Economy and culture are not two watertight compartments, but closely interrelated social spheres; the economic categories and legal rules of the EC Treaty include cultural activities whenever these present a transnational economic dimension.'

[21] Case 155/73, *Giuseppe Sacchi* [1974] ECR 409.

[22] Ibid., at para 10, in which the Court referred to 'televised commercial advertising' as having the character of a service. The Court did not consider the application of Article 49 to the facts of the case, not having been asked by the referring court to do so.

[23] The provisions guaranteeing the free movement of goods and workers have tangential effects upon the television industry but they are less likely to impact directly upon systems of audio-visual regulation.

control the public broadcasters' activities. Article 86(1) (ex 90), however, extends Articles 81 and 82 to state measures applicable in the case of public undertakings and undertakings that have been granted special or exclusive rights. As a result, provisions of national audio-visual regulation which are in some way connected to anti-competitive actions by these categories of undertaking are also subject to control.

The other competition rule to have played a part in the audio-visual sector is Article 87 (ex 92). This provision declares incompatible with the common market 'any aid granted by a Member State or through State resources in any form whatsoever which distorts or threatens to distort competition by favouring certain undertakings or the production of certain goods', at least 'insofar as it affects trade in goods'. Its relevance arises from states' promotion of national cultural policy through the funnelling of privileged income streams to the public broadcasters.

The balance between these economic norms and national cultural policies is struck by the various derogations available to Member States under EC law. Which derogations will apply depends upon the rule of EC law in issue, and the nature of the national measure to which it is applied. They vary in the extent of their capacity to accommodate objectives of cultural policy.

As for the free movement rules, the derogations available have traditionally been understood to depend upon whether or not the national measure in question discriminates on the basis of nationality. According to the established rule, discriminatory national rules can only be defended by reference to the derogations expressly contained in the Treaty. In the context of Articles 43 and 49, Article 46 (ex 56) protects national rules 'providing for special treatment of foreign nationals on grounds of public policy, public security or public health'. The EC case law relating to television suggests that cultural policy considerations will not be deemed to fall within the ground of public policy, but is somewhat equivocal, leaving flexibility, in a difficult case, for a broader construction of the derogation.[24] Some recent case law also suggests a willingness,

[24] In Case 352/85, *Bond van Adverteerders* [1988] ECR 2085, Mancini AG was firmly of the opinion that cultural policy objectives did constitute grounds of public policy (at 2118 (1st col)), whereas in his opinion in Case C-288/89, *Stichting Collectieve Antennevooziening Gouda* [1991] ECR I-4007, offered a few months subsequently, Tesauro AG doubted whether cultural policy could fall under Article 46 (at 4025 (2nd col)–4026 (1st col)). In neither case did the Court pronounce on this question: in the former case, it preferred to find that the national measures were disproportionate; and in the latter case, it was faced with non-discriminatory measures. However, in its judgment in Case C-211/91, *Commission v Belgium*, [1992] ECR I-6757, the Court stated categorically (at recital 10) that cultural policy objectives did not fall within any of the grounds for exemption permitted by Article 46. In Case C-17/92, *Fedecine* [1993] ECR I-2239, van Gerven

on occasion, to expand the range of justifications available in respect of discriminatory measures, but it remains unclear when such a relaxation is permissible and what types of justification it will encompass.[25]

Non-discriminatory national rules which are caught by the free movement rules can be justified on the basis of the express derogations, but will also escape an application of the free movement rules if they can be shown to serve an overriding requirement in the public interest. The pursuit of cultural policy objectives can definitely constitute one such requirement.[26]

Another defence, available when either a free movement or competition rule is used to challenge the regulation or conduct of a particular broadcaster, is provided by Article 86(2), if it can be shown that the broadcaster is 'charged with the operation of a service of general economic interest', and that the EC rule in issue would 'obstruct the operation, in law or in fact of the particular tasks' with which the broadcaster is assigned. The case law suggests that a Member State, as well as the broadcaster itself, may rely on Article 86(2).[27] The European Commission has offered as a definition of general interest services 'market services which the Member States subject to specific public service obligations by virtue of a general interest criterion'.[28] It has recognized that television has a general interest dimension within the meaning of Article 86(2), on account of its 'central role in the functioning of modern democratic societies, in particular in the development and transmission of social values'.[29] The Court of Justice has also accepted the potential

AG urged 'flexibility' on the question of whether discriminatory provisions could be justified on cultural policy grounds (at para 27). The Court in that case was somewhat equivocal, observing (at recital 20) that 'cultural policy is not one of the justifications set out in Article [46]' but then proceeding to base itself on the purely economic nature of the objective pursued.

[25] In several cases, the European Court of Justice has appeared willing to permit the justification of discriminatory state measures on environmental grounds, but has failed explicitly to recognize or explain the departure from established case law. See the case law cited in Case C-379/98 *Preussenelektra* [2001] ECR I-2099, at para 227 of AG Jacobs' Opinion. The Advocate General argues in favour of overtly expanding the categories of justification available in respect of discriminatory measures to include environmental considerations. See paras 226–233 of the Opinion. The Court held the discriminatory measure at issue in *Preussenelektra* to be capable of justification but did not expressly acknowledge the novelty of its approach.

[26] See, e.g., Case C-288/89, *Stichting Collectieve Antennevooziening Gouda* (n 24, above) at para 23 of the judgment.

[27] See the discussion of the recent case law in Buendia Sierra, *Exclusive Rights and State Monopolies under EC Law* (Oxford: OUP, 1999), 294–8.

[28] See the *First Communication on Services of General Interest in Europe* (OJ [1996] C 281/3). The *Second Communication* on the same topic, n 1 above, adopted the same definition by reference.

[29] See *Second Communication on Services of General Interest in Europe*, n 1 above, at Annex 1. See also the *First Communication*, n 28 above, at para 51.

applicability of Article 86(2) to defend cultural policy goals in the audio-visual sector.[30]

Lastly, as regards Article 87, some types of aid, specified in Article 87(2), are completely exempted from the prohibition on state aids, while other types, listed in Article 87(3), may be exempted at the Commission's discretion. Article 87(3)(d), which was inserted by the Treaty of Maastricht, allows the exemption of 'aid to promote culture and heritage conservation'. Trading conditions and competition in the Community must not be affected 'to an extent that is contrary to the common interest', however.

All of these derogations are narrowly construed, and will only apply to a national measure which is proportionate, in that it is both suitable to meet the objective on the basis of which it claims the benefit of a derogation, and that it pursues that objective in the manner least restrictive of the interests protected by EC law.[31] In the case of the free movement provisions, a national measure will not be proportionate if the policy objective which it pursues is substantially met by the regulatory arrangements already in place in the state of origin.[32] The national measure must also accord with the general principles of EC law, a category which includes fundamental rights drawing their inspiration in part from the European Convention on Human Rights (ECHR).[33] Of special relevance in the context of television is the right to freedom of expression. Some national cultural policies may therefore be denied the protection of a derogation which they would otherwise enjoy if it can be shown that they unjustifiably limit freedom of expression. Account will be taken of the jurisprudence relating to Article 10 of the ECHR, which has itself fixed limits to the range of permissible cultural policies available to European states.[34]

Initially, the economic rules of the Treaty had no real impact on television regulation. In a situation of almost universal monopoly, there were few private litigants with an interest in challenging the status quo. Moreover, EC law was widely understood to give the Member States a free hand in deciding whether an activity should be allocated to the market, or should be conducted by a state monopoly within the public part of the mixed economy. This understanding

[30] Para 15 of *Sacchi*, n 21 above, may be read as referring to Article 86(2). More recently, see Joined Cases T-528/93, T-542/93, T-543/93, and T-546/93, *Metropole Television SA and Reti Televisive Italiane SpA and Gestevision Telecinco SA and Antena 3 de Television v Commission of the European Communities* [1996] ECR II-649.

[31] See, e.g., Case C-55/94, *Reinhard Gebhard* [1995] ECR I-4165, at para 37 of the judgment.

[32] See, e.g., AG Mancini's opinion in *Collectieve Antennevoorziening Gouda*, n. 24 above, at recital 14.

[33] See Case C-260/89 *ERT* [1991] ECR I-2925, paras 41–43 of the judgment.

[34] For discussion of the relevant case law, see Craufurd Smith, n 17 above, at 135–41.

rested in part on the belief that monopolies enjoyed an *a priori* exclusion from the application of EC law.[35] Also, it derived from an interpretation of the substantive provisions of EC economic law, which in any event meant that monopolies would not infringe them.[36] Thus, for so long as national audiovisual regulation was built around monopoly, the possibility that television was an economic activity capable of engaging the free movement and competition norms was a matter of purely academic interest. With liberalization, however, the door was opened to a more extensive application of EC law, which has since come significantly to affect the strategic choices open to Member States in pursuing their cultural policies toward television.

(i) The strategy of cultural closure

Since the early 1990s, the notion that the EC Treaty rules had no application to legal monopolies has been comprehensively refuted. First, the idea that there was any *a priori* exclusion as a consequence of Articles 86(1) and 295 (ex 222) was rejected by the Court of Justice in the telecommunications terminal equipment case of 1991.[37] At the same time, the competition and free movement norms have been reinterpreted in such a way as to apply to many monopoly rights.[38]

[35] A number of factors went to preserve monopolies against challenge under the Treaty rules. First, Article 86(1) refers to 'undertakings to which Member States grant special or exclusive rights', and goes on to provide that in respect of these undertakings, Member States must not enact or keep in place measures contrary to other Treaty rules. This reference was initially understood by many to mean that the granting of such special or exclusive rights could not itself be questioned in EC law. Article 295 was seen as confirming legal monopolies' immunity, with its guarantee that the Treaty 'shall in no way prejudice the rules in Member States governing the system of property ownership'.

[36] The free movement rules were until the 1980s interpreted as outlawing the discriminatory treatment of out-of-state interests. Monopolies were considered to be non-discriminatory because they prevented both domestic and out-of-state undertakings from setting up in competition with the monopolist. The competition rules enshrined in Articles 81 and 82, although addressed to undertakings, were also applicable to state measures in the context of undertakings enjoying special or exclusive rights by virtue of Article 86(1). However, some violation of the competition rules would need to be shown before a state measure could be challenged, and it was difficult to see how the mere grant of an exclusive right could violate those rules. No agreement between undertakings was involved such as would engage Article 81. A dominant position would be created, but Article 82 requires not only the existence of such a position but also evidence of its abuse.

[37] In case 202/88, *France v Commission* [1991] ECR I-1223, the Court emphasized, at para 22 of the judgment, that although Article 86(1) 'presupposes the existence of undertakings which have certain special or exclusive rights, it does not follow that all the special or exclusive rights are necessarily compatible with the Treaty. That depends on different rules, to which Article [86(1)] refers.'

[38] The free movement rules are now understood to cover non-discriminatory restrictions. A legal monopoly clearly restricts free movement, by preventing the output of a particular industry to be supplied by anyone other than the monopolist, and by preventing other companies from

As a result of these developments in the Court of Justice's jurisprudence, both private parties and the Commission have been able to use EC law to whittle away at the exclusive rights traditionally granted to public broadcasters. EC law has therefore come to enshrine a clear policy against the strategy of cultural closure, and has contributed to its progressive abandonment across Europe. Articles 43 and 49 and the competition rules work in complementary fashion, each allowing different groups of litigants to challenge varying types of cultural closure. Article 49 has been used to challenge national monopolies that attempt to exclude the provision of services by undertakings established in other Member States.[39] More recently, Article 43 has been deployed to attack the conferral of an *internal* private broadcasting monopoly as an unjustifiable restriction on the freedom of out-of-state broadcasters to establish themselves within the state in question.[40] Lastly, the competition rules, and in particular the combined application of Articles 86(1) and 82, allow national monopolies to be challenged by nationals of the Member State in question, despite the lack of the cross-border element which would be required by the free movement provisions.[41]

The possibility remains that a strategy of cultural closure might enjoy the benefit of one of the derogations. It is unlikely, however, that broadcasting monopolies will be easily justified. The fact that so few states now regard such a strategy as necessary renders it harder to claim that it is a proportionate method of advancing cultural policy goals. A consideration of the general principles of EC law would strengthen this conclusion, given that the ECHR jurisprudence on freedom of expression is itself negative towards cultural closure.[42]

setting up within the Member State in which the monopoly operates. There are anyway suggestions in some of the case law that monopolies should be understood as inherently discriminatory in character, given that they involve the conferral of an advantage upon a national undertaking (in the form of an exclusive right) which excludes potential competitors from out-of-state. See discussion in Buendia Sierra, n 27 above, at 223–8. As regards the competition rules, the mere granting of a monopoly has been found in a number of circumstances to breach Article 86(1), operating in conjunction with Article 82. See Buendia Sierra, ibid., at 182–6.

39 See Case C-288/89, *Stichting Collectieve Antennevoorziening Gouda*, n 24 above.

40 See Commission Decision 97/606/EC of 26 June 1997 pursuant to Article 86(3) EC (ex 90(3)) on the exclusive right to broadcast television advertising in Flanders (OJ [1997] L 244/18).

41 See Case C-260/89, *ERT*, n 33 above.

42 The case law of the Community courts regarding the possibility of justifying a strategy of cultural closure does not supply that much guidance, but it tends to suggest that derogations will not readily assist states in defending strategies of cultural closure. In *ERT*, n 33 above, the Court of Justice left the question of whether the retransmission monopoly was defensible for the national court to decide. In the Dutch media law cases, n 24 above, the Court of Justice declined to apply any of the derogations, holding that the proffered defence was in reality economic in character. In a challenge to the Commission's Decision 97/606/EC, n 40 above, the Court of First

(ii) The strategy of availability

By assisting in the removal of strategies of cultural closure, EC law has contributed to the displacement of the public broadcasters from their erstwhile status as sole providers of television. The application of the Treaty norms thus far described has not, however, entailed an impact upon the internal organization and funding structure of the public broadcasters, and therefore leaves intact the ability of Member States to use public broadcasters to ensure the general availability of public service output.

During the course of the 1990s, however, it became apparent that Article 87, the provision of the Treaty banning state aids, applied to the public broadcasters.[43] A number of complaints[44] were made to the Commission by private television channels. They alleged that the funding supplied by the state for their public counterparts was an illegal state aid within the meaning of Article 87(1). They also asserted that the funding in question was either disproportionate, in that it was not necessary to meet the public service obligations in return for which it was supplied, or was not in fact used to fund programming having a public service character.[45]

This gave rise to fears amongst the supporters of public service broadcasters that EC law would now insinuate itself much deeper into their practices, controlling when and how far states might use public broadcasters to pursue a strategy of availability. Such was the level of concern that states such as France, which were most committed to an extensive cultural policy, sought to protect the position of the public service broadcasters by lobbying to amend the Treaty. The outcome of this pressure was the Protocol on Public Broadcasting, which was annexed to the EC Treaty by the Treaty of Amsterdam. This legally binding declaration states that the EC Treaty's provisions 'shall be without prejudice to the competence of the Member States to provide for the funding of public service broadcasting insofar as such funding is granted to broadcasting organisations for the fulfilment of the public service remit as conferred, defined and organised by each Member State'. Such funding must not, however, 'affect trading conditions and competition in the Community to an

Instance refused to overturn the Commission's assessment, arrived at in the context of an Article 86(3) decision, that the private broadcasting monopoly was not a proportionate method of advancing the goal of media pluralism. See Case T-266/97, *Vlaamse Televisie Maatschapij NV* [1999] ECR II-2329.

[43] The first complaints to this effect were received by the Commission in 1992. See Craufurd Smith, R, 'State Support for Public Service Broadcasting', *Legal Issues of Economic Integration*, 28(1) (2001), 3, at 6.

[44] By 2001, more than 10 such complaints had been made.

[45] Craufurd Smith, n 43, above, at 6.

extent which would be contrary to the common interest'. While the Protocol clearly emphasizes the Member States' competence to define and organize their own public service broadcasting institutions, it equally clearly does not exclude the application of the state aid rules altogether. Thus, at most, it served as a warning to Court and Commission not to adopt too constraining an approach to public service broadcasters, without putting an end to the oversight of EC law.

Aware of the profound political sensitivity of the issues raised by the state aid complaints, the Commission initially attempted to exclude the application of the state aid rules on the basis that the funding supplied to public service broadcasters was consideration for the broadcasters' having fulfilled their public service remit, and therefore not state aid at all.[46] This approach ran into difficulty when the Court of First Instance struck down a Commission decision to this effect. The Court held that any payment which would not have obtained under normal market conditions would amount to an aid within the meaning of Article 87, regardless of the purposes for which it had been made.[47] Subsequent Commission decisions therefore proceeded on the basis that public service funding constituted a state aid unless awarded under an open and objective system of competitive tendering amongst broadcasters, in which case no competitive distortion would result.[48]

On this approach, given that public service funding is nearly always supplied to a specific institution in the absence of any tendering process, the legality of such funding would turn on whether it could be justified either under Article 87 itself, or under Article 86(2), the exemption for services of general economic interest. The Commission has resisted applying Article 87(3)(d), which gives it a discretion to exempt aid intended to promote culture and heritage conservation, leaving Article 86(2) as the only avenue of justification. After early attempts to specify with some precision what aspects of broadcasting could be considered to constitute a service of general economic interest, the Commission now appears to have accepted that it is largely for the Member States to determine the boundaries of the general interest in relation to broadcasting. In its recently published guidelines relating to the application of the state aid rules in the context of public service broadcasting,[49] the Commission asserts only a right to control the definition of public service broadcasting at the margins, guarding against abusive interpretations which cannot credibly be related to the 'democratic, social and cultural needs of each society'.[50]

[46] Case NN-141/95, OJ [1997] C 67/10.

[47] Case T-46/97, *SIC v Commission* [2000] ECR II-2125.

[48] Craufurd Smith, n 43 above, 10–11. [49] OJ [2001] C 320/04. [50] Ibid., at para 36.

Such an approach appears consonant with the terms of the Protocol, but it does not remove the potential for EC law to affect the funding arrangements of public service television. Article 86(2) also requires Member States to show that the aid supplied to public service broadcasters is both necessary for, and proportionate to, the general interest task with which they are assigned. As a consequence, Member States must define with some precision what actually falls within the public service remit of their broadcasters, and must set up some system of oversight in order to verify that funds do not exceed what is required in order to fulfil that remit.

The European Court of Justice has meanwhile recently returned to the question of whether funding to perform a public service task is necessarily a state aid. In the case of *Altmark*,[51] which concerned subsidies in the field of public transport, the Court held that such funding should be analysed as compensation rather than aid provided that various conditions were met.[52] First, the firm receiving the funding must actually have public service obligations to discharge, and those obligations must be clearly defined. Secondly, the parameters on the basis of which the compensation is calculated must be established in advance in an objective and transparent manner. Thirdly, the compensation must not exceed what is necessary to cover all or part of the costs incurred in the discharge of the public service obligations. The Court makes clear that a detailed level of accounting supervision is necessary to meet this condition. Lastly, where the firm in question is not chosen pursuant to a public procurement procedure, the level of compensation needed must be determined on the basis of an analysis of the costs which a typical and efficiently run firm would have incurred in meeting the public service obligations at stake.

Applying the Court's analysis in *Altmark* to the situation of the public service broadcasters, it is clear that their funding will not always constitute aid. However, the conditions which must be met to avoid an application of the state aid rules look similar to those which would need to be fulfilled in order to invoke Article 86(2). The status of public service broadcasting under the state aid rules would not therefore appear to have been greatly modified by recent developments in the case law.[53]

[51] Case C-280/00 [2003] 3 CMLR 12.

[52] See paras 87–93, and the dispositive part of the judgment.

[53] The only significant difference between an analysis under Article 86(2) and one which involved an application of the *Altmark* conditions is that under the latter, if funding is found not to constitute aid, there will be no obligation to notify the funding to the Commission pursuant to Article 88(3), even where it cannot be characterized as existing aid.

EC law can therefore be seen, in relation to the strategies of availability which are now carried forward by the public service broadcasters, to require discussion at the national level about what are the precise cultural policy objectives pursued in relation to television. The Commission's guidelines make clear that this discursive exercise must reach conclusions which are transparent and public.[54] It should ideally include an independent regulatory body that will ensure that the reflection does not too easily elide cultural policy with the interests of the cultural producers.[55] Thus, the primary Treaty rules, even when not directly constraining national cultural policy in the audio-visual sphere, exercise a wider influence, opening cultural policy up to justificatory scrutiny.

(iii) Strategies of cultural preference

With the abandonment of strategies of outright cultural closure, and the growth of a more sophisticated regulatory component to national audio-visual policy, questions have arisen as to how far states may legitimately design their regulatory arrangements in such a way as to favour national cultural output. It is clear that, under EC law, rules which on their face confer advantages exclusively upon domestic cultural products or producers will breach the rule against discrimination on the basis of nationality which lies at the heart of the free movement provisions. Where discrimination is in play, the possibilities for justifying rules of this character are, at least on a traditional analysis, limited to the express derogations included in Article 46. If it is correct that cultural policy cannot be brought within any of the heads of Article 46, several very widespread and fundamental features of national audio-visual regulation, such as language quotas, must carry rules, and perhaps even preferential access to spectrum, may fall foul of EC law.[56]

There are three possible solutions to the danger that EC law might therefore excessively constrain national cultural policy choices. The first, which has been adopted in the case of must carry rules, is to include in EC legislation provisions that confer a specific permission upon states to preserve discriminatory features of their national cultural policies.[57] The second, available to the Community courts themselves, would be to expand the category of public policy to incorporate at least some types of cultural policy objective, a possibility not completely ruled out in the existing case law.[58] The third would be to accept that even discriminatory measures may be justified on the basis of

[54] Ibid., paras 37–39. [55] Ibid., paras 41–43. [56] See de Witte, n 11 above, at 254–5.

[57] See Article 31 of Directive 2002/22/EC, the Universal Service Directive (OJ [2002] L 108/51). [58] See n 24, above.

some additional categories of justification not explicitly listed in the Treaties, including cultural policy. Such a solution would involve explicitly acknowledging and extending the development in the case law of the European Court of Justice which appears already to have occurred, *de facto*, in relation to national environmental initiatives.[59]

(iv) Strategies of uniformity

A final strategy comprising national cultural policies towards television involves the imposition of uniformly applicable rules upon all broadcasters of a particular type. Such a strategy may be either global, applicable to all services and providers, whether domestic or out-of-state, or it may limit itself to domestic services or providers. Prior to the 1980s, such rules would have been regarded as beyond challenge in EC law. Now, however, the free movement norms apply to non-discriminatory restrictions. As a consequence, Article 49, guaranteeing the free movement of services, catches any uniformly applicable rule which extends to cross-border as well as to national service providers. Such would include the broadcast of a television channel from state A to B, either directly to the public or to a cable company for onward distribution, as well as the supply of a television programme by a producer in state A to a broadcaster for transmission in state B. In addition, other types of service besides the supply of television itself may be in play. Most notably, the supply of advertising airtime will constitute the provision of a service across a national border if it is sold to an out-of-state advertiser. Consequently, generally applicable rules regulating how much advertising may be seen, and when it may be shown, will constitute restrictions caught by Article 49, even if their application is confined to domestic broadcasters.

Because in the case of such uniformly applicable national rules, discrimination will not normally be in issue, appeal can be made to a wider range of justificatory grounds, of which cultural policy is undoubtedly one. In the early days of market opening, the case law suggested a generous application of the proportionality criterion. In *Debauve*, for instance, even a total ban on television advertising was deemed proportionate, given the significant divergence in national regulatory practices in this regard.[60] More recently, with the introduction of harmonizing EC legislation, aimed at creating an internal market in television, a stricter approach will likely be taken even in respect of those national regulations which are not precluded by the EC legislation itself.

The fact that the free movement rules apply only to situations comprising a 'cross-border element' affords Member States a potentially significant zone of

[59] See n 25 and the accompanying text, above.

[60] Case 52/79, [1980] ECR 833.

internal regulatory autonomy. Many of the most popular television services in a Member State will continue to be supplied by domestic broadcasters, given the demand for local content and the continued dominance of the free-to-air channels.[61] Given that the regulation of these services will, often, not involve any cross-border element, Member States remain free to adopt an approach of their own choosing, thereby retaining their unmoderated influence over the lion's share of the audio-visual output consumed nationally.

Whether this internal regulatory autonomy will avail states in practice depends, however, upon their ability to prevent their domestic broadcasters from using Article 43 to relocate themselves in another Member State, in order either to escape rules which are uniformly applicable to internal broadcasters, or to gain the standing under Article 49 to challenge rules which are uniformly applicable to domestic and out-of-state broadcasters alike. EC law offers some protection to Member States in these circumstances. In the case of *van Binsbergen*,[62] the Court of Justice held that a Member State was permitted to take measures to prevent a service provider from relying on Article 49, provided, first, that the services were directed 'mainly or principally' at that state's territory; and, secondly, that the service provider's purpose in operating from outside that state was to avoid the professional rules of conduct which would be applicable to him if he were established within that state. Subsequent cases have applied this doctrine in the context of broadcasting.[63] Although its application remains in a number of respects uncertain,[64] it has provided some

[61] Such channels are usually of higher quality, supply a wider range of content, have the benefit of familiarity, ease of access, and, of course, cost nothing.

[62] Case 33/74, [1974] ECR 1299.

[63] In Case C-148/91, *Vereniging Veronica Omroeporganisatie* [1993] ECR I-487, the Court of Justice upheld provisions of The Netherlands media law designed to prevent domestic broadcasters either establishing themselves in other states, or supplying services to out-of-state broadcasters. In Case C-23/93, *TV10 SA* [1994] ECR I-4795, the Dutch regulator, the Commissariaat voor de Media, was permitted to apply domestic regulations to a broadcaster operating out of Luxembourg but aiming its services specifically at the Dutch market.

[64] To offer two examples, the Court has indicated that the conduct of the broadcaster must be improper or wrongful, but has not specified what it means by this, other than to state that wrongfulness falls to be assessed on a case-by-case basis. See *TV10*, above n 63, at para 21; *Veronica*, above n 63, at para 13. The Court also appears to suggest that for the anti-circumvention rule to apply, the national rules at stake must be in pursuit of a general interest objective recognized as such by EC law. See, e.g., *TV10*, paras 19–21. Although cultural policy objectives have been so recognized, it is uncertain whether EC law requires any detailed scrutiny of the national rules to check that they qualify as such, and that they are proportionate. If so, a Member State would gain no benefit from pleading the anti-circumvention doctrine, having to justify its domestic arrangements in exactly the same way as it would if they were being tested under Article 49. See Craufurd Smith, R, 'The Establishment of Companies in European Community Law: Choice of Law or Abuse of Rights?', *European Current Law Year Book*, [1999], lxii, at lxv.

protection of internal regulatory autonomy in the audio-visual sector. It is expressly acknowledged in the recitals to the amended Television Without Frontiers Directive, implying that, in the view of the Community legislators, it is of continued relevance to the sector, despite harmonizing legislation.[65]

(b) EC legislation in the audio-visual sphere—the Television Without Frontiers Directive

The use of the primary Treaty norms to integrate the European audio-visual market ran up against certain inherent limitations. States were able to justify many national measures, especially those pursuing a strategy of uniformity in respect both of domestic and cross-border services. The consequential patchwork of divergent national regulatory objectives and mechanisms had the effect of fragmenting the internal market, requiring service providers to devote much effort to tailoring their output to each national regulatory framework before they could develop a presence in more than one country. The proponents of a pan-European audio-visual marketplace therefore came to advocate a legislative solution, which would introduce a shared platform of regulatory measures to cut away at least some of the national variety. Although national cultural policy constituencies were never enthusiastic at the loss of control entailed by Community legislative intervention, their opposition was muted by a greater concern at the prospect of judicial harmonization effected through a more stringent application of the proportionality test.

Accordingly, agreement was reached upon the so-called 'Television Without Frontiers' Directive,[66] which remains the most important Community legislative initiative in the audio-visual sector, and which will form the focus of the present discussion. Its enactment under Articles 47(2) (ex 57(2)) and 55 (ex 66), the Treaty bases for coordinating provisions relating to establishment and services, emphasizes its economic justification. However, here as in other areas, EC law and policy have been obliged, in their pursuit of market integration, to adopt and carry forward the objectives inspiring the national regulatory barriers to integration. Many of the provisions of the Directive can therefore be understood as accommodating preoccupations of cultural policy.[67]

[65] See Line Hell Hansen, 'The Development of the Circumvention Principle in the Area of Broadcasting', *Legal Issues of European Integration*, 2 (1998), 111–38.

[66] Directive 89/552/EEC (OJ [1989] L 298/23), as amended by Directive 97/36/EC (OJ [1997] L 202/60).

[67] See de Witte, n 11 above, at 275: 'The growing entanglement of the European Community with culture by means of its common market competences provides an excellent illustration of "spillover" and possibly a partial vindication of functionalist theories of integration . . . A functional linkage is made by the actors of the Community system between the original task of

(i) A Community strategy of uniformity and its consequential constraints upon national strategies of uniformity

Much of the Directive consists of a set of harmonized standards which Member States are required to apply to the broadcasters operating within their jurisdiction.[68] The Directive therefore partially harmonizes the regulatory component of national audio-visual policies, pursuing a kind of strategy of uniformity at the Community level. Most of the minimum standards which it enshrines operate in areas that were already subject to some regulation at the national level. They therefore cater to existing national preoccupations, of a kind undoubtedly related to cultural policy. For instance, the Directive places limitations on the commercial element of television. Advertisements must be clearly demarcated.[69] They are also restricted in duration and frequency,[70] and they cannot interfere with the integrity and value of programmes.[71] Similarly, sponsorship must not affect the 'responsibility and editorial independence of programmes',[72] and is completely banned in respect of news and current affairs coverage. The rules for the protection of minors and public order also mirror traditional limitations upon certain extreme forms of content.[73] While these standards are, then, directed within the broad field of cultural policy, they lie at its margins, achieving a convergence only at the crudest and most quantitative stratum of national regulation, where cultural policy merges with consumer protection measures and with the criminal law. The Court of Justice has held, moreover, that the Directive's rules are to be construed restrictively as incursions upon broadcasters' fundamental freedom to provide services.[74]

The imposition of these standards has a multiple effect upon national cultural policies. First, it partially constrains the cultural policy of the state having jurisdiction over a given broadcaster by requiring it to maintain in place a floor of harmonized standards. States are prevented from deregulating in respect not only of broadcasters aiming their services at other Member States, but also purely domestic broadcasters.[75] At the same time, they remain free to

achieving economic integration and a new side-task of developing cultural policy initiatives in order to ensure an appropriate overall balance.'

[68] Directive 89/552/EEC, n 66 above, Article 3(2). [69] Ibid., Article 10(1).

[70] Ibid., Articles 11(3), (4), and (5), 18, and 18a. [71] Ibid., Article 11.

[72] Ibid., Article 17. [73] Ibid., Articles 22, 22a.

[74] See Case C-6/98, *Pro Sieben* [1999] ECR I-7599 at paras 28–30 of the judgment. However, the recent judgment in Case C-245/01, *RTL Television* (not yet reported), delivered on 23 October 2003, may suggest a somewhat more generous approach to the interpretation of the Directive's restrictions upon broadcasters' activities.

[75] Member States are, however, permitted by Article 20 of the Directive not to apply certain of the provisions of the Directive to 'broadcasts intended solely for the national territory which cannot be received, directly or indirectly by the public, in one or more other Member States'.

require television broadcasters under their jurisdiction to comply with more detailed or stricter rules in the areas covered by the Directive.[76]

Secondly, the Community strategy of uniformity constrains the activities of *receiving* states. Article 2a(1) limits the freedom of receiving states to regulate services produced by an out-of-state broadcaster 'within the fields co-ordinated' by the Directive. The Directive therefore strengthens and develops the control already accomplished by the free movement provisions over national rules which are uniformly applicable to out-of-state as well as domestic broadcasters.[77] Whereas under the free movement provisions, national rules might be justified provided they were shown to be proportionate means of pursuing legitimate public policy objectives, under the Directive such national rules are entirely prohibited in so far as they fall within the Directive's coordinated fields. The extent of this additional control obviously turns upon how broadly these 'fields' are to be construed. On the basis that specific rules of the Directive arguably advance cultural policy goals, the Commission submitted in *Commission v Belgium*[78] that there was no longer any scope for Member States to regulate broadcasts from other states on cultural policy grounds.[79] The Court avoided pronouncing on the question, preferring to strike down the rules in question as disproportionate restrictions on the free movement of services.[80] It therefore remains unclear whether states in principle retain any competence since the enactment of the Directive to regulate out-of-state broadcasts on cultural policy grounds.

(ii) A Community strategy of cultural preference?

In one respect, at least, the harmonized standards contained in the Directive go beyond the re-regulation of areas already covered at the national level. Article 4 requires that 'where practicable, and by appropriate means . . . broadcasters reserve for European works a majority proportion of their transmission time'.[81] This European content requirement is a novelty: none of the Member States prior to the Directive's promulgation pursued content quotas

[76] Article 3(1), Directive 89/552/EEC, n 66 above.

[77] A small degree of flexibility is introduced into this constraining aspect of the Directive, by Article 2a(2), which permits receiving states to take measures in respect of out-of-state television broadcasts which 'manifestly, seriously and gravely infringe' the provisions relating to the protection of minors and public order. This derogation has various procedural safeguards built in, in order to allow Commission monitoring.

[78] Case C-11/95, ECR [1996] I-4115.

[79] Ibid., Opinion of Lenz AG, at para 64.

[80] Ibid., judgment of the Court, paras 54–55.

[81] Gameshows, news, sports, adverts, teletext, and teleshopping are not to be counted when calculating whether the majority threshold of European works has been reached (Article 4(1), Directive 89/552/EEC, n 66 above).

relating to *European* (as opposed to national) works. The measure cannot therefore be viewed as merely another of the 'three hundred pieces of the internal market mosaic', but instead appears to constitute an independent initiative of Community cultural policy.[82] On examination, however, the rule has been drafted in vague and aspirational terms, in a manner which undermines its effectiveness. Its core obligation applies only in so far as practicable, and is to be 'achieved progressively, on the basis of suitable criteria' and 'having regard to the informational, educational, cultural and entertainment responsibilities' of a broadcaster to its viewing public. The provision was further blunted by the statement, included in the Council minutes at the time of its adoption, that the obligation it imposed was political in nature.[83] Somewhat ironically, therefore, it exerts a stronger force in restraining receiving states from imposing any secondary control in defence of the European content requirement which it enshrines than it imposes upon the transmitting state to meet that requirement in the first place.

(iii) A Community facilitation of national cultural policy

Not all of the Directive's provisions contribute to a harmonized set of minimum standards which all Member States are mandated to enforce. The listed events provision,[84] inserted as part of the 1997 package of amendments, is intended to facilitate a particular type of cultural policy measure at the national level, while leaving Member States the option of whether to invoke it. Each Member State may designate important national events. The other Member States are then required to ensure that broadcasters within their jurisdiction do not exercise exclusive rights pertaining to the designated events in such a way that a substantial proportion of the public in the Member State in question are deprived of the possibility of watching those events on free television. The provision appears designed to provide Member States with a method for advancing a strategy of availability by regulatory means, without imposing any obligation to do so.

(iv) An obligation to extend the national strategy of uniformity to domestic broadcasters targeting other states

As well as guaranteeing the harmonized rules laid down in the Directive, Member States are also required to apply their domestic rules to all broadcasters within their borders, including those directing their services in all or in

[82] de Witte, B, 'The European Content Requirement in the EC Television Directive—Five Years After', *The Yearbook of Media and Entertainment Law*, 1 (1995), 101.

[83] Ibid., 114.

[84] Directive 89/552/EEC, n 66 above, Article 23a.

part at other Member States.[85] This obligation of uniformity bolsters the Directive's central focus upon mutual recognition[86] with a safeguard against states attracting broadcasters to establish in their territory by exempting them from domestic rules in so far as they target another state. Each state can be confident that other states will already have applied a package of regulatory measures to services crossing national borders, thereby ensuring that key public policy concerns have been met. There are two reasons, however, why this obligation is of less significance than it might appear. First, the obligation does not require uniformity across all types of television service. Member States can and do, therefore, impose different levels of obligation on their free-to-air television stations than they do upon their cable or satellite operators. At most, the Directive prevents them from differentiating, within a given category, between services directed at a domestic or an out-of-state audience. Secondly, the logic of mutual recognition may be less effective in relation to cultural policy than, say, product safety, because of the wide variety of preoccupations and emphases pursued by different states in the cultural policy sphere. Even if a service provided from a neighbouring Member State is subject to quite an intensive level of control to ensure its compatibility with the neighbouring state's cultural policy, the outcome may not enshrine the particular cultural policy objectives pursued in the receiving state.

(v) A discursive forum

Lastly, the Directive also contributes to the discursive aspect to EC law and policy within the audio-visual sphere by establishing a contact committee of television regulators with a broad remit to consult on issues of relevance to the audio-visual sector in Europe.[87] This development provides a forum for deliberation between national regulators and the European Commission. The scope for discussion is explicitly extended beyond the business of administering the Directive, to include also 'any development within the sector on which an exchange of views appears useful'.[88] It adds an institutional dimension to the underlying process of reflection set in train by European involvement in television regulation, opening a two-way channel of communication. On the one hand, the group may provide an avenue for national regulators to make their opinions felt at the Community level, ensuring that various conceptions of national cultural policy prevalent at the national level are not ignored. On the other hand, the emergent breed of independent television regulators, already encouraged by EC competition and state aids rules, may

[85] Ibid., Article 2(1).
[86] See de Witte, n 82 above, at 105.
[87] Directive 89/552/EEC, n 66 above, Article 23a.
[88] Ibid., Article 23a(2)(f).

acquire through their affiliation with the Community institutions a more critical perspective, which recognizes the need to adapt cultural policy to ensure that other public policy objectives are not unduly hampered.

(c) EC subsidies and support programmes

The final manner in which the European Community has made its presence felt in the audio-visual sector is through support schemes designed specifically to boost television and film production in Europe, the most important of which have been the three MEDIA programmes: MEDIA I (1990–1995), MEDIA II (1996–2000), and the current MEDIA plus (2001–2005). In principle, given the importance of the institutional component, backed by subsidies, as a mainstay of the more ambitious elements of national audio-visual policies, one might expect these various Community initiatives to promote a more positive European cultural policy. Yet for a number of reasons, this has not been the case.

First, the sums of money involved have been small by comparison either with the subsidies provided for television and film production at the national level, or Community research and development initiatives in the field of audio-visual equipment.[89] For political reasons, such funding as there is has often also been divided across a number of the Member States, further diluting the sums involved.[90]

Secondly, the programmes have primarily been grounded in an industrial policy agenda of overcoming various practical obstacles to cross-border initiatives, with only secondary attention paid to the nature of the content produced.[91] This is apparent from the legal bases chosen to justify the MEDIA programmes. At the time when MEDIA I was introduced, there was still no cultural funding competence in the Treaty, and it was therefore not surprising that Article 308 (ex 235) should have been used.[92] By the time that MEDIA II was introduced, however, Article 151(5) (ex 128(5)) allowed for the adoption of incentive measures to promote the aims and objectives referred to in that Article, which include 'encouraging cooperation between Member

[89] See Levy, D, *Europe's Digital Revolution* (London: Routledge, 1999), 49. By way of example, he compares the budget for MEDIA II (less than 100 million ecus per annum) with the licence fee income received by EU public service broadcasters in 1995 (9.4 billion ecus) and the audio-visual trade deficit with the US ($6 billion). The current MEDIA plus programme has a budget of €350 million (for development, distribution, and promotion) and €50 million (for training) over a five-year period.

[90] Ibid.

[91] See Goldberg, D, Prosser, T, and Verhulst, S, *EC Media Law and Policy* (London: Longman, 1998), 79–83.

[92] See Council Decision 90/685/EEC (OJ [1990] L 380/37).

States, and, if necessary, supporting and supplementing their action in [the area of] artistic and literary creation, including in the audio-visual sector'.[93] However, the two decisions upon which MEDIA II was based[94] were adopted under Article 157 (ex 130), in the industry title, and Article 150 (ex 127), which establishes the Community's vocational training policy. The same treaty bases were used for the decisions underpinning MEDIA plus.[95]

These limitations reflect a wider lack of political consensus as to the appropriateness of funding cultural production at a European level. The Member States are more content to allow a minimal industrial policy initiative in relation to television than they are to see the Community developing its own cultural policy programme for the sector.

4. Conclusion—towards a Community cultural policy for television?

The EC integration process has contributed to the transformation of national cultural policies in the audio-visual sector, manifesting a clear and consistent policy towards national cultural policies, which spans the judicial development of the Treaty rules, Community legislation, and the various incentive measures, and which comprises two distinctive aspects.

First, Community interventions show a constraining aspect, which delimits and controls the range of applicable strategies for advancing cultural policy objectives. As regards the institutional component of national cultural policy, the primary Treaty norms are applied with particular force to any strategy of cultural closure. The Community's constraining aspect has had its most sustained and pervasive impact, however, in relation to the regulatory component of national arrangements. The strategy of cultural preference is curtailed given the very limited scope accorded to Member States for derogation. The Television Without Frontiers Directive then exerts an equally rigorous control over the strategy of uniformity. It requires Member States to impose its harmonized core of controls on all broadcasters within their jurisdiction and to apply their own internal regulatory rules without distinction to broadcasters

[93] See Article 151(2).

[94] Council Decision 95/563/EC (OJ [1995] L 321/25); Council Decision 95/564/EC (OJ [1995] L 321/33).

[95] See Corrigendum to Council Decision 2000/821/EC (OJ [2000] L 13/34); Council Decision 163/2001 (OJ [2001] L 26/1).

who target either a domestic or an out-of-state audience. It also prevents Member States from applying regulatory obligations to services coming from out-of-state, at least in so far as those obligations fall within a field coordinated by the Directive.

Secondly, the Community has exercised a more discursive influence on national cultural policies. In the context of the primary Treaty rules, the shift from constraint to discussion may be achieved in part by widening the range of justificatory possibilities open to Member States. Partly, also, it may be accomplished through a more permissive application of the proportionality criterion. By moderating the rigour of Community judicial oversight, particular elements of national cultural policy may be treated with tolerance, but they are nonetheless subjected to a degree of scrutiny. Member States must, as a minimum, explain the objectives pursued by a particular measure, and must show that the measure is at once rationally related to those objectives *and* pursues them at minimum cost both to the internal market and the fundamental rights enshrined in the general principles of EC law. The balance between judicially mandated discussion and the more directly constraining aspect of EC law has shifted over time in favour of the latter. National measures advancing a strategy of global uniformity were initially subjected to a more discursive oversight, given the more generous derogations available in the absence of discrimination. However, with the enactment of the Television Without Frontiers Directive, such measures are more directly and intensively controlled. The discursive aspect of EC law is therefore now largely confined to the institutional component of national cultural policy. The Public Service Broadcasting Protocol devolves the task of defining the legitimate remit of the public service broadcasters almost entirely to the Member States. The involvement of EC law is therefore limited to a requirement that states perform a range of discursive operations. The discussion set in train by EC law takes place within an emerging Community policy network which may assist in sustaining and promoting sectoral discussion. The Commission advocates the establishment of independent regulators. Community legislation then brings regulators together in the contact group, supplying one of several European forums for mutual learning, peer review, and debate amongst national audio-visual policymakers.

In assessing the impact of EC law upon national cultural policies, it is important to remember that expansive cultural policies typically reside in the institutional and not the regulatory component of national audio-visual arrangements. Thus, the intensive regulatory control established by EC law has not, for the most part, had a significant impact on the capacity of Member

States to pursue such expansive policies. While the discursive impetus supplied by EC law may be felt as an uncomfortable intrusion by national public broadcasters already incommoded by national political and competitive pressures, the task of recasting the public service mission and its methods in a form better adapted to present-day conditions is a necessary and inevitable stage in ensuring its survival.

Whilst EC law and policy have therefore developed a policy towards national cultural policies, they have not succeeded in generating an independent European cultural policy. Re-regulatory legislation has harmonized only the crudest quantitative components of national cultural policy. The only innovative obligation, the European content requirement, is not rigorously enforced. The subsidy arrangements promote an industrial policy towards cultural production rather than a content-oriented cultural policy. The sums involved are in any event too small to make their presence felt. Against this assessment, it might be argued that EC law's impact in the opening up of national television arrangements to a broader range of services amounts in itself to a kind of cosmopolitan cultural policy, in which the cultural possibilities of Europeans are expanded.[96] Nor does this cornucopia of choice consist exclusively of unmoderated commercial expression: given that public service broadcasting is left intact, many of the services which citizens are able to access thanks to the removal of national barriers to the free flow of television will be the outcome of another country's cultural policy in the audio-visual sphere.[97] However, while considerable cultural advantages may flow from breaking down the walled gardens of national cultural policy, it is nonetheless

[96] See, for an example of an attempt to develop a culturally oriented justification for opening up the European audio-visual market, Schwartz, I, 'Broadcasting and the EEC Treaty', *ELR*, [1986], 7. He justifies the application of the economic rules of the EC Treaty in the context of television partly by reference to Article 2 of the Treaty, and the objective of fostering 'closer relations between the States belonging to [the Community] which it identifies' (at 17). He then argues against allowing any derogation in respect of national regulatory arrangements pursuing a policy of national preference in the following manner (at 30, emphasis added): 'Special treatment in one Member State for transmissions broadcast to it from another Member State could not be justified either on the grounds that they concerned, affected or influenced economic, cultural or political life in that country. For *this is their precise purpose as endorsed in the EEC Treaty . . . and recognised under EEC law.* The dialogue between different cultures and their interpenetration and cross-fertilisation, nurtured as they are by radio and television, do not pose a threat to a country's public policy but preserve it from isolation, one-sidedness and nationalism by imparting a European dimension.'

[97] Ibid., at 15: ' . . . [T]elevision is . . . in all Member States a function or public function or special public service . . . The organisation of television as a . . . service in the public interest in each of these States can therefore scarcely be jeopardised by cross-frontier television traffic between these states.'

difficult to regard the contribution of European integration as manifesting a cultural policy in its own right. For one, it does not comprise any scheme for directing the character of European public culture. Further, whilst it has tolerated and accommodated national cultural policies, it has not actively promoted them.

Are there convincing arguments for a more positive European cultural policy in the audio-visual sphere? One argument to this effect departs from the importance of public culture to the meaningful and effective operation of democracy. It is argued that liberal democratic states flourish when political institutions and processes are underpinned by a set of widely shared cultural orientations. These orientations may not run very deep, but without them it is difficult to sustain the types of deliberation which are needed to ensure that voters are adequately informed and able to make their preferences count. Examples include the existence of media which constitute a shared point of reference for a large section of the population and which serve to foster an understanding of complex issues, explore and showcase the opposing positions, drawn from all of the main currents of opinion, and probe the activities of those in power as a guard against corruption, incompetence, and failure. The European political process already deals with many topics of the highest importance, but the democratic accountability of European institutions is arguably less than that of national legislatures and executives. Alongside formal changes to the institutions and procedures of European politics, efforts to increase democratic legitimacy would also necessarily entail, on this view, efforts to stimulate the emergence of a widely shared media resource. Without such a resource, even if the role of democratic decision procedures in the Community legislative process was strengthened, the Community would still lack democratic legitimacy.

More boldly, it might be argued that a shared sense of identity is also important in a democracy, in order to foster the sense of trust and mutual responsibility which is necessary to ensure that voters and politicians transcend their personal interests and act in the common good. In particular, a correlation is sometimes asserted between a willingness to sustain social support mechanisms and a shared sense of belonging. If this is correct, and political integration at the Community level is to extend to the solidaristic component which is claimed to distinguish Europe from other models of developed capitalist societies, a thicker European public culture would need to be built around such commonalities as may already exist.

Such arguments have led some commentators to advocate a more ambitious cultural policy programme at the European level. Cederman, for example, concludes that 'it seems hard to avoid advocating *direct identity-promotion* if only in the more distant future',[98] a policy which would include the 'Europeanization' of the media sector.[99] However, there are formidable practical objections to any programme which attempted simply to replicate extensive national cultural policies in the audio-visual sphere.

First, as Crouch notes, a strategy of cultural closure is not now tenable. Whereas in previous periods the introduction of new communications technologies moved the focus of cultural activity from the localized to the national level, we now operate in an era of 'already achieved internationalism', which could not now be reversed.[100] Even if reversal were possible, it would be incompatible with the commitment to a free society in which the right to receive and impart information is respected.

Secondly, the national public service broadcasters made a major contribution to the reconstruction of public culture in European states after the Second World War, but they went to work on communities which already shared significant features in common, including, for the most part, a shared language. Whatever Europeans share in common, it is demonstrably thinner. There is therefore the risk that even if European policies succeeded in generating a supply of programming reflective of a cultural policy for Europe, there would be no real demand for it.

Thirdly, it is important to note the delicate arrangements which have developed over time within European countries for advancing cultural policy goals. The more ambitious goals of national cultural policy have been delivered via intermediate institutions the autonomy of which has been carefully guarded, and the effectiveness of which has depended upon the accumulation over time of a stock of conducive organizational culture. Efforts to devise a European cultural policy would therefore require not just support mechanisms but also the development of an institutional framework. Whether European integration has the constitutional resources to create and to insulate broadcasting institutions at this juncture in its history must be doubted.

Fourthly, the idea of an expansive national cultural policy is under great challenge at the national level. The idea of public service broadcasting is now a contested one. In part, this is the consequence of an increased confidence in the capacity of markets to arrive at acceptable outcomes. In part also, it results from a loss of faith in the existence of any uncontentious cultural agenda

[98] Cederman, L-E, 'Nationalism and Bounded Integration: What it Would Take to Construct a European Demos', *EUI Working Paper*, (2000), 34, at 26.

[99] Ibid., at 23.

[100] Crouch, C, *Social Change in Western Europe* (Oxford: Oxford University Press, 1999), at 395.

which the state might pursue. Lastly, it derives from an uncertainty as to how far it will be feasible to ensure any credible influence for public service offerings given the current technological changes, increasing the number of services available, with the likely consequence of some audience fragmentation. It is unlikely that ambitious European cultural policy initiatives in the audio-visual sphere will succeed in the absence of a credible and current model for such initiatives at the national level.

Given the unlikeliness of a European cultural policy equivalent to national audio-visual arrangements, the question then arises whether alternative measures, better adapted to the current situation, might be adopted to take us in the direction of a Europeanized audio-visual media. As Cederman recognizes, such measures might best begin outside the audio-visual sphere. He proposes educational reforms in the first instance, designed to remove language barriers and reform the school curriculum so as to supply a European context to discussions. 'Once "Europeanized",' he suggests, 'citizens with a broader cultural horizon and better language skills start to enter the media "market place," [and] the conditions for all-European mass media might finally materialize.'[101]

Further, it is important to note the potential of the existing deliberative aspect of the EC legal involvement in the television sector as a stimulus to interchange, leading to a slow but steady convergence in attitudes towards public service broadcasting. By testing public service broadcasting, EC law may strengthen its rationales. Broadcasters and Member States must clarify the cultural policy objectives that underpin public involvement in the audio-visual sector. The integration process is also creating various arenas in which regulators at national and Community levels, states, and broadcasters can exchange opinions and formulate shared positions. On these still modest foundations, a more ambitious Community cultural policy, supplementing the existing national arrangements, might eventually be built.

[101] Cederman, n 98 above, at 26.

7

Language Law of the European Union: Protecting or Eroding Linguistic Diversity?

*Bruno de Witte**

1. Introduction

The decision to adopt a *common currency* in order to replace the national currencies of most European Union countries was a major operation from which the participant states expected considerable economic benefits as well as a reinforcement of the European Union's political cohesion. The adoption of a *common language* for Europe would, arguably, entail even greater economic benefits, since linguistic diversity is a practical obstacle to the operation of a common European market and to the effective implementation of common policies. It would also, arguably, boost the sense of European identity and, hence, the social and political cohesion of the European Union. However, there are factors that explain why the adoption of a common currency was possible whereas the adoption of a common language is unthinkable. The common currency is a new currency, separate from the earlier national currencies, whereas a common language could, realistically speaking, only be one of the existing languages—in fact, only English. Only eccentrics keep dreaming of adopting Esperanto, Latin, or some other 'neutral' language in order to replace the national languages of Europe. Moreover, whereas the shift to a common currency was a costly but relatively painless operation that was successfully accomplished in a time span of a few months, the shift to a common language would take at least two generations. All this explains why the adoption of a common European language is not, and has never been, a goal of European federalists.

* Professor of EU Law, European University Institute, Florence.

Another choice was made originally in the European integration process, and it has often been confirmed since. That choice entailed that the fundamental aims which the Member States sought to achieve through their integration in the European Union, namely political security and economic prosperity, should not go to the detriment of social cohesion and cultural distinctiveness. The preservation of the existing linguistic diversity among the countries participating in the European Union is a core element of this basic understanding. This interpretation is not self-evident. Niamh Nic Shuibhne notes, in her recent book on European Union language law, that 'there are two prevailing but opposing interpretations of the fact of linguistic diversity: it is either celebrated as a manifestation of humanity and free expression, an invaluable cultural asset; or it is denounced as a divisive obstacle, a hollow—and costly—ideal that thwarts the achievement of true European unity'.[1] The official interpretation is clearly the former. The European Union institutions, and the governments of the EU Member States, unanimously *celebrate* linguistic diversity. For a long time, this celebration happened in 'soft' policy documents but did not find an echo in the fundamental legal norms of the European Communities. Yet, increasingly, respect for linguistic diversity has come to be expressly affirmed as a fundamental value of the European integration process. It is now mentioned in the European Treaties themselves, in the EU Charter of Rights and Freedoms, and continues to be embraced in countless policy documents of the Commission, the Council, and the European Parliament.

Article 149 of the EC Treaty (inserted by the Treaty of Maastricht in 1992) specifies that the Community's competence in education must respect the Member States' 'cultural and linguistic diversity'. It is not clear, from the wording of this Treaty Article, whether recognition is given to the value of diversity *among the states* or also, more broadly, to the value of diversity *among and inside the states*. The latter view, which includes intra-state diversity, finds support in the parallel Article 151 EC (also introduced by the Treaty of Maastricht), which limits the powers of the Community in the field of *culture* by requiring respect for the states' 'national and regional diversity'. The word 'linguistic' is not repeated in this Article, but one may safely conclude from a combined reading of the Treaty provisions on education and culture that linguistic diversity is considered a value worth preserving, not only at the European level (as between the various states of Europe) but also within each separate country of the European Union. Article 22 of the Charter of

[1] Nic Shuibhne, N, *EC Law and Minority Language Policy. Culture, Citizenship and Fundamental Rights* (The Hague/London: Kluwer Law International, 2002), at 1.

Fundamental Rights of the European Union, proclaimed in December 2000, confirms this Treaty language and extends it beyond the policy fields of culture and education by affirming in general terms: 'The Union shall respect cultural, religious and linguistic diversity.'

The insistence on this value indirectly implies that linguistic diversity is vulnerable. It may also be a sign of the bad conscience of the drafters of these documents, who may be aware that the European integration process may, in many different ways, contribute to an erosion of linguistic diversity in Europe, so that a countervailing commitment to its preservation is needed. The object of this chapter is to explore this ambiguous role of the European Union, an organization that claims to respect and protect linguistic diversity, but also, by its action or inaction, lets it crumble. This ambiguity is present at four distinct levels, or policy arenas, which will be looked at separately in sections 3. to 6. of this chapter. The *first arena* (below, section 3.) is the regime of language use in the institutions of the European Union. This regime is marked by the recognition of a formal equal status of a large number of official languages, combined with the privileged use of a small number of them (English and French essentially) in particular institutional contexts, and with complete ignorance of regional, minority, and immigrant languages. The *second arena* (section 4.) is regulation of official languages (that is, the languages to be used in transactions with and within public administration and public services) in the Member States of the EU. The leading principle is that of the autonomy of Member States to organize this as they wish, with only very limited interference from the side of the EU designed to ensure equal treatment of EU citizens. In this manner, the EU passively respects the linguistic diversity *among* its Member States, allowing some of those states to freely pursue linguistic uniformity (rather than diversity) *within* their borders. The *third arena* (section 5.) is the regulation of private language use, that is, the use of languages outside the sphere of public administration. Here again, the Member States are in principle free to intervene, but European Community law limits their autonomy whenever it interferes with free trade and the internal market. The principle of 'free movement of languages' within the internal market is itself ambiguous. It may be conducive to greater variety of language use within each country, but it may also threaten the position of the weaker parties on the 'market for languages'. The *fourth arena* (section 6.) is the European Union's own language policy, or rather the scattered elements of such a policy. Despite the dominant competence of the Member States, there is a limited complementary competence for the European Union which it could use actively to promote the value of linguistic diversity. However, the reality is disappointing.

Partly due to the jealous control of the Member States, but partly due also to the lack of resolve of the EU institutions, that policy is not very effective. These four sections will be preceded by section 2., situating EU law within the broader legal context of national language law and the emerging contribution of the Council of Europe. This, again, is a recognition of the fact that the role of EU law in this field is complementary to that of the Member States and, indeed, to that of other international organizations.

Having outlined the approach proposed in this chapter, I should add that the writers who have dealt with language and EU law have chosen very different ways of organizing their subject matter. This is not one of the traditional fields of EU law literature with canonical concepts and classical doctrinal controversies, and it may be useful, therefore, to provide, at this point, a very brief overview of the literature. It can be divided into three rather distinct strands.

The *first strand* deals with the 'languages of EU law' rather than the EU law on languages. The multilingual character of European Union law is one of its essential characteristics. Although this is often forgotten in the day-to-day application of EU law (and, indeed, in the day-to-day writing about EU law), written norms of EU law are enacted in multiple languages, and the meaning of these norms must be understood by reference to all the language versions of the norm. Discrepancies between language versions of the Treaty or of an EU act often give rise to distortions in their application, and to questions of interpretation posed before the European Court of Justice (ECJ).[2] This multilingual context has not merely given rise to technical questions of interpretation; it may have had a broader impact on the way the Court understands and applies European law. Thus, John Usher suggests that 'it is to a large extent language problems which have led the European Court to use a purposive rather than a literal approach to the interpretation of Community legislation'.[3]

The *second strand* in the literature deals with the *régime linguistique* of the European Union, that is, with the legal principles and practice regulating the use of languages within the various institutions and bodies of the European Union, and in the relations between these institutions and the citizens.[4]

[2] See the comprehensive analysis by Van Calster, G, 'The EU's Tower of Babel—The Interpretation by the European Court of Justice of Equally Authentic Texts Drafted in More than One Official Language', *Yearbook of European Law*, 17 (1997), 363; among the many shorter notes on this matter, see Usher, J A, 'Languages and the European Union', in M Anderson and E Bort (eds), *The Frontiers of Europe* (London: Pinter, 1998), 222; Barents, R, 'Law and Language in the European Union', *EC Tax Review*, (1997), 49.

[3] Usher, n 2 above, at 225.

[4] Contributions dealing specifically with this question include: Milian-Massana, A, 'Le régime linguistique de l'Union européenne: le régime des institutions et l'incidence du droit communautaire sur la mosaïque linguistique européenne', *Rivista di diritto europeo*, (1995), 485; and Lopes

The *third strand* deals with the impact of EU law on the regulation of language use within the Member States. Two main issues have been the object of special attention at this level, mainly because ECJ judgments or EC legislation gave them prominence: the role of language rules in consumer protection, and the extent to which language rules and requirements act as a source of discrimination against citizens of other EU countries.[5] These questions are sometimes dealt with in the broader context of the development of a European cultural policy,[6] and also (in some more recent contributions) in the context of minority protection by the European Union.[7]

The theme addressed in the first of these three strands of legal writing is quite distinct from the other two. It involves questions of legal method and legal theory rather than of cultural law and policy and, therefore, does not fit within the scope of the present volume. The other two strands, taken together, deal with what may be termed the *language law of the European Union*, that is, the set of EU legal norms that regulate the use of languages.[8]

Sabino, A, 'Les langues dans l'Union européenne—enjeux, pratiques et perspectives', *Revue trimestrielle de droit européen*, (1999), 159.

[5] See, among others: Boch, C, 'Language Protection and Free Trade: The Triumph of the *Homo* McDonaldus', *European Public Law*, 4 (1998), 379; and Palermo, F, 'The Use of Minority Languages: Recent Developments in EC Law and Judgments of the ECJ', *Maastricht Journal of European and Comparative Law*, 8 (2001), 299.

[6] See, in particular, Loman, A, Mortelmans, K, Post, H, and Watson, S, *Culture and Community Law: Before and After Maastricht* (Deventer: Kluwer Law and Taxation, 1992); McMahon, J A, *Education and Culture in European Community Law* (London: Athlone Press, 1995); de Witte, B, 'The Cultural Dimension of Community Law', in *Collected Courses of the Academy of European Law*, vol. IV, book 1 (1995), 229; Brossat, C, *La culture européenne: définitions et enjeux* (Bruxelles: Bruylant, 1999).

[7] E.g.: Fenet, A, 'Le droit européen des minorités', in Fenet, A, Koubi, G, Schulte-Tenkhoff, I, *Le droit et les minorités*, 2nd edn (Bruxelles: Bruylant, 2000), 115; Toggenburg, G, 'A Rough Orientation through a Delicate Relationship: The European Union's Endeavours for (its) Minorities', *European Integration online Papers*, 4 (2000), n. 16; Toggenburg, G., 'A Trinity of Relationships Between Minorities and the European Union. Is the Newest Player in the Field Simply Adolescent or Contradictory *per definitionem*?', *Journal of European Integration* (forthcoming); Hilpold, P, 'Minderheiten im Unionsrecht', *Archiv des Völkerrechts*, 39 (2001), 432. For earlier essays on the same subject, see Martín Estébanez, M A, 'The Protection of Ethnic, Religious and Linguistic Minorities', in Neuwahl, N and Rosas, A (eds), *The European Union and Human Rights* (The Hague/London: M Nijhoff, 1995), 133; and de Witte, B, 'The European Community and its Minorities', in Brölmann, C, Lefeber, R, and Zieck, M (eds), *Peoples and Minorities in International Law* (Dordrecht: M Nijhoff, 1993), 167.

[8] The most comprehensive combined treatment of these two strands of EU language law is to be found in Nic Shuibhne, n 1 above. Shorter essays combining these two aspects of EU language law are: Fenet, A, 'Diversité linguistique et construction européenne', *Revue trimestrielle de droit européen*, 37 (2001), 235; and Ortolani, A, 'Lingue e politica linguistica nell'Unione europea', *Rivista critica del diritto privato*, (2002), 127.

They form the specialist *legal* branch of the broader stream of social science literature dealing with the language policies of the European Union and the evolution of linguistic diversity in Europe.[9] At the same time, they form the specialist *European Union* branch of the literature dealing with language law and linguistic rights from a national, comparative,[10] and international law[11] perspective.

2. The legal regulation of linguistic diversity in contemporary Europe

(a) A comparative view of the major trends of language law in European countries

The pattern of primary language use in Europe has remained rather stable over the past half century, the period in which the European integration process has unfolded. However, against this background of overall stability, one can identify three sociolinguistic trends that are modifying established patterns of language use. New norms of language law were enacted in order to give recognition to these new linguistic realities, or, on the contrary, in order to restrain them.

[9] Coulmas, F (ed), *A Language Policy for the European Community: Prospects and Quandaries* (Berlin: Mouton De Gruyter, 1991), 1; Labrie, N, *La construction linguistique de la Communauté européenne* (Paris: Editions Champion, 1993); de Swaan, A, *Words of the World. The Global Language System* (Cambridge, Polity Press, 2001), ch 8.

[10] Comparative language law is an undeveloped area of legal writing. Among the most notable writings taking a genuine comparative law approach is: Milian-Massana, A, *Derechos lingüísticos y derecho fundamental a la educación. Un estudio comparado: Italia, Belgica, Suiza, Canada y España* (Madrid: Editorial Civitas, 1994) (dealing with language rights in education). More often, comparative language law is embedded within the broader context of a comparative study of minority protection law—see, e.g., Hilpold, P, *Modernes Minderheitenrecht. Eine rechtsvergleichende Untersuchung des Minderheitenrechtes in Österreich und in Italien unter besonderer Berücksichtigung völkerrechtlicher Aspekte* (Wien: Manz, 2001).

[11] The most comprehensive treatment of language in international human rights law is by de Varennes, F, *Language, Minorities and Human Rights* (The Hague: Kluwer Law International, 1996). See also Dunbar, R, 'Minority Language Rights in International Law', *International and Comparative Law Quarterly*, 50 (2001), 90. In addition, language rights occupy pride of place in the numerous writings on international minority protection; see among many others: Thornberry, P, 'Minority Rights', *Collected Courses of the Academy of European Law*, vol. VI, book 2 (1997), 307; Henrard, K, *Devising an Adequate System of Minority Protection. Individual Human Rights, Minority Rights and the Right to Self-Determination* (The Hague: M Nijhoff, 2000); Pentassuglia, G, *Minorities in International Law: An Introductory Study* (Strasbourg: Council of Europe Publishing, 2002).

The first trend is the emergence of *successful language preservation* movements. For many years, the use of regional and minority languages was declining in most states, and the tendency towards linguistic uniformity seemed unstoppable. Even as late as in the late 1970s, Riccardo Petrella predicted, with regret, that even such widely spoken languages as Catalan or Basque would gradually disappear.[12] Since then, there has been a reassertion of regional and of minority languages and a growth of the number of speakers of some of those languages, including Catalan, Basque, and Welsh. The assimilation of minority languages is no longer an overall European trend; instead there is a chequered pattern, with some minority languages gaining strength whereas others continue to decline.

A second trend is the *increase of linguistic diversity through immigration*. In the whole post-1945 period, Western Europe has witnessed waves of immigration which have led to a large increase of foreign-born persons in the resident population of these countries. In most cases, this also meant an increase in linguistic diversity. In contrast with earlier expectations, there is ample evidence of post-migration language maintenance among such groups.[13]

A third trend was hardly noticeable in the immediate post-Second World War period, but has become more visible in recent decades: the *spread of English as a second language* throughout Europe. As noted by Abram de Swaan:

> Within the countries of Europe, increasingly, a state of diglossia exists: in most domains of society, the national language continues to predominate, but in other spheres the supercentral linking language predominates. Quickly growing numbers of Europeans have learned English and speak it as their second language.[14]

In the course of this process, English also influences the *corpus* of the other European languages. However, English has so far not replaced the other European languages in their function of primary language of interpersonal communication.

These three trends are not equally strong in all parts of Europe. The phenomenon of new multilingualism caused by immigration is typical for Western Europe and is much less noticeable in the countries of Central and Eastern Europe, whereas the increased secondary use of English is more marked in the Scandinavian countries and The Netherlands than in France and Spain. Portugal, to take another example, does not have autochthonous

[12] Petrella, R, *La renaissance des cultures régionales en Europe* (Paris: Entente, 1978).

[13] On the factors contributing to this language maintenance, see Cheesman, T, 'Old and New Lesser-Used Languages of Europe: Common Cause?', in O'Reilly, C (ed), *Language, Ethnicity and the State*, vol. 1 (Basingstoke: Palgrave, 2001), 147, at 154–7.

[14] de Swaan, n 9 above, at 151.

linguistic minorities, and most of its immigrants, until very recently, spoke Portuguese upon arrival, so that this country has mainly been affected by the third trend, and even then, less so than other countries of Europe.

These three sociolinguistic trends have been accompanied by corresponding developments in the *language law* of European countries.

(i) Recognition of regional and minority languages

From the 1970s onwards, but more clearly from the 1980s, there have been numerous constitutional and legislative changes, and new trends in the case law of courts, giving *recognition to* the multilingual character of countries with sizeable *regional and minority languages*. Where this recognition was accompanied, as in Spain, by the devolution of powers to newly established regions, language law is increasingly being made at the regional rather than at the national level. In Catalonia, Euskadi, Galicia, Valencia, and the Balearic Isles, regional legislation was adopted in order to restore the use of the respective regional language as a normal means of public and private communication, to compensate for the active suppression of these languages under Franco's dictatorship. Hence, these laws are commonly called 'linguistic normalization laws' *(Leyes de Normalización lingüística)*.[15]

In Catalonia, a second-generation *Ley de Política Lingüística* of 7 January 1998 is possibly the most comprehensive piece of language legislation in Europe today. It deals with the 'traditional' subject matter of the use of languages in and with public administration, public education, and the public media (all areas in which it now gives some priority to Catalan over Spanish), but it also deals in a rather detailed way with the use of languages in private business and social activities.[16] In Italy, specific language regimes have been in place for many years for the largest territorial minorities; they were recently complemented by a general law on the protection of linguistic minorities in Italy.[17]

[15] For a synthetic view, in English, of the particularly ambitious language policy of Catalonia, see Keating, M, *Nations against the State. The New Politics of Nationalism in Quebec, Catalonia and Scotland*, 2nd edn (Basingstoke: Palgrave, 2001), at 165–76. For a comprehensive analysis, see Poggeschi, G, *Le nazioni linguistiche della Spagna autonomica* (Padova: CEDAM, 2002), particularly ch 3.

[16] For an analysis of this law, see Poggeschi, n 15 above, at 134–87, and Milian-Massana, A, 'Comentarios en torno de la Ley del Parlamento de Cataluña 1/1998, de 7 de enero, de Política Lingüística', *Revista de Administración Pública*, nr 157 (2002), 337. For an account in English of the political debate surrounding the adoption of the new law, see Costa, J, 'Catalan Linguistic Policy: Liberal or Illiberal?', *Nations and Nationalism*, 9 (2003), 413.

[17] Law No 482 of 15 December 1999; for a brief commentary, see Richard, P, 'La loi-cadre sur la protection des minorités linguistiques historiques en Italie: entre sincérité et opportunité', *Revue française de droit constitutionnel*, (2001), 55. More generally: Piergigli, V, *Lingue minoritarie e identità culturali* (Milano: Giuffrè, 2001).

There are also long-established regimes of official plurilingualism in countries such as Belgium, Switzerland, and Luxembourg, where the main principles of language law were set out in the early part of the twentieth century, but whose language legislation was further developed and diversified in recent decades. In Switzerland, in particular, the recent global revision of the Constitution in 1998 involved a codification and strengthening of the country's constitutional commitment to linguistic diversity. This constitutional codification will be examined in more detail in a separate paragraph below, as it may serve as an empirical and normative model for the European Union. In Central and Eastern Europe, developments have been uneven in the last decade, and many countries are still waiting for a stable legal framework for dealing with linguistic minorities. A characteristic example is Slovakia, which saw a succession of overlapping and coexisting laws, including a rigid Slovak-only law adopted in 1995 under the Mečiar Government and a more balanced law on the use of minority languages adopted in 1999.[18]

(ii) Languages and migrants

The creation of new linguistic minorities through the settlement of migrants has not led to the same amount of new language laws. The dominant view in most European countries was, and still is, that no specific language rights are needed for 'new' minorities, even when many of the members of that minority have acquired the citizenship of their state of residence. Rather, the existing language laws of their country of residence should apply to them. Special migration-related language rules, such as they exist, often aim at imposing linguistic conditions or duties, rather than rights. Proficiency, or at least adequate knowledge, of the national language is a traditional condition for the naturalization of foreigners, and it has tended to be imposed with more rigour in recent years. Recently, a number of countries have also started to develop 'integration programmes' involving duties for migrants to follow training courses in the language of the host country, and often make access to public benefits dependent on participation in these language immersion programmes.[19]

[18] See the analysis of these phases and of the reasons for the repeated changes by Daftary, F, and Gál, K, 'The New Slovak Language Law: Internal or External Politics?', *ECMI Working Paper No 8*, September 2000.

[19] These language immersion programmes are dubious from a human rights perspective; see the analysis by De Gucht, K, 'Inburgering door verplicht aanleren van de streektaal en de bescherming van de mensenrechten', *Tijdschrift voor bestuurswetenschappen en publiekrecht* (1997), 151.

(iii) Legislation advancing the use of national language

Some countries have enacted language legislation to advance the use of the national language against growing foreign linguistic influence, particularly that of English. The best-known example, though it is not the only one,[20] is the French *Loi Toubon* of 1994, imposing the use of French in a wide range of public service and economic activities, including product information and advertising.[21] Its application is supervised by a special administrative body; it leads to specific administrative controls and occasionally to fines for its breach.[22] In a sense, such policies echo the traditional use (also, and particularly, in France) of language regulation as an instrument for the consolidation of national identity. Whereas the target of such policies used to be regional languages within the country, it is now the external threat represented by the dominant world language. The *Loi Toubon* had been preceded, two years earlier, by the enactment of a new provision in the Constitution stating that '*La langue de la République est le français*'. This constitutional amendment happened to be adopted at the same time as the amendments allowing for French ratification of the Treaty of Maastricht. There was no necessary connection between these two amendments (as the Maastricht Treaty did not contain any provision that could directly affect the position of French). Yet, for the proponents of the new language article, there was a strong symbolic connection, because they conceived of the French language as a bulwark of national identity that needed strengthening in the face of growing European unification.[23]

(b) An emerging European minimum standard: the Council of Europe instruments

These developments of *national* language law are situated in a legal context that is common to all European countries, and that consists of two main

[20] See also the Polish law of 7 October 1999 on the protection of the Polish language. For a commentary in French, see the Poland page of the *Aménagement linguistique* website of the *Université Laval:* www.tlfq.ulaval.ca/axl/europe/pologne-3pol-polonais.htm.

[21] *Loi du 4 août 1994 relative à l'emploi de la langue française*, in *Journal Officiel de la République française* of 5 August 1994, p 11392. For a comprehensive view of this statute in the context of the evolution of French language law, see Pontier, J M, *Le droit de la langue française* (Paris: Dalloz, 1997).

[22] See the figures and explanations in the annual reports to the French Parliament prepared by the supervisory body, the *Délégation à la langue française et aux langues de France.* These reports can be accessed on the website of the Ministry of Culture: www.culture.gouv.fr/culture/dglf.

[23] A commentator of the constitutional amendment of 1992 put the connection between Maastricht and the French language as follows: 'Le droit de vote et d'éligibilité accordé à des non-français aux élections municipales, la disparition programmée du franc et l'impossibilité pour la France de contrôler ses frontières extérieures, de manière autonome, devaient faire

elements: international human rights and minority protection instruments, and European Union law. The latter is the central subject of this chapter, but the impact of EU law needs to be briefly situated within the broader context of the human rights and minority protection obligations imposed on EU states. The main sources of such obligations are the European Convention of Human Rights and the 'twin conventions' of the Council of Europe that entered into force in 1998: the European Charter for Regional or Minority Languages, and the Framework Convention on National Minorities.[24]

The European Convention of Human Rights contains a provision prohibiting discrimination on grounds of language in the exercise of the rights of the Convention, and it also guarantees a right for the accused to use an interpreter if he or she cannot understand the language of criminal proceedings. However, it does not lay down general standards for the use of languages, and does not contain any specific minority rights. Despite this absence of specific attention to languages and minorities, there has been, in recent years, a 'burgeoning' minority rights jurisprudence of the European Court of Human Rights.[25] General human rights listed in the Convention are being explored and tested by applicants from minority groups as to their implicit 'minority protection' potential. Questions of language use have been raised only sporadically. Yet there is no doubt, for instance, that restrictions on the use of a particular language (say, Kurdish in Turkey) in private broadcasting or print media would be considered by the Court as restrictions on freedom of expression, a right guaranteed in Article 10 of the Convention. In *Association Ekin v France*, the Court held that French legislation allowing for the administrative seizure of foreign publications or publications in a foreign language (as opposed to 'Franco-French' publications) was a violation of Article 10.[26]

émerger la revendication d'une garantie permanente pour la langue française.' (Debbasch, R, 'La reconnaissance constitutionnelle de la langue française', *Revue française de droit constitutionnel* (1992), 457, at 461)

[24] It would go too far to examine the impact of the corresponding universal instruments, particularly the UN Human Rights Covenants and, as far as language rights are concerned, especially Article 27 of the UN Covenant on Civil and Political Rights. See de Varennes, n 11 above, ch 5; see also the other literature mentioned in n 11 above, as well as Ramu, S, 'Le statut des minorités au regard du Pacte international relatif aux droits civils et politiques', *Revue trimestrielle des droits de l'homme*, (2002), 587.

[25] The terms are borrowed from Gilbert, G, 'The Burgeoning Minority Rights Jurisprudence of the European Court of Human Rights', *Human Rights Quarterly*, 24 (2002) 736.

[26] European Court of Human Rights, judgment of 17 July 2001, App No 39288/98, *Association Ekin v France*. See the case comment by Julien-Laferrière, F, 'L'incompatibilité du régime des publications étrangères avec la Convention européenne des droits de l'homme', *Actualité Juridique Droit Administratif*, (2002), 52.

Whereas the Framework Convention on National Minorities includes some linguistic rights within the broader context of its minority protection provisions, the European Charter for Regional or Minority Languages[27] is more directly relevant since it focuses directly and exclusively on the regulation of the use of languages. It applies to 'autochthonous' languages, excluding expressly the languages of migrants.[28] The Charter's main characteristic is its *à la carte* approach. Not only are state parties free to indicate the 'regional and minority languages' to which they wish to make the Charter provisions applicable, but they also have considerable discretion in picking and choosing from among the many, rather detailed, substantive provisions of the Charter.[29] The Charter is therefore a very flexible instrument, requiring the contracting states to undertake only those obligations that they are positively willing to undertake, with the expectation that a process of emulation among states will get underway.

Both the Framework Convention and the Charter on Languages entered into force in 1998 and contain binding obligations for the states parties, among which are included a majority of the Member States of the EU. However, the provisions of these two treaties do not appear capable of direct effect in the national legal order. Their international supervision mechanisms seem fairly modest, since they do not lead to binding judicial or quasi-judicial decisions. Periodical state reports on the application of the Conventions are to be submitted to the Committees of Experts that were set up under each. These Committees have taken a rather dynamic approach to their task. They establish a dialogue with the governments concerned, visit the country and speak to minority groups, and do not hesitate to make statements as to whether the states have adequately complied with their obligations. These statements can then lead to recommendations adopted by the Committee of Ministers of the Council of Europe.[30] Pressure is thus exerted on the states to adopt best practices as formulated by the expert bodies.[31]

[27] Adopted on 5 November 1992, *European Treaty Series* No 148.

[28] For a critique of this exclusion, see Cheesman, n 13 above, at 149–53.

[29] On the Charter, see Fenet, n 7 above, at 206–13, and Thornberry, n 11 above.

[30] These various reports and recommendations can be found on the website of the Council of Europe at: www.coe.int/T/E/human_rights/minorities and www.coe.int/T/E/Legal_Affairs/Local_and_regional_Democracy/Regional_or_Minority_languages.

[31] For an account of the incipient monitoring practice of the Framework Convention, see Hoffmann, R, 'Protecting the Rights of National Minorities in Europe. First Experiences with the Council of Europe Framework Convention for the Protection of National Minorities', *German Yearbook of International Law*, 44 (2001), 237. See also the earlier study by Pentassuglia, G, 'Monitoring Minority Rights in Europe: The Implementation Machinery of the Framework Convention for the Protection of National Minorities—With Special Reference to the Role of the Advisory Committee', *International Journal on Minority and Group Rights*, (1999), 417.

One may note that the Council of Europe instruments played a distinctive role in the preparation of the recent enlargement of the European Union. They offered benchmarks for assessing whether the applicant countries offered adequate protection to their minorities, which is one of the political criteria for accession formulated in 1993 by the European Council meeting at Copenhagen. In certain cases, the role of the EU has been decisive. For instance, the 'carrot' of accession to the EU was instrumental in the adoption of the relatively liberal Slovak law on the use of minority languages in 1999.[32]

Apart from this specific role, those Conventions form an important site for the gradual development of a minimum standard with regard to the legal position of regional and minority languages. In fact, the decision to ratify these two instruments prompted a number of European countries to adopt new laws on the protection of minority languages, so that one could witness a mini-wave of new minority protection legislation in the late 1990s.[33] However, it is too early to conclude that these two Conventions form the basis of a genuinely common European law on minority protection and language rights. In fact, several countries have refrained from ratifying one or both of them, and in France they have been officially rejected as incompatible with national constitutional principles. The French *Conseil Constitutionnel* declared in a decision of 1999, on rather spurious grounds, that the envisaged ratification of the Charter for Regional or Minority Languages would be contrary to the Constitution (and the same assessment would apply *a fortiori* for the Framework Convention on National Minorities).[34] France is thus among the few countries (with Belgium and Greece) that refuse to ratify either of these two Conventions. This reluctance of some Member States of the EU has also prevented the Council of Europe Conventions from shaping the European Union's own 'domestic' language policy.

[32] Daftary and Gál, n 18 above, at 32 ff. There is a growing literature on this theme, including the following: Pentassuglia, G, 'The EU and the Protection of Minorities: The Case of Eastern Europe', *European Journal of International Law*, 12 (2001) 3; Hilpold, n 7 above, at 444–53; de Witte, B, 'Politics versus Law in the EU's Approach to Ethnic Minorities', in Zielonka, J (ed), *Europe Unbound. Enlarging and Reshaping the Boundaries of the European Union* (London: Routledge, 2002), 464.

[33] See, e.g., the Italian law of 1999 mentioned in n 17 above, the Slovak law of 1999, and the Swedish Law on national minorities of 1999, which was immediately followed by two specific Laws providing for the use of the Finnish and the Sami language.

[34] See Fraisseix, P, 'La France, les langues régionales et la Charte européenne des langues régionales et minoritaires', *Revue française de droit administratif*, 17 (2001), 59.

(c) *A mature system and possible model: the constitutional regime of linguistic diversity in Switzerland*

The global constitutional revision that was enacted in Switzerland in 1998 codified existing constitutional principles and redefined some of them. The new constitutional text contains a combination of fundamental rights and institutional principles aimed at preserving the unique plurilingual character of Switzerland, in which one can identify four essential building blocks:[35]

1. The recognition, in Article 4 of the Constitution, of four national languages (German, French, Italian, and Romansh), despite the fact that the numbers of speakers of these languages are vastly different.[36] Three of these languages are recognized as full official languages at the federal level, whereas there is a more limited right to use Romansh in dealing with federal authorities (Article 70, para 1).
2. The cantons have the competence to designate their own official languages, while taking into account the 'territoriality principle', meaning that the existing and traditional pattern of language use should be preserved (Article 70, para 2). Most cantons are officially unilingual, three of them are bilingual, and one is trilingual.
3. The freedom to use the language of one's choice is recognized as a fundamental right (Article 18).[37]
4. The cantons have a general competence for cultural affairs, but the federal government has the power and duty to complement cantonal action in order to protect linguistic diversity, with particular reference to the plurilingual cantons and to the cantons Ticino (where most Italian speakers live) and Graubünden (where the Romansh speakers live) (Article 70, paras 4 and 5, in conjunction with Article 69).

While recognizing the factual and legal differences between Switzerland and the European Union, it does not seem entirely unreasonable to compare them with regard to the constitutional treatment of linguistic diversity. Since the European Union is an organization composed of (at least) two layers of

[35] For detailed commentary, see Ehrenzeller, B, Mastronardi, Ph, Schweizer, R, and Vallender, K (eds), *Die Schweizerische Bundesverfassung—Kommentar* (Zürich: Schulthess, 2002), particularly the comments on Articles 4, 18, and 70 of the Constitution (all written by Kägi-Diener, R).

[36] At the census of 1990, 65 per cent of the resident population indicated German as their main language, as against 19.2 per cent French, 7.6 per cent Italian, and a mere 0.6 per cent Romansh (Bundesamt für Statistik, *Statistisches Jahrbuch 2000*, at 418 ff.).

[37] Article 18 is one of the shortest articles of the Constitution. It states, in French: 'La liberté de la langue est garantie.'

government, like Switzerland, and since it has formally committed itself to linguistic diversity, one might want to examine whether it has adopted constitutional rules and principles, either explicit or implied, that approach the 'Swiss model'.

3. The multilingual European institutions: the doctrine of equality and its practical accommodation

The European institutions function in many languages. This institutional multilingualism embodies, in a symbolic and practical way, the equality between the Union's Member States. It also reflects the value of democratic governance, since it guarantees that legislative, executive, and judicial powers transferred from the Member State level to the European level shall be exercised there in languages that are accessible to the citizens of all Member States. The principled choice for plurilingualism is not clearly expressed in the text of the European Treaties. However, an indirect expression of that principle can be found in Article 21 EC, which includes (since the Treaty of Amsterdam) a right for citizens of the Union to use any of the 12 'Treaty languages' for dealing with the institutions of the European Union.[38]

The clause of the Amsterdam Treaty gives due recognition to the national languages of the Member States. It also corresponds to the existing long-standing practice of the European Union. Indeed, a very similar rule was set out in the very first Regulation ever adopted under the EEC Treaty, namely Council Regulation 1/58 on the use of languages by the Community institutions.[39] The Council then adopted the principle, which is still valid today, that the national

[38] Article 21, third indent: 'Every citizen of the Union may write to any of the institutions or bodies referred to in this Article or in Article 7 in one of the languages mentioned in Article 314 and have an answer in the same language.' The 'bodies or institutions referred to' are the European Parliament, the Commission, the Council, the Court of Justice, the Court of Auditors, and the Ombudsman. Article 314, the last Article of the EC Treaty, states which language versions of the Treaty are to be authentic versions; the languages listed are: Dutch, French, German, Italian, Danish, English, Finnish, Greek, Irish, Portuguese, Spanish, and Swedish. I could not find, in the Treaty of Accession, a provision that amends Article 314 so as to expand this list with the nine new official languages. Whatever the wording of the Treaty, the intention of the negotiators of the Treaty of Accession must have been that the right granted by Article 21 will, after accession, also extend to Czech, Estonian, Hungarian, Latvian, Lithuanian, Maltese, Polish, Slovak, and Slovenian.

[39] *Journal Officiel des CE*, 1958, 385. The Regulation was adopted pursuant to Article 217 EEC Treaty (now Article 290 EC Treaty), which states: 'The rules governing the languages of the

languages of the Member States were to rank equally as official and working languages of the European Communities, subject to more detailed arrangements to be adopted by each institution separately. This rule was extended later on to the national languages of all the states acceding to the Communities[40] and, at Maastricht, it was also extended to the second and third pillars of the European Union.[41] Still, the inclusion of a *right* to use these languages, as part of the citizenship rights reforms enacted by the Treaty of Amsterdam, is not insignificant. It lends an entrenched constitutional status, in part at least, to a linguistic regime that hitherto was regulated by an act of secondary Community law (although, in truth, the existing regime was already firmly entrenched, thanks to the unanimity requirement imposed by Article 290 EC for the adoption of the relevant Council regulation).[42] The Amsterdam language clause is also important because it renews the original commitment of the Member States to linguistic diversity, at a time when the cost of the language regime has become incommensurably higher than in 1958. Cautious recommendations for a simplification of the Union's linguistic regime, made now and then in recent years, were ignored in the Treaties of Amsterdam and Nice. The most recent Treaty of Accession has simply extended the existing linguistic regime to the future Europe of 25 Member States, modifying Regulation 1/58 so as to add nine additional official languages, including even Maltese.[43] Even now, the

institutions of the Community shall, without prejudice to the provisions contained in the rules of procedure of the Court of Justice, be determined by the Council, acting unanimously.'

[40] An exception was made for Irish. There is an authentic version in Irish of the founding Treaties, but Irish was not included among the official and working languages when Regulation 1/58 was modified upon the accession of the UK, Ireland, and Denmark (Section XIV of Annex I to the Act of Accession, OJ [1972] L 73/122). As for Letzeburgesch, it became an official language of Luxembourg many years after that country helped found the European Communities, and this language was not subsequently added to the list of Regulation 1/58.

[41] See the Articles 28 and 41, EU Treaty.

[42] The unanimity rule also applies to the determination of the language regime of the European Court of Justice, because the rules of procedure of the ECJ used to require a unanimous Council decision for their amendment. The Treaty of Nice did remove the unanimity requirement for most modifications of the Court's rules of procedure, but it excepted the language regime, which continues to be subject to the unanimity rule. It is planned to transfer the language regime from the rules of procedure to the Statute of the ECJ (see Article 64 of the Protocol on the Statute of the Court of Justice, as added by the Treaty of Nice). Modifications of the Statute will (unlike modifications of the rules of procedure) continue to be subject to the unanimity rule. The planned relocation of the Court's language regime, from the rules of procedure to the Statute, is therefore further evidence of the constitutional importance and political sensitivity of language regulation in the EU. The language regime of the Court is presently to be found in Articles 29 to 31 of the Rules of Procedure of the European Court of Justice and Articles 35 to 37 of the Rules of Procedure of the Court of First Instance (codified versions), OJ [2003] C 193/1.

[43] Treaty of Accession, Annex II, section 22 (document AA 2003 final of 3 April 2003, p 2473).

exponential increase of translation and interpretation costs, and the growing danger of communication failures between actors in the European policy-making and implementation process, could not outweigh the commitment to linguistic diversity and equality among the Member States.

Between 1958 and now, the commitment to linguistic diversity has, in fact, radically changed in its tone and its implications. In 1958, it was a *pragmatic solution* that the EEC took in the same way as other international organizations that must decide on their language regime.[44] The rather liberal option adopted then in the EEC, which did not sacrifice any of its Member States' national languages, was taken at a rather low cost, because it meant that a co-official status was being given to four languages only. Today, the commitment to the equality of Europe's national languages has become a *constitutional principle* of paramount importance, which is extended to 20 languages, and therefore lays a heavy burden on the Union's institutional machinery.

However, the principle does not guarantee full equality between all the languages of the European Union. It applies to the national languages of the Member States, and not to regional languages, some of which have more speakers than some of the national languages (compare Catalan with Danish), nor to languages of migrant communities, which are also spoken by numerous EU citizens.

Moreover, the leeway left to each of the institutions by Article 6 of Regulation 1/58, namely that they could make practical accommodations of the equality norm, has been used very extensively. The day-to-day reality of the European Union shows a rather different picture than the principles outlined above.[45] It is widely known that the internal working languages of the Commission services are English and French, to the almost total exclusion of the other languages (although German is formally the Commission's third working language, it is very seldom used). It is also known that the European Court of Justice has so far conducted its deliberations in French, and that much of its preparatory work takes place exclusively in French.[46] Increasingly,

[44] On the language regimes of international organizations, see Tabory, M, *Multilingualism in International Law and Institutions* (Alphen: Sijthoff & Noordhoff, 1980), and, for a brief overview, Schermers, H and Blokker, N, *International Institutional Law*, 3rd edn (Dordrecht: M Nijhoff, 1995), at 256–62.

[45] See Nic Shuibhne, n 1 above, at 12–21; Bruha, T, 'Rechtliche Aspekte der Vielsprachigkeit: Vertrags-, Amts-, Arbeits- und Verkehrsprachen in der Europäischen Union', in Bruha, T and Seeler, H J (eds), *Die Europäische Union und ihre Sprachen* (Baden Baden: Nomos, 1998), 83.

[46] See, e.g., Mancini, G F and Keeling, D T, 'Language, Culture and Politics in the Life of the European Court of Justice', *Columbia Journal of European Law*, (1995), 397, at 397–8; Sevón, L, 'Languages in the Court of Justice of the European Communities', in *Scritti in onore di Giuseppe Federico Mancini*, vol II (Milano: Giuffrè, 1998), 933.

policy documents emanating from the European institutions are placed on the Internet site of the EU in a few language versions only.[47]

There is also a tendency to restrict the range of languages to be used in newly-established bodies of the European Union. In its *Kik* judgment of 12 July 2001,[48] the European Court of First Instance (CFI) rejected a complaint against the language regime of the Office for Harmonization in the Internal Market (OHIM: a body that is also known as the EU trademark agency and that has its seat in Alicante). In the interest of expediency, the Council Regulation setting up the OHIM requires that all persons filing an application for a Community trademark (an application which itself can be made in any of the official languages of the EU) must designate a second language to be chosen from among five official EU languages (English, French, German, Italian, or Spanish) in the event that their trademark application is contested in proceedings for opposition, revocation, or invalidity. Ms Kik, a Dutch trademark lawyer, refused to choose from among these five privileged languages. She rather indicated Dutch as her language for proceedings, whereupon her trademark application was rejected by the Office for failure to comply with the language regime. In support of her action for annulment of this negative decision, she argued that the Regulation, by restricting the choice of languages, was in breach of the principle of non-discrimination.

The CFI rejected this claim. It distinguished the case of a body such as OHIM from that of the EU institutions, by stating that Council Regulation 1/58 applied to the latter but not to the former. It made the sweeping statement that 'the rules governing languages laid down by Regulation No 1 cannot be deemed to amount to a principle of Community law'. Since, according to the Court, there is no overarching principle of equality of Community languages, Regulation No 1 only deals with the institutions directly regulated by its terms, and for all other bodies and agencies (including OHIM) the rules of language use can freely be decided in the legal act by which they are created. The Court then addressed the applicant's separate argument that the language regime of the OHIM was in breach of the (unwritten) principle of non-discrimination because it treated speakers of the smaller Community languages less favourably than the speakers of the five most widely spoken languages. The Court also rejected this claim and held that

> in pursuing the objective of determining the language of the proceedings where parties who do not share the same language preference fail to agree, the Council must be

[47] See the Commission's reply to Written Question E-02012/02 by C Ripoll y Martinez de Bedoya (MEP), OJ [2003] C 92 E/3.

[48] Court of First Instance, Case T-120/99, *Christina Kik v Office for Harmonisation in the Internal Market (Trade Marks and Designs)*, judgment of 12 July 2001.

considered to have made an appropriate and proportionate choice, even if the official languages of the Community were treated differently.[49]

Clearly, the CFI gave precedence to the interest of ensuring the efficient functioning of the trademark office over that of protecting the linguistic interests of applicants from smaller EU countries. The importance of the *Kik* judgment is that, unless it is overruled on appeal by the Court of Justice, it excludes the existence of a constitutional principle of language equality and thereby paves the way for the EU legislator to create differentiated language regimes for the various EU agencies—but not for the institutions referred to in Article 21 EC, for which citizens have a constitutional right to use any of the official EU languages. Along the same lines, a protracted battle was recently waged about the language regime of the future Community patent system. The question of whether or to what extent the free choice of languages in patent procedures can be limited was one of the main stumbling blocks during the negotiations on the Community Patent Regulation.[50]

Still, despite the institutional practices, informal arrangements, and limited exceptions mentioned above, the European Union is an extraordinarily polyglot organization, and it continues to operate the most elaborate and sophisticated machinery of translation and interpretation in the whole world. Thousands of European Union officials operate this machinery and the system manages to facilitate comprehension, despite the unavoidable delays in decision-making that it causes, and despite occasional errors and legal ambiguities. For the actors of the system, multilingualism has subtle consequences. It forces participants in meetings of the Commission, the Council, or the Parliament to be brief and simple, and it hinders intensive discussion. This may be a source of misunderstandings, but may also, paradoxically, help to defuse the conflicts and cultural tensions that might arise if all actors had easy access to each other's languages.[51]

[49] Ibid., para 63. An appeal is pending, at the time of writing, before the Court of Justice (Case C-361/01 P). For detailed discussion of this case, see Gundel, J, 'Zur Sprachenregelung bei den EG-Agenturen—Abschied auf Raten von der Regel der "Allsprachigkeit" der Gemeinschaft im Verkehr mit dem Bürger?', *Europarecht*, (2001), 776; and Campailla, S, 'Regime linguistico dinanzi all'UAMI: il fine giustifica i mezzi', *Diritto pubblico comparato e europeo*, (2001), 1966.

[50] At the time of writing, this Regulation was still not formally adopted. For a view of the complexity of the language question in the European patent system, see Ullrich, H, 'Patent Protection in Europe: Integrating Europe into the Community or the Community into Europe?', *European Law Journal*, 8 (2002), 433, at 468–71.

[51] Abélès, M, 'Homo communautarius', in Kastoryano, R (ed), *Quelle identité pour l'Europe? Le multiculturalisme à l'épreuve* (Paris: Presses de la Fondation Nationale des Sciences Politiques, 1998), 43, at 56. It could even be argued (perhaps too optimistically) that the cultural and linguistic diversity among its members gives to the debates in the European Parliament a uniquely deliberative character (see Eriksen, E O, and Fossum, J E, 'Democracy through Strong Publics in the European Union?', *Journal of Common Market Studies*, 40 (2002), 401, at 413).

The enlargement of the European Union has prompted new efforts for reforming the language regime. The Seville European Council, in June 2002, asked the Council of Ministers 'to study the question of the use of languages in the context of an enlarged Union and practical means of improving the present situation without endangering basic principles'. The Council did present a short note in December 2002,[52] but clearly further thought will have to be given to this question. In the coming years, the European Union will probably seek to streamline its present regime of 'controlled multilingualism'. It will try to restrict the occasions at which interpretation and the translation of documents is required in its internal operation, within the legal limits set by the official language regime and the political limits set by the governments of countries speaking languages other than English and French. In the external domain, that of relations between EU institutions and the citizens, the existing arrangements will hardly be modified, since the right to use any of the EU official languages is guaranteed by primary law. A sore point, in this respect, is the fact that speakers of regional and minority languages are excluded from the full benefit of this right. If this is a fundamental right (as it clearly is after its incorporation in the EU Charter of Fundamental Rights), then how can one justify that it is granted to those who speak Maltese and not to those who speak Catalan?[53]

4. The use of languages in the public sector: Member State autonomy and equal treatment of European citizens

Every national legal system has its own language policy, even those systems that do not have *language laws* that are openly acknowledged as such. Indeed, a choice must necessarily be made, if only implicitly, of the language(s) that must be used by the legislature, the courts, and the administrative authorities, and the languages of communication in public schools, public broadcasting, and other public services. A choice for the use of a particular language in these institutional contexts also implies that citizens are expected to understand and to use, in their turn, the same language when addressing these public authorities and dealing with these public services. In some cases, this choice merely consists in selecting a standard version of a language, as opposed to the many

[52] Council of the European Union, *Use of languages in the Council in the context of an enlarged Union*, Doc 15334/1/02, REV 1, 6 December 2002.

[53] See Nic Shuibhne, n 1 above, at 253.

dialect forms of the language that many people use in their daily activities. However, whenever two or more *separate languages* are spoken by sizeable groups of persons living within one state, a selection must be made as to which of those will be an *official language* for public transactions. Again, this choice is not necessarily enacted in a formal legal document. In many European countries, including Germany, Italy, the United Kingdom, The Netherlands, and Sweden, there is no general constitutional rule stating explicitly which is the official language of the country. Even in France, a country known for having pursued a policy of linguistic uniformity over a long period of time, it took until 1992 before an article was included in the Constitution stating that French is the 'language of the Republic'.

One consequence of the selection of one or more official languages in a country or region is that the public service in that country or region should be competent to deal with the demands made by the citizens through the official language(s). Where there is a regime of official bilingualism (as in several Spanish regions, in South Tyrol, in Brussels, in many areas of Wales, etc.) this requires a choice between different models of linguistic organization of the various public services and administrations. One approach is to provide for some form of internal language specialization, so that the *service* as a whole is able to respond in the appropriate language whereas its employees do not systematically need to be proficient in both languages. However, in many cases, national or regional laws require every *individual official* to have the capacity to work in both languages, and to communicate with the population in both languages. As a logical consequence, bilingual skills are imposed as a condition for employment or promotion in the service. There has been widespread litigation, in domestic law, on the validity of such linguistic conditions for access to public employment, but, by and large, national courts have found them permissible for being the most efficient way of allowing the public service to function in both official languages.[54]

[54] In Spain, this question was addressed in a judgment of the *Tribunal Constitucional* (nr 46 of 1991), in which the Court recognized the constitutional validity of a Catalan law requiring oral and written proficiency in both Catalan and Spanish. See also the doctrinal analysis by Agirreazkuenaga, I, 'Reflexiones jurídicas sobre la oficialidad y el deber de conocimiento de las lenguas', in *Estudios sobre la Constitución española. Homenaje al prof. Garcia de Enterria*, vol II (Madrid: Editorial Civitas, 1991), 683. For Ireland, see: *The State (Cussen) v Brennan, per* Henchy J, [1981] *Irish Reports* 181, at 194. However, the fact that Irish is recognized as an official language (and even, according to Article 8 of the Constitution, as the 'first official language') does not, in practice, guarantee a universal right for citizens to use Irish for official purposes; see Nic Shuibhne, N, 'The Constitution, the Courts and the Irish Language', in Murphy, T and Twomey, P (eds), *Ireland's Evolving Constitution, 1937–97: Collected Essays* (Oxford: Hart Publishing, 1998), 253.

In principle, EU law does not affect the power of the Member States to determine freely whether, and to what extent, they allow the use of a plurality of languages for public purposes. The Member States can either opt for a system of rather strict linguistic uniformity (as do France and Germany), or give wide official recognition to regional and minority languages (as do Spain, Italy, and the United Kingdom). This is a matter left to their own choice with which the European Union does not interfere. As a consequence, imposing proficiency in one or more particular languages as a condition of recruitment to public employment is also allowed by Community law. However, official language rules are not entirely immune from the impact of Community law. They must be applied without discrimination against citizens of other EU countries.

The fact that linguistic conditions of employment could function as indirect discrimination against foreigners was recognized early on in Regulation 1612/68 on the free movement of workers. Article 3 of the Regulation prohibits indirect discrimination resulting from actions having as their exclusive or principal aim or effect to keep nationals of other Member States away from the employment offered. To this rule a qualifying statement is added, namely, that the prohibition does 'not apply to conditions relating to linguistic knowledge required by reason of the nature of the post to be filled'. The question therefore is whether a particular requirement of linguistic proficiency is genuinely related to the function concerned, or, rather, is a condition the aim or effect of which is to exclude foreigners, in particular EU citizens.

This issue was addressed by the European Court of Justice in a high-profile case decided in 1989, the *Groener* case.[55] Irish law imposes the requirement that candidates for a permanent post in public education should demonstrate an adequate knowledge of the Irish language. A Dutch applicant for the job, Anita Groener, having failed the test, alleged that this requirement effectively excluded EU citizens from applying for any of these jobs and was therefore a form of indirect discrimination falling under the prohibition of Article 3 of Regulation 1612/68. There seemed to be very good reasons to hold this view given the particular facts of the case. The job for which Ms Groener applied, that of teacher of painting in the College of Marketing and Design in Dublin, did not in fact require her to speak Irish at any time, and therefore knowledge of that language was not a functional necessity. However, the Court of Justice gave a remarkably wide interpretation to the language clause of Regulation 1612/68. Because Irish was an official language of the country, Ireland was

[55] ECJ, Case 379/87, *Groener v Minister for Education and the Dublin Vocational Education Committee* [1989] ECR 3967.

allowed to require its knowledge from all teachers, even those who would not be called to use it in the course of their work, on condition that the required level was not set too high. The Court did not read Article 3 of the Regulation as laying down a purely functional test (that is, 'is knowledge of the language necessary for the day-to-day performance of the job?'), but as allowing for consideration of the broader constitutional background and the language policy priorities of the Member States. There has been much speculation about the implications of the *Groener* judgment, beyond the specific case of Ireland and of employment in public education.[56] The judgment certainly expressed sensitivity on the part of the Court for the national identity concerns of the Member States, even before such concerns were formally incorporated in primary law by the Treaty of Maastricht. However, no blank cheque is given to the Member States and their regions. It is rather the idea of *relative national autonomy* that prevails. Whenever a language criterion is used in recruitment for a particular job, the suspicion arises that it may be indirectly discriminating against EU citizens. If litigation starts, it is for national courts and the ECJ to decide whether the language knowledge is actually required and, if so, whether or not it is set at a disproportionately high level. As to the latter point, the Commission recently stated that the condition, frequently used in announcements of recruitment, that candidates should be 'native speakers' of a particular language, is a form of indirect discrimination against citizens of other EU countries which is prohibited by EC law.[57]

The scope of the prohibition of discriminatory language conditions has recently been extended in two directions. Its substantive scope has been extended from public to private employment conditions, and its personal scope is, still timidly, being extended from EU citizens to other categories of foreigners. The extension of the principle of non-discrimination on grounds of nationality to private sector employment was probably not intended by the drafters of the EEC Treaty, but it was clearly affirmed in a recent judgment of the European Court of Justice, namely in the *Angonese* case that had been referred to it for a preliminary ruling by a court in Bolzano, Italy. Access to employment in a bank in Bolzano was made dependent upon a showing of adequate knowledge of both Italian and German, the two official languages in South Tyrol. This, the Court found, was a direct and acceptable consequence

[56] For a detailed analysis of the implications of the judgment, see Nic Shuibhne, n 1 above, at 80–104.

[57] See Commission Communication of 11 December 2002, *Free Movement of Workers—Achieving the Full Benefits and Potential*, COM(2002) 694, at p 7: 'The Commission considers that while a very high level of language may, under certain strict conditions, be justifiable for certain jobs, a requirement to be mother tongue is not acceptable.'

of the minority protection regime enacted in this region of Italy (even though it concerned employment in a private bank), but the additional requirement that evidence of bilingualism could be provided only by means of a local certificate was held to be an indirect discrimination against citizens from other EU countries, and hence in breach of EC law.[58] The judgment has become famous for its sweeping statement that the right to free movement has full horizontal application, that is that private persons are bound to respect the freedom and must abstain from discrimination against EU citizens. As in public sector employment, language skills may be imposed on citizens of other European Union countries only to the extent that they are necessary for the performance of the function concerned.

The protection against language discrimination in recruitment and conditions of employment now arguably applies to many *third country nationals* as well, on the basis of the Race Discrimination Directive of 2000.[59] Linguistic proficiency requirements that are not justified by the nature of the job could be considered as an indirect form of racial or ethnic discrimination in the terms of the Directive. The Race Discrimination Directive also intends its provisions to apply horizontally. Indeed, its main concern is to combat discrimination in formally private legal relations and in social life in general. So, the imposition of language conditions or requirements by private employers could amount to indirect discrimination on the grounds of race and ethnic origin. Similarly, employment conditions unduly prohibiting the use of minority languages during work could be indirect discrimination on grounds of race.[60]

The material scope of the Race Directive is not limited to employment but extends to discrimination (by both public authorities and private persons) in the fields of education, housing, and social protection. The Directive thereby follows the model of Regulation 1612/68, which also set a wide scope for the

[58] ECJ, Case C-281/98, *Angonese v Cassa di Risparmio di Bolzano*, judgment of 6 June 2000, [2000] ECR I-4083. See the comment by Lane, R and Nic Shuibhne, N, in *Common Market Law Review*, 37 (2000), 1237.

[59] Council Directive 2000/43 implementing the principle of equal treatment between persons irrespective of racial or ethnic origin, OJ [2000] L 180/22. Third country nationals are within the personal scope of this Directive, although only half-heartedly; see Brown, C, 'The Race Directive: Towards Equality for *All* the Peoples of Europe?', *Yearbook of European Law*, 21 (2001–2), 195, at 209–12.

[60] An example from practice is the decision of the Dutch Equal Treatment Commission (*Commissie Gelijke Behandeling*) of 28 March 2000. It held that the internal rules of firms that impose the use of Dutch as the language of communication among the workforce could be disproportional and therefore discriminatory. This is the case, e.g., where no linguistic conditions have been formulated upon recruitment for the job (the text of the decision is on the website of the CGB, www.cgb.nl/oordelen/tekst/2000–15).

protection of EU citizens against nationality discrimination. In fact, the consequences of the equal treatment principle affect the official language regime of the Member States in more subtle ways than only by requiring justification of language conditions for employment. In several rulings, the Court of Justice held that if Member States or regions provide for the right to use a minority languages for public transactions (as, for example, in court proceedings), then that right should be extended to EU citizens who happen to speak that same language. Thus, an Austrian visitor in South Tyrol may use German in court proceedings, even though this right was only intended for the German-speaking minority of the area.[61]

5. The use of languages in the private sector: Member State autonomy and the linguistic freedom of economic actors

One effect of linguistic diversity in Europe is to make communication across national boundaries more difficult. Therefore, language differences act as an obstacle to the movement of persons and ideas; and even the diffusion of linguistically neutral images and objects is hampered by linguistic diversity, if only because they are accompanied by linguistic messages (as with text accompanying films and television programmes). In economic terms, one could say that linguistic diversity creates additional transaction costs that would not arise within a linguistically homogeneous area.

To this economic and social cost of linguistic diversity, a further political and legal cost is added by the language policies adopted by national and regional governments. Such language policies increasingly extend outside the traditional field of official language use (considered in the previous section) and also apply to private language use. This legal regulation of language use in economic and social life can be seen as a *distortion* of the linguistic patterns that would spontaneously result from the informal interaction between private

[61] ECJ, Case 137/84, *Ministère Public v Mutsch* [1985] ECR 2681; Case C-274/96, *Criminal proceedings against Horst Otto Bickel and Ulrich Franz* [1998] ECR I-7650. See the comments by Nic Shuibhne, n 1 above, at 71–9 and 278–84, and by Palermo, n 5 above. The second of these two Court cases, like the Angonese case decided by the ECJ two years later, dealt with the complex language regime of the Italian province of South Tyrol. Generally, on the EU-compatibility of South Tyrol language laws, see Toggenburg, G, 'Diritto comunitario e tutela delle minoranze in provincia di Bolzano. Due aspetti inconciliabili di un (unico) sistema?', in *L'ordinamento speciale della Provincia autonoma di Bolzano* (Padova: CEDAM, 2001), 139.

persons. It can also be seen, alternatively, as a useful or necessary *correction* of the dominant position occupied by some of the parties in an economic or social transaction. A prominent example of an interventionist language law is the French *Loi Toubon*, which imposes the use of French (as opposed, essentially, to English) in the sale, promotion, and advertisement of all goods and services. Another example, in a different sociolinguistic context, is the Catalan language law of 1998 that seeks to extend the societal use of Catalan (as opposed, essentially, to Spanish) by imposing language obligations on broad categories of private persons.[62]

In this context, the balance between Member State autonomy and EU intervention is struck differently from the way it is struck with regard to language use in the *public* sector. To the extent that persons from other EU states, or goods or services imported from other EU states, are involved, policies targeting private language use may conflict with EC law. One could put the nature of the tension in the following very general terms: because the EC Treaty aims at removing barriers to economic activity within the internal market, and because language is the medium of practically all economic activity, the EC Treaty indirectly acts as a source of linguistic rights for the participants in transnational economic activities. The Treaty, together with the free movement of goods, services, and persons, also guarantees a *free movement of languages*, and thus recognizes a functionally limited *liberté de la langue* comparable to that of Article 18 of the Swiss Constitution.[63] Linguistic policies pursued by national or regional governments that form a barrier to the cross-border trade of goods and services, and cross-border mobility of persons, are *prima facie* suspect.

Language regulation is thus a typical example of a more general phenomenon whereby the 'conversion of long-standing national markets into integrated cross-border markets requires the exercise of intrusive control over functions previously assumed to be the natural preserve of the state'.[64] Language policy is no longer a discrete compartment of Member State autonomy as it is officially claimed to be, but is yet another national policy that is exposed to the standards of European trade law. The existence of this 'conflict zone' between language protection and free trade was revealed by a number of European Court rulings over the years. In each of those cases, the Court

[62] See Milian Massana, A, 'La réglementation linguistique dans le domaine socio-économique: perspectives catalane et comparée', *Revue générale de droit*, 30 (1999/2000), 329.

[63] See n 37 above.

[64] Weatherill, S, *Law and Integration in the European Union* (Oxford: Clarendon Press, 1995), at 225.

was called to balance the interest of ensuring trade liberalization and the mobility of persons within the common market, as against the competing public policy interest, advanced by the Member State concerned, to pursue the language policy of its choice. The same kind of balance must be struck by the Community *legislator*, whenever an impediment to the functioning of the internal market, instead of being brought before the courts, is addressed by means of harmonizing legislation at the European level. The Community legislator then has to decide the appropriate degree of deregulation or, alternatively, Europe-wide re-regulation in matters of language use. In this context, linguistic freedom is like other freedoms: genuine freedom for all may need some degree of intervention, given the unequal starting points of those engaged in linguistic communication.[65]

In relation to the free movement of persons, this issue arises when linguistic conditions are being imposed for the exercise of certain *private professions*. In such cases, the language condition is not the consequence of the selection of an official language for that state or region, but is inspired by the need to guarantee effective communication between the professional and his or her clients or patients. In the *Haim* case, the European Court of Justice affirmed, in general terms, that imposition of non-discriminatory language requirements on self-employed EU citizens may be justified. In the particular case of Salomone Haim (an Italian dentist seeking to practise his profession in Germany), the Court held that

> the reliability of a dental practitioner's communication with his patient and with administrative authorities and professional bodies constitutes an overriding reason of general interest such as to justify making the appointment as a dental practitioner under a social security scheme subject to language requirements.[66]

The Commission now proposes to make this into a general rule for the recognition of professional qualifications. In its proposal for recasting the various directives on the recognition of diplomas into one single directive,[67] it inserted an Article dealing with knowledge of languages. Paragraph 1 of the Article states that '[P]ersons benefiting from the recognition of professional qualifications shall have a knowledge of languages necessary for practising the profession in the host Member State', whereas para 2 adds that '[T]he Member States shall ensure that, where appropriate, the beneficiaries acquire

[65] See Nic Shuibhne, n 1 above, at 3.

[66] ECJ, Case C-424/97, *Salomone Haim v Kassenzahnärztliche Vereinigung Nordrhein*, judgment of 4 July 2000, [2000] ECR I-5123, para 59.

[67] Commission proposal for a Directive of the European Parliament and of the Council on the recognition of professional qualifications, COM(2002)119 of 7 March 2002, Article 49.

the language knowledge necessary for performing their professional activity in the host Member State.' The latter phrase is very ambiguous. It is probably not meant to imply that host states should offer free language courses to migrant professionals, but it may prevent the host states from simply denying access to a profession, without further ado, to a migrant whose language competence is temporarily deficient.

The issue of linguistic regulation of private commercial activities drew most attention in the context of the adoption of a number of *consumer protection directives*. The oldest and most widely known of these instruments is Directive 79/112 on labelling of consumer products.[68] Its Article 14 (now amended) dealt with the linguistic dimension of labelling in a rather ambiguous way. It stated that the Member States may (and must) prescribe that labelling should be in a language which the consumer can easily understand, unless he or she is sufficiently informed otherwise about the characteristics of the product. Some countries traditionally have much stricter rules, and often prescribe the use of the national language in all cases and for all products. This creates additional packaging costs for multinational firms, and may generally hinder their cross-border marketing strategy. After a number of judgments delivered by chambers, the Court of Justice confirmed its pro-business interpretation of Article 14 in a plenary court judgment of 12 September 2000 in the *Geffroy and Casino France* case.[69] Criminal proceedings had been brought in France against a supermarket and one of its managers (Mr Geffroy) for offering for sale cola with English-language labels, rather than the required French-language labels. In its preliminary ruling, the ECJ held that the general imposition of the use of French for the labelling of foodstuffs contravened the EC Directive, because the latter merely imposes the use of a language which is easily comprehensible to the consumer in the particular context of the sale. It must be decided case by case whether, in the absence of labelling in the national language, consumers are sufficiently informed about the nature of the product. Although the judgment merely confirmed earlier Court rulings on the same question, it caused quite a stir, because this producer-friendly doctrine of the Court was applied for the first time in the particularly delicate French context.[70] Subsequently, the Commission

[68] OJ [1979] L 33/1. See, on the question of the use of languages for labelling purposes, Chapter 3 by Niamh Nic Shuibhne in this volume.

[69] ECJ, Case C-366/98, *Yannick Geffroy and Casino France*, judgment of 12 September 2000, [2000] ECR I-6579.

[70] See the very critical comment on this case by a French language law expert: Pontier, J M, 'Le juge communautaire, la langue française et les consommateurs', *Le Dalloz* (2001) nr 18, 1458.

brought an infringement action against France to force it to change the law in accordance with the Court's judgment.[71] This, however, involves only a minor aspect of the *Loi Toubon*. The Commission has, so far, refrained from challenging many other provisions of that French statute which could seem equally suspect from a Community law point of view.[72]

Partly as a reaction to the Court's case law, the Community legislator modified the language provision of the labelling Directive, through an amendment adopted in 1997 which is now codified in Article 16 of Directive 2000/13 on the labelling, presentation, and advertising of foodstuffs.[73] According to para 2 of this Article, the Member States are allowed to stipulate that information shall be provided to consumers in one or more languages to be determined by each Member State, although they may not exclude the additional use of other languages.[74] Some other consumer directives (those on time-sharing and on life assurance) go further and require the contract to be concluded in the language of the state where the consumer resides, whereas still other directives regulating consumer contracts do not refer to language at all.[75]

It seems fair to say that, at present, neither the European Court of Justice nor the political institutions have dealt with the question of language barriers to trade in a comprehensive and convincing manner. Moves of the Court of Justice or the EU's political institutions that appear to curtail the states' language policies are viewed with particular suspicion in several of these states, and nowhere more than in France. An expression of this distrust is the fact that the highest French courts have recently decided to make up their own minds on the compatibility of national language legislation with Community trade law, without entering into a judicial dialogue with the ECJ. The French *Cour de Cassation* (criminal chamber) confirmed the fines that had been imposed, on the basis of the *Loi Toubon*, on a distributor of electric festoons imported from Germany for having sold these products without an accompanying notice written in French. The French Supreme Court accepted that this was a restriction of the free movement of goods, but considered the restriction to be justified by reasons of consumer protection. In its view, this conclusion was so evident that there was no need to ask for a preliminary ruling by the

[71] Commission Press Release IP/02/1155 of 25 July 2002.

[72] For a critical view in the literature, see Albers, J and Zwaak, L, 'The Trouble with Toubon: Language Requirements for Slogans and Messages in the Light of Article 30 EC', *European Law Review*, (1996), 71.

[73] OJ [2000] L 109/29.

[74] A similar provision was included in Directive 99/44 on certain aspects of the sale of consumer goods and associated guarantees (OJ [1999] L 171/12, Article 6(4)).

[75] Roth, W-H, 'Transposing "Pointillist" EC Guidelines into Systematic National Codes—Problems and Consequences', *European Review of Private Law*, (2002), 761, at 766.

European Court of Justice.[76] The *Conseil d'Etat*, the highest French administrative court, took a similar attitude in a decision of 8 April 1998. The case involved the compatibility with Community law of the French radio quotas regulation, according to which at least 40 per cent of songs broadcast on French radio stations must be *chansons d'expression française*. The court acknowledged that this constituted a restriction of intra-Community trade, both of the free movement of goods (music recordings) and of the free movement of services (pre-packaged music programmes). It held, however, that these restrictions were justified for reasons of national cultural policy, and that the 40 per cent requirement was not disproportional. In doing so, the *Conseil d'Etat* applied the test formulated by the European Court of Justice but omitted to refer a preliminary question to the ECJ, for fear probably that the ECJ would reach a different conclusion as to the necessity of the restriction.[77]

6. A complementary competence for the EU to protect and promote linguistic diversity

There is no explicit competence for the EU to develop a comprehensive language policy. There are a number of fragmentary Treaty bases that, together, constitute a complementary EU competence, but this has not been used to develop a coherent language policy for the European Union. More particularly, the timid action of the EU positively to favour the preservation of linguistic diversity has not brought substantial benefits to the languages that need most protection—the regional and minority languages.

(a) Language policy competences of the EC

The way the powers of the European Community in the field of education and culture are defined puts heavy emphasis on their subsidiary nature. According to both Articles 149 and 151 EC, action by the Community shall be there (only) for 'supporting and supplementing' the action of the Member States. Moreover, the Community is not allowed to enact 'any harmonization of the laws and regulations of the Member States' in these fields. To the extent

[76] Cass Crim 26 April 2000, *Nizard*, No 2600. See Simon, D, 'Utilisation des langues et protection du consommateur—Les guirlandes électriques n'éclairent pas nécessairement les juges . . . ', *Europe—Editions du Juris-Classeur* (March 2001), p 18.

[77] Conseil d'Etat, 8 April 1998, *Sté SERC Fun Radio, in Revue française de droit administratif* (1999), 209 (and the interesting conclusions of the *Commissaire* Sylvie Hubac, ibid., 194).

that EU language policy is part of educational or cultural policy, it is caught by the restrictive wording of Articles 149 and 151. Still, those two Articles do provide both a direct and an indirect foundation for a positive EU language policy.

The *direct foundation* is provided by the fact that they allow for the enactment of incentive measures in order to achieve the aims set in the Articles. Whereas incentive measures may not amount to harmonization, it is not clearly spelled out, in a positive way, what they are. In practice, they have taken the form essentially of so-called action programmes, through which the European Union is funding projects proposed either by the Member State authorities, or by private actors and organizations within the framework of policy objectives set at the European level. Among those objectives, Article 149(2) lists one of particular relevance, namely 'developing the European dimension in education, particularly through the teaching and dissemination of the languages of the Member States'.

The *indirect foundation* is hidden in the text of Article 151(4). This so-called horizontal integration clause stipulates that '[T]he Community shall take cultural aspects in account in its action under other provisions of this Treaty.' This anodyne phrase recognizes an important reality that pre-dates the Treaty of Maastricht, namely the fact that cultural policy (and, particularly, language policy) objectives may be achieved under other EU policy headings. In fact, EU language law norms have been typically enacted, both before and after Maastricht, on the basis of such 'other provisions' of the EC Treaty, rather than as part of EU cultural or educational policy properly speaking. This practice was addressed, and approved, by the ECJ in a case dealing with the correct choice of the legal basis for the Community's programme to promote linguistic diversity in the information society.[78]

However, this indirect approach contains an inherent limitation. In the system of EU competences as it was patiently constructed by the ECJ through its many 'legal basis' cases, the main content of EU legislation should always correspond to the specific aims or object mentioned in the Treaty Article that serves as its legal basis. Therefore, language regulation cannot be enacted for its own sake, but only as an integral part of a measure whose central aim is defined otherwise. In this way, a limited ('ancillary') power to harmonize national language laws can be construed, so that national language laws can be affected sideways by forming the object of European legislation whose central aim is non-linguistic.

[78] ECJ, Case C-42/97, *European Parliament v Council*, judgment of 23 February 1999, [ECR] 1999 I-869.

This regulatory phenomenon finds its 'natural home' in internal market law. EC legislation harmonizing national laws in order to facilitate the free movement of persons, goods, or services may contain language provisions to the extent that divergence between national language law impedes the functioning of the internal market by restricting one of the freedoms or distorting conditions of competition. One of the oldest but still most striking examples is the Directive of 1977 on the language education of migrant children.[79] This Directive imposes on the Member States a duty to organize special language education for children of EU migrants in order to facilitate these EU citizens' integration in the country of their residence. The special educational entitlements relate to both the language of the country of origin and the language of the host country. The implementation of this Directive has been very erratic, and the control on its implementation by the Commission very feeble, which is partly due to the 'soft' language used in its substantive provisions. Nevertheless, it presents a rather intrusive form of EU language regulation that was justified by the aim of facilitating the free movement of workers. The functional powers of the Community thus served as a vehicle for legislation dealing with a subject matter, language policy, that one would have thought to be within the residual jurisdiction of the Member States. Today, with the heightened political impact of the doctrine of subsidiarity, such a Directive would probably not be enacted by the EU institutions, although the underlying reasoning, that internal market powers may justify the enactment of language policy measures, is still perfectly valid. This reasoning underlies the language provisions in the consumer protection directives and recognition of diplomas directives discussed above (in section 5.), which were enacted under the internal market powers of the European Community. It could form the basis, in the future, for more ambitious attempts of the EU to tackle the linguistic dimension of market integration and of the mobility of persons.

(b) A hesitant minority languages policy

For many years, the European Community budget offered some modest financial support to projects aiming at 'the promotion and preservation of regional and minority languages and cultures'. This budget line B3–1006 was created in 1982 at the insistence of the European Parliament and was continued year after year as a 'pilot programme'.[80] The European Bureau for Lesser

[79] Council Directive 77/486, OJ [1977] L 199/32.

[80] The story is recounted by Ó Riagáin, D, 'The European Union and Lesser Used Languages', in 3 *International Journal on Multicultural Societies* (2001), No 1, www.unesco.org/most/jmshome.htm.

Used Languages was set up for the purpose of accompanying the implementation of the programme.[81] However, in a judgment of 12 May 1998, the European Court of Justice annulled a Commission scheme of financial grants for projects to fight social exclusion.[82] The general point made by the Court in that ruling was that significant EC expenditure required the prior adoption of a basic act by the EC legislative authority. The judgment therefore caused the end of a series of Community funding programmes covered by an annual budget heading but not based on a legislative act setting out the goals and instruments. One of those budget headings that fell victim to this judgment was the long-standing EC funding programme for regional and minority languages, which thereby came to an abrupt end.

Following this judgment, the Commission considered the feasibility of proposing a genuine multi-annual action programme for the benefit of regional and minority languages, which would put funding for this purpose on a firm footing.[83] Although the European Parliament, the traditional champion of minority interests in the EU, supported the plan, several Member States in the Council working groups did not, so that nothing came of it.[84]

In the absence of a dedicated minority languages funding programme, the funding has been continued in a piecemeal and indirect way. In 2001, money was made available on a one-off basis, and for rather ephemeral events, in the framework of a special 'European Year of Languages' project.[85] Currently (in the 2003 budget), support is provided for two particular bodies: the European Bureau for Lesser-Used Languages, and the Mercator research and documentation centres.[86] They are part of the Commission's funding for a miscellaneous group of 'Institutions of European interest'.[87] In addition, projects

[81] See the website of the Bureau, www.eblul.org. It publishes a periodical Contact Bulletin dealing with minority language questions in the European Union context. On the history and role of the Bureau more generally, see Ó Riagáin, D, 'Many Tongues but One Voice: A Personal Overview of the Role of the European Bureau for Lesser Used Languages in Promoting Europe's Regional and Minority Languages', in O'Reilly, n 13 above, 20.

[82] Case C-106/96, *United Kingdom v Commission* [1998] ECR I-2729.

[83] Commission Notice, *Support from the European Commission for measures to promote and safeguard regional or minority languages*, OJ [1999] C 125/14.

[84] Since, presumably, Article 151 EC would have been the legal basis, or one of the legal bases, of the programme, it would have required the unanimous agreement of all Member State delegations. See Ó Riagáin, n 80 above, at 8.

[85] Decision 1934/2000 of the Parliament and the Council of 17 July 2000, OJ [2000] L 232/1.

[86] There are three such Mercator centres: Mercator Education (in Leeuwarden), Mercator Legislation (in Barcelona), and Mercator Media (in Aberystwyth).

[87] EU budget for 2003, item A-3015. The amount of appropriations for 2003 is €1,050,000.

can provisionally be funded under the general heading 'Preparatory cooperation measures in the fields of education and youth policy'.[88]

In order to circumvent the misgivings of several Member States against a separate minority languages programme, the Commission's latest plan is to include support for regional and minority languages in a broader 'action plan on language learning and linguistic diversity'. Such a plan was called for in a Council Resolution of 14 February 2002,[89] and was being drawn up by the Commission in the summer of 2003. According to the plan, financial support for linguistic diversity projects would be made available as part of the current EU funding programmes. This part of the Commission's plan is open to the criticism that, by failing to create a dedicated funding base for linguistic diversity projects, and instead funding them from existing programmes with multiple policy goals, there is a danger of dilution. It could also be seen, in a more positive light, as the attempt to develop a global vision of the question of linguistic diversity in Europe (integrating the needs of both national and minority languages) and of mainstreaming this concern for linguistic diversity in other EU policies.

This plan corresponds, to some extent, to the current state of things. Linguistic diversity is present, as an aim or as an object of special consideration, in the description of several EC programmes. Thus, one of the objectives of MEDIA plus, the well-funded programme for the development, distribution, and promotion of European films, is 'to support linguistic diversity'.[90] The *Culture 2000* programme has, among its many goals, that of 'supporting the translation of literary, dramatic and reference works, especially those in the lesser-used European languages and the languages of central and east European countries'.[91] The most important example is the *Socrates* programme in the field of education. It incorporates the formerly separate *Lingua* programme dedicated to the improvement of language skills of students and pupils and to language teacher training, by means of mobility grants and the development of language learning materials. The objective of the *Lingua* part of the *Socrates* programme is 'to promote a quantitative and qualitative improvement of the knowledge of languages of the European

[88] See EU budget for 2003, explanation under budget line B3-1000: 'An amount of €1,000,000 is destined for the promotion and safeguard of regional and minority languages, dialects and cultures.'

[89] Council Resolution of 14 February 2002 on the promotion of linguistic diversity and language learning in the framework of the implementation of the objectives of the European Year of Languages 2001, OJ [2002] C 50/1.

[90] Decision 821/2000 of 20 December 2000, OJ [2000] L 336/82.

[91] Decision 508/2000 of 14 February 2000, OJ [2000] L 63/1, Annex II, I b.

Union, in particular those languages which are less widely taught, so as to lead to greater understanding and solidarity between the peoples of the European Union and promote the intercultural dimension of education'.[92] This statement could give the mistaken impression that regional and minority languages are included. In fact, the Annex of the *Socrates* Decision makes clear that only the official languages of the European Community are covered, together with Irish and Letzeburgesch. On the basis of the European Economic Area (EEA) Agreement, Norwegian and Icelandic were also included. Therefore, the special priority given to the 'less widely taught' languages does not refer to the regional and minority languages (such as Catalan, Basque, and Welsh). This is odd, because improved knowledge of these languages seems equally able to 'lead to greater understanding among the peoples of the European Union', which is the declared underlying aim of *Lingua*. There is an obvious double standard here, which contradicts and annihilates the modest EU funding for minority language projects.

The question is whether the Commission's proposed new approach, of mainstreaming linguistic diversity concerns in a variety of existing programmes, will lead to an increase of overall funding. The financial amounts allocated over the years to language-related projects were very limited. For their immediate beneficiaries, this European funding is meaningful, but the overall impact of this on the preservation of linguistic diversity is negligible. Whereas the European Parliament is traditionally pleading for increased funding of media, culture, and education programmes, the Council has always been very reluctant. In the particular case of the *Culture 2000* programme, which is potentially important due to its broad scope, Council decision-making is by unanimity, in accordance with Article 151 EC. The United Kingdom, for one, has not shown any interest in substantial funding for measures to promote linguistic diversity. This is quite understandable since these measures are, in fact, to a very large extent aimed at limiting the expansion of the use of the English language.

The EU Charter of Fundamental Rights, adopted in 2000, did not modify the legal and political situation. Apart from the general consideration that the Charter is supposed not to add any new competences for the European Union, the drafters of the Charter also declined to include minority protection rights despite proposals made by various non-governmental organizations, such as the Minority Rights Group International.[93] As early as 1981, the

[92] Decision 253/2000 of 24 January 2000, OJ [2000] L 28/1, Article 2, sub (b).

[93] CHARTE 4478/00 (contribution by the Minority Rights Group), on the Charter website: http://db.consilium.eu.int/DF. See Schwellnus, G, 'Much Ado About Nothing? Minority

European Parliament adopted a resolution calling for the drawing up of a 'Bill of Rights' for linguistic minorities.[94] Twenty-three years later, there still is no such document. It is true that minority protection instruments have, since then, been adopted within the wider framework of the Council of Europe, and there is probably no need for the European Union to duplicate such efforts. Still, in view of the prominent role of minority rights alongside other human rights in the EU's external policy, particularly towards the candidate countries, one would have expected at least some reflection of it in a Charter which intended to enact a comprehensive and up-to-date codification of fundamental rights.

7. Conclusion

There is EU language law, undoubtedly, but one may doubt whether there is a genuine EU language policy. There are elements of a constitutional framework for such a policy in the EC Treaty, in Council Regulation 1/58, in the Charter of Rights, and in unwritten general principles of Community law. However, these various elements have not grown into a coherent whole. There is no comprehensive reflection on the language question in the European institutions, nor has the Commission ever drafted a White or Green Paper setting out its overall views on the matter. The Convention on the Future of the European Union has produced a draft constitutional treaty that does not innovate in language matters either. Whereas there is no doubt that the European Community has an environmental policy, a consumer protection policy, and a social policy (even though their content may be criticized), it is far less obvious that there is such a thing as a European language policy.

There is certainly evidence of what could be called a *negative language policy* of the EU. Community law is often considered to be a 'sword of Damocles', constantly menacing the integrity of Member-State language policies.[95] Although in principle Member States and their regions can freely define and implement their own language policies, and in particular their own linguistic minority policies, European Community law interferes with their autonomy. It does so mainly through the application of a broad principle of equal treatment of EU citizens (and, increasingly, of third country nationals as well) and

Protection and the EU Charter of Fundamental Rights', *Constitutionalism Web-Papers* No 5/2001, http://les1.man.ac.uk/conweb.

[94] OJ [1981] C 287/106.

[95] Fenet, n 7 above, at 226.

through the underlying ethos of internal market law which makes language regulation of private economic transactions a suspect restriction of trade. The Court of Justice has recognized that cultural policy (*Fedicine*), the protection of a national language (*Groener*), and the protection of minorities (*Bickel and Franz*, *Angonese*) are all legitimate interests that may justify a restriction of trade and even indirect discrimination against EU citizens. However, these restrictions must always pass a proportionality test that leaves the courts as the final arbiters of the compatibility of state language laws with EC law. So, whereas the European Union does not attempt to redefine the general approach taken by the Member States in language matters, specific elements of these language policies are affected by the European Union.

There is much less evidence of a *positive language policy*. The overall aim of such a policy is uncontroversial and constantly reaffirmed: the protection of linguistic diversity. However, there is a double standard at work, which leads the EU to privilege certain languages (the official languages of the EU) over others. The European Union spends some funds on projects designed to overcome language barriers in Europe and on projects designed to foster the use and knowledge of 'lesser used' languages. This feel-good funding is very limited, though, and probably does not even counterbalance the language shift (to the detriment of the weaker languages) caused by the general economic and social dynamics of the European integration process.

8

Reflections on Education and Culture in EC Law

*Julian Lonbay**

1. Introduction

Few would doubt that education is inextricably linked with culture. Indeed its cultural sensitivity is one of the reasons why it is, in large measure, excluded from the sphere of EC competence, though not completely as we shall see. Traditionally it has been dealt with more within the inter-governmental confines of the Council of Europe.[1] After a brief look at the competence of the European Union in the sphere of education this chapter sets out the context of educational activities in European law. It then evaluates the emergence of European activities in the field of education which impinge on cultural identity. The actors in the emerging scene are not only the conventional European institutions, though they play a role, but rather comprise many non-state infra-national actors. The growing convergence through sub-state actors indicates a deepening of the European Union and also provides evidence of common cultural ambitions in the sphere of education.

* School of Law, the University of Birmingham.

[1] In particular, the major programmes to support the emerging democracies in Central and Eastern Europe that focused on Education and Training of European Citizens, dealing with human rights, democracy, history teaching, and developing a European dimension in teaching: e.g., Council of Europe Report to the ENIC-NARIC Joint Networks meeting (Valletta, June 2002); see further http://culture.coe.int/restricted/ccher/eng/ecesu.ses.html.

2. Competence

This chapter does not look in detail at the formal competence of the EU itself vis-à-vis education.[2] Despite its clearly limited jurisdiction,[3] which arguably has got more limited, in some respects,[4] over time with the Maastricht Treaty amendments,[5] the EU nevertheless does have a marked direct, as well as an indirect, impact on educational systems. It has, moreover, kick-started a series of informal soft-law and Open Method of Coordination (OMC) processes[6] and activities that have taken on a life of their own.

Article 149 EC stipulates that:

1. The Community shall contribute to the development of quality education by encouraging cooperation between Member States and, if necessary, by supporting and supplementing their action, while *fully respecting the responsibility of the Member States for the content of teaching and the organisation of education systems and their cultural and linguistic diversity.*[7] (emphasis added)

[2] For a fuller view see de Witte, B, 'The scope of Community Powers in Education and Culture in the Light of Subsequent Practice', in Bieber, R and Ress, G (eds), *The Dynamics of EC Law* (Baden Baden: Nomos, 1987), p 261; Lonbay, J, 'Education', in *European Union Law Reporter*, 4 (Bicester: CCH, 1997), 13001; Peiter van der Mei, A, *Free Movement of Persons within the European Community* (Oxford: Hart, 2003).

[3] It was not even mentioned in the first Treaty of Rome. The European Court of Justice in the *Gravier* and *Erasmus* judgments widely interpreted the competence of the EC in relation to training and education, and Member States thereafter clipped the wings of the EC in this sphere in the subsequent Maastricht Treaty. See Case 293/83, *Gravier v City of Liège* [1985] ECR 73; Case 242/87, *Commission of the European Communities v Council of the European Communities* [1989] ECR 1425.

[4] Harmonization of content was ruled out by the Maastricht Treaty revisions which added Articles 126 and 127, subsequently re-numbered in the Treaty of Amsterdam to Articles 149 and 150 EC.

[5] Articles 149 EC and 150 EC; see n 7 below and accompanying text.

[6] See n 70 below and accompanying text.

[7] Article 149(2) EC states:

Community action shall be aimed at:

—developing the European dimension in education, particularly through the teaching and dissemination of the languages of the Member States;

—encouraging mobility of students and teachers, inter alia by encouraging the academic recognition of diplomas and periods of study;

—promoting cooperation between educational establishments;

—developing exchanges of information and experience on issues common to the education systems of the Member States;

—encouraging the development of youth exchanges and of exchanges of socioeducational instructors;

—encouraging the development of distance education.

Article 149(3) states: 'The Community and the Member States shall foster cooperation with third countries and the competent international organisations in the field of education, in particular the Council of Europe.'

Article 149(4) EC provides:

In order to contribute to the achievement of the objectives referred to in this Article, the Council:

—acting in accordance with the procedure referred to in Article 251, after consulting the Economic and Social Committee and the Committee of the Regions, shall adopt incentive measures, *excluding any harmonisation of the laws and regulations of the Member States*;

—acting by a qualified majority on a proposal from the Commission, shall adopt recommendations. (emphasis added)

At the European Council Lisbon Summit in March 2000[8] the Council called upon the Member States, in line with their constitutional rules, the Council, and the Commission to take the necessary steps within their areas of competence to meet the following targets:[9]

—a substantial annual increase in per capita investment in human resources;

—the number of 18 to 24 year olds with only lower-secondary level education who are not in further education and training should be halved by 2010;

—schools and training centres, all linked to the Internet, should be developed into multi-purpose local learning centres accessible to all, using the most appropriate methods to address a wide range of target groups; learning partnerships should be established between schools, training centres, firms, and research facilities for their mutual benefit;

—a European framework should define the new basic skills to be provided through lifelong learning: IT skills, foreign languages, technological culture, entrepreneurship, and social skills; a European diploma for basic IT skills, with decentralised certification procedures, should be established in order to promote digital literacy throughout the Union;

—define, by the end of 2000, the means for fostering the mobility of students, teachers, and training and research staff both through making the best use of existing Community programmes (Socrates, Leonardo, Youth), by removing obstacles, and through greater transparency in the recognition of qualifications and periods of study and training; to take steps to remove obstacles to teachers' mobility by 2002 and to attract high-quality teachers;

[8] *Education and training for living and working in the knowledge society*, para 25. Europe's education and training systems need to adapt both to the demands of the knowledge society and to the need for an improved level and quality of employment. They will have to offer learning and training opportunities tailored to target groups at different stages of their lives: young people, unemployed adults, and those in employment who are at risk of seeing their skills overtaken by rapid change. This new approach should have three main components: the development of local learning centres, the promotion of new basic skills, in particular in the information technologies, and increased transparency of qualifications. The Presidency Conclusions may be found at: http://ue.eu.int/presid/conclusions.htm.

[9] Ibid., para 26.2.

—a common European format should be developed for *curricula vitae*, to be used on a voluntary basis, in order to facilitate mobility by helping the assessment of knowledge acquired, both by education and training establishments and by employers.

The careful list of addressees in the Council's call reflects the sensitivity surrounding competences in this field. The extensive set of targets indicates the scope of action in this field. The addition of the right to education[10] to the Charter of Fundamental Rights of the EU[11] adds very little given its currently declaratory status and relative lack of imagination. It makes clear that compulsory education should be free, and that the right to education includes vocational and continuing training, and the right to found educational establishments.

3. Education, culture, and citizenship

Education is a very broad concept.[12] The European Court of Human Rights considered that:

[Education] is the whole process whereby, in any society, adults endeavour to transmit their beliefs, culture and other values to the young, whereas teaching or instruction refers in particular to the transmission of knowledge and to intellectual development.[13]

Education can include all upbringing and socialization of the young, as well as adults,[14] though more commonly now it is associated with teaching and learning in schools and universities.[15] Education can also be seen to have social

[10] Article 14, 'Right to education' provides:

1. Everyone has the right to education and to have access to vocational and continuing training.
2. This right includes the possibility to receive free compulsory education.
3. The freedom to found educational establishments with due respect for democratic principles and the right of parents to ensure the education and teaching of their children in conformity with their religious, philosophical and pedagogical convictions shall be respected, in accordance with the national laws governing the exercise of such freedom and right.

[11] OJ [2000] C 364/1.

[12] Peters, R S, 'Education and the Educated Man', *Proceedings of the Philosophical Society of Great Britain*, 4 (1970), 5.

[13] *Campbell and Cosans v The United Kingdom*, judgment, Series A No 48 (1982). The Court took a broad view of education: 'The use of corporal punishment may, in a sense, be said to belong to the internal administration of a school, but at the same time it is, when used, an integral part of the process whereby a school seeks to achieve the object for which it was established, including the development and moulding of the character and mental powers of its pupils.'

[14] Janne, H, 'Future Policy', *Education and Culture*, 19 (1972), 14.

[15] Niewenhuis, H, 'Le role de l'école dans l'education à la culture', *Cahiers de Pedagogie et d'orientation professional*, 16 (1957), 69.

aims allowing individuals to 'better themselves'.[16] Inculcating 'desirable qualities' in someone is a key aim of education.[17] What is desirable depends upon the social and cultural context within which the educational processes take place. This context historically has primarily been nationalistic.[18] Indeed in most countries mandatory education of future citizens is regarded as a key duty of the state and as an important right and duty of citizens.[19] The formative process of education is recognized as one of the aims of education.[20] In the United States early cases talked of the importance of education in 'Americanizing the mongrel hordes'.[21] This 'moulding' of citizenry is a common aspect of educational systems, and has also been recognized by the European Court of Human Rights in Strasbourg, notably in the *Belgian Linguistics*,[22] *Kjeldsen*,[23] and *Campbell and Cosans*[24] cases. In these cases the Court importantly recognized the role of state in moulding its citizens but ensuring at the same time that there were limits:

> ... the State, in fulfilling the functions assumed by it in regard to education and teaching, must take care that information or knowledge included in the curriculum is conveyed in an objective, critical and pluralistic manner.[25]

There are also key safeguards for parental rights.[26]

One of the main rationales for mandatory state education has been to have informed citizens who can participate in democracy.[27] In its early days the EU

[16] See, e.g., the UN Committee on Economic, Social, and Cultural Rights, General Comment on the right to education, E/C 12/99/10.

[17] Peters, n 12 above.

[18] Hans, N, Comparative Education, 3rd edn (London: Routledge & Kegan Paul, 1958), at p 9; Piaget, J and Weil A-M, 'The Development in Children of the Idea of Homeland and of Relations with Other Countries', *Int. Soc. Sciences Bull*, 3 (1951), 561. A study by Jahoda failed to reproduce Piaget's results: Jahoda, G, Children's Conceptions of Nationality: A Critical Study of Piaget's Stages', *Child Development*, 35 (1964),1081.

[19] Lonbay, J, 'Towards Educational Rights' in Blackburn, R (ed), *Rights of Citizenship* (London: Mansell, 1993), p 215.

[20] Lonbay, J, 'State Control of Education', in Gardner, P (ed), *United Kingdom Law in the 1990's* (London: UKNCCL, 1990), p 293.

[21] It is nonetheless clear that the liberty interests of parents and guardians to direct the upbringing and education of children under their control was to be respected. So attempts to 'Americanize mongrel hordes' by insisting on attendance at district public schools in Oregon was struck down. *Pierce v Society of the Holy Names of Jesus and Mary, Pierce v Hill Military Academy* 268 US 510, 45 S Ct 571 (1925).

[22] *Belgian Linguistics* case, judgment, Series A No 6 (1968).

[23] *Kjeldsen, Busk Madsen and Pedersen*, judgment, Series A No 23 (1976).

[24] *Campbell and Cosans v UK*, n 13 above.

[25] *Kjeldsen*, n 23 above.

[26] Ibid.; cf. Lonbay, J, 'Implementing the Right to Education in England', in Hill, D and Beddard, R (eds), *Economic, Social and Cultural Rights: Progress and Achievement* (London: Macmillan Publishers, 1992), ch 9, p 163.

[27] *Doe v Plyler* 457 US 202 (1982).

lacked its own citizens as such, but with the Maastricht Treaty this was technically rectified,[28] and with the growing case law of the Court,[29] and with a Constitution on the way,[30] the EU has made steps towards establishing its own citizenry with substantive rights.[31] As the Court stated in *Grzelczyk*: 'Union citizenship is destined to be the fundamental status of nationals of the Member States'.[32]

However, the European Court of Justice (ECJ) is cautious and respectful of Member States' rights when it comes to any imposition on national prerogatives of a cultural nature, especially in the sphere of education.[33] One of the clearest examples of this was the *Groener* case, where the Court made it clear that it recognized Ireland's competence in relation to the important task of education:

> The importance of education for the implementation of such a policy must be recognised. Teachers have an essential role to play, not only through the teaching which they provide but also by their participation in the daily life of the school and the privileged relationship which they have with their pupils. In those circumstances it is not unreasonable to require them to have some knowledge of the first national language.[34]

Advocate General Darmon had stated in his Opinion that:

> It seems to me that every State has the right to try to ensure the diversity of its cultural heritage and, consequently, to establish the means to carry out such a policy. Such means concern primarily public education.[35]

[28] Article 18 EC *et seq.* See Reich, N, 'Union Citizenship—Metaphor or source of rights?', *ELJ*, 7 (2001), 4; De Groot, G-R, 'Latin-American European citizens: Some Consequences of the Autonomy of the Member States of the EU in Nationality Matters' (editorial), *MJ* (2002), 115; Oliveira, C, 'Workers and Other Persons: Step-by-step from Movement to Citizenship', *CMLRev*, 39 (2002), 77; Reich, N and Harbacevica, S, 'Citizenship and Family on Trial: a Fairly Optimistic Overview of Recent Court Practice with Regard to Free Movement of Persons', *CMLRev*, 40 (2003), 615; Jacqueson, C, 'Union Citizenship and the Court of Justice: Something New under the Sun? Towards Social Citizenship', (2002) 27 *ELRev* 260.

[29] Notably Case C-184/99, *Rudy Grzelczyk v Centre public d'aide sociale d'Ottignies-Louvain-la-Neuve* [2001] ECR I-6193; Case C-413/99, *Baumbast R v Secretary of State for the Home Department* [2002] ECR I-7091; and Case C-224/98, *D'Hoop* [2002] ECR I-6191.

[30] http://europa.eu.int/futurum/index_en.htm.

[31] A development visible early on from the free use made of Article 12 EC in the Court's case law, see e.g. Case 186/86, *Cowan v Trésor Public* [1989] ECR 195, discussed by Tridimas, T, *The General Principles of EC Law* (Oxford: Oxford, 1999), at p 84. Proposal for a European Parliament and Council Directive on the right of citizens of the Union and their family members to move and reside freely within the territory of the Member States, COM(2003) 199(01).

[32] Case C-184/99, n 29 above, at para 31.

[33] Lonbay, J, 'Education and Law: The Community Context', *European Law Review* 14 (1989), 363; Lenaerts, K, 'Education in European Community Law after Maastricht, *CMLRev*, 31 (1994), 7.

[34] Case 379/87, *Groener v Minister for Education and the City of Dublin Vocational Education Committee* [1989] ECR 3967, at para 20.

[35] Ibid.

Whilst the European Union now has a citizenry, it is composed of citizens of the Member States. One could assert that the European Union lacks homogeneity in the sense of an identity[36] and is clearly not a state itself but a collection of nations, defying easy classification.[37] Each Member State retains its own language[38] and culture, particularly as regards education. Whilst there has been some development of European icons,[39] the Preamble to the Treaty famously calls for 'a closer union of peoples' in the plural,[40] a wording carried over into the Preamble of the Charter of Fundamental Rights of the EU.[41] Whilst there has been some movement towards creating a European dimension in education,[42] these moves are largely of a voluntary and informal nature and had, initially, a relatively small impact. Soysal[43] found a growing sense of identity where familiar civic ideals (from nation states) have found a new repository in the European Union. Interestingly, the manifestations are in sectors (re-writing history books, for example) which are beyond the formal competences of the EU altogether. The work is taking place in the context of UNESCO and the Council of Europe, together with non-governmental organizations and others. The EU's lack of competence and relative ineffectiveness is marked.[44]

4. Funding and soft law approaches

Whilst one can see the heavy impact on educational and training regimes of the European Community's Single European Market rules on professional mobility (below), one can also see much progress in increased cross-border

[36] Lonbay, n 19 above; Smith, A, 'National Identity and the Idea of European Unity', *International Affairs*, (1992), 55.

[37] Weiler, J, *The Constitution of Europe* (Cambridge: CUP, 1999), ch 8.

[38] Promotion of multilingualism is an avowed aim of the EU; see European Commission, *Promoting Language Learning and Linguistic Diversity: An Action Plan 2004–2006*, COM(2003) 449 final.

[39] The Euro, the flag, the look-alike passport, etc.

[40] Weiler, J, 'To be a European Citizen: Eros and Civilisation', in Weiler, n 37 above; Barber, N, 'Citizenship, Nationalism and the European Union', *ELRev* (2002), 241.

[41] See n 11 above.

[42] Lonbay, n 33 above, details some of the early attempts to add a European dimension in education.

[43] Soysal, Y N, 'Locating Europe', *European Societies*, 4 (2002), 265.

[44] Ibid., at p 270 *et seq.*; Theiler, T, 'The European Union and the "European Dimension" in Schools: Theory and Evidence', *European Integration*, 21 (1999), 307. A sample of EU activity can be seen on their collection of European resources for schools: http://futurum.eun.org/eun.org2/eun/en/SpringSite_Information/content.cfm?ov=27979&lang=en&id_area=512&oid=27979.

interaction, cooperation, and a growing mutual trust resulting from the significant influence brought to bear through the power of funding permitted under the EC Treaty.[45] The famous Socrates/Erasmus mobility programme,[46] for example, has ensured the mobility of over a million European students.[47] There is a plethora of similar programmes.[48] The EU has also helped to fund an ever-increasing level of knowledge exchange. It has done this largely through its NARIC network[49] and the Eurydice[50] system.

The EU's education-related programmes have funded considerable cross-border activities in the field of education[51] that have in turn spun off into promoting European dimensions in schools, universities, and also within the professions in the context of their educational activities. Thus, much of the off-agenda activity relating to the development of educational commonalties has a source, perhaps indirectly, in the formal activities of the EU.

Under the Lisbon strategy the Community should now use 'the open method of coordination' in this field. Its use has been more effective than might have been imagined. The lack of direct competence vis-à-vis changing the structure of national educational systems has led, at the higher education level, to a non-EU process of integration and to the searching out of commonalities. It is

[45] E.g., the budget for the *e*Learning programme is under discussion in the European Parliament with €44,000,000 expected to be the resulting compromise.

[46] http://europa.eu.int/comm/education/programmes/socrates/socrates_en.html.

[47] The programme is to extend beyond European borders under the Commission's 2004–2008 proposal, COM(2002) 401, and will include the creation of European masters programmes (Erasmus mundus masters). The Erasmus mundus extension was approved in a first reading by the European Parliament in April 2003, and political agreement was reached in the Council at its May 2003 meeting. It will create a European equivalent to the US Fulbright scholarships.

[48] Phare; Tempus (http://europa.eu.int/comm/education/tempus/index.html); Leonardo da Vinci (http://europa.eu.int/comm/education/leonardo-en.html); Tacis; the European Training Foundation, all involved funding of educational exchanges and common programmes. The Commission developed its plans in a public consultation document in November 2002, 'The future development of the EU education, training and youth programmes after 2006', http://europa.eu.int/comm/education/newprogconsult/. This document conveniently gives summaries of all the programmes to date.

[49] The NARIC (National Academic Recognition Information Centres) regime was supported by the Commission initially in 1984, and after the establishment of the Erasmus programme in 1987 the NARIC became part of the Erasmus programme. They form an information resource for all those in the education sector. http://europa.eu.int/comm/education/programmes/socrates/agenar_en.html

[50] Eurydice is the European network for information on education; it promotes the exchange of information on education systems and on national policies in the field of education and contributes to increasing mutual understanding and cooperation between the 15 Member States of the European Union. It was established in 1976. See http://www.eurydice.org/.

[51] Including a new database opened in December 2002 giving job and learning opportunities in Europe; see http://www.Ploteus.net/.

recognized, in this process, that a European Higher Education Area framework should have a common structure which would include taking account of workload, level, quality, and profile of topics studied.[52] Importantly, it should also consider some of the aims of higher education, such as preparation of students for the labour market, the creation of active citizens for democracy, personal development and fulfilment, and support of advanced knowledge base.[53] Such a framework would also facilitate the task of 'recognition' authorities.[54]

This process of change goes under the name of the Sorbonne Bologna process.[55] This started with a four nation statement, the Sorbonne Declaration, turning the following year into the famous 29-state Sorbonne Bologna Declaration,[56] now followed, post-Berlin,[57] by 40 states, that has launched the rolling process whose aims are succinctly set out below.

5. The aims of the Sorbonne Bologna process

The key aim of the Sorbonne Bologna process is to create a European space for higher education by 2010. In order to do this it is recognized that mobility of students should be eased and the transportability of qualifications encouraged.

[52] Bergan, n 86 below. There are Working Groups spawned from the Bologna process, developing generic and programme-specific descriptors to help measure 'levels' at the Bachelor/Master division, and account must be taken of the Joint Quality Initiative (an informal network for quality assurance) which has developed the Dublin descriptors (also known as the Amsterdam consensus); see Adam, S, 'Qualification structures in European higher education', at the Danish Bologna Seminar 27–28 March 2003, e.g., http://www.bologna-berlin2003.de/en/bologna_seminars/copenhagen.htm; http://www.videnskabsministeriet.dk/cgi-bin/docshow.cgi?doc_id = 138030&doc_type = 831&leftmenu = NYHEDER.

[53] Bergan, n 86 below, at p 12.

[54] Kristensen, B (Copenhagen meeting 2003), see n 52 above.

[55] Knudsen, I, 'Introduction to the Sorbonne Bologna Declaration', *ELFA Newsletter* (2001), 25; Lonbay J, 'University Training: The implications of the Bologna Declaration for the UK', *Rassegne forense*, 35 (2002), 89, for a brief introduction in the context of legal studies, also Reich, N, 'Recent Tends in European Legal Education: the Place of the European Law Faculty Association', *Penn State International Law Review*, 21 (2002), 21, and Vanistendael, V, 'Legal Education in Europe and the Challenge of the Sorbonne Bologna Declaration', *ELFA Newsletter* (2001), 48. ELFA, 'For a European Space of Legal Education', can be found at http://elfa.bham.ac.uk/. See Lourtie, P, 'Furthering the Bologna Process', for a report on the Bologna process up to May 2001; for the Prague 2001 meeting, http://www.bologna-berlin2003.de/pdf/Lourtie_report.pdf; see generally the Berlin website, http://www.bologna-berlin2003.de/, and Reports from the Graz meeting at http://eua.uni-graz.at/documents.html.

[56] This can be seen on the ELFA website at http://elfa.bham.ac.uk/; a major repository of information on the process is found on the Berlin website, n 55 above. The next major conference will take place in Bergen on May 2005.

[57] http://www.bologna-berlin2003.de/en/communique_minister/index.htm.

Existing EU programmes (such as Socrates, Erasmus, NARIC, ENIC,[58] and the Mutual Recognition regimes) (as well as the key transparency instruments—the European Credit Transfer System (ECTS) and the Diploma Supplement (Lisbon Convention)[59]) are to be brought into play to reinforce these aims. The overall objective is to increase the attractiveness and competitiveness of the European higher education sector and to enhance the employability of graduates by allowing increased portability of qualifications, thus helping to create a true European labour market.[60] An indirect aim is also to improve the competitiveness of European higher education in the world education market.

The instruments of implementation for this process include, first, ensuring that degrees are easily readable and comparable. Secondly, to reorganize European higher education to ensure that it is in two phases: an undergraduate phase followed by postgraduate phase.[61] The third is to encourage credit accumulation and transfer systems (ECTS) and, fourthly, to adopt quality assurance processes.[62] This whole process is taken forward by a series of follow-up groups meeting to discuss sub-themes[63] and take the process forward by agreeing aims and standards. These are brought to plenary meeting for discussion and approval, the next of which is scheduled for Bergen in May 2005.[64] National Ministries, taking their cue from this process, introduce changes to national law to achieve the aims of the Sorbonne Bologna process. For an example from the field of legal education, in higher education one can see that in most Continental countries a bachelor-level degree is being created of only three years' duration.[65] In many cases the three-year law degree does not comply with the traditional requirements for access to training for

[58] http://www.enic-naric.net.

[59] The Convention on the Recognition of Qualifications concerning Higher Education in the European Region, 1997, ETS 165, was developed by the Council of Europe and UNESCO; http://conventions.coe.int/. See n 152 below and accompanying text for further details.

[60] The Lisbon mantra, of making the Union the most dynamic, competitive, sustainable knowledge-based economy, enjoying full employment and strengthened economic and social cohesion, made this a clear object of reform in the educational sphere; COM(2002) 14 final (15 January 2002). These aims were rededicated at the Barcelona Conference 2002, and refined, with urgency, in European Commission, 'Education and Training 2010', COM(2003) 685 final (11 November 2003).

[61] A research phase has been added at the Berlin Conference. The Berlin communiqué expresses the hope that the structural alignment will have been started by all countries by 2005.

[62] A European Network for Quality Assurance (ENQA) was created recently with membership from EU states.

[63] http://www.bologna-berlin2003.de/en/bologna_seminars/conferences.htm

[64] http://www.bologna-bergen2005.no/

[65] In Italy, Belgium, and the Netherlands for example.

the legal profession(s).[66] One result of the reduction in number of years has been the creation of masters' degrees of one or two years' duration. This gives rise to an opportunity to have a common master's element across Europe, potentially.[67] For law, the topics covered could include European Union law, European human rights law, and the Brussels/Lugano Conventions, and so on. Change is in the air and, with some considerable effort, some commonality might be achieved in some of these matters at the master's level. In parallel, one can report that there are academic teams working on textbooks setting out common themes in contract and tort derived from the different national legal orders.[68] In other words, potentially, in the future, law could be taught in a non-national way across Europe, or at least in a comparative way, thus potentially facilitating cross-registration to Bars. One can see from this example the strong impact that European developments are having in the sphere of education despite its formal exclusion from the scope of the Treaty.

The changes were imposed in a top-down fashion with little or no opportunity for debate amongst those affected. In Austria professors of law even threatened strike action.[69] This is a further illustration of the break-down in openness and accountability that plagues European policy and law-making processes. Though at one level it is an 'open' process, at once informal, intergovernmental, and infra-national, it is also semi-intergovernmental and very powerful, acting to a large extent outwith both the EU and national control. It is now considered to be part of the Open Method of Coordination[70] launched

[66] In the Netherlands, e.g., see Kasteelen, M, 'Implementing the Sorbonne Bologna process at Utrecht Law School', presentation given at the Birmingham ELFA Conference, February 2003.

[67] A prospect promoted as an idea by the European Law Faculties Association (ELFA), in its position paper on the Sorbonne Bologna process; see ELFA, 'For a European Space of Legal Education', n 56 above.

[68] Generally see de Witte, B and Forder, C, *The Common Law of Europe and the Future of Legal Education* (The Hague: Kluwer, 1992), and its follow-up, Faure, M, Smits, J, and Schneider, H, *Towards a European Ius Commune in Legal Education and Research* (Antwerp: Metro, 2002); Beale, H and Lando, O (eds), *Principles of Contract Law* (2 vols) (Dordrecht, London: M Nijhoff, 2000); and van Gerven, W, Lever, J, and Larouche, P (eds), *European Tort Law—a Casebook* (Oxford: Hart, 2000). See van Gerven, W, 'A Common Framework of Reference and Teaching', *EJLE*, 1 (2004) 1.

[69] See Kasteelen, n 66 above, and Braekhus, H and Husabe, O, 'The impact of the Sorbonne Bologna Declaration on Legal Education in Norway', *EJLE* 1 (2004), 43. (The paper was presented at the Conference of the European Law Faculties Association (ELFA) in Birmingham, 2003; http://elfa.bham.ac.uk.)

[70] On the Open Method of Coordination (OMC), see: Zeitlin, J, 'Opening the Open Method of Coordination', at the Committee of the Regions Conference on *The Open Method of Coordination: Improving European Governance?*, Brussels, 30 September–1 October 2002, http://www.cor.eu.int/pdf/omc/zeitlin.pdf; Radaelli, C M, 'The Open Method of Coordination: A New Governance Architecture for the European Union?', a Preliminary Report for the

at the Lisbon Summit,[71] though the process started before March 2000. The European Commission plays an important role in the process:[72] its activities range from funding[73] and undertaking studies[74] to supporting Sorbonne Bologna Seminars, setting European benchmarks,[75] and adapting its own programmes to achieve the Sorbonne Bologna aims.[76] The Education Council has itself adopted a series of concrete objectives for educational systems.[77]

Swedish Institute for European Policy Studies, March 2003, http://www.sieps.su.se, p 8. Generally, on OMC and education, see: http://europa.eu.int/comm/education/policy_en.html. *The Detailed work programme on the follow-up of the objectives of education and training systems in Europe*, Council Document, OJ [2003] C142/1, sets out the scheme for achieving 13 key educational objectives.

[71] The Lisbon agenda is broader than the Sorbonne Bologna process which focuses on higher education, e.g., COM(2001) 501 final, where the Commission adopted a work plan to implement the educational aims set out during the Swedish presidency. European Commission, *The concrete future objectives of education systems*, COM(2001) 59 final.

[72] Witness its earlier Communications, e.g., the White Paper on education and training, *Teaching and learning—towards the learning society*, COM(95) 590 final, and *Towards a Europe of knowledge*, COM(97) 563 final.

[73] E.g., the Tuning Educational Structures project, see further n 86 below, and a series of pilot projects in the Sorbonne Bologna process, such as credit transfer, European masters, and quality assurance. See European Commission, n 48 above, p 16.

[74] European Commission, *Investing efficiently in education and training: an imperative for Europe*, COM(2002) 779 final (10 January 2003).

[75] *Communication from the Commission of 20 November 2002 on European benchmarks in education and training: follow-up to the Lisbon European Council*, COM(2002) 629 final. The Education Council in May 2003 adopted a series of five benchmarks, e.g., the goal of decreasing the number of early school leavers to under 10% and increasing the amount spent on research and development to 3% of GDP, 8430/03 (Presse 114), at http://ue.eu.int/.

[76] E.g., the Socrates programme has been adapted to support (financially) the introduction of the Diploma Supplement. See generally, European Commission, *From Prague to Berlin: the EU contribution—Progress Report*, at http://www.bologna-berlin2003.de/pdf/updated_report.pdf (1 August 2002); European Commission, *From Prague to Berlin: the EU contribution—Second Progress Report*, at http://www.bologna-berlin2003.de/pdf/Text2_KOM.pdf (12 February 2003). In 2002 it adopted an *Action Plan for Skills and Mobility*, COM(2002) 72 final, that included improving better ICT-based education systems, and increased European level quality control information. It also included a series of measures to improve occupational mobility, geographic mobility, and to improve information flows. See also European Commission, 'From Berlin to Bergen: The EU Contribution', http://www.bologna-berlin2003.de/pdf/Berlin_ Bergen.pdf 8 November 2003.

[77] *Council conclusions of 13 July 2001 on the follow-up of the report on the concrete future objectives of education and training systems*, OJ [2001] C 204/6; *Council conclusions of 14 February 2002 on the follow-up to the report on the concrete future objectives of education and training systems in view of the preparation of a joint Council/Commission report to be presented to the Spring 2002 European Council*, OJ [2002] C 58/1; http://ue.eu.int/newsroom/LoadDoc.asp?MAX = 1&BID = 92&DID = 69473&LANG = 1; *Detailed work programme of the Council on the follow-up of the objectives of education and training systems in Europe* OJ [2002] C 142/1. These follow on from the Commission's *Report from the Commission of 31 January 2001: The concrete future objectives of education systems*, COM(2001) 59 final.

These recognize the overtly cultural nature of education. For example, the Education Council in February 2001 adopted a Report in which the Council notes the principle that an important role of education is to promote the humanistic values shared by our societies. The Education Council has also considered the general aims which society attributes to education and training:

- the development of the individual, who can thus realize his or her full potential and live a good life;
- the development of society, in particular by fostering democracy, reducing the disparities and inequities among individuals and groups, and promoting cultural diversity;
- the development of the economy, by ensuring that the skills of the labour force correspond to economic and technological evolution.[78]

In May 2003 the Education Council adopted a series of five European benchmarks in education.[79]

The success of the Sorbonne Bologna process has led to an attempt to develop a similar 'Bruges' process with vocational education and training,[80] launched at the Barcelona Summit (March 2002). This will focus on transparency, recognition, quality, and guidance in vocational training, attempting to development a credit transfer scheme as well as common principles for validating non-formal learning.[81]

Another indirect impact on Member States' educational competences and control is the Commission's strategy on new labour markets. This includes removing and tackling skills barriers as well as skills gaps. The Lisbon strategy to create a new labour market by 2005 included recognition of skills acquired at work and the reinforcement of life-long learning. In an earlier White Paper[82] the main barrier was recognized, *inter alia*, as cultural. Removing barriers to mobility meant increasing researchers' mobility and educational workers' mobility. One result of the pressure to create a single labour market[83] and

[78] *Report from the Education Council to the European Council on the concrete future objectives of education and training systems* (February 2001), http://register.consilium.eu.int/pdf/en/ 01/st05/05980 en1.pdf.

[79] IP/03/620. Press release 8430/03 (Presse 114), 2503rd Council Meeting.

[80] See the draft Council Resolution on the Promotion of Enhanced European Cooperation in Vocational Education and Training (6 December 2002), Doc 14343/02.

[81] European Commission, http://europe.eu.int/comm/education/bruges/index.html.

[82] White Paper, *Teaching and learning—towards the learning society* (Luxembourg, 1996). Report from the Commission, *Implementation of the White Paper 'Teaching and learning—towards the learning society'*, COM(1999) 750 final.

[83] As opposed to the public interest aspects of education. See further n 81 above and accompanying text.

the Sorbonne Bologna process[84] is the move towards an outcomes approach in teaching and learning,[85] that is to say, looking at outputs rather than inputs when measuring the result of education or training.[86] This helps to tie in the educational and training processes to the labour market. The competency approach is also more likely to find commonality than looking at input factors such as duration of course, hours, and topics of study, etc. The EU itself has funded major studies in which cooperation and coordination in seven disciplines—chemistry, physics, business, education sciences, geology, history, and mathematics—are taking place, led by academics from Groningen and Deusto. The project is on-going and can be seen as adjacent to the Sorbonne Bologna process; it aims to bring about European convergence in the relevant subject areas, and can be viewed as a pilot scheme.[87] Creating convergence through commonly accepted outcomes[88] is not at all the same as creating a rigid, Europe-wide curriculum.

6. The free movement of educational actors

The European Community's influence on education and training in Member States is brought to bear directly through its rules on establishing the Single

[84] See above n 55 and accompanying text.

[85] Eurydice, *Key Competencies: A developing concept in general compulsory education* (2002), http://www.eurydice.org/.

[86] This trend was noticed in the tuning project: *Tuning educational structures in Europe, Final Report Phase* 1, at p 29, http://www.relint.deusto.es/TuningProject/index.htm, and, more generally, at http://europa.eu.int/comm/education/policies/educ/tuning/tuning_en.html, but also by the European Universities Association (EUA); see Rauhvargers, A and Tauch, C, *Survey on Masters Degrees and Joint Degrees in Europe* (Brussels: EUA, 2002); Bergan, S, *Report of the Conference on Qualification Structures in European Higher Education*, København, 27–28 March 2003, Council of Europe, http://www.vtu.dk/fsk/div/bologna/Koebenhavn_ Bologna_ Reprot_final.pdf.

[87] The ECTS regime, now widely adopted across Europe, started off with a small pilot of similar nature. Generally, see Adams, S, 'Credit Recognition and Transparency in Transnational Education', *European Journal of Legal Education*, 0 (2001), 35.

[88] Accountants and medics have developed competency-based approaches: see International Federation of Accountants, 'Guidance on competency-based education, http://www.ifac.org/News/LastestReleases.tmpl?NID = 1051504944143375O; and, e.g., that developed by Dr Julian Bion for intensive care medicine, at http://www.ics.ac.uk/competency.html. The latter is being extended by a Leonardo project to the EU and beyond, see CoBaTriCe under the auspices of the European Society of Intensive Care Medicine, http://www.esicm.org/. The Quality Assurance Agency has agreed benchmarks covering degree courses in the UK, http://www.qaa.ac.uk/crntwork/benchmark/benchmarking.htm.

European Market. Here a series of cases and legislation, designed to free mobility of individuals, have developed into a right of free movement for students[89] and pupils.[90] This initially was largely linked to vocational training,[91] and workers[92] and their families[93] were favoured, but over time it has become broader, covering educational provision in its wider aspects and for all Community nationals.[94] Cross-border participation in each other's education and training systems inevitably has a cultural rub-off on participants. Individuals have a right of free movement to receive education and training in other Member States,[95] particularly in relation to vocational training. The EC Single Market rules also allow cross-border movement of teachers and university professors, who, having the status of Community nationals, are entitled to move as 'workers'.[96] Community law also mandates free movement for educational courses and even institutions,[97] in principle, as they are providing educational services (Article 49 EC)[98] or establishing educational bodies (Article 43 EC). This is dealt with further below regarding transnational education.

[89] The free movement of students largely being the creation of the ECJ in Case 152/82, *Forcheri* [1983] ECR 2323, Case 293/83, *Gravier* [1985] ECR 593, and Case C-357/89, *Raulin* [1992] ECR I-1027, ultimately topped off by Directive 93/96, OJ [1993] L 317/59, Case C-85/96, *Martinez Sala* [1998] ECR I-2691, and Case C-184/99, *Rudy Grzelczyk* [2001] ECR I-6193.

[90] As the scope of the EC Treaty includes 'education' now, albeit in a restricted manner, Article 12 EC should equally apply to access to schools. As a practical matter this is unlikely to be significant, as school-age children rarely travel without parents or guardians and, if they are with their families, access to schooling is part of their rights as children of EU migrants. Moreover, one of the earliest Directives dealing with education was designed to help integrate the migrant worker's family, Directive 77/486/EEC on the education of the children of migrant workers, OJ [1977] L 199/32, though it also preserved the culture of the child by ensuring education in the home state language. See Cullen, H, 'From Migrants to Citizen? European Community Policy on Intercultural Education', *ICLQ*, 43 (1996), 109.

[91] Defined in Case 293/83, *Gravier* [1985] ECR 593, Case 24/86, *Blaizot* [1988] ECR 379, and Case 263/86, *Humbel* [1988] ECR 5365; Lonbay, n 2 above.

[92] Article 39 EC; Council Regulation 1612/68, OJ 1968 (II), Eng spec ed, p 475.

[93] Regulation 1612/68, n 91 above, Articles 10–11.

[94] *Rudy Grzelczyk*, n 29 above; Case C-7/94, *Gaal* [1995] ECR I-1031; Case C-224/98, *D'Hoop* [2002] ECR I-6191; Case C-413/99, *Baumbast R v Secretary of State for the Home Department* [2002] ECR I-7091; and pending Case C-413/01, *Franca Ninni-Orasche v Bundesminister für Wissenschaft, Verkehr und Kunst*, Opinion of Advocate General Geelhoed (27 February 2003), judgment (6 November 2003).

[95] Directive 93/96, OJ [1993] L 317/59.

[96] Case 66/85, *Lawrie Blum* [1986] ECR 2121, Case C-4/91, *Bleis* [1991] ECR I-5627, and Case 33/88, *Allué* [1989] ECR 1591.

[97] Case 147/86, *Commission v Greece* [1988] ECR 1637.

[98] Case 263/86, *Belgian State v Rene Humbel and Marie-Therese Edel* [1988] ECR 5365.

7. Transnational education

The market place created by EU rules has seen the emergence of transnational education. This is defined by the ENIC-NARIC[99] working group on Franchised Qualifications[100] as 'those programmes or courses of study, or parts of programmes or courses of study, in which students are located in a different country from the one in which the awarding and/or sponsoring institution is based'.

There are six or seven modes of provision of transnational education, ranging from branch campuses to distance learning, etc.[101] They include the mobility of students and teachers,[102] which is clearly encouraged by the flagship EU Socrates programme. The emergence of transnational educational regimes clearly signals that globalization of education is becoming an increasing reality.[103] Within the EU the Single Market rules strengthen its legality and diminish the state's capacity to resist such competition in this sensitive sector. (The process of transnational education clearly diminishes Member State autonomy and sovereignty in this sphere.[104]) Although there are advantages in terms of choice and accessibility and the internationalization of education, the disadvantages include the fear of both states and educational 'consumers' of lower standards, and worries about consumer protection and, of course, cultural 'contamination'. What if the language of instruction is non-national, for example? These worries are to some extent addressed by

[99] http://www.enic-naric.net/.

[100] This was instituted in 1997 as a UNESCO/Council of Europe ENIC/NARIC Network group; see Wilson, L and Vlasceanu, L, 'Transnational Education and Recognition of Qualifications', in *Internationalisation of Higher Education: an Institutional Perspective* (Bucharest: UNESCO-CEPES Papers on Higher Education, 2000), at p 75, also available at http://www.cepes.ro/.

[101] Kaufmann, C, 'The Recognition of Transnational Education Qualifications', Seminar on Transnational Education, Malmö, 2–3 March 2001, www.cfwb.be/infosup/Charger/chkte.pdf; Adam, S, *Transnational Education Project Report and Recommendations*, Confederation of European Union Rectors' Conferences, March 2001, http://www.crue.org/espaeuro/transnational_education_project.pdf.

[102] See generally, European Commission, *Strategies in Favour of Mobility within the European Research Area*, COM(2001) 331 final.

[103] The UNESCO-CEPES database on transnational providers reported over 140 educational programmes from 100 higher education institutions in June 2002; 'UNESCO-CEPES Database on Transnational Educational Providers—a Progress Report', Joint ENIC-NARIC Meeting, Valetta, June 2002; http://www.cepes.ro/.

[104] It is noteworthy that the 1997 Lisbon Convention provides in Article VI.5: 'Each Party may make the recognition of higher education qualifications issued by foreign educational institutions operating in its territory contingent upon specific requirements of national legislation or specific agreements concluded with the Party of origin of such institutions.'

unilateral controls and guidance issued by countries that 'export' educational services,[105] as well as the UNESCO-Council of Europe Code of Good Practice in the provision of transnational education.[106] There are also serious questions regarding how to recognize the outputs of transnational educational collaboration.[107] EC law, whilst permitting cross-border establishment of educational courses and institutions, as well as the movement of students, nevertheless also permits Member States to control such education on 'public interest' grounds.[108] These clearly include quality control.

In Greece, 74 per cent of degree courses on offer were from transnational providers.[109] This is partially the result of limited access for Greeks to home-grown higher education: only 15 per cent of applicants passed the Greek university access test.[110] It is clear that EC internal market law allows a right to provide cross-border education. Issues arising from such provision include how the results of such provision are to be accredited, how the degrees are to be recognized, what the guarantees of quality assurance are, whether Member States can prevent the use of non-national languages on such courses. In Belgium, for example, only 'official' studies authenticated by law are recognized,[111] thus no private institutions can have their diplomas recognized for academic purposes. Foreign degrees may be recognized if they are official (part of that state's national system) and the studies take place in that state. Is this compatible with internal market law? Many of the issues are outwith the EC's remit and are being tackled through OMC and, in particular, the Sorbonne Bologna process, described above. For legal studies the European

[105] E.g., the *Quality Assurance Code of Practice: Collaborative provisions* of the UK Quality Assurance Agency, http://www.qaa.ac.uk/, and *The Code of Ethical Practice in the Offshore Provision of Education and Educational Services* devised by the higher education institutions of Australia, http://www.avcc.edu.au/news/public_statements/publications/code.htm.

[106] This was adopted by the Committee of the Convention on the Recognition of Qualifications concerning Higher Education in the European Region (a creature of the 1997 Lisbon Convention) at its second meeting at Riga, 6 June 2001: http://www.cepes.ro/. See also the Recommendation on criteria and procedures for the assessment of foreign qualifications, devised by the UNESCO-CEPES Working Party on criteria and procedures for the assessment of foreign qualifications created in 1995, available on the same website.

[107] Within the Socrates programme this is tackled by the ECTS system. See generally, http://europa.eu.int/comm/education/programmes/socrates/ects_en.html.

[108] Case C-147/86, *Commission v Greece* [1988] ECR I-1637.

[109] 42% of these were from the UK. Adam, n 100 above, p 24.

[110] Machados dos Santos, S, *Introduction to Transnational Education*, http://www.esib.org/ commodification/documents/machadosdossantos.htm.

[111] One hundred and thirty providers were teaching 28,000 students. Machado, S and Kaufmann, C, 'The Recognition of Transnational Education Qualifications', paper given at the Seminar on Transnational Education, n 101 above.

Law Faculties Association (ELFA) has established a Committee to investigate and report on quality assurance, accreditation, and assessment (QUAACAS) issues.

In the *Neri* case,[112] Italian administrative practices effectively forbade the recognition of degrees awarded to Italians in Italy who had followed a course in Italy provided by the European School of Economics (ESE) and validated by an English university. Courses pursued by Italians in the UK would have been recognized only if the Italians were resident in the UK. This clearly is a breach of Article 43 EC as it renders the ESE courses in question less attractive to students.[113] However, such restrictions may be justified either if they fall within one of the exceptions specifically provided for in the Treaty, or, in so far as they apply in a non-discriminatory manner, if they serve overriding requirements relating to the public interest, are suitable for securing the attainment of the objective which they pursue, and do not go beyond what is necessary in order to attain it.[114] Italy did regulate its own private university courses and therefore a blanket non-recognition was disproportionate and thus disallowed.

8. Individual rights for educational actors

Community citizens also have a right to use the fruits of their learning elsewhere in the European Union.[115] The EU has created a system for the mutual recognition of qualifications,[116] a system currently under revision.[117] In its creation there has been a potent mix of judicial activism and legislative leapfrogging based in part on judicial rulings. Whilst respecting national

[112] Case C-153/02, *Valentina Neri v European School of Economics*, Opinion of Advocate General Jacobs, 10 April 2003, judgment 13 November 2003.

[113] Case C-55/94, *Gebhard*, n 125 below.

[114] Opinion of Advocate General Jacobs, n 112 above, at para 46.

[115] Case 222/86, *Union Nationale des Entraineurs et Cadres Techniques Professionels du Football v Heylens* [1987] ECR 4097; Case C-19/92, *Kraus* [1993] ECR I-663; Case C-340/79, *Vlassopoulou* [1991] ECR I-2357, cf. *Belgian Linguistics case* at n 22 above.

[116] Schneider, H, *Die Anerkennung von Diplomen in der Europäischen Gemeinschaft* (Antwerp, Baden-Baden: Maklu/Nomos, 1995); Lonbay, J, 'The Mutual Recognition of Professional Qualifications in the EC', in Hodgin, R (ed), *Professional Liability Law and Insurance*, 2nd edn (London: LLP, 1999), p 1; Pertek, J, *La reconnaissance des qualifications dans un espace européen des formations et des profesions* (Brussels: Bruylant, 1998).

[117] Proposal for a Directive of the European Parliament and of the Council on the recognition of professional qualifications, COM(2002) 119 (7 March 2002), OJ [2002] C 181/183. See generally http://elixir.bham.ac.uk/.

patterns and impositions in relation to the content of education in accordance with Articles 149 and 150 EC, Member States must nonetheless for professional purposes recognize an individual's qualifications, knowledge, and experience, as far as possible.

9. Indirect impact through the educational requirements of regulated professions

It is clear that Member States, in the absence of harmonization of national rules regulating access to the professions, retain the right to control access to their professions as they see fit.[118] This is reinforced by Article 47(2) EC, which requires a unanimous vote by Member States for any Directive which would involve amendment in any Member State of principles 'laid down by law governing the professions with respect to training and conditions of access for natural persons'.[119] However, the exercise of these regulatory powers must respect the freedoms granted by Articles 43 and 49 EC (freedom to provide services) and must not undermine the mutual recognition Directives or other requirements of Community law.[120]

Articles 39 and 43 EC may be used by Community citizens as another route of entry to professions in cases where the Directives on mutual recognition cannot be applied. In the *Vlassopoulou* case,[121] which arose before Directive 89/48/EEC[122] was in force, a 'qualified lawyer' from Greece (*dikigoros*) applied to join the German Bar. The German Bar rejected her application as

[118] Case C-61/89, *Bouchoucha* [1990] ECR I-3551; Joined Cases 193/97 and 194/97, *De Castra Freitas and Escallier* [1998] ECR I-6747; Case C-108/96, *Macquen* [2001] ECR I-837.

[119] Moreover, Articles 149 EC and 150 EC specifically exclude any harmonization of laws and regulations of Member States dealing with the content of education and training, 'respecting the responsibility of the Member States for the content of teaching and the organisation of educational systems' and 'vocational training'.

[120] Case C-58/98, *Josef Corsten* [2000] ECR I-7919.

[121] Case C-340/89, *Vlassopoulou* [1991] ECR I-2357 and Case C-238/98, *Hocsman* [2000] ECR I-6623.

[122] Directive 2001/19/EC of the European Parliament and of the Council of 14 May 2001 amending Council Directives 89/48/EEC and 92/51/EEC on the general system for the recognition of professional qualifications and Council Directives 77/452/EEC, 77/453/EEC, 78/686/EEC, 78/687/EEC, 78/1026/EEC, 78/1027/EEC, 80/154/EEC, 80/155/EEC, 85/384/EEC, 85/432/EEC, 85/433/EEC, and 93/16/EEC concerning the professions of nurse responsible for general care, dental practitioner, veterinary surgeon, midwife, architect, pharmacist, and doctor, OJ [2001] L 206/1.

she did not have the relevant German qualifications. However, the ECJ indicated, applying Article 43 EC (ex 52 EEC), that her abilities and knowledge all had to be taken into account in assessing her application. The German Bar could not simply reject her. They had to assess her, find out what knowledge or abilities were missing, and could then evaluate her (by test or otherwise) on those missing areas alone.[123] This was a 'finished product' case,[124] but it established that the Treaty itself, by Article 43 EC, gave migrants a right to have their qualifications assessed, if they come from a relevant profession.

The *Gebhard* case[125] reinforces the *Vlassopoulou* ruling, indicating that the right of establishment granted to individuals by Article 43 EC requires host state competent authorities to assess knowledge and qualifications.[126] As the ECJ stated at paras 36–37:

> Where the taking-up or pursuit of a specific activity is subject to such conditions in the host Member State, a national of another Member State intending to pursue that activity must in principle comply with them. It is for this reason that Article 57 [now 47] provides that the Council is to issue directives, such as Directive 89/48, for the mutual recognition of diplomas, certificates and other evidence of formal qualifications or, as the case may be, for the coordination of national provisions concerning the taking-up and pursuit of activities as self-employed persons.
>
> It follows, however, from the Court's case law that national measures liable to hinder or make less attractive the exercise of fundamental freedoms guaranteed by the Treaty must fulfil four conditions: they must be applied in a non-discriminatory manner; they must be justified by imperative requirements in the general interest; they must be suitable for securing the attainment of the objective which they pursue; and they must not go beyond what is necessary in order to attain it (see Case C-19/92, *Kraus v Land Baden-Wuerttemberg* [1993] ECR I-1663, para 32).

In para 38 of the *Gebhard* decision the ECJ continued, citing *Vlassopoulou* and *Thieffrey*:

> . . . in applying their national provisions, Member States may not ignore the knowledge and qualifications already acquired by the person concerned in another Member State . . . they must take account of the equivalence of diplomas . . . and if necessary

[123] Followed in Case C-319/92, *Salomone Haim v Kassenzahnärztliche Vereinigung Nordrhein* [1994] ECR I-425 (known as Haim I).

[124] This principle was used in *Haim* I, n 123 above—a dentistry Directive case—showing that it is applicable even to professions covered by Directives. See also *Hocsman*, n 121 above, and Case C-31/00, *Conseil National de l'Ordre des Architectes v Nicholas Dreesen* [2002] ECR I-663.

[125] Case C-55/94, *Reinhard Gebhard v Consiglio Dell'Ordine Degli Avvocati e Procuratori di Milano* [1995] ECR I-4165.

[126] This case, too, involved a 'finished product'.

proceed to a comparison of knowledge and qualifications required by their national rules and those of the person concerned.

Thus, obligations contained in Article 43 EC certainly include the requirement to evaluate the professional qualifications of a migrant professional.[127] This case law has recently been reinforced. In the *Hocsman* case[128] the ECJ stated that:

> . . . Article 52 of the EC Treaty (now, after amendment, Article 43 EC) is to be interpreted as meaning that where, in a situation not regulated by a directive on mutual recognition of diplomas, a Community national applies for authorisation to practise a profession access to which depends, under national law, on the possession of a diploma or professional qualification, or on periods of practical experience, the competent authorities of the Member State concerned must take into consideration all the diplomas, certificates and other evidence of formal qualifications of the person concerned and his relevant experience, by comparing the specialised knowledge and abilities certified by those diplomas and that experience with the knowledge and qualifications required by the national rules.

The case was followed in *Dreesen*.[129] Here the issue was whether the competent authority could '*Vlassopoulou* assess' Dreesen, using Article 43 EC, when there was a Directive in the field which he was not covered by. The ECJ stated, at para 27:

> It follows that Member States must comply with their obligations as regards mutual recognition of professional qualifications arising from the Court's interpretation of Articles 43 EC and 47 EC (see, in particular, Vlassopoulou, Haim and Hocsman), in examining any application for authorisation to practise a profession, access to which depends, under national legislation, on the possession of a diploma or professional qualification or on periods of practical experience, where the diploma held by the Community national is not the subject of automatic recognition under a directive on the mutual recognition of diplomas, even if such a directive has been adopted in the professional field in question.

The existence of a mutual recognition Directive which covers a particular profession would not prevent the operation of Article 43 EC where such a Directive, in fact, did not operate in a particular case.[130] Under the general mutual recognition Directives and under Article 43 EC the host state competent

[127] *Vlassopoulou*, n 121 above; Case C-31/00, *Dreesen*, n 124 above.

[128] *Hocsman*, n 121 above.

[129] *Dreesen*, n 124 above.

[130] Case C-232/99, *Commission v Spain* [2002] ECR I-4235, at paras 22 and 25. Cf. Case C-234/97, *Teresa Fernández de Bobadilla v Museo Nacional del Prado, Comité de Empresa del Museo Nacional del Prado and Ministerio Fiscal* [1999] ECR 4773.

authority should compare the migrant's knowledge and skills with those required for the exercise of the relevant host profession.[131] All the migrant's knowledge and experience should be assessed, in the light of national requirements for the exercise of the profession.[132] As a result of the case law cited above, a similar requirement would flow in cases of migrant professionals not covered by a Directive. Thus, on the face of it, it would appear that a migrant is entitled to have his qualifications and experience assessed under Article 43 EC and compared to the host state's knowledge and qualification requirements for the equivalent profession.

It is clear that Member States retain autonomy, in the absence of EC law,[133] in designating what professions are, and their powers to determine their spheres of activity, reserved powers, and modes of entry.[134] EC law requires proper consideration of migrants falling outwith the mutual recognition Directives, and the case law to date has dealt with migrants who were in fact pursuing equivalent professions: thus in *Haim I*,[135] *Vlassopoulou*, *Hocsman*, and *Dreesen*, the applicants were all members of an equivalent regulated profession.[136]

There is an institutional dissonance and dis-balance of cultural inputs here. Directive 89/48/EEC provides no real definition of what is an equivalent profession, referring in Article 3 simply to the 'profession in question'. Article 4 of Directive 89/48/EEC, which deals with compensation measures, makes it clear that the professions would not always completely overlap, as it talks of 'substantial differences' in the diplomas. Article 4(b) of Directive 89/48/EEC

[131] Article 1(g) of Directive 89/48/EEC requires: '... In order to permit this test to be carried out, the competent authorities shall draw up a list of subjects which, on the basis of a comparison of the education and training required in the Member State and that received by the applicant, are not covered by the diploma or other evidence of formal qualifications possessed by the applicant.'

[132] Case C-110/01, *Malika Tennah-Durez*, Opinion AG Jacobs (6 June 2002). This case concerned a doctor who had undertaken over 12 years of training and professional activity, and was decided on 19 June 2003.

[133] EC law crops up in many guises, thus a requirement of educational qualifications to join a profession is affected by European competition law; see, Commission Communication, *Report on Competition in Professional Services of* 9 February 2004, COM (2004) 83 final (available at http://europa.eu.int/eur-lex/en/com/cnc/2004/com2004_0083en01.pdf). A parallel Commission Communication on the competitiveness of business-related services and their contribution to the performance of European enterprises of 4 December 2004, COM(2003) 747 final (available at http://europa.eu.int/eur-lex/en/com/cnc/2003/com2003_0747en01.pdf), supports the draft Directive on Services in the Internal Market, which itself is seeking to eliminate 'entry barriers'; COM(2004) 2 final/3.

[134] *Macquen*, n 118 above and related text. Case C-294/00, *Deutsche Paracelsus Schulen für Naturheilverfahren GmbH v Kurt Gräbner* [2002] ECR I-6515.

[135] *Haim I*, n 123 above.

[136] In any event they are entitled to full reasons and a right of appeal; Case 222/86, *UNECTEF v Heylens* [1987] ECR 4097.

allows the competent authority of the Member State to insist that the incoming professional:

> complete an adaptation period not exceeding three years or take an aptitude test:
>
> —where the matters covered by the education and training he has received as laid down in Article 3(a) and (b), differ substantially from those covered by the diploma required in the host Member State, or
>
> —where, in the case referred to in Article 3(a), the profession regulated in the host Member State comprises one or more regulated professional activities which are not in the profession regulated in the Member State from which the applicant originates or comes and that difference corresponds to specific education and training required in the host Member State and covers matters which differ substantially from those covered by the diploma adduced by the applicant, or
>
> —where, in the case referred to in Article 3(b), the profession regulated in the host Member State comprises one or more regulated professional activities which are not in the profession pursued by the applicant in the Member State from which he originates or comes, and that difference corresponds to specific education and training required in the host Member State and covers matters which differ substantially from those covered by the evidence of formal qualifications adduced by the applicant.
>
> If the host Member State intends to require the applicant to complete an adaptation period or take an aptitude test, it must first examine whether the knowledge acquired by the applicant in the course of his professional experience is such that it fully or partly covers the substantial difference referred to in the first subparagraph.[137]
>
> Should the host Member State make use of this possibility, it must give the applicant the right to choose between an adaptation period and an aptitude test. By way of derogation from this principle, for professions whose practise requires precise knowledge of national law and in respect of which the provision of advice and/or assistance concerning national law is an essential and constant aspect of the professional activity, the host Member State may stipulate either an adaptation period or an aptitude test. . . .

So it is clear from this that professions that 'underlap' can have 'missing parts' compensated by the Article 4 compensation measures as, for example, in the case of solicitors in England and Wales by an aptitude test, the Qualified Lawyers Transfer Test (QLTT). But this principle cannot be extended too far. If there is a minor element missing it can work, but if the 'mores' or activities, or modes of practice of the professions are too far apart, or, put alternatively, if they only overlap but a little, then it would not be reasonable to allow rights of entry through the Directive or Article 43 EC mechanisms. This conclusion is bolstered by the draft, revised, and consolidating mutual recognition

[137] Inserted by Directive 2001/19/EC, OJ [2001] L 206/1.

'Proposal for a Directive of the European Parliament and of the Council on the recognition of professional qualifications'.[138]

Article 4 of the proposed Directive gives additional insight into what is the same profession by defining it in para 2:

Article 4 Effects of recognition

1. The recognition of professional qualifications by the host Member State allows the beneficiary to gain access in that Member State to the same profession to [*sic*] that for which he is qualified in the home Member State and to practise it in the host Member State with the same rights as its nationals.
2. For the purposes of this Directive, the profession which the applicant wishes to pursue in the host Member State is the same as that for which he is qualified in his home Member State if the activities covered are similar.

This definition of what is the 'same' profession gives a functional test: are the activities similar? However, there are limits to this general principle. Article 4(3) states:

3. Where the profession for which the applicant is qualified in the home Member State constitutes an autonomous activity a profession covering a wider field of activities in the host Member State and where the difference cannot be made up by a compensatory measure referred to in Article 14, the recognition of the applicant's qualifications gives him access to that activity alone in the host Member State.

Thus, if the professions are not too far apart, compensation measures can be applied and the migrant, if successful, can join the host state profession. If they are too far apart then the migrant will be permitted to practise as a home state professional only, with access to the reserved activity in question.[139] This principle is followed in the draft revised Directive, currently under consideration in the decision-making process, and it is reflected in Article 14 that deals with compensation measures:

Article 14 Compensation measures

1. Article 13 does not preclude the host Member State from requiring the applicant to complete an adaptation period of up to three years or to take an aptitude test if:
   (a) the duration of the training of which he provides evidence under the terms of Article 13, paragraph 1 or 2, is at least one year shorter than that required by the host Member State;

[138] Proposal for a Directive of the European Parliament and of the Council on the recognition of professional qualifications, COM(2002) 119 final (7 March 2002). This is currently still in draft and being amended in the EC's decision-making process. The text cited is from this COM doc.

[139] If this provision does not survive the legislative process, a case currently before the Court of Justice might instill it as a matter of general Community law; Case C-330/03, *Colegio de Ingenieros de Caminos, Canales y Puertos v Administración del Estado*, OJ [2003] C 226/11.

(b) the training he has received covers substantially different matters than those covered by the evidence of formal training required in the host Member State;

(c) the regulated profession in the host Member State comprises one or more regulated professional activities which do not exist in the corresponding profession in the applicant's home Member State within the meaning of Article 4(2), and that difference consists in specific training which is required in the host Member State and which covers substantially different matters from those covered by the applicant's attestation of competence or evidence of formal training.

2. If the host Member State makes use of the option provided for in paragraph 1, it must offer the applicant the choice between an adaptation period and an aptitude test. Where a Member State considers, with respect to a given profession, that it is necessary to derogate from the requirement, set out in the previous subparagraph, that it give the applicant a choice between an adaptation period and an aptitude test, it shall inform the other Member States and the Commission in advance and provide sufficient justification for the derogation.

   If, after receiving all necessary information, the Commission considers that the derogation referred to in the second subparagraph is inappropriate or that it is not in accordance with Community law, it shall, within three months, ask the Member State in question to refrain from taking the envisaged measure. In the absence of a response from the Commission within the above-mentioned deadline, the derogation may be applied.

3. For the purpose of applying paragraph 1(b) and (c), 'substantially different matters' means matters of which knowledge is essential for practising the profession and with regard to which the training received by the migrant shows important differences in terms of duration or content from the training required by the host Member State.

4. Paragraph 1 shall be applied with due regard to the principle of proportionality. In particular, if the host Member State intends to require the applicant to complete an adaptation period or take an aptitude test, it must first ascertain whether the knowledge acquired by the applicant in the course of his professional experience in a Member State or in a non-member country, is of a nature to cover, in full or in part, the substantial difference referred to in paragraph 3.

Under Article 14(1)(a), (b), or (c), the home state profession would be able to impose compensation measures (as it can under Directive 89/48/EEC). Article 14(3) of the proposed Directive gives a better indication of what is meant by 'substantially different'. The definitions and tests of 'same profession' in the proposed Directive give an indication of how the European Court of Justice might interpret Article 43 EC.[140]

[140] In the famous *Vlassopoulou* case, n 121 above, the ECJ knew of the then draft Directive 89/48/EEC and this steered its interpretation of (then) Article 52 EEC (now Article 43 EC).

If the profession of the migrant is sufficiently different in scope then there could be no transmutation into a member of the host state profession for such a professional, using the Directive 89/48/EEC itself. The proposed Directive, in Article 4(3), indicates that in this situation the migrant should be allowed to pursue his activity (not bearing the professional title sought). This could bring about regulatory mayhem if adopted.

If a case can be considered as a non-Directive case then there is more latitude as regards 'compensation measures' as long as any imposition is reasonable. In *Haim I* and *Vlassopoulou*, it was clear that the competent authorities had to assess the applicants' professional experience, but that, should they have found it lacking, they could nonetheless impose additional training requirements. These must themselves be proportional, and cannot be excessive.[141]

A further non-EU input into education in the Member States has come from professional associations. The creation of a pan-European marketplace and the need to respond at a European level has led to most professional bodies organizing themselves at a European level.[142] The coordination and cooperation by professional bodies has also led to cooperation in the education sphere. This has partly come about through the necessity to implement Community Directives on mutual recognition of qualifications. This requirement meant that professional associations at the European level had to understand how each others' education and training systems operated. Having discovered this commonality—in some cases it was relatively easy to see—professional associations at the European level themselves agreed on a common regime for certain qualifications. One can see this with the engineers, for example.[143] For other professions, commonality came at the behest of the sectoral directive system.[144]

Furthermore, it is quite clear from the *Bobadilla* case,[145] which has been reinforced by the *Morgenbesser* case,[146] that the impact of Article 43 EC in opening access to Bar training, or the Bar itself, to 'semi-finished' trainee

[141] Case C-285/01, *Isabel Burbaud v Ministère de l'Emploi et de la Solidarité*, Opinion of Advocate General Stix-Hackl (12 September 2002), ruling on 9 September 2003.

[142] Cf. Lonbay, J, 'Governmental and Professional Power and Influence in Legal Education in Europe', in Becher, T (ed), *Governments and Professional Education* (The 1993 Society for Research into Higher Education Conference Proceedings), (Maidenhead: Open UP, 1993), p 76.

[143] http://www.feani.org/euring.html.

[144] The sectoral Directives on doctors, nurses, dentists, pharmacists, and other professions are all currently undergoing a consolidating reform, see n 117 above and accompanying text.

[145] Case C-234/97, *Teresa Fernández de Bobadilla v Museo Nacional del Prado, Comité de Empresa del Museo Nacional del Prado and Ministerio Fiscal* [1999] ECR 4773, noted at *ICLQ*, 50 (2001), 170.

[146] Advocate General Stix-Hackl in Case C-313/01, *Christine Valia Morgenbesser v Consiglio dell'Ordine degli avvocati di Genova* (20 March 2003), judgment 13 November 2003.

lawyers is likely to increase. Similar rules apply, *mutatis mutandis*, to other professions. In *Morgenbesser*, a case involving a French qualified law graduate seeking access to professional legal training in Italy, Advocate General Stix-Hackl in her Opinion concluded that competent authorities of Member States had a duty to assess all qualifications, including university qualifications[147] and professional experience, that a migrant held. The Court agreed, adding that these could be acquired anywhere, and had to be assessed by the competent authority itself. In the assessment itself the Court concluded that competent authorities could take into account different environments in which the education and training took place with respect to both the legal environment of the profession and its fields of activities.[148] If, in the resulting comparison, it is likely that there are missing elements, then the host state competent authority can ask the migrant to demonstrate that he or she has acquired the necessary knowledge, competence, and qualifications.[149] Member State competent authorities cannot simply require the national qualification without fully explaining why. An unreasoned and automatic refusal would be contrary to Community law.

The innovative element here could be that half-trained professionals would have a right to be assessed for access to 'final stage' training. Most systems are insufficiently flexible to cope with new entry points half way through the training process. Without some form of commonality or recognition of each others' systems, the administrative burden caused by such free movers will be considerable. Thus, the EC law pressure, arising from the cross-border rules, on domestic institutions to converge and make more transparent their training regimes is considerable and leads to cross-border cooperation and coordination efforts at an infra-national level. In the case of lawyers this is taking place within the Council of Bars and Law Societies of the European Union (CCBE) and ELFA.[150]

For the legal professions the CCBE and European Bars Federation (FBE) have both adopted resolutions on the training of lawyers,[151] and are currently in the process of reviewing their education and training to see whether a 'common platform' might be conceivable for European lawyers.[152] Factors

[147] Cf. Case C-19/92, *Kraus* [1993] ECR I-663.

[148] Advocate General Stix-Hackl, n 142 above, at para 96.

[149] Ibid., para 97.

[150] See, e.g., the guidance of the CCBE on the *Morgenbesser* case, http://www.ccbe.org/.

[151] These can be found on their websites: the CCBE website at http://www.ccbe.org/ and the FBE website at http://www.fbe.org/. See, for an introduction, Lonbay J, 'The Educational work of the CCBE and FBE', *European Journal of Legal Education*, 0 (2001), 43.

[152] COM(2002) 119. The revised and consolidating Directive envisages such agreed 'common platforms' as being a gateway to 'automatic' recognition.

leading to this review include the necessity of implementing the general diplomas Directive 89/48/EEC, including for the new accession states. Additionally, the CCBE is taking into account that at the academic stage the developments occurring in the Sorbonne Bologna process are having a serious impact on the structure of higher education across Europe, as described above.

Though European policy talks of converging and adjusting educational provision by enhancing the mobility of the 'consumers' of education, the actual creation of rules allowing a free labour market itself works backwards to impose considerable pressures on the education 'market'. Thus the very lengthy, rigid, and extensive law courses (and training) required in some countries are challenged by the fact that one can now, for example, become a *Rechtsanwalt* in Germany without completing the *Staatsexamen*.[153] Thus the labour market liberalization calls into question an educational regime that has not really been significantly altered for some time.[154] The Single Market rules indirectly help to manipulate the education sector, thus shifting the long-entrenched cultural assumptions of important professional actors. It is clear that the European Commission also intends to use competition law against what it sees as restraints of trade in professional rules.[155]

10. Academic recognition

There have been no cases yet in the sphere purely of academic recognition for admission to courses, but Article 12 EC, as interpreted in the recent citizenship cases,[156] would indicate that states, and the competent authorities within them, should lean over backwards to assess the qualifications of migrant students in their admission policies and practice. Direct or indirect discrimination based on nationality in this area would be likely to violate EC rules.

A separate but important non-EU source of law in this area is the Lisbon Convention of 1997.[157] This is a UNESCO/Council of Europe Convention that has been ratified by 22 'Bologna' states[158] and which sets out a series of principles and rules for academic recognition of qualifications that give access

[153] By virtue of the EC law on lawyers, notably by the operation of Directives 95/5/EC and 89/48/EEC, together with Article 43 EC.

[154] Reidel, J, 'The Reform of Legal Education in Germany', *European Journal of Legal Education*, 0 (2001), 3; Kohler, J, 'From Bologna to Prague—the Case of Social Sciences and Humanities' at http://www.uni-nordverbund.de/html/3pub/bologna.html (6 October 2002).

[155] See n 133. [156] See n 28 and following. [157] See n 59. [158] 1997 ETS 165.

to universities,[159] and recognition of both periods of study[160] and resultant higher education qualifications.[161] Under its provisions holders of academic qualifications of one state have a right to have access to assessment of these in another state,[162] discrimination is disallowed,[163] and the burden of proof is on the body making the assessment when qualifications are held to be inadequate, as Article VI(1) provides:

To the extent that a recognition decision is based on the knowledge and skills certified by the higher education qualification, each Party shall recognize the higher education qualifications conferred in another Party, unless a substantial difference can be shown between the qualification for which recognition is sought and the corresponding qualification in the Party in which recognition is sought.

The Lisbon Convention also contains a series of information[164] and transparency provisions,[165] including provisions relating to the Diploma Supplement.[166] The Berlin communiqué[167] indicates that Diploma Supplements should be issued in a 'widely spoken' European language and be available free to all graduating students from 2005.

11. Conclusions

The EC Single European Market rules have helped to open the Member States' educational arenas as a marketplace. The EC has granted cross-border access to education provision for students, by encouraging and granting rights of mobility to educational actors, both teachers and students, as well as educational institutions and/or their educational programmes themselves. It has regulated the recognition of professional qualifications, pursuing the goals of a mobile, skilled, and educated labour force. It has also facilitated transnational provision of education and recognized the commercial elements in education.

[159] Article IV. See also the *Recommendation on international access qualifications*, adopted at the First Meeting of the Committee of the Lisbon Convention on the Recognition of Qualifications Concerning Higher Education in the European Region, Vilnius, 16 June 1999.

[160] Article V. [161] Article VI. [162] Article III(1). [163] Article III(2).

[164] Article III(4) and Articles VIII and IX.

[165] Article III(2) states: 'Each Party shall ensure that the procedures and criteria used in the assessment and recognition of qualifications are transparent, coherent and reliable.'

[166] Article IX(3). The Diploma Supplement was developed by the Council of Europe, EC Commission, and UNESCO. It is essentially an extended description of qualifications that sets out the context in which a qualification is awarded. [167] See n 57 above.

The EC has additionally had a very strong indirect effect on the content of education and training. The mutual recognition mechanisms have in fact caused professional bodies, in their European groupings,[168] to compare notes and start to draw together their education and training commonalities. The comparative examination of qualifications and knowledge, skills and competence, all further cross-cultural understanding of how professions operate and make clearer the similarities (and differences) in their educational and training regimes. This increases mutual trust and cooperation. The co-coordinator system established by the general mutual recognition Directives also helps to promote this transparency in a horizontal fashion.[169] It is clear, therefore, that the Community has in fact had a major impact on the education and training provisions of Member States. This ranges from professions and governments implementing the mutual recognition Directives, to improving procedures for receiving migrant professionals, both processes requiring an understanding of the migrants' educational baggage, to educational institutions providing cross-border services.

The EC has also promoted a European dimension to national curricula, in particular by funding research and integrative policies, by developing educational resources, and also by using OMC methods. But the lack of true citizens and a true identity to promote has left it floundering somewhat in terms of 'inculcating values', and the EU is in any event forcibly excluded from harmonizing or dealing with the content of education directly.

Moreover, control over the resulting need for cooperation in the field of accreditation, quality assurance, and assessment etc., is not to be found at the EU level. The European Council, and to some extent the Commission, has exhorted all sorts of ambitious actions, but Member States and international and infra-national bodies control parts of the process that is now quite rapidly developing and shaping the evolving standards. Non-EU bodies—the Council of Europe, UNESCO-CEPES—control part of the process. Non-EU law is applicable in parts, such as the Lisbon Convention. Non-governmental organizations, universities, students, and professional bodies all have inputs into the process.

The downside of this is that the processes of change in these fields are seemingly devoid of European level, political, and administrative scrutiny. Moreover, because they occur at an infra-national, occasionally intergovernmental, level they are subject to only weak domestic political controls. As a result, some rapid changes can take those involved by surprise. Not all

[168] E.g., the CCBE: http://www.ccbe.org.

[169] See Lonbay, n 116 above.

constituencies are necessarily formally involved in the emergence of new standards that takes place outside the normal national/European decision-making processes, outwith even the pillar structure of the European Union. This seems to be a somewhat ironic result given that Member States refused EC competence precisely in order to protect their sovereignty and cultural diversity. Of course, the soft informal processes are subject to the national veto of non-action.

A side-effect of the EC rules, combined with the activities of non-EC actors in this sphere, has been the emergence of pan-European groups through which a considerable increase in cooperation, exchange of knowledge, and cross-border mobility takes place. As a result of all these activities there is a growing level of mutual trust and the beginnings of the creation of European identity in a real and concrete way. Thus, paradoxically, a key EC aim is fulfilled by the EC itself not being allowed to take, and not taking, action. One can truly say that education is playing its part at the European level in creating a closer union of the peoples of Europe, with all their cultural baggage.

Part IV

Culture, Identity, and European Integration

9

Article 151 EC and European Identity

*Rachael Craufurd Smith**

1. Introduction

The references in Article 151 of the EC Treaty to the 'common cultural heritage', the 'culture and history of the European peoples', and to 'cultural heritage of European significance', lend support to the view that one of the rationales for the Article was to increase popular identification with a distinct geographical or cultural area, namely 'Europe', in order to foster support for a political entity, the European Union. As we have seen in Chapter 2, the belief that culture is capable of playing this integrative role dates back to the Tindemans and Adonnino Reports, and finds reflection in many recent official Community documents.[1] The Council's 2002 resolution on the role of culture in the development of the European Union, for example, states that 'the common dimensions and mutual knowledge of cultures in Europe, in a society based on freedom, democracy, solidarity and respect for diversity, are essential components of citizens' support for, and participation in, European integration'.[2] If Article 151 is interpreted as authorizing measures designed to promote European integration then this will have a significant impact on the focus and direction of Community activity in the cultural field. It may also, ultimately, have an impact on national identity, and for this reason Member States are likely to monitor developments and funding in this area closely.

But is a European identity, or at least some form of identification with Europe, necessary for the survival or future development of the European Union; and what form might this identity take? The European Union may

* School of Law, University of Edinburgh. I would like to thank Sean Smith for his valued comments on this chapter.

[1] Chapter 2, above, n 4.

[2] Council Resolution of 21 January 2002 on the Role of Culture in the Development of the European Union, OJ [2002] C 032/2, recital six.

not yet fit neatly into established definitions of the state, but it encompasses a set of political institutions, has its own judicial system, and is increasingly being drawn into areas of policing and defence.[3] Most importantly from our perspective, these political institutions depend on the continuing support of European Union citizens: Member States may obstruct the Union's operations in order to appease national sentiment, even ultimately reject association with it; Treaty amendments must be approved by domestic referenda in certain countries; while the legitimacy of the European Parliament depends upon its democratic mandate. If it is the case that individuals positively identify only with those political entities which resonate in some way with their own sense of history, and that this identification is essential for popular support, then the prospects for further European integration, given Europe's cultural diversity and divided past, would appear extremely slim.[4] Absent shared traditions, symbols, even a common history, there will be little on which to forge a sense of *European* community.[5]

Although nations may be built up from below on the basis of a shared culture, they may also be the product of deliberate political fashioning.[6] If Europe has little in the way of a common culture on which to draw, a conclusion which, as the following paragraph indicates, is contested, it nevertheless

[3] For discussion of what constitutes a state, see Gellner, E, *Nations and Nationalism* (Blackwell: Oxford, 1983), p 3, and with regard to the difficulty of categorizing the European Union, Schlesinger, P, 'Europeanness: A New Cultural Battlefield?', excerpted in Hutchinson, J and Smith, A D, *Nationalism* (Oxford: Oxford University Press, 1994), pp 315–25; and Weiler, J H H, *The Constitution of Europe, 'Do the New Clothes have an Emperor?'* (Cambridge: Cambridge University Press, 1999), pp 270–8.

[4] For the importance of this resonance even in constructed nations, see Smith, A D, *Nationalism and Modernism* (Routledge: London, 1998), p 129. David Miller suggests that national identity requires the existence of 'a community (1) constituted by shared belief and mutual commitment, (2) extended in history, (3) active in character, (4) connected to a particular territory, and (5) marked off from other communities by its distinct public culture': Miller, D, *On Nationality* (Oxford: Oxford University Press, 1995), p 27.

[5] For a sceptical approach to the existence of a common European culture, see Karnoouh, C, 'Europe: Common Heritage and Differences', in Council of Europe, *Forward Planning: The Function of Cultural Heritage in a Changing Europe*, p 29, at http://www.coe.int/T/E/Cultural_Co-operation/Heritage/Resources/ECC-PAT(2001)161.pdf.

[6] Gellner, E, above n 3, at pp 48–9, argues that this fashioning sometimes draws on pre-existing cultures, sometimes invents them, and often obliterates them. Lars-Erik Cederman helpfully identifies four theoretical approaches to the role of culture and politics in the formation of identity: ethnonationalism, pannationalism, bounded integration, and postnationalism. These vary in the extent to which identity is considered to be a product of pre-existing social and cultural factors or a deliberate construction: Cederman, L-E, 'Political Boundaries and Identity Trade-Offs', in Cederman, L-E (ed), *Constructing Europe's Identity, The External Dimension* (London: Lynne Rienner, 2001).

embraces a rich repository of traditions on which a sense of identity could possibly be founded. In seeking to 'nation build' in this way the Union faces, however, a central difficulty: to select symbols or traditions from any one Member State entails rejecting those from other Member States. Political realities preclude such a deliberate process of selection in the European Union context. It is pertinent that the architectural designs on the euro notes are abstract, and do not depict specific buildings located in a given country.[7]

The possibilities may not, however, be as limited as the foregoing discussion suggests. There are a number of shared cultural values or practices on which a specifically European identity might be constructed, obviating the need to prefer one country's cultural heritage over that of another. As Paul Kearns notes in the concluding chapter of this volume, distinct European traits can be identified. In the arts, for example, 'European classical composers have always written to common rules of structure and harmony; European playwrights have regularly drawn on Greek drama; there have always been distinctively European visual-artistic canons'.[8] Similarly, Anthony Smith points to a common European cultural heritage centred on 'Roman law, Judeo-Christian ethics, Renaissance humanism and individualism, Enlightenment rationalism and science, artistic classicism and romanticism, and above all, traditions of civil rights and democracy'.[9] The European Union is, however, restricted in its ability to construct an 'imagined community' on the basis of this common culture, in that it has limited influence over the mass media or state education systems, disseminators of culture which the Member States continue to guard carefully.[10] Community cultural policy can nevertheless play a role in the dissemination of such ideas by promoting individual access to cultural initiatives that emphasize this shared intellectual patrimony.

The term 'culture' is here given a broad reading to embrace not only concrete manifestations of the past—archaeological sites, art, furniture or clothing, etc.—but also the ideas and values which animate a particular society. In consequence, the phrase 'common cultural heritage' in Article 151(1) could be interpreted as covering certain political aspirations, given that there undoubtedly exist distinct political *values* that are currently recognized as fundamental by the Member States and the European Union.[11] These values

[7] Though the euro coins do allow for national references.

[8] See below, Chapter 13, at text accompanying n 24.

[9] Smith, A D, *National Identity* (Harmondsworth: Penguin, 1991), p 11.

[10] On the role of the print media in forging identity, see Anderson, B, *Imagined Communities* (London: Verso, 1991).

[11] Though arguably not for those who see a radical disjunction between culture and politics, on which see Eagleton, T, *The Idea of Culture* (Oxford: Blackwell, 2000), p 21.

include respect for democracy, fundamental rights, and the rule of law, values which find affirmation in the case law of the Court of Justice, in the preamble to and Article 6 of the Treaty on European Union, and, most recently, in the European Union Charter of Fundamental Rights.

Some support for this interpretation of Article 151 may be gleaned from the fifth paragraph of the preamble to Decision 508/2000/EC establishing the Culture 2000 programme.[12] This provides '[i]f citizens give their full support to, and participate fully in, European integration, greater emphasis should be placed on their common cultural values and roots as a key element of their identity and their membership of a society founded on freedom, democracy, tolerance and solidarity.' Similarly, in the introduction to the Commission's 1987 Communication on *A Fresh Boost for Culture*, Europe's cultural identity was said to be 'nothing less than a shared pluralistic humanism based on democracy, justice and freedom'.[13]

Parallel issues have recently been considered within the auspices of the Council of Europe, which is called on in Article 1 of its statute to protect and promote 'the ideals and principles' that constitute the 'common heritage' of its members. Peter Wagner has advocated that the Council should move away from what he considers to be a de-politicized understanding of the term 'cultural heritage', one which embraces merely the 'preservation (and techniques for the preservation) of monuments (objects) and practices associated with national traditions'. Instead he argues that the Council should seek to 'redefine "cultural heritage" as part of a project to establish a common European identity through and in a variety of themes/issues and policy fields . . . the political approach shifts the *meaning and significance* of the Council's heritage work to include "human rights"'.[14]

Though culture has been used for political ends from the very origins of human society, it is questionable whether it should be so used today. Indeed, this instrumental use of culture is not without some risk to the European polity. Attempts to include a reference to Christianity in the preamble to the draft European Constitution caused heated opposition from secular and other religious groups. The text adopted in June 2003 by the European Convention

[12] European Parliament and Council, *Decision No 508/2000/EC Establishing the Culture 2000 Programme*, OJ [2000] L 63/1.

[13] Foreword by Carlo Ripa de Meana to European Commission, *A Fresh Boost For Culture in the European Community*, (1987) 20 *Bull EC*, supp 4/87, at p 5.

[14] As Claude Karnoouh has noted, '[t]hough it bears the same name, Europe no longer has much in common factually, existentially or phenomenologically with the Europe of a thousand years ago or less. It is a new entity, with a new history and a new view of its origins and hence of its heritage': see above n 5, at p 35.

was less divisive, stating that it drew its inspiration from 'the cultural, religious and humanist inheritance of Europe'.[15] To identify certain cultural manifestations as 'common' to all Europeans may block out, or minimize, the counter-currents and forces which have opposed them in the past. The English common law, for example, drew not only on Roman law but also on Islamic and earlier chthonic legal traditions;[16] Enlightenment rationalism often foundered in the face of religious conviction; while civil rights and democracy have, over the span of European history, been honoured more in the breach than in the observance. Moreover, the representation of these values as part of our *present* culture suggests a concrete realization too often belied by continuing intolerance and human rights abuses.

Even if an awareness of these cultural trends can help us to understand many aspects of modern European society, the insights they offer are only partial. Culturally, Europe is now much more diverse as a result of immigration and world trade, and with future rounds of enlargement this will become even more marked. A sense of commitment to the European Union is unlikely to be forged, at least for many of Europe's inhabitants—particularly, one might guess, among the young—through a backward-looking focus on specific artistic movements or intellectual trends. Such a focus is potentially alienating, if not divisive.

For Joseph Weiler, the Union's political institutions move into dangerous territory when they attempt to forge a sense of European identity. Weiler reminds us that the European Communities were built on the ruins left by the Second World War and argues that the role of the European Union should be to overcome and contain national allegiances, rather than seek to replicate them at a higher level: 'the conceptualization of a European demos should not be based on real or imaginary trans-European cultural affinities of shared histories nor on the construction of a European "national" myth of the type which constitutes the identity of the organic nation'.[17] Instead, he argues for the creation of a distinct and separate form of identification, founded on 'European transnational affinities to shared values which transcend the ethno-national diversity'.[18] Though, as we have noted above, these transnational affinities may themselves be considered cultural, for Weiler their normative

[15] Draft Treaty Establishing a Constitution for Europe, CONV 850/03 of 18 July 2003, available at http://european-convention.eu.int/docs/Treaty/cv00850.en03.pdf.

[16] Glenn, H P, *Legal Traditions of the World* (Oxford: Oxford, 2000), ch 7.

[17] Weiler, above n 3, p 344.

[18] Ibid., p 346 *et seq*. Jürgen Habermas has also advocated a form of 'constitutional patriotism', founded on a common allegiance to human rights and constitutional principles: 'Citizenship and National Identity: Some Reflections on the Future of Europe', *Praxis International*, 12 (1992–3), 1.

quality stems from the nature of the values they espouse, and is not dependent on whether they were widely respected in the past or find reflection in modern-day Europe.

Ultimately, a history of common traditions and symbols may not be crucial for the development of political identity. Rather than looking backwards to a questionable shared past, identification with the European Union may instead be forged through a forward-looking emphasis on common goals, the existence of a 'common space' within which individuals and goods can circulate freely, and the need to act together to respond to shared economic, security, and environmental challenges.[19] *Legitimacy*, rather than identification, may be derived from the nature of the European Union's objectives—the preservation of peace among its Member States, the establishment of a pan-European market economy, a high level of environmental protection, social justice, and equality, etc.—and from the way in which these objectives are implemented in practice.

Such an approach could, if required, be supported by a limited number of distinct Community events or symbols, freed from nostalgia for the past, of the sort which we see today. One can here point to Europe Day, the EU flag, and the Ode to Joy anthem.[20] Though such European initiatives may elicit as much amusement as a sense of identification, parallels may nevertheless be drawn with the institutionalization of the French Republic in the aftermath of the French Revolution.[21] Anything historical that was likely to be divisive was avoided and only a few symbols were introduced, such as the tricolour, the 'Marsellaise', and Marianne. It is arguable that, over time, these symbols have made up in potency what they lack in number.

Historical parallels have their weaknesses, however, in that French state symbolism was backed by powerful manifestations of state organization and authority in the everyday lives of French men and women. Symbols here served to represent, as a form of shorthand, something which was concrete and largely understood. Though the European Community has undoubtedly had an enormous impact on the lives of Member State nationals— for example, outlawing discriminatory working practices and facilitating access to foreign

[19] Roche, M, 'Citizenship, Popular Culture and Europe', in Stevenson, N (ed), *Culture and Citizenship* (London: Sage, 2001), p 74. Roche recognizes that Community cultural policies in, for example, the fields of tourism and sport can have a significant impact on individual identity.

[20] With the consent of the Council of Europe, the European Community adopted the same blue flag with gold stars from 1986. Shared use emphasizes the common European focus of the two institutions, but may also lead to confusion as to their respective roles.

[21] Hobsbawm, E, 'Mass-Producing Traditions: Europe, 1870–1914', in Hobsbawm, E and Ranger, T (eds), *The Invention of Tradition* (Cambridge: Cambridge University Press, 1983).

goods and services—the European provenance of these developments has frequently been hidden. This is a result not only of deliberate government obfuscation, but also of a system of Community law which requires directives to be implemented using domestic legislation. Those measures which have been labelled 'European' in the press have frequently been of the ridiculous 'bent cucumber' variety. Absent responsible coverage in the mass media (and some states clearly have a worse track record in this respect than others) or educational curriculum, the European Union enjoys a fragmented, transitory existence in the public's imagination, an existence which even the most carefully crafted symbols will do nothing to bring to life. A rather different reason for the adoption of such symbols by the Community suggests an outward- rather than inward-looking strand to Community cultural policy. To date, European identity has been considered from the perspective of the European citizen, but the introduction of quasi-state symbolism—a flag, an anthem, etc.—may render the Community an identifiable political unit to the outside world.

Certain provisions in Article 151 are consequently particularly pertinent to the question of European identity and are considered in more detail below. The often vague or oblique use of language reinforces the suspicion that contentious issues were recognized but left largely unresolved. From this perspective, Article 151 is far from marginal in that, along with the Treaty provisions on citizenship, it poses fundamental questions about the political nature and future direction of the European Community.

2. Article 151 as the basis for promoting a European identity

(a) Bringing the common cultural heritage to the fore: Article 151(1)

Much of the previous discussion regarding the relationship between culture and European identity is directly relevant to the reference to 'common culture' in Article 151 and will not be repeated here. To the extent, however, that the Member States can be said to share a common culture, be it an allegiance to certain political and spiritual values, or the existence of certain musical, artistic, or literary traditions, then Article 151(1) calls on the Community to promote it. Before proceeding further it is necessary to consider the relevance of the word 'common' in this context. Apart from the sense of 'vulgar' or 'popular', the term can be understood as meaning 'occurring often', or 'shared by . . . more than one', or 'belonging to . . . or affecting, the whole community or the public'.[22] It appears that the Commission understands the term in the second, less demanding sense of 'shared . . . by more than one'. So, for example, the Art Nouveau Network, set up under the Culture 2000 Programme, currently links participating cities from eight EU Member States and a number of Central and Eastern European countries. The influence of art nouveau was more pronounced in certain European cities, such as Brussels, Paris, or Barcelona, than in others, and it also had an impact far beyond the borders of the present European Union, in, for example, the United States. It would seem, therefore that Europe's 'common culture' need be neither common to all the Member States, nor unique to Europe: it is sufficient that it finds reflection in a certain number of Member States. If the Commission were to adopt a more demanding approach, requiring that there be a presence in all the Member States, then the impact of Article 151(1) would be greatly diminished, particularly as the European Union expands to take in new members.

But clearly, many cultural manifestations will not be 'common' even in the more expansive sense identified above, in that an important function of culture is to differentiate one group from another. This may explain why one of the Community's stated aspirations for its cultural policy is to foster 'unity in diversity'.[23] This somewhat perplexing phrase would appear to constitute an injunction to the citizens of the Member States to stand together *despite* their cultural diversity.[24] The term 'common cultural heritage' may push this idea one stage further, by suggesting that all of Europe's cultural heritage is the common patrimony of its citizens. The common cultural heritage is not merely a collection of diverse cultural manifestations—'your' culture and 'my' culture—but 'your' culture is also presented as being in some way now also 'my' culture.

Reclassification in this sense does not seek to obliterate or marginalize certain cultural forms in the search for European identity; instead it universalizes culture, or, more accurately, 'Europeanizes' it. In such a context the only intelligible boundary that can be drawn is a geographic one, one that delimits the European Union from the rest of the world.[25] But it is far from clear why a

[22] Allen, R E (ed), *Concise Oxford Dictionary of Current English*, 8th edn (Oxford: Oxford University Press, 1990).

[23] See discussion of this idea in Collins, R, *Broadcasting and Audio-visual Policy in the European Single Market* (London: John Libbey, 1994), at p 46.

[24] It is also understood in the sense of 'unity and diversity', suggesting that the Community should support and highlight those aspects of European culture which can be said to be truly common, as well as take pride in and respect those elements which are diverse.

[25] Collins, above n 23, states that if the European Community 'is culturally unified then its unity exists only at a level of generality insufficient to differentiate Europeans (or strictly citizens of the European Communities) from other major world economies'.

Scot would feel any more *European* because she eats an Italian meal or watches a Spanish bullfight on television, though she might feel in some way Italian or Spanish. Even if one were to focus on major cultural achievements, or particularly if one does so, the sense of identification remains problematic. Is it, for example, realistic to suppose that the same Scot might regard the Eiffel Tower as *European*, as opposed to or in addition to being French, and thus part of *her* common cultural patrimony? And why stop here: why should achievements such as the Eiffel Tower be considered merely of European as opposed to, say, world significance?

Though problematic for the reasons indicated, it does seem that Article 151 was intended to lay the foundations for the delimitation by the European Community of a European cultural patrimony: a common cultural heritage, of which all Europeans can be proud and, a not unimportant point, support financially.[26] Initiatives such as the 'European City of Culture' reveal how Community assistance can prove financially and culturally advantageous at the national level, while at the same time encouraging individuals to attribute to the designated cities a European significance, linking them with other cities named in the same year or in the past on a conceptual European map.[27] Such initiatives are also likely to encourage tourism and to have economic spin-offs for the cities concerned. The reference to 'common' may also indicate that there is an obligation on the Member States not only to preserve the objects in question, but also to ensure a degree of public access. A similar conclusion was reached as long ago as 1954 in the Council of Europe European Cultural Convention, which provides in Article 5 that '[e]ach Contracting Party shall regard the objects of European cultural value placed under its control as integral parts of the common cultural heritage of Europe, shall take appropriate measures to safeguard them and shall ensure reasonable access thereto'.[28]

The attempt to create a common concern for, and interest in, Europe's diverse cultural heritage is unlikely to be opposed by the Member States, but it is possible that this approach could, in certain contexts, prove rather more problematic for them. When, for example, the Commission first started to consider domestic rules designed to prevent the export of national art treasures, it suggested the abolition of the traditional concept of 'national heritage' and

[26] Building on the work already done in this area by UNESCO and the Council of Europe.

[27] See also the 'European Capital of Culture' programme, detailed in *Decision No 1419/1999/EC of the 25 May 1999, Relating to the Years 2005–2019*, OJ [1999] L 166/1.

[28] Council of Europe, European Cultural Convention of 19 December 1954, European Treaty Series No 18, available at http://conventions.coe.int/. It is noticeable that many of the phrases used in Article 151 EC and discussed in this chapter are far from new, having already featured in other international documents.

the creation of a new concept of 'Community heritage'.[29] It followed that where such works were taken from one EC country to another, the country of origin should not feel that it had been impoverished or suffered a loss. It is not, perhaps, surprising that the measures finally adopted in this area make no reference to 'Community heritage' and instead refer to '*national treasures* possessing artistic, historic or archaeological value'.[30]

(b) Improvement of the knowledge of the culture and history of the European peoples: Article 151(2)

Article 151(2) requires one to focus on a separate, though related, issue, namely *who* should be regarded as European. The Treaty itself offers no guidance as to the ambit of the highly contentious phrase 'European peoples', an ambit which varies depending on whether geographic or cultural criteria are employed.[31] From a geographical perspective, the phrase could be read as extending to any distinct social group located within the territorial boundaries of the European Union, even if small in number and fragmented across the Member States, such as the Roma people. In this latter formulation the category could consequently extend to immigrant communities originating outwith the geographic area of the European Union, from India, say, or China, however recent their settlement within its borders. It will also fluctuate over time as the borders of the European Union expand. Alternatively, the term might be understood as referring only to national groups, leading to an emphasis on those historical and cultural factors considered to be characteristic of a particular state or nation, an approach which could lead to regional or local cultures being sidelined.[32]

[29] European Commission, *Communication on Stronger Community Action in the Cultural Sector*, (1982) 15 *Bull EC*, supp 6/82, p 8.

[30] Council Directive 93/7 of 15 March 1993 on the Return of Cultural Objects Unlawfully Removed from the Territory of a Member State, OJ [1997] L 60/59, emphasis added. For detailed discussion of Community initiatives in this area, see Chapter 5 by Andrea Biondi in this volume.

[31] For wide-ranging discussion of European identity, see Jansen, T (ed), *Reflections on European Identity*, European Commission Working Paper, 1999.

[32] For Ernest Gellner the nation has both a cultural and a voluntaristic element: two men are of the same nation if and only if they share the same culture, understood as 'a system of ideas and signs and associations and ways of behaving and communicating', and if they also *recognize* each other as belonging to the same nation: above n 3, p 7. The Committee of the Regions in its *Opinion on the Kaleidoscope 2000 programme*, CdR 145/95, para 2.7, voiced its concern that the Commission unduly emphasizes national as opposed to regional or local cultures. In its subsequent *Opinion on Culture and Cultural Differences and their Significance for the Future of Europe*,

A different approach would be to read the paragraph as referring only to those social groups, whether or not primarily located within the European Union, whose culture can in some sense be said to be 'European'. This would require one to determine which social practices or beliefs are distinctively European, drawing on some form of 'common cultural heritage' along the lines discussed in the preceding section. The possibilities here are considerable and, putting to one side political objectives, it is not clear why one should be restricted to the spiritual, political, or artistic canons identified by Paul Kearns and Anthony Smith. John Gray, for example, has controversially suggested that the 'countries of the European Union share the images they all absorb from Hollywood movies more than they do any aspect of each other's cultures': perhaps, then, our common culture is an American one?[33] America has consciously used its highly successful film and television industries to further its political and economic objectives, and it is not implausible to see the promotion of a European people and a European identity as, at its most basic, just one aspect of similar political and economic aspirations on the part of the European Union.

As indicated above, this particular cultural perspective could nevertheless extend to embrace groups located outside the European Union, provided they share 'European' characteristics. The Council of Europe currently numbers 45 Member States, including the Russian Federation, Turkey, and Switzerland, which some regard as merely extending Europe's borders 'to what can be considered Europe's historico-cultural roots'.[34] This approach equally necessitates consideration of the way in which the cultures of new Member States or immigrant communities feed into, or alter, 'European' identity. Is Islam, for example, part of Europe's culture; and might our answer to that alter depending on whether or not Turkey becomes a member? It is interesting to note that although Article 49 of the Treaty on European Union states that '[a]ny *European State* which respects the principles set out in Article 6(1) may apply to become a member of the Union' (emphasis added), the key 1993 Copenhagen criteria for admission require solely the existence of a democratic political

COM 7/004, it identified a number of large regional entities, such as the coastal areas of the Mediterranean, whose identity falls between the national and European.

[33] Gray, J, *False Dawn, The Delusions of Global Capitalism* (London: Granta Books, 1998), p 57. It certainly appears that Europeans prefer to watch American films and television programmes rather than programmes produced in other European countries. As with Europe, however, America is a land of many cultures, and one should be wary of simplistic references to 'American' culture.

[34] Wagner, P, 'From Monuments to Human Rights: Redefining "Heritage" in the Work of the Council of Europe', in Council of Europe, above n 5, at p 11.

system, compliance with fundamental rights and the rule of law, a functioning market economy, and the adoption of pre-existing Community rules and regulations. The priorities here are evidently political and economic, rather than cultural. As François Heisbourg has recently observed: '. . . if a country fulfils the Copenhagen criteria, it can join the club; and therefore Morocco (which applied in 1987) or Tunisia or Israel, or a democratic Iraq may some day follow Turkey. I assume that some sort of geographic continuum will be seen as desirable, in order to avoid extending to New Zealand or Chile.'[35]

But why should dissemination of the culture and history of the European peoples be a Community objective? Understood too narrowly, or used to promote a particular form of European identity, such a policy could, as we have noted, prove divisive. Understood more broadly, in order to illuminate the various forces which have shaped modern Europe and the diverse cultures of which it is composed, such a policy might prove beneficial; in particular, it could render European integration less threatening to the individuals who are experiencing it at first hand. The free movement of goods and persons across Europe exposes individuals to alternative ways of living both through their relocation or travel abroad and as a result of exposure to new communities established within their country. Given that such exposure may engender fear or hostility, cultural initiatives can play a useful role in helping the Community to combat racism and xenophobia.

Secondly, greater understanding of Europe's diverse cultures not only opens up new options for one's own life, it may also lead to a better appreciation of the preoccupations and concerns of other countries. At the political level this may encourage respect for compromises or approaches that one's own country might not favour. David Miller discusses the question of empathy among Europeans in his book *On Nationality*.[36] He notes that in Eurobarometer surveys carried out in the 1980s most people gave affirmative replies to very general and personally costless questions such as: '[i]f one of the countries of the EC finds itself in major economic difficulties, do you feel that other countries (including your own) should help it or not?' In contrast, most gave negative answers to the more specific question whether they personally were prepared to make an individual sacrifice, such as paying a little more tax, to help another country of the EC experiencing major economic difficulties.

But although greater awareness of different cultures may foster understanding and a degree of empathy towards other 'European peoples', this is by

[35] Heisbourg, F and Grant, C, 'How should Europe respond to the new America?', in *Prospect*, April 2003, pp 16–20, at p 17.

[36] Miller, above n 4, at pp 160–61.

no means certain. As always, the crucial question is: who is doing the telling, and why? The briefest study of European history reveals that its constituent states have spent much of the past fighting with, and attempting to subjugate, each other. Indeed, the one thing they do appear to have had in common was a sense of mutual rivalry and suspicion. Knowledge of this past can be used to fuel national pride, with an emphasis on battles won and hardship endured, as well as to reinforce distrust of other nations. Alternatively, it can be used, as indeed it is, in order to emphasize the benefits of European union, through which states have overcome their past enmities and learned to work together to increase prosperity. In *The Origins of European Identity*, a book supported by the European Commission and written with young people in mind, the authors chart a gradual process of 'political progress', culminating in the creation of the European Union.[37] European identity is seen as resting on a largely positive heritage of artistic creativity, democracy, and western philosophical thought. There is, interestingly, no mention of the contribution that the slave trade made to European prosperity, nor of the impact on subject nations of Member State empires.

Though history of this type may make Europeans feel good about themselves, it does little to help them understand the contingent nature of the present political situation, nor the forces which could unsettle it. Moreover, Community initiatives designed to increase 'knowledge of the culture and history of the European peoples' that directly undercut Member State attempts to maintain their own distinct national identities, are likely to be resisted. Though the Community consequently appears poorly placed to redress the nation-centred version of history propounded by the Member States, this is perhaps not such a loss if it would merely replace one politically motivated narrative with another.

The Community also has an economic, as opposed to political, rationale for the dissemination of information about the diversity of European culture. Such knowledge encourages individuals to exploit the opportunities opened up by the internal market by, for example, moving to another Member State to take up work or to visit on holiday. We have also suggested that there may

[37] Couloubaritsis, L, De Leeuw, M, Noël, E, and Sterckx, C, *The Origins of European Identity* (Brussels: European University Press, 1993). Yasemin Soysal suggests that, rather than direct attempts on the part of the Community institutions to exert an influence, it has been the process of networking among academics and experts at the European level which has affected the national curricula of the Member States. Networking of this type appears, e.g., to have led to a shift in focus in the history curricula, with national concerns and interests becoming relativized and placed within a broader European framework of analysis: Soysal, Y N, 'Locating Europe', *European Societies*, 4/3 (2002), 265.

be a belief that the development of a particular 'European' sensibility will lead consumers to prefer European, as opposed to American or Asian, goods or services. As individuals come to perceive Europe as a single area of opportunity, a kind of 'giant supermarket', so their identification with their state of origin may weaken.[38] Rather than create a sense of allegiance to the European Union, however, this could instead lead to identification with the host country in which the individual is based or has significant contacts.

Knowledge of other cultures can also lead to innovation and enhance creativity. The reference to a 'flowering' of national cultures in Article 151(1) may be seen in this forward-looking, evolutionary way. Member States are likely to approve the idea of innovation, in that a varied and rich cultural environment offers both economic and social benefits. They will nevertheless wish to maintain a bedrock of values that are national, regional, or in some way indigenous in an attempt to differentiate their political unit from others. But where should the balance be struck, as a matter of European Community policy, between, on the one hand, preserving established traditions and distinctive ways of life and, on the other hand, promoting exchange and the development of new cultural forms? It is possible that Member States intended Article 151, with its reference in paragraph 1 to respect for national and regional diversity, to indicate that the preservation of existing cultures should be prioritized over the uncertain benefits of cultural evolution. Moreover, use of the term 'cultures' in the phrase 'flowering of the cultures of the Member States' suggests that Community action would be legitimate to prevent one country's culture being submerged by that of another.

This discussion feeds into a much broader debate concerning the commodification of culture and the potential levelling impact on culture of market forces. On one side are those who consider that, with a global economy, products and services will increasingly become standardized as the multinationals squeeze out competition through vigorous advertising and promotion of their brand.[39] Over time, almost all aspects of life will become commercialized and subject to market forces: government revenues will be squeezed and the remaining public spaces and institutions, museums and parks, even schools, will gradually be given over to retail outlets and sponsorship.[40]

[38] A term used by Miller, above n 4, at p 165.

[39] Klein, N, *No Logo: No Space, No Choice, No Jobs* (London: Flamingo, 2000). Though globalization may lead to the standardization of certain products and services, John Gray, above n 33, at pp 58–60, has argued that capitalism's corporate culture will continue to vary markedly from one country to the next.

[40] Arguably these states will be the lucky ones—for countries unable to attract investment capital, poverty and exclusion will be exacerbated: Gray, above n 33, p 58.

A more optimistic, less deterministic view considers the influence of globalization to be 'not all predictable and not all bad'.[41] From this perspective, individuals are not simply sponges, soaking up the values purveyed by global culture, but have critical facilities that enable them to accept or reject what is on offer. The cultural specificity of many goods and services renders them unlikely to succeed on a world market, and those that do are often modified on reception by the host culture.[42] Exposure to foreign lifestyles and ways of thinking need not lead to the total destruction of indigenous cultures but rather to a process of creative hybridization, what Roland Robertson has termed 'glocalization'.[43] Even McDonald's products, it has been noted, undergo modification to reflect local culinary practices.[44] Moreover, many European countries have a long history of both emigration and immigration: over time they have become a patchwork of diverse cultures. As individuals become increasingly mobile, they carry with them practices and values that are integral to their own identity. Though these practices may be modified as a result of exposure to the new environment, or themselves modify that environment, they may also be refined in a process of self-differentiation. The consequences of cultural interaction can consequently be quite unpredictable, leading not only to the extinction or hybridization of cultural practices, but also to their mutual regeneration.

It is unlikely that the Member States intended to initiate this particular debate at Community level by agreeing Article 151. When contributing 'to the flowering of the cultures of the Member States' and taking 'cultural aspects into account in its action under other provisions of this Treaty' within the terms of Article 151, the Community institutions cannot, however, avoid these complex issues which must be both clearly articulated and addressed. When considering globalization the Community tends to focus, first, on the impact of global forces on the European Union as a political and economic unit and, secondly, on how the Community's external policies, for example in the field of development aid, should be altered in the light of these same

[41] Lull, J, *Media, Communication, Culture, A Global Approach*, 2nd edn (Cambridge: Polity, 2000), p 229.

[42] Gray, above n 33, at p 60, suggests, e.g., that media companies such as MTV, which vary their content to suit different cultures, can expect to remain global; while CNN, if it remains Americocentric, will be 'no more than one national media company among many others'.

[43] Robertson, R, 'Glocalization: time-space and homogeneity-heterogeneity', in Featherstone, M and Lash, S (eds), *Global Modernities* (London: Sage, 1995). Discussed by Lull, above n 41, pp 249–53, and Beck, U, *What is Globalization?* (Cambridge: Polity, 2000), pp 47–52.

[44] Lull, above n 41, p 250. In India, e.g., the company offers vegetable nuggets. For consideration of why the 'McDonaldization of the world thesis is wrong', see Beck, above n 43, at pp 42–7.

forces.[45] Consideration is also given as to whether forms of social, environmental, and financial management developed by the European Union might not serve as useful models for other regions. This tendency to analyse the situation from the perspective of the European Union as a discrete unit can also be seen in the cultural context. Globalization is regarded primarily as an external threat to the Community, to be addressed in international fora such as the World Trade Organization, rather than as a complex set of economic, political, and social developments at work within the European Union itself.[46] Article 151 could thus prove useful in encouraging the adoption by the Community of a more inward-looking perspective on the cultural and social problems posed by globalization.

(c) Dissemination of the culture and history of the European peoples: Article 151(2)

The reference to the dissemination of culture in Article 151(2) points to another cultural policy objective, namely the facilitation of access to, or democratization of, culture. This objective, which was recognized by the Commission as far back as the 1970s,[47] has links with the idea of cultural rights enshrined in Article 27 of the Universal Declaration of Human Rights and Article 15 of the International Covenant on Economic, Social, and Cultural Rights.[48] The right to participate in a country's cultural life, as well as to manifest and pass on one's own culture, has been considered an aspect of citizenship.[49] The dissemination of culture is here regarded as stemming from

[45] See, e.g., European Commission working document, *Responses to the Challenges of Globalisation: A Study on the International Monetary and Financial System and on Financing for Development*, SEC(2002) 185 final, and European Commission, *Communication on Promoting Core Labour Standards and Improving Social Governance in the Context of Globalisation*, COM(2001) 416 final.

[46] See European Commission, *Communication on the First European Community Framework Programme in Support of Culture (2000–2004)*, COM(1998) 266 final, p 3. This issue is discussed in more detail by Rosamond, B, 'Discourses of Globalization and European Identities', in Christiansen, T, Jorgensen, K E, and Wiener, A (eds), *The Social Construction of Europe* (London: Sage, 2001), p 158.

[47] European Commission, *Communication on Community Action in the Cultural Sector*, (1977) II *Bull EC*, supp 6/77.

[48] For discussion of the recognition of cultural rights in international law, see Eide, A, 'Cultural Rights as Individual Human Rights', in Eide, A, Krause, C, and Rosas, A (eds), *Economic, Social and Cultural Rights: A Textbook* (London: Nijhoff, 1995), p 229. See also Articles 4–6 of the UNESCO Universal Declaration on Cultural Diversity, adopted by UNESCO's General Conference on 2 November 2001.

[49] For a wide-ranging discussion of the relationship between culture and citizenship, see Stevenson, E (ed), *Culture and Citizenship* (London: Sage, 2001).

European citizenship, as opposed to feeding into and supporting it, in the way outlined in the sections above. This, however, raises difficult questions regarding access to cultural resources, such as the media, and rights to multi-cultural education, questions to which the Member States would undoubtedly prefer to provide answers, in accordance with their own distinct histories and constitutional traditions, at the domestic level.[50]

The scope for Community/Member State conflict becomes apparent when one asks to *which* culture or cultures one has a right of access. This is not merely a question of high culture or low culture. The Committee of the Regions answers this in its opinion on intercultural education in terms of access to the culture of one's own ethnic or social group, in addition to that of the dominant culture of the relevant state.[51] It argues not only that ethnic minorities should have an opportunity to learn the values of their own culture, but that the cultural and linguistic rights of migrant workers and immigrants should be taken fully into account when developing education policy.[52] Such opinions indicate how the enthusiastic pursuit of policies designed to enhance the dissemination of culture could once again prove highly contentious for the Member States, raising as they do thorny issues concerning integration and multi-culturalism.[53]

(d) Conserving cultural heritage of European significance: Article 151(2)

Similar questions can be raised with regard to the phrase 'cultural heritage of European significance' in Article 151(2). Though clearly pursuing the laudable aim of restoring and saving objects of historical or architectural importance, this head of action may also have been intended to feed into and foster the development of a distinct concept of 'European culture'. Once again,

[50] For a discussion of cultural rights and citizenship, see Roche, above n 19, p 74, in particular at p 78; and on the role of civic education in transmitting national identity to the incoming generation, see Miller, above n 4, at pp 180–81.

[51] Committee of the Regions, *Opinion on Intercultural Education*, Cdr 194/96 final. Article 5 of the 1995 Council of Europe Framework Convention for the Protection of National Minorities, European Treaty Series No 157, requires contracting parties to take steps to enable national minorities to 'maintain and develop their culture, and to preserve the essential elements of their identity, namely their religion, language, traditions and cultural heritage'.

[52] On which see also Cullen, H, 'From Migrants to Citizens? European Community Policy on Intercultural Education', *ICLQ*, 45 (1996), 109.

[53] *Council Resolution of 25 July 1996 on Access to Culture for All*, OJ [1996] C 242/1, called on the European Commission to carry out research into the problems which certain groups encounter in accessing culture.

there is no attempt to identify the criteria which should be used to determine what is of 'European significance'. Might not a worthless or mundane artefact be of such significance where it increases our knowledge of how people lived, or live, even in a restricted area of what is now the European Union? Or must the object have an iconic status, like the Eiffel Tower, and be recognized as culturally important throughout all the Member States? To date, Community funds have been specifically allocated, as in the Kaleidoscope and Raphaël programmes, to projects which are likely to have wide symbolic value. The Community has, for example, helped finance the restoration of the frescoes in the Basilica of St Francis of Assisi in Italy, monuments on the road to Santiago di Compostela, and world famous historic sites such as Mount Athos.

3. Conclusion

It will be apparent from the preceding section that the development of Community cultural policy raises difficult questions concerning European identity and the political nature of the European Union itself. Philip Schlesinger, writing in 1992, observed with considerable foresight that '[c]ulture is . . . going to be one of the key political battlefields in the 1990s'.[54] There is little sign, in the twenty-first century, that the field has yet been vacated. Article 151, with its open-ended references to 'common cultural heritage', 'European peoples', and 'cultural heritage of European significance', offers considerable scope for culture to be used instrumentally for political purposes. Most cultural policy is, of course, instrumental; it is rarely based simply on a desire to promote culture for culture's sake. Indeed, the variety of meanings ascribable to the term 'culture' renders such instrumentality all but inevitable. Nevertheless, deliberate use by the European Community of Article 151 in an attempt to further European integration runs the risk not only of distorting Community cultural policy, but also of increasing, rather than reducing as intended, the sense of alienation felt by certain sectors of Europe's population.

The never too far distant preoccupation with European integration undoubtedly has the potential to distort the application of Article 151. It is a preoccupation that requires one to grapple with, on one view even create, the notion of 'Europeanness'. Such an endeavour distracts attention from other, less synthetic justifications for Community intervention in the cultural field.

[54] Schlesinger, above n 3, at p 22.

Preservation of an archaeological site may, for example, prove to be important because, in the words of the European Convention on the Protection of the Archaeological Heritage, it helps us 'to retrace the history of mankind and its relation with the national environment'; an object or building may be important because it displays a key evolution in style; a book or painting may be valuable because of the skill of the author or artist and the insight it gives into our own, or past, societies.[55] Such knowledge may tell us very little about what it is to be 'European' but quite a lot about what it was like to live at a particular time, in a particular place. Admittedly such criteria involve difficult qualitative assessments, but the Community is not required to work from scratch or in isolation. As we have noted, the Community has a long history of supporting culture and is able to build, as it has done, on the considerable expertise developed over the years by organizations such as the Council of Europe and UNESCO.

But Community cultural policy should not solely be focused on preservation, and it is possible to point to a number of instrumental uses to which culture can be put which arguably have greater legitimacy than its use as a vehicle to promote European identity. There is, for example, much to be said for Community initiatives designed to increase access to, and enhance understanding of, other cultures; to promote innovation; or encourage employment and social regeneration in deprived areas through support for culture. The pursuit of such objectives are, of course, not without their own distinctive risks. For example, attempts to promote employment or social regeneration may result in culture being regarded merely a means to an economic end, leading to those cultural manifestations which are not commercially viable being sidelined or ignored. In the same vein, greater familiarity and interest in the culture of other peoples and countries may lead to uncontrolled tourism and the ultimate destruction of the very culture which the visitor wishes to experience.

Concern over the direction of Community cultural policy finds clear reflection in various opinions produced by the Committee of the Regions, which, it must be noted, has a distinct political agenda of its own. The Committee sees the Community's role as furthering 'the integration of every cultural group into *local* society', rather than the creation of a new, overarching European identity.[56] It regards as questionable Community attempts to impose such an

[55] Council of Europe, European Convention on the Protection of the Archaeological Heritage, European Treaty Series No 143, Article 1, available at http://conventions.coe.int/.

[56] Committee of the Regions, *Opinion of 13 March 1998 on Culture and Cultural Differences and their Significance for the Future of Europe*, COM 7/004, emphasis added.

identity from above, driven by commercial or political considerations. The 'Europeanization' of day-to-day life could, in its view, weaken established local and regional identities. An awareness of how political considerations can shape Community intervention is also apparent in its comments on Community proposals to renew the Kaleidoscope project, ultimately overtaken by the Culture 2000 programme. The Committee noted, for example, that, as formulated, emblematic, high-profile projects would tend to be supported even though such projects usually receive substantial local or national support.[57] This would be to the 'detriment of work emanating from the grass roots'.[58] The Culture 2000 programme continues to earmark a proportion of its funds for projects with high symbolic value, designed to 'strike a significant chord with the people of Europe and help to increase their sense of belonging to the same community as well as making them aware of the cultural diversity of the Member States'.[59]

The Committee also questioned the need for cooperation among groups from as many as three Member States, in that links within countries may prove to be as valuable as external contacts. Under the Culture 2000 programme this Community dimension has been reinforced: cooperation agreements must involve participants from either three or, for multi-annual projects, five participating states. It is certainly the case that cooperation may prove highly valuable, generating economies of scale and leading to the transmission of expertise and knowledge. Many projects, such as the Art Nouveau Network, discussed in section 2.*(a)* above, clearly invite a cooperative approach. Nevertheless, Community political considerations appear to be influencing the kind of projects that are being funded, possibly to the detriment of authentic, yet smaller-scale initiatives.

This chapter has sought to highlight some of the dangers and complexities inherent in using cultural policy in order to foster a sense of European identity. It has, in particular, been suggested that there are other, less contentious objectives which can usefully occupy the Community and which, indeed, the Community is already pursuing in the cultural field. This is not to discount the potential for Community cultural policy to bring into question or relativize established identities, for example, the national identities so carefully crafted by the Member States, but the Community should seek to avoid a similarly

[57] Committee of the Regions, *Opinion of 25 April 1995 on the Proposal for a European Parliament and Council Decision establishing a programme to support artistic and cultural activities having a European Dimension Kaleidoscope 2000*, CdR 145/95.

[58] Ibid., para 2.10.

[59] *European Parliament and Council Decision No 508/2000/EC Establishing the Culture 2000 Programme*, OJ [2000] L 63/1, at Annex 1, 1.3.

instrumental use of culture for its own political ends. Whatever the merits of this view, the Community needs to be explicit on this point, given the capacity for political ends to be hidden behind the more anodyne, day-to-day procedures of awarding grants and determining priorities. Those who drafted Article 151 may have skirted round the issue of European identity; such a luxury is not available to those who are required to implement it.

10

Long-term Resident Third Country Nationals in the European Union: Institutional Legacies and Evolving Norms

*Theodora Kostakopoulou**

1. Introduction

One of the most important challenges facing democratic polities concerns the relationship between the constitutional commitment to civic equality, on the one hand, and the public recognition of 'difference', on the other. Democratic theory cannot ignore the 'politics of recognition' of cultural, national, ethnic, religious, racial, gender, sexual, and other identities, even though the latter appears to call into question the traditional conception of democratic society as a bounded polity based on the ideal of universal and 'monochrome' citizenship. The non-citizen residents' demands for political inclusion and recognition have been viewed as a problem and/or a threat by the EU Member States[1] whose very constitution relies on a 'trinity of unity,' that is, a unitary territory, a unitary force, and a unitary people.[2] Yet, despite concerns about the long-term impact of the politics of recognition on the sense of common belonging and unity, it is generally acknowledged that democracy cannot be enhanced unless political and social institutions and structures become more

* Manchester School of Law, University of Manchester. This chapter is a revised version of my article on ' "Integrating" non-EU migrants in the European Union', which appeared originally in the *Columbia Journal of European Law*, 8(2)(2002), 181.

[1] See generally Castles, S, 'How Nation-States Respond to Immigration and Ethnic Diversity', *New Community*, 21(3) (1995), 293–308; Castles, S and Miller, M J, *The Age Of Migration: International Population Movements in the Modern World* (London: Macmillan, 1993).

[2] Diez, T, 'International Ethics and European Integration', *Alternatives*, 22 (1997), 287.

attentive to, and reflective of, the claims made by minority constituencies for socio-political inclusion and cultural recognition.[3]

In the European Union, barriers to free movement and residence are increasingly removed for Union citizens. Long-term resident third country nationals, however, have been relegated to the periphery of the emerging European civil society. The only EU citizenship rights they enjoy on the same footing as Community nationals are the rights to petition the European Parliament and to complain to the European Ombudsman. In post-Amsterdam Europe, possession of Member State nationality remains a qualifying criterion for eligibility to the benefits afforded by Community rules.[4] In addition, only a small percentage of third country nationals can claim derived rights as family members of Union citizens, as employees of Community based providers of services providing services in another Member State, or as beneficiaries of the differential and partial rights entailed by the Association and Cooperation agreements concluded by the European Community and third countries.[5] Kees Groenendijk is, therefore, correct to argue that Community law has unintentionally legitimized the unequal treatment of ethnic minorities.[6] Such treatment is difficult to justify considering that long-term third

[3] See Parekh, B C, *Rethinking Multiculturalism* (London: Macmillan, 2000); Connolly, W, 'Pluralism, Multiculturalism and the Nation-State: Rethinking the Connections', *J Pol Ideologies*, 1 (1996), 53; Habermas, J, 'Citizenship and National Identity: Some Reflections on the Future of Europe', *Praxis Int'l*, 12 (1992), 1–19; id., 'Struggles for Recognition in Constitutional States', *Eur J Phil*, 1 (1993), at 128, 128–54; Marion Young, I, *Justice and the Politics of Difference* (Princeton: Princeton University Press, 1990).

[4] 'Every person holding the nationality of a member state shall be a citizen of the Union. Citizenship of the Union shall complement and not replace national citizenship.' (Treaty Establishing the European Community [TEC], Article 17(1)) See also the Declaration on Nationality of a Member State which was annexed to the Final Act of the Treaty on European Union.

[5] The discussion focuses on the process of political incorporation of long-term non-citizen residents who do not derive rights from Community law. The paper does not address the position of third country nationals who enjoy Community law rights as family members of Union citizens, employees of undertakings providing services in another Member State, or beneficiaries of the association and cooperation agreements signed by the Community and third countries. For a discussion of the last, see Willy, A, 'Free Movement of Non-EC Nationals: A Review of the Case-Law of the Court of Justice', *Eur J Int'l L*, 3 (1992) 53; Evans, A, 'Third Country Nationals and the Treaty on European Union', *Eur J of Int'l L*, 5 (1994), 199; Peers, S, 'Towards Equality: Actual and Potential Rights of Third Country Nationals in the European Union', *CMLRev*, 33(1) (1996), 7–50; Guild, E (ed), *The Legal Framework and Social Consequences of Free Movement of Persons in the European Union* (The Hague: Kluwer Law International, 1999); Staples, H, *The Legal Status of Third Country Nationals Resident in the European Union* (The Hague: Kluwer, 1999).

[6] See Groenendijk, K, 'Security of Residence and Access to Free Movement for Settled Third Country Nationals under Community Law', in Guild, E and Harlow, C (eds), *Implementing Amsterdam* (Oxford: Hart Publishing, 2000), 226.

country nationals are an integral part of the European community, *de facto* members of and contributors to the flourishing European societies.

The exclusionary scope of Union citizenship has been criticized[7] and the merits of replacing the 'subjective standard of nationality by the objective standard of residence or domicile'[8] have been defended by both academics and non-governmental organizations (NGOs). Although national executives oppose the extension of Union citizenship to long-term resident third country nationals, the latter are no longer mere objects of policy and vulnerable dependants. A more liberal approach is gradually replacing the Council's favoured intergovernmental restraint mode of integrating such persons, owing to a combination of factors, such as European Parliament interventions, intense lobbying by pro-migrant NGOs, academic reaction against the deficiencies of Justice and Home Affairs Cooperation I (the so-called Third Pillar of the Treaty on European Union), and the spill-over effect of the logic of market integration.

The partial Communitarization of the Third Pillar, one of the most important innovations of the Amsterdam Treaty,[9] marked the beginning of a third phase in the development of a European immigration policy.[10] The Schengen *acquis* has been incorporated into the Union, and most of the provisions of the *acquis* concerning the free movement of persons have been allocated a legal base in Title IV of the Treaty Establishing the European Community (TEC). Empowered both constitutionally and institutionally,[11] the Commission has

[7] See O'Keeffe, D, 'Union Citizenship', in O'Keeffe, D and Twomey, P (eds), *Legal Issues of the Maastricht Treaty* (Chichester: Wiley, 1994); Kostakopoulou, T, 'European Citizenship and Immigration After Amsterdam: Silences, Openings, Paradoxes', *J Ethnic & Migration Studies*, 4 (1998), 639–56; eds., 'The European Citizenship Menu: Modes and Options', *J Eur Pub Policy*, 7 (2000), 477–92; La Torre, M (ed), *European Citizenship—An Institutional Challenge* (The Hague: Kluwer, 1998); Martiniello, M, 'European Citizenship, European Identity and Migrants: Towards the Postnational State?', in Miles, R and Thranhardt, D (eds), *Migration and European Integration: The Politics of Inclusion and Exclusion in Europe* (London: Pinter, 1995), 37–52; Wiener, A, *Citizenship Practice: Building Institutions of a Non-State* (Oxford: Westview, 1998).

[8] Nascibene, B (ed), *Nationality Laws in the European Union* (London: Butterworths, 1995); see also Peers, S, 'Building Fortress Europe: The Development of EU Migration Law', *CMLRev*, 35 (1998), 1236, 1268–70.

[9] The Treaty was signed on 2 October 1997 and entered into force on 1 May 1999.

[10] During the first phase (1985–1991) national governments embarked upon a process of ad hoc and informal intergovernmental cooperation. The second phase (1992–1998), introduced by the Treaty on European Union, introduced a form of 'diluted' intergovernmentalism; links were established with the Community institutions, but it accorded leading actor status to national governments.

[11] Emek Ucarer notes the importance of leadership resources and the creation of a new Directorate-General on Justice and Home Affairs: 'Sidekick No More: The Commission's Evolving Role and Agency in Justice and Home Affairs', paper presented at ECSA 7th International Conference, Madison, Wisconsin, 31 May– 2 June 2000.

taken advantage of the structural shift from the intergovernmental pillar and proposed instruments which are likely to improve the position of long-term resident third country nationals.[12] Although it may be premature to talk about a genuine paradigm shift in the Community's approach to migration, it is certainly the case that addressing the inequitable position of long-term resident third country nationals has become a priority in the Community's policy agenda. The special meeting of the European Council at Tampere (October 1999) acknowledged that the European Union must ensure the fair treatment of third country nationals who legally reside on its territory and that 'a more vigorous integration policy' aimed at 'granting them rights and obligations comparable to those of Union citizens' is needed.[13]

But what does a 'vigorous integration policy' entail? Evidently, the 'integration' of minority communities within the European Union cannot have the same meaning as in national-statist jurisdictions. An important difference between the European Community and national publics is that the former is a community of multifarious minorities entangled in a project that exerts a profound impact upon their nature and organization. Since the European Union is neither an extension, nor the mirror image of national jurisdictions, it is plausible to argue that its model of pluralism does not have to resemble national models of pluralism. In many respects, European developments prompt a rethinking of the connection between the state, the nation, and pluralism in its various forms, and invite us to consider the possibility of transcending these connections. Accordingly, the vocabulary of integration may not be apposite to issues of European membership issues, and its replacement with that of democratic equality and inclusion should be considered.

Interestingly, the Tampere discourse on 'fair treatment of third country nationals' stands in sharp contrast to the intergovernmental restraint mode of the Justice and Home Affairs Council's non-binding 1996 Resolution on the integration of long-term resident third country nationals.[14] Similarly, one observes a discursive shift in the Commission's interpretation of the meaning and terms of integration of long-term resident third country nationals in pre-Tampere and post-Tampere initiatives. The latter suggest the possibility of

[12] At Tampere the Commission was invited to prepare a scoreboard of progress towards realizing the objectives of creating an 'area of freedom, security and justice'. The scoreboard was presented in March 2000 and has been subsequently updated: COM (2000) 167, 24 March 2000; COM (2000) 782, 30 November 2000. It contains a summary of objectives, the action needed to achieve them, the responsibility for these actions, the likely timetable, and the current state of play.

[13] European Council, *Tampere Presidency Conclusions*, SN 200/99, Brussels, 16 October 1999.

[14] See Council Resolution 96/80/01, OJ [1996] C 80/2 (concerning the status of third country nationals who reside on a long-term basis in the territory of the Member States).

a harmonized national denizenship status for long-term resident third country nationals coupled with the grant of European denizenship.

In this chapter I critically examine these developments and argue that the claims of long-term resident third country nationals should not be seen as demands for better integration, but rather for their recognition as legitimate recipients of justice and democratic equality. True, it is a welcome development that after more than four decades of European integration, long-term resident third country nationals are now being portrayed as rightful participants with equal rights and opportunities in the workplace and society at the national level, and are granted free movement rights.[15] The Commission's proposed directive concerning the status of third country nationals who are long-term residents will soon become a legally binding instrument, albeit in a diluted form.[16] However, this initiative does not fully embrace a participatory model of incorporation that gives third country nationals a stake in the European polity. Realizing the latter requires subjecting the Member States' definition of 'who makes up the European people' to a normative test and mustering the political will to give all settled residents a stake in the success of the project of 'post-national' democracy.[17] For 'civic citizenship' is an oxymoron and cannot really be a substitute for political membership. In this respect, promoting democratic inclusiveness in the European Union and recognizing the claims of long-term resident third country nationals to inclusion and equality require keeping discussions about the evolution of Union citizenship on the agenda.

2. Contending liberal and intergovernmental visions of integration at the Community level

In post-Maastricht Europe, matters related to long-term resident third country nationals were dealt with via the means provided for by the Third Pillar of

[15] See Commission proposal for a Council Directive 28/08, OJ [2001] C 240/79 (127 final).

[16] The Council reached political agreement on the draft Directive at its 2514th meeting in Luxembourg, in June 2003: Justice and Home Affairs Council Meeting, Luxembourg, 5 June 2003, 9845/03 (Presse 150).

[17] On the theme of postnationalism, see Shaw, J, 'The Emergence of Postnational Constitutionalism in the European Union', *J Eur Pub Policy*, 6 (1999), 579, 579–97; see also Chalmers, D, 'Postnationalism and the Quest for Constitutional Substitutes', *Journal of Law and Society*, 27 (2000), 178, 178–217.

the Treaty on European Union (TEU).[18] The intergovernmental character of this cooperation, coupled with the absence of democratic control and judicial scrutiny, ensured the continuation of the long tradition that had accustomed national elites to see cultural difference as a problem for social integration. Difference was perceived as undermining social cohesion and as leading to the weakening of the fabric of society. Integration of long-term resident third country nationals was to be achieved by introducing stricter rules and instilling greater conformism.

According to the Council's 1996 Resolution on the Status of Third-country Nationals who Reside on a Long-term Basis in the Territory of the Member States, integration was to be promoted because it 'contributes to greater security and stability, both in daily life and in work, and to social peace in the various Member States'—and not because it was required by principles such as fairness, democracy, and respect for cultural diversity.[19] The Resolution provided that third country nationals (refugees under the Geneva Convention were excluded) could be recognized as long-term residents after lawful and uninterrupted residence of 10 years in the territory of the Member State concerned. In considering an application for residency status, which could be valid for a 10-year or unlimited period, national authorities could take into account 'the level and stability of the means of existence which the applicant demonstrates, in particular whether (s)he had health insurance, and the conditions for exercising an occupation'.[20] This provision gave national authorities discretion to refuse residence authorization to those with an interrupted employment record, without examining whether the interruptions had been voluntary or involuntary. Member States could refuse to renew the residence authorization on the grounds of prolonged absence (which could be no less than six consecutive months), expulsion, or fraudulent possession of the residence authorization.[21] Under the Resolution, long-term residents would enjoy

[18] For a critique, see O'Keeffe, D, 'Recasting the Third Pillar', *CMLRev*, 32 (1995), 893, 893–920; Beiber, R and Monar, J (eds), *Justice and Home Affairs in the European Union: The Development of the Third Pillar* (Brussels: Interuniversity Press, 1995).

[19] Council Resolution 96/80/01, above n 14.

[20] Ibid., at Title IV(2).

[21] The provisions concerning cancellation or non-renewal of residence authorizations resemble the provisions entailed by Council Directive 64/221 on the coordination of special measures concerning the movement and residence of foreign nationals which are justified on the grounds of public policy, public security, or public health. In line with Articles 2 and 3(1) of Directive 64/221, Title VI of the Resolution stated that the expulsion measure shall be based exclusively on the personal conduct of the individual concerned. This means that previous criminal convictions shall not in themselves constitute grounds for the taking of such measures, and that the applicant's criminal behaviour or activities must be sufficiently harmful in order to pose a genuine and

unlimited travel in the territory of that Member State and the same rights as nationals of the host state with regard to working conditions, trade union membership, housing, social security, emergency health care, and compulsory schooling. They 'should be able to obtain authorization to engage in gainful activities'; but would not have unfettered access to all occupations, except where expressly permitted by Community law.[22] Hence, third country nationals would not enjoy free movement rights and would have no protection against discrimination as regards access to employment, enjoyment of the same social and tax advantages as national workers, and access to training in vocational schools and retraining centres.[23] The Resolution treated long-term resident third country nationals as a subject class, that is, as objects of governmental policy. The model of integration underpinning it was one of qualified membership in the civil society and hierarchization. This framework was ultimately sustained as an instrument of state sovereignty.

The Commission's approach during this period was cautious. It did not hesitate to pinpoint the deficiencies of the Third Pillar, but at the same time it refrained from asserting long-term resident third country nationals as democratic subjects. Following the commencement of legal proceedings by the European Parliament (EP) under Article 175 EC (now Article 232 EC) for failing to present the necessary proposals for legislation as required by Article 7a EC (now Article 14 EC),[24] the Commission proposed a draft Directive which granted lawfully resident third country nationals the right of visa-free travel for short stays not exceeding three months.[25] This proposal drew on Article 21

sufficiently serious threat to the requirements of public policy affecting one of the fundamental interests of society. See Case 30/77, *R v Bouchereau* [1977] ECR 1999; Case 350/96, *Clean Car* [1998] ECR I-2521. In any case, the requirement of personal conduct can never justify deportation as a general preventative measure. See Case 67/74, *Bonsignore v Oberstadtdirektor der Stadt Köln* [1975] ECR 297. But the Resolution makes no reference to procedural rights and safeguards, such as those afforded to Community nationals under Articles 6, 7, 8, and 9 of Directive 64/221.

[22] Council Resolution 96/80/01, above n 14, at Title VII.

[23] Compare the generous provisions of Council Regulation 1612/68. Council Regulation 19/10/EEC, OJ [1968] L 257/2.

[24] See Case 445/93, *European Parliament v Commission* [1994] ECR C1/24.

[25] The Commission adopted three proposals with the view to attaining the objective set out in Article 14 (ex Article 7a) of the TEC: first, Council Directive amending Directive 68/360/EEC and Directive 73/148/EEC (concerning the abolition of restrictions on movement and residence within the Community for Community workers and for professionals and service providers respectively, COM (95) 0348-C4–0357/95–95/0202(COD)); secondly, Proposal for a Council Directive on the elimination of controls on persons crossing internal frontiers, COM (95)0347-C4–0468/95–95/0201(CNS); and thirdly, Proposal for a Council Directive on the right of third country nationals to travel in the Community, COM(95) 0346-C4–04420/95–95/0199(CNS),

of the 1990 Schengen Implementing Convention, which provided for a similar right.[26] The exercise of the right to intra-EU travel would depend on the possession of a valid residence permit and travel document, and of sufficient means of subsistence to cover both the period of the intended stay or transit and the resident's return to the Member State of departure or a third state. Indeed, the requirement of self-sufficiency was rather excessive given that economically non-active EU citizens are required to be self-sufficient in order to exercise their right of residence only, not their right to travel.[27] Although the draft Directive did not secure the Member States' approval, it nevertheless provided an important resource, which was utilized at Amsterdam and found its way into Article 62(3) of the TEC. The latter Article grants nationals of third countries the right of free circulation within the Union for short stays not exceeding three months.

The Amsterdam Treaty also ended the uncertainty as to whether the requirement of the abolition of border controls (Article 14 of the TEC) applies to third country nationals: Article 62(1) of the TEC imposed a clear obligation on the Council to adopt within a five-year period the necessary measures for the removal of 'any controls on persons be they citizens of the Union or nationals of third countries, when crossing internal borders'. This covers both long-term residents and newly admitted persons. More importantly, according to the Action Plan of the Council and the Commission, within a period of five years from the entry into force of the Treaty, the Council has to adopt measures concerning the conditions of entry and residence, and standards of procedures for Member State issuance of long-term visas and residence permits, including those for the family reunion.[28] Measures defining the rights and conditions under which long-term resident third country nationals may reside in other Member States will be adopted by the Council acting unanimously on a proposal from the Commission, or on the initiative of a Member State.[29]

the amended proposal which was adopted by the Commission on 17 March 1997, OJ [1997] C 139, 6.5.97; COM(97) 106.

[26] Schengen Implementing Convention 1990, (1991) 30 ILM 84.

[27] See Council Directive 90/364, OJ [1990] L 180/26 (on the right of residence); Council Directive 90/365, OJ [1990] L 180/28 (on the rights of residence for employees and self-employed persons who have ceased their occupational activity); Council Directive 93/96, OJ [1993] L 317/59 (on the right of residence for students). See also Joined Cases 286/82 and 26/83, *Luisi and Carbone v Ministero del Tesoro* [1984] ECR 377, [1985] 3 CMLR 52.

[28] See Joint Action Plan on how best to implement the provisions of the Treaty of Amsterdam establishing an area of freedom, security, and justice, OJ [1999] C 19/1, 9; see also TEC Article 63(2)(a).

[29] See TEC Article 64(4).

The creation of Community law competence (albeit not an exclusive one) in matters relating to third country nationals is a welcome development, if only because it opens up the possibility for a qualitative shift in the basic orientation of the Member States' migration policy.[30] The Commission manifested its policy entrepreneurialism early. Before the Treaty of Amsterdam was ratified, the Commission proposed a Convention on the Rules for the Admission of Third Country Nationals to the Member States of the Union, using as a legal base Articles K1(3)(a) and (b) and K3(2)(C) of the TEU.[31] The draft Convention marked an attempt to regulate the entry of third country nationals to the Member States of the Union for long stays (that is, for periods exceeding three months) and to improve the position of long-term resident third country nationals in the EU. The explanatory memorandum stated that integration of long-term resident third country nationals is an imperative dictated by the democratic and humanitarian tradition of the Member States, thereby echoing the pro-migrant agenda suggested by NGOs.[32] To this end, long-term resident status should be granted to those third country nationals (including refugees under the Geneva Convention) who have lived legally in a Member State for at least five years and have the right to residence for another five years.[33] Recognition of long-term resident status results in the following rights: the right to free movement in the state of residence; increased protection against expulsion; authorization to reside there for all purposes set out in Titles VI and VII and to engage in all economic activities covered by the Convention; and the right to enjoy the same treatment as Union citizens with regard to access to employment or self-employment, training, trade union rights, the right of association, and access to housing and schooling.[34] Long-term resident third country nationals could apply for employment in another Member State in response to a vacancy, and, if they obtain a work contract, will be entitled to move there—assuming that the post

[30] See Kostakopoulou (1998), n 7 above. The Schengen *acquis* has been incorporated into the Union. Its provisions and decisions concerning the abolition of controls at the internal borders, free movement of persons, long- and short-term visas, the crossing of external borders, third country nationals (TCNs), and carriers sanctions have been allocated a legal base in the First Pillar. See Council Decision 1999/435/EC, OJ [1999] L 176/1. The *acquis* is not binding on the UK and Ireland, but the UK has agreed to participate in aspects of the Schengen *acquis* and of Title IV of the TEC which do not conflict with the British frontier control policy. Denmark has opted out from Title IV of the TEC and therefore those Schengen provisions integrated into the First Pillar will have the status of public international law.

[31] See Commission Proposal for a Decision on Establishing a Convention on Rules for the Admission of Third Country Nationals to the Member States of the European Union 07/11, OJ [1997] C 337/9.

[32] See Explanatory Memorandum, p II.

[33] See Commission Proposal 07/11, above n 31, Article 32.

[34] See ibid., at Article 34.

cannot be filled by EC nationals or legally resident third country nationals who are part of the labour market of that Member State.[35] After two years of residence there, third country nationals will be recognized as long-term residents in that state and lose their status in the previous state.[36] The consequences of the possible loss of resident status in the original state of residence—where third country nationals have family ties and property—were not fully addressed by the Commission, which, in its effort to appease governmental sensitivities, continued to treat resident migrants as the 'property' of the original state of residence or the host Member State.

More favourable terms for third country nationals were contained in Title VII of the Convention dealing with family reunification.[37] The provisions of the Title made no differentiation between long-term resident third country nationals and first admissions: third country nationals who are legally resident in a Member State for at least a year upon the date of submitting the application for family reunion have the right to family reunion.[38] Notwithstanding the draft Convention's favourable terms, however, its provisions on family reunion did not institutionalize parity between Union citizens and third country nationals: the requirements for admission of family members entitled to be reunited were more restrictive, and the category of family members included only spouses and children below the age of majority;[39] spouses and children could not engage in economic activities for the first six months of residence; and spouses and children were to be excluded if it was assessed that the sole purpose of the marriage or adoption was entry to the state.[40]

A few months before the Amsterdam Treaty entered into force, the Commission proposed two Directives on Extending the Freedom to Provide

[35] See Commission Proposal 07/11, above n 31, at Article 35(1).

[36] See ibid., at Article 35(2) and (3).

[37] Earlier initiatives include the 1993 Resolution on the harmonization of national policies on family reunification (2828/1/93 WGI 1497 REV I) and the 1997 Resolution on measures to combat marriages of convenience, 16/12, OJ [1997] C 382/1.

[38] See Commission Proposal, above n 31, Article 24. Family members of Union citizens, who have or have not exercised the right to free movement, would also be entitled to family reunification under Article 10 of Council Regulation 1612/68, OJ [1969] L 257/2. This solved the problem of 'purely internal situations', that is, of the state of affairs where Community nationals who have not exercised their free movement rights cannot invoke the more favourable Community provisions on family reunion against their state of origin. Notably, in its proposal for a European Parliament and Council Regulation amending Council Regulation No 1612/68, the Commission has broadened the definition of 'spouse' so as to include cohabitees who are recognized as spouses under the legislation of the host Member State. Additionally, in the event of dissolution of marriage with a Community national, family members who are TCNs would not lose their right of residence in a host Member State, provided that they have lived there for three consecutive years: Commission Proposal 98/0394, OJ [1998] C 344/9.

[39] See Commission Proposal, above n 31, at Article 24.

[40] See ibid., at Article 28.

Cross-border Services to Third Country Nationals established within the Community and on the Posting of Workers who are Third Country Nationals for the Provision of Cross-border Services.[41] It also recommended the amendment of Regulation 1408/71 (EEC), thereby extending Community coordination of social security schemes to employed and self-employed persons who are insured in a Member State and who are not Community nationals.[42]

3. The Tampere discourse

The Commission's liberal initiatives, coupled with sustained lobbying by pro-migrant NGOs and calls for a more positive approach to migration flows by academics, affected the process of framing migration issues. The special meeting of the European Council at Tampere, in October 1999, which was dedicated to the elaboration of principles underpinning the establishment of an Area of Freedom, Security, and Justice, signalled the 12 Member States' willingness to develop common policies on asylum and immigration, including the integration of long-term resident third country nationals. According to the Tampere Presidency Conclusions, 'a more vigorous approach should aim at granting them rights and obligations comparable to those of EU citizens. It should also enhance non-discrimination in economic, social and cultural life and develop measures against racism and xenophobia.'[43] Approximation of the legal status of long-term resident third country nationals to that of EC nationals would entail the grant of 'a set of uniform rights which are as near as possible to those enjoyed by EU citizens; e.g., the right to reside, receive education and work as an employee or self-employed person as well as the principle of non-discrimination vis-à-vis the citizens of the state of residence'.[44]

The application of rights-based approach to issues concerning long-term resident third country nationals is seen to signal that the EU has realized

[41] See Commission Proposal for a Council Directive extending the freedom to provide cross-border services to third-country nationals established within the Community, COM (1999) 3 final (March 1999), amended by Doc 500PC0271 (02) (February 2001). The UK believes that the proposal should have been based on provisions of Title IV and not on Article 59 of the TEC that requires qualified majority voting and co-decision, and it accuses the Commission of undermining its opt-out from Tile IV of the TEC. See also Commission Proposal on the posting of workers who are third-country nationals for the provision of cross-border services, COM (1999) 3 final (March 1999), amended by COM(2000) 271 (May 2001).

[42] See Council Regulation 1408/71, OJ [1998] C 6.

[43] *Tampere Presidency Conclusions*, above n 13.

[44] Ibid., at 5.

that '. . . long-term resident third country nationals, irrespective of their nationality should not be treated as second class citizens, but are entitled to equal treatment, secure residence rights and the option of full citizenship'.[45] The absence of any reference to rights of mobility within the Union in the Tampere Presidency Conclusions, coupled with the statement that 'long-term resident third country nationals should be offered the opportunity to obtain the nationality of the Member State in which they are resident', however, seems to suggest that national executives maintained the view that ethnic and cultural diversity was to be contained within self-enclosed 'authentic' national communities and regulated by national jurisdictions in accordance with some minimum set of principles and rights designed to keep civil societies going.

The foregoing view did not coincide with the Commission's vision of integration. Believing that family reunification is a necessary means of successful integration, the Commission took the first initiative in the field of migration since the entry into force of the Treaty of Amsterdam by proposing a Directive on family reunification.[46] The legal basis of the Directive has been Article 63(3)(a) of the TEC. The draft Directive sought to harmonize national legislation in this area by granting the right to family reunification[47] to all third country nationals—including refugees under the Geneva Convention of 1951 and persons enjoying subsidiary protection[48]—who reside lawfully in a Member State and hold a residence permit for at least a year regardless of the purpose of their residence. The draft Directive also covered Union citizens who have not exercised their right to free movement and whose situation had hitherto been subject solely to national rules. According to the draft Directive, family members who would be eligible for family reunification include the applicant's spouse or cohabitee (who may be of the same sex), their children and the children of just one of the spouses or partners under his or her actual custody and responsibility, relatives on the ascending line, and children of full age who have no family support in the country of origin and are dependent on the applicant.[49] The right to family reunification would be subject to conditions such as the availability of adequate accommodation, sickness

[45] See Groenendijk, above n 6, at 234.

[46] See COM (1999) 638 final, amended by COM(2000) 624 final. According to the Commission, 'the presence of family members makes for greater stability and deepens the roots of these people, since they are enabled to lead a normal family life': COM (99) 638 final, 3.

[47] In this respect, it differs from the 1993 Resolution, above n 37.

[48] The amended proposal excluded persons enjoying subsidiary protection from the scope of the Directive: COM (2000) 624, Article 3(2).

[49] See draft Directive, above n 46, at Article 5. Notably, this is more restrictive than Article 10 of Council Regulation 1612/68.

insurance, and stable and sufficient resources. Public policy, domestic security, and public health considerations are permissible bases for refusing entry or residence. Member States would also enjoy discretion to set a qualifying period of up to one year before the applicant may exercise the right to family reunification.[50] All family members would enjoy access to education, but the nuclear family (that is, spouses and children) would have access to employment, self-employed activities, and to all forms of vocational training.[51] Access to social and tax advantages was excluded from the scope of the Directive. An autonomous right of residence was given to members of the nuclear family after four years of residence, although there was a possibility for early application upon separation, divorce, or death. After one year of residence, if the applicant was in a particularly difficult situation, the Member States would be obliged to issue an autonomous residence permit. For other family members dependent on the applicant, the Member States retained the possibility of granting autonomous status. As regards remedies, Article 16 provided for a right to appeal to the courts in the event of infringement of rules and procedures relating to family reunification.

Unfortunately, these favourable provisions did not find their way into the final text of the Directive, which was adopted by the Council on 22 September 2003.[52] Instead of preserving the unity and stability of family communities, national executives attached restrictive conditions to the exercise of the right to family reunification which render it devoid of substance. In particular, Article 8 of the Directive requires migrants to have resided lawfully in the territory of a Member State for a period not exceeding two years before being joined by family members. A Member State may also provide for a further waiting period of no more than three years between the submission of an application for family reunification and the issue of a residence permit to the family members, owing to considerations relating to the 'reception capacity' of the country. Such provisions not only prevent family life, but they also confirm the unequal treatment of long-term resident third country nationals. In addition, they are likely to lead to the reduction of more favourable existing national provisions.[53]

[50] See ibid., at Article 10. [51] See ibid., at Article 12.

[52] Council Directive 2000/83 was adopted on 22 September 2003 and was published on 3 October 2003; OJ [2003] L 251/12. Ireland, the UK, and Denmark have not participated in the adoption of the Directive.

[53] See Brinkmann, G, 'Family Reunion: Third Country Nationals and the Community's New Powers', in Guild and Harlow, above n 6, at 241–66. But cf. Boeles, P, 'Directive on Family Reunification: Are the Dilemmas Resolved?', *European Journal of Migration and Law*, 3 (2001), 61, 66.

The personal scope of the Directive has also been restricted; it does not apply to Union citizens who have not exercised their right to free movement. Persons enjoying subsidiary protection, temporary protection, and asylum seekers are also excluded. Further, unmarried or registered partners and their children, dependent ascendant relatives of the applicant or spouse with no other means of family support in the country of origin, and adult unmarried children of the applicant or spouse/unmarried partner 'who are objectively unable to provide for their own needs on account of their state of health' are not automatically eligible for family reunification. It is for the Member States to adopt legislation authorizing the entry and residence of these categories of third country nationals.[54] Such a decision does not bind other Member States should these people decide to reside in their territory in the future. Furthermore, the possibility of limiting the right to family reunification of children over the age of 12, who arrive independently from the rest of their family, in light of considerations concerning their 'capacity for integration', the restrictive measures concerning applications for family reunification of polygamous households, and the derogation enabling Member States to request that applications concerning family reunification of minor children have to be submitted before the age of 15, all demonstrate national executives' outmoded conception of 'integration' and their unwillingness to create the institutional preconditions for the democratic inclusion of migrant communities.[55]

The conditions set by the Directive for the exercise of the right to family reunification now include 'stable and regular resources which are sufficient to maintain the applicant and the members of his/her family, without recourse to the social assistance system of the Member State concerned', in addition to possession of sickness insurance covering all risks and adequate accommodation. In relation to the substantive rights of family members, Article 14(2) envisages the possibility of Member States setting a time limit of no more than 12 months, 'during which Member States may examine the situation of their labour market before authorizing family members to exercise an employed or self-employed activity'. Lastly, the qualifying period of residence

[54] Article 4(2) and (3) of Council Directive 2003/86.

[55] See also Council Directive 19/07, OJ [2000] L 180, implementing the principle of equal treatment between persons irrespective of racial or ethnic origin; Council Directive 02/12/EC, OJ [2000] L 303. It is interesting to note that Directive 2000/43 reflects the Commission's view that successful integration of third country nationals requires action against racism and xenophobia, but it does not cover discrimination on the basis of nationality, despite the calls for its inclusion made by the European Parliament and NGOs. The Directive is also without prejudice to provisions concerning the entry and residence of third country nationals and their access to employment and occupation (Article 3(2)).

required for the grant of an autonomous right of residence to family members has been raised to five years,[56] and the conditions concerning the grant and duration of an autonomous residence permit will be established by national laws. All these provisions fall short of placing third country nationals on equal terms with European Union citizens.

4. The Commission's Communication on a Community Immigration Policy: a paradigm shift?

In line with the Tampere mandate and in an attempt to go beyond the piecemeal approach to the legislative programme set out in Article 63 of the TEC, the Commission issued a Communication on a Community Immigration Policy in November 2000.[57] In this Communication, the Commission set out a comprehensive, flexible, and more liberal framework for the regulation of migration. It acknowledged the economic benefits of migration and emphasized the value of cultural diversity. The EU was described as 'by its very nature a pluralistic society', but with

> fundamental shared principles and values: respect for human rights and human dignity, appreciation of the value of pluralism and the recognition that membership of society is based on a series of rights but brings with it a number of responsibilities for all of its members be they nationals or migrants.[58]

The Commission justified the need for a 'new approach to immigration' and the corresponding shift in policy orientation on the basis of:

1. the new constitutional framework of the Migration Title and the centrality of these policies to the internal market;
2. the changing economic context of the Union and the existence of labour and skill shortages in the Member States; and
3. demographic concerns about low fertility rates and the ageing European population.

The impact of sustained lobbying by pro-migrant NGOs and the input of academics can be also be detected in the text.[59]

[56] See Article 15(1) of Council Directive 2003/86.

[57] See Commission Communication to the Council and the European Parliament on Community Immigration Policy, COM(2000) 757 final (22 November 2000).

[58] Ibid., at 20.

[59] E.g., it is stated that 'such a proactive immigration policy should be based on the recognition that migratory pressures will continue and that there are benefits that orderly immigration can

The Commission's suggested framework for a common migration policy focused on such areas as: admission to the EU for humanitarian reasons and the development of a European asylum system; admission of economic migrants; integration of legally resident third country nationals; coordinated action against illegal migration; and the development and implementation of migration policy in partnership with the countries of origin and transit. The principles underpinning the common legal framework for admission were transparency and rationality, differentiated rights according to the length of stay, clarity and simplicity of application and assessment procedures, and the availability of information to potential migrants. With regard to admission, the Commission proposed a flexible scheme, whereby the Member States would set out indicative admission targets in line with projected labour shortages, changing economic conditions, and the impact of existing policies on domestic arenas. In compiling their reports for the Commission, the Member States would have to involve the social partners, regional and local authorities, as well as all other actors involved in the integration of migrants. The Commission would produce a synthesis of the national reports. On the basis of the Commission's report, the Council would then lay down the principles of the common approach to be implemented within the next period. The Communication also proposed the establishment of a European information point, a website containing full information on admission policies and contact details for national authorities, information on employment opportunities, and conditions of entry and residence. The main concerns arising from the proposed linkage between admission and employment policy are that indicative targets could easily become quotas distinguishing desirable from undesirable migration and restrictive trends could easily slip into the framework.

The Communication also stated that a 'hard' definitive core of rights should be available to migrants on arrival, with this core of rights possibly extending with the length of stay—ultimately culminating in long-term resident status. Long-term resident status would include security of residence and the right of abode in another Member State. In this respect, the Communication used the EU Charter of Fundamental Rights as a reference point for the creation of 'civic citizenship' and the possibility of granting free movement rights to long-term resident third country nationals. 'Enabling migrants to acquire

bring to the EU, to the migrants themselves and to their countries of origin'. Ibid., at 13. On p 15, the Commission notes that 'the underlying principle of an EU immigration policy must be for different purposes that persons admitted should enjoy broadly the same rights and responsibilities as EU nationals, but that these may be incremental and related to the length of stay provided for in their entry conditions'. See also ibid., at 6–7, 9–11, and 22.

such [civic] citizenship after a minimum period of years might be a sufficient guarantee for many migrants to settle successfully into society or be a first step in the process of acquiring the nationality of the Member State concerned.'[60]

While integration issues fall within the competence of the Member States, the Communication opened up the possibility for the involvement of civil society in line with the principle of partnership among all actors involved and of coordination of action at the national and local levels. The EU could assist the process by developing a 'pedagogical strategy', promoting the exchange of information and good practice, and the development of guidelines or common standards for integration measures.

Notwithstanding the progressive nature of the Communication, the issue of political inclusion was not addressed. The proposed harmonization of national denizenship rules did not include local electoral rights (which are available in The Netherlands, Sweden, Ireland, Denmark, Finland, and in Spain and Portugal on the basis of reciprocity). National denizenship and the possibility of a European denizenship may widen the circle of 'belongers' to the civil society, but do not reduce political exclusion. Long-term resident third country nationals are not recognized as full members and equal participants in the European and national polities.

5. The Nice Settlement and the 'civic citizenship' approach

The importance of ensuring the fairer treatment of third country nationals was underlined by the 2000 Intergovernmental Conference. Although the Treaty of Nice extended the scope of qualified majority voting into 27 areas,[61] including free movement of Union citizens under Article 18 of the TEC, judicial cooperation in civil proceedings (with the exception of aspects relating to family law) is the only area of Title IV of the TEC to which qualified majority voting will apply.[62] A partial and deferred switch to qualified majority voting was agreed to at Nice. An amendment to Article 67 EC provided that

[60] See Commission Communication, above n 57, at 19–20.

[61] See Treaty of Nice Amending the Treaty on European Union, The Treaties Establishing the European Communities and Certain Related Acts, 10/03, OJ [2001] C 80, available at http://europa.eu.int/igc2000. The Treaty was officially signed on 26 February 2001.

[62] See TEC Article 65.

co-decision and qualified majority voting would apply to measures laying down common rules on asylum policy, but only after the Council has unanimously adopted legislation defining the common rules and main principles in the matter.[63] A Protocol was also annexed to the Treaty whereby the partners agreed that as of 1 May 2004, measures in the field of administrative cooperation would be adopted by qualified majority voting and consultation with the European Parliament.[64] In addition, Member States issued a declaration on Article 67 of the TEC, stating that measures setting out the conditions for the free circulation of third country nationals for short visits, illegal immigration, and illegal residence will be adopted by qualified majority voting and co-decision from 1 May 2004 onwards.[65] The same procedure may apply to measures and procedures concerning the carrying out of checks on persons crossing the external borders of Member States, provided that agreement has been reached on the field of application of these measures.[66] Lastly, the political declaration confirmed the Member States' intention to apply qualified majority voting to the other areas of the Title or parts of them as of 1 May 2004, or as soon as possible thereafter.

The European Council at Nice also took note of the progress on all aspects of the policy formulated at Tampere and approved the European Social Agenda, which emphasized the need to promote social integration.[67] According to paragraph 23 of Annex I, legally resident third country nationals should be 'integrated satisfactorily.' 'Satisfactory integration' is to be achieved by granting third country nationals rights and obligations comparable to those of Union citizens, implementing effective Community legislation combating all types of discrimination, and developing exchanges of experience and good practice on national integration policies and anti-discrimination policies. At Nice, the Council, the Commission, and the Parliament also jointly proclaimed the European Union Charter of Fundamental Rights.[68] The Charter did not redress the inequitable position of long-term resident

[63] See TEC Article 63(1) and (2)(a); see also Treaty of Nice, Article 2(4).

[64] See Protocol on Article 67 of the Treaty Establishing the European Community, 10/03, OJ [2001] C 80, at 69.

[65] See Declaration on Article 67 of the EC Treaty, 10/03, 2001 OJ (C 80), at 77–8.

[66] See TEC Article 62(2)(a).

[67] See Nice European Council, *Presidency Conclusions*, Press Release: Brussels (8/12/2000) Nr 400/1/00. Available at http://europa.eu.int/council/off/conclu/index.htm.

[68] See Charter of Fundamental Rights of the European Union 18/12, OJ [2000] C 264. Although several states wished to amend Article 6 of the TEU at Nice so that a reference could be included to the Charter of Fundamental Rights, the IGC decided not to incorporate the Charter into the Treaty. According to the Declaration on the future of the Union, which is annexed to the Treaty of Nice, this issue will be on the agenda of the 2004 IGC.

third country nationals. Apart from universal human rights, third country nationals enjoy the rights to good administration (Article 41), access to documents (Article 42) and non-judicial means of redress through complaints to the Ombudsman (Article 43), and petitions to the European Parliament (Article 44). The Charter also recognizes the right of migrant workers, authorized to work in Member States, to working conditions equivalent to those of Union citizens (Article 15(3)) and protection against unjustified dismissal. Yet it also reaffirmed the prevailing confinement of a core of civic and political rights to Union nationals, notwithstanding the fact that Article 45 stated that 'freedom of movement may be granted, in accordance with the Treaty establishing the EC, to nationals of third countries legally resident in the territory of a Member State'.[69] Although it could be argued that the inclusion of Article 45 is symbolically significant in that it demonstrates that a consensus is beginning to emerge with regard to the possibility of extending mobility rights to long-term resident third country nationals, the Charter itself is not distinguished by 'a morality of aspiration' which would include expanded rights for long-term resident third country nationals.

6. Revisiting the status of long-term resident third country nationals: the Commission's proposed Directive

Using the Charter as a point of orientation and an additional source of inspiration, the Commission proposed a Council Directive on the Status of Third Country Nationals who are Long-term Residents on 13 March 2001.[70] The legal bases of the Directive are Articles 63(3)(a) and 63(4) EC.[71] The Directive is designed to harmonize national laws governing the conditions for the acquisition and the scope of long-term resident status, and to grant long-term resident third country nationals the right of residence in the other Member States. Harmonization is justified on both normative (that is, to ensure equality of treatment with Union citizens) and pragmatic grounds. The latter include considerations of the needs of the employment market, the effective attainment of the internal market, and the enhancement of economic

[69] European Social Agenda, Article 45.

[70] See Commission Proposal for Council Directive 28/08, above n 15.

[71] Considering that the Directive can only be adopted by unanimity, Member States might react and argue that the Community's *acquis* concerning Article 63(4) is thin, particularly since the Amsterdam negotiations excluded legislation on access to the labour market.

and social cohesion (Articles 2 and 3(1)(k) of the TEC) by ensuring the integration of third country nationals.

The harmonization of national legislation involves the establishment of common Community rules governing the long-term resident status of third country nationals throughout the Community. However, the Commission makes it clear that it follows the 'minimum harmonization' approach. This means that the Directive will act as 'a floor', thereby allowing the Member States to put in place more favourable conditions for the acquisition of permanent status and expanded rights.[72] In addition, the Directive will not affect more favourable provisions entailed by the Community, or mixed agreements concluded with third countries.[73] The proposal is also without prejudice to favourable provisions contained in the European Convention on Establishment, the European Social Charter, and the European Convention on the Legal Status of Migrant Workers.

The principle underpinning this Directive is that domicile generates entitlements both in the forms of equalization of the treatment of third country nationals with nationals of the host Member State in socio-economic life and enhanced protection against expulsion, as well as rights of mobility within the Union. This is reflected in the personal scope of the Directive, which covers all long-term and legally resident third country nationals, including Geneva refugees and family members of Union citizens, thereby empowering them to exercise individually the right to reside in another Member State.[74] The Directive does not apply to asylum seekers, persons enjoying subsidiary or temporary protection,[75] students, seasonal workers, cross-border service providers, workers posted by cross-border service providers, and diplomats.

After five years of continuous legal residence[76] a Member State is obliged to grant long-term resident status to third country nationals who have stable and

[72] See Commission Proposal for Council Directive 28/08, above n 15, at Articles 14, 12(2). For a detailed discussion of national laws entailing more favourable provisions, see House of Lords, Select Committee on the European Union, 5th *Report on the Legal Status of Long-Term Resident Third Country Nationals*, Session 2001–2002, 6 November 2001, HL Paper 33, paras 13–16.

[73] See Commission Proposal, above n 15, at Article 3(4).

[74] See ibid., at Article 3. The United Kingdom has decided not to opt into the proposed Directive owing to policy considerations about border control and control over admissions. In addition, 'the Government does not support the extension of the right of free movement to legally resident third country nationals': see Home Office Minister Lord Rooker's statement in the House of Lords on 23 July 2001, HL Paper 33, at paras 26, 30–35, above n 72.

[75] The Commission intends to submit a proposal for a Directive on the extension of the long-term resident status Directive to persons enjoying subsidiary protection.

[76] The five-year residence period has been criticized, given that Decision 1/80 of the EC-Turkey Association Council and ILO Convention No 143 require shorter periods of residence.

adequate resources to meet their own subsistence needs and those of their family members, and who are covered by sickness insurance.[77] Refugees and third country nationals born in the territory of a Member State are exempt from the test for resources and sickness insurance.[78] Absences from the territory of the Member State for less than six consecutive months, or owing to important and specific reasons (military service, secondments for work purposes, serious illness, maternity, research or studies), will not be regarded as interrupting the period of residence. Apart from the derogation provided for in Article 7 for public policy and domestic security considerations along the lines of Council Directive 64/221, the Member State must grant long-term resident status automatically where the acquisition criteria are met.[79] Applicants must lodge an application accompanied by documents proving that the applicant meets the necessary conditions contained in Articles 5 and 6. The competent national authorities must examine the application within six months after it is lodged. The long-term resident status can be withdrawn only on certain grounds set out in the Directive, namely: absence from the territory for more than two consecutive years, fraudulent acquisition of status, adoption of an expulsion measure under the conditions set out in Article 13, and acquisition of long-term resident status in a second Member State.[80] The status cannot be withdrawn in the events of unemployment and reliance on public funds. Procedural guarantees against the withdrawal of status are provided for by Article 11. As proof of the right of residence, a long-term EC residence permit will be issued, valid for 10 years and renewable automatically on expiry. This practice will be uniform throughout the Community.[81] As the permit is not constitutive of the right of residence, its expiry can never constitute a ground for deportation.[82]

Long-term resident third country nationals will enjoy enhanced protection against expulsion[83] and are entitled to equal treatment as regards access to

[77] See Directive, above n 15, at Articles 5, 6. [78] See ibid., at Article 6(2).

[79] See ibid., at Article 8(3). The grant of the status to a qualifying applicant is thus mandatory.

[80] See ibid., at Article 10.

[81] This will be in accordance with the specifications laid down by the Council Regulation proposed by the Commission on 23 March 2001, 2001/0082 (CNS), COM (2001) 157 final.

[82] See Case 48/75, *Royer* [1976] ECR 497, [1976] 2 CMLR 619; Case 175/79, *Stanislaus Pieck* [1980] ECR 2171, [1980] 3 CMLR 220.

[83] Article 13 sets out the provisions concerning protection against expulsion. These draw on Directive 64/221 and the relating jurisprudence. Similarly, Article 13(4) is inspired by decisions of the European Court of Human Rights relating to Article 8 ECHR. Article 13(5) provides for a judicial redress procedure against an expulsion decision, and Article 13(6) states that legal aid should be given to long-term residents lacking adequate resources. Lastly, emergency expulsion decisions against long-term residents are prohibited under Article 13(7).

employment and self-employed activity, conditions of employment and working conditions, education and vocational training, including study grants, recognition of qualifications, social security and health care, social assistance, social and tax benefits, access to goods and services including public and private sector housing, freedom of association and union membership, and free access to the entire territory of the Member State concerned. Although this list seems impressive, in reality it confirms the existing core of socio-economic rights granted by the Member States to permanent settlers as well as to EU and EEA nationals. Civic involvement and participation does not extend to the political field, however: electoral rights are excluded from the material scope of the Directive. Nonetheless, Article 12(2) states that Member States may extend the benefit of equal treatment to matters that are not referred to in Article 12(1).

Chapter III of the Directive outlines the conditions for the exercise of the right of residence in a Member State other than the one that granted the long-term resident status, thereby implementing Article 63(4) of the TEC and reflecting Article 45(2) of the European Union Charter of Fundamental Rights. Long-term resident third country nationals, who are not service providers or posted workers,[84] have the right to reside in a second Member State for long stays in order to pursue an economic activity as employed or self-employed persons, for study or vocational training purposes, or for all other purposes, provided that they are self-sufficient and have sickness insurance.[85] By analogy with EC law in the field of free movement of workers, temporary incapacity for work as a result of illness or accident, involuntary unemployment, and entitlement to unemployment benefits in case of unemployment do not constitute grounds for the loss of worker status.[86] In cases of voluntary unemployment in order to embark on vocational training, the ECJ's ruling in *Lair* applies; that is, there must be a link between the previous employment activity and the training to be pursued.[87]

When the application for a residence permit is lodged, the authorities in the second Member State may require documentary evidence. An exhaustive list of the items of documentary evidence is contained in Article 17(2)–(4), thereby limiting the national authorities' discretionary power. The right to enter the territory of another and to reside there presumably applies to work

[84] Their legal status is governed by the relevant Commission proposals. See Council Directive 28/08, above n 15, at Article 15(3).

[85] See ibid., at Articles 15, 16(1).

[86] See Council Directive 68/360, OJ [1968] L 257, at Article 7(1).

[87] See Council Directive 28/08, above n 15, at Article 16(2); Case 39/86, *Lair v Universität Hannover* [1988] ECR 3161, [1989] 3 CMLR 545.

seekers, by analogy to *Antonnisen*.[88] The family members of the long-term resident may accompany him or her to the second Member State, or join him or her there, on condition that they already formed a family in the first Member State. If the family was not constituted in the first Member State, the Council Directive on family reunification will apply.[89]

A Member State may refuse applications for residence on the grounds of public policy, domestic security, or public health. The proposal also provides for a series of procedural guarantees, such as a statutory period for examining applications for residence permits, arrangements for notifying interested parties, redress procedures, and conditions governing expulsion. With respect to the last, Article 25(2) of the proposed Directive provides that expulsion decisions may not be accompanied by a permanent ban on residence. As soon as they enter the second Member State, long-term residents will enjoy all the benefits that they enjoyed in the first Member State under the same conditions as nationals,[90] with the exception of social assistance and maintenance grants for study.[91] Family members are entitled to the rights conferred by Article 12 of the proposed Council Directive for family reunification, that is: access to education, to employment or self-employment, and to vocational training.

Long-term residents living in the second Member State will retain their status in the first Member State until they have acquired the same status in the second Member State. If they wish, they may, after being legally resident in the second Member State for five years, apply to be considered as long-term residents in that Member State. The first Member State will be obliged to readmit, together with their family members, long-term residents whose residence permits have been withdrawn by the second Member State.

Evidently, the draft Directive regards integration as dependent upon the maintenance of existing and the creation of new social and economic spaces for personal projects at both the national and European levels. National denizenship goes hand in hand with European denizenship (see Figure 1 below). The grant of the latter represents a major step towards inclusion. Asserting the freedom of long-standing residents and enhancing their security,

[88] See Case 292/89, *R v Immigration Appeals Tribunal, ex parte Antonissen* [1991] ECR I-745. Having said that, however, I share the criticism that the position of long-term residents in a second Member State before acquiring a residence permit is not satisfactorily explained in the Directive. On this see HL Report 33, para 50, above n 72.

[89] See Council Directive 2000/83, above n 52.

[90] According to the draft Directive's Recital (17), 'the rights enjoyed by the persons concerned in the second Member State should be similar to those enjoyed by citizens of the Union when they exercise their right of free movement': above n 15.

[91] See draft Directive 28/08, above n 15, at Article 24.

Figure 1: Actual and potential pathways to political inclusion

National Denizenship	→	National Citizenship
↓		↓
European Denizenship	(*f*→)	European Citizenship

however, takes precedence over creating the institutional preconditions for their participation in political life. In the eyes of the drafters, national denizenship is likely to lead to national citizenship and, thus, to European citizenship. At the same time, however, the grant of European denizenship leaves open the possibility of potential future extension of European citizenship to long-term resident third country nationals.

7. Conclusion

The European Union is an experimental polity; it has neither a fixed structure nor a determinate telos. Rather, it is the product of history, imaginative design, conflict, and compromise. As such, it brings with it the presence of the past with all its intellectual baggage—be it in the form of ideas, concepts, presumptions, policy tools, or organizing principles—and a burden of expectation. By the latter I mean the expectation to transform statism and nationalism, to reconfigure the identities of its constituent units, and to turn aliens and old enemies into associates. And yet the borrowing of concepts (for example, integration) and policies (for example, the fields of citizenship and migration) from the national-statist context limits the capacity to talk about new developments and to make advances on democratic governance at the European level. Nationality has commonly been taken as a proxy for defining the political community, and the transplantation of this principle to the European level has resulted in the exclusion of Europe's long-standing residents of migrant origin. However, the situation is changing. EU institutions have realized that the solution to the issue of long-term resident third country nationals lies in the recognition of their ethical standing and the refusal to treat them as mere objects to be dealt with according to whim. The post-Tampere developments and the Commission's proposals for Council Directives recognize long-term resident third country nationals as rights holders to be treated equally in the workplace and society. Although the vocabulary of integration still dominates this discussion, the preceding paragraphs have shown the merits of replacing it with a pluralistic mode of incorporation that is guided by the dialectic of recognition, inclusion, and respect for differences. But embracing the latter would also require efforts to incorporate long-term resident third country nationals politically and to recognize them as full members and equal participants in democratic governance.

Part V

Culture and the European Union's External Relations: Trade and Aid

11

Preserving and Promoting Differences? The External Dimension of Cultural Cooperation

*Joseph A. McMahon**

1. Introduction

Convinced that the diversity of traditions and cultures has for centuries been one of Europe's riches and that the principle of tolerance is the guarantee of the maintenance in Europe of an open society respecting the cultural diversity to which we are attached.[1]

This 1993 Declaration goes on to acknowledge that cultural cooperation was essential to the creation of a cohesive yet diverse Europe. Such cooperation, involving schemes in partnership with public authorities and the community at large, would occur in five areas: education, the media, cultural action, the protection and enhancement of cultural heritage, and the participation of young people. In particular it was recognized that states 'should create the conditions necessary for persons of national minorities to develop their culture while preserving their religion, traditions and customs'.[2] The parties to this Declaration included not only the then 12 Member States of the Community, but also future members Austria, Finland, and Sweden, and the acceding countries of Central and Eastern Europe. The Declaration began: 'We, Heads of State and Government of the Member States of the Council of Europe . . . '

In exploring the external dimension of the Community's activities in the field of culture it is impossible to ignore the activities of the Council of

* Professor of International Trade Law, the Queen's University of Belfast.

[1] Preamble, Vienna Declaration 1993. The text of the Vienna Declaration is available at http://culture.coe.fr/welcome/eng/ecopsom.html.

[2] This would also involve work beginning on drafting a protocol complementing the European Convention on Human Rights in the cultural field (Appendix II of the Vienna Declaration).

Europe. The most important elements of these activities are those arising out of the 1954 European Cultural Convention.[3] The Convention recognized the existence of a 'European culture' which a policy of common action would safeguard and develop. Under Article 1 of the Convention, each Contracting Party is required to take 'appropriate measures to safeguard and encourage the development of its national contribution to the common cultural heritage of Europe'. Cooperation, effected through the Council for Cultural Cooperation, focused on the five areas noted above, and the various programmes were supported through a Cultural Fund. The history of cultural cooperation under the Convention has been marked by five distinct phases of activity: reconciliation, mutual recognition, establishment of common terminology, a shared approach to find solutions, and joint action.[4] The re-organization of the activities of the Council for Cultural Cooperation in 1996 had to take into account the emergence of a cultural policy within the Community. This policy was not seen as a threat to the role that the Council of Europe had developed as Article 151 EC (ex Article 128) explicitly recognized the role of the Council of Europe.

Indeed, the Commission, in its first Communication on Cultural Policy in 1977, realized that action taken by the Community in the sphere of culture would be complementary to that of other international organizations, such as the Council of Europe.[5] In its 1982 assessment of its activities in the cultural sector, the Commission:[6]

> . . . considered, and still considers, that Community action in the cultural sector should be both complementary and subsidiary to what is already being done internationally. There is therefore no duplication with the efficiently run activities of organisations like the Council of Europe, for which the development of culture is a prime objective.

This was endorsed by the first formal meeting of the Council and Ministers of Cultural Affairs within the Council in June 1984, where broad agreement was reached on five areas for future cultural cooperation, which included cultural cooperation with 'non-member countries'.[7] Beyond these countries and the

[3] Available on Council of Europe website, http://www.coe.int. See Resolution No III on European Cultural Cooperation adopted by the fourth Conference of European Ministers responsible for Cultural Affairs (1984) and Recommendation 1216 (1993) adopted by the Council of Europe's Parliamentary Assembly on European Cultural Cooperation, inviting the Community to accede to the European Cultural Convention.

[4] See Grosjean, E, *Forty Years of European Cultural Co-operation*, available at the following website: http://www.coe.int/T/F/coopération_culturelle/Commun/40Cceng.asp, 2–5.

[5] *Community Action in the Cultural Sector*, EC Bulletin Supp 6/77, 6.

[6] *Stronger Community Action in the Cultural Sector*, EC Bulletin Supp 6/82, 7.

[7] EC Bulletin 6-1984, point 2.1.63.

Council of Europe, it was also recognized that it was necessary to cooperate with international organizations that were working in the area.[8] It came as no surprise that a limited external competence would be attributed to the Community whenever the Treaty incorporated a reference to a specific policy on culture. Article 151(3) EC states: 'The Community and the Member States shall foster cooperation with third countries and the competent international organisations in the sphere of culture, in particular the Council of Europe.'

The first Commission Communication on culture after the Treaty of Maastricht, outlining the future scope of Community action in the field of culture, proposed three areas of activity.[9] These are a Community contribution to the flowering of culture in the frontier-free area, bringing the common cultural heritage to the fore by providing support for specific areas, and, lastly, increased cooperation with non-member countries and international organizations.[10] The Conclusions of Ministers of Culture meeting within the Council in November 1992 on the Commission Communication did not define the precise scope of future activities, although they endorsed the Commission's proposals for the future direction of the Community's cultural activities.[11] However, the Council continued by pointing to the limited financial resources available for these activities, leading it to emphasize the complementary nature of Community activity in this area. Indeed, such activity is placed below that which could be achieved at national or regional level, on the one hand, and at international level, on the other hand.

The issue of financial resources has been addressed in the Culture 2000 programme, which established a single financing and programming instrument for cultural cooperation for the period up to the end of 2004.[12] Article 1(f) sets as an objective for Community action 'the fostering of inter-cultural dialogue and mutual exchange between European and non-European cultures', and Article 2(c) lists as one of the types of cultural actions and events 'special cultural events with a European and/or international dimension'. The programme may, according to Article 7, include participation by, and cooperation

[8] E.g., in the copyright area, the Berne and Rome Conventions that are administered by the World Intellectual Property Organization.

[9] COM (92) 149, *New Prospects for Community Cultural Action*, 1.

[10] As examples of the internationalization of Community activity in the field of culture, it is possible to point to the European City of Culture scheme, instituted in 1985, which has already been extended to other European countries. In parallel with this event there is to be a European Cultural Month to be held each year in a European city outside the Community, OJ [1990] C 162/1.

[11] OJ [1992] C 366/1.

[12] Decision 508/2000 establishing the Culture 2000 programme, OJ [2000] L 63/1. Proposals have been made for the continuation of the programme until the end of 2006.

with, third countries and joint actions with relevant international organizations, such as the Council of Europe.[13] Shortly after the Decision of the European Parliament and the Council establishing the Culture 2000 programme, the Commission launched a major reform of the Community external assistance programme.[14] Informed by Article 177 EC on development cooperation policy, the primary emphasis of the Community's external assistance would become the alleviation of poverty and the better integration of developing countries into the world trading system.[15]

The reformed external assistance programme will inform the Community's cooperation strategy with third countries. The 1992 Commission Communication on culture recognized that a breakthrough had been made in this area by the inclusion of provisions on cultural cooperation in various agreements concluded by the Community with third countries.[16] Given the increasing number of agreements including provisions on cultural cooperation, the Commission considered that it would be necessary to ensure that such provisions fitted within a more coherent framework and that the provisions were actually applied in the concerned countries. The following section of this chapter outlines the culture provisions of cooperation agreements concluded with the countries of Africa, the Caribbean, and the Pacific (ACP), Europe, and the Mediterranean, before discussing cultural cooperation arising from the Asia-Europe Meeting (ASEM). It ends with an assessment of whether or not a coherent framework has actually been established.

2. Cooperation Agreements

(a) The Lomé and Cotonou Agreements

One of the earliest examples of cultural cooperation with third countries can be found in the 1990 Lomé Convention, Article 139 of which states, *inter alia*, that:

Such co-operation shall aim at promoting, in the interests of dialogue, exchange and mutual enrichment and, on the basis of equality, a better understanding and greater

[13] By virtue of Article 7, cooperation with third countries is dependent on the additional funds being made available. One project, involving Egypt, was funded in the first round of projects. For details see http://www.europa.eu.int/comm/culture/coop.pdf.

[14] Commission Communication on the reform of the Management of External Assistance (16 May 2000).

[15] See Report on the Implementation of the European Commission's External Assistance, available at http://europa.eu.int/comm/europeaid/reports/status_report_2001_en.pdf.

[16] See above, n 9, at p 16.

solidarity between ACP governments and peoples on the one hand, and between ACP and Community governments and peoples on the other.

The principal areas of cooperation were listed in Articles 145–149 as including the promotion of cultural identities and inter-cultural dialogue, safeguarding the cultural heritage, the production and distribution of cultural goods, cultural events, and, lastly, information and communications. Under the Convention, the ACP state had to request the inclusion of cultural cooperation within the scope of the national indicative programmes that formed the basis of financing cooperation between the Community and the ACP.[17] The cultural dimension had to embrace all areas and be reflected in all development projects and programmes. Moreover, it was designed to back up the policies and measures adopted by the ACP states to enhance their human resources, increase their own creative capacities, and promote their cultural identities. As for the financial support provided under the national indicative programmes, in over 10 years of cooperation, 380 cultural projects were funded through the European Development Fund at a cost of €116 million.[18]

The fundamental revision of the Lomé IV Convention effected through the Cotonou Agreement led to a major restructuring of the relationship between the Community and the ACP countries.[19] Article 27 of the Cotonou Agreement on cultural development provides that the aims of cultural cooperation shall be:

i) integrating the cultural dimension at all levels of development cooperation;
ii) recognizing, preserving, and promoting cultural values and identities to enable inter-cultural dialogue;
iii) recognizing, preserving, and promoting the value of cultural heritage, supporting the development of capacity in this sector; and
iv) developing cultural industries and enhancing market access opportunities for cultural goods and services.

Paragraphs 121 to 126 of the Compendium providing policy guidelines in specific areas of cooperation, signed at the same time as the Cotonou Agreement, deals with the implementation of Article 27.[20] The Compendium

[17] Applications for funding could also be made on a regional basis and specific procedures existed for the three areas: assistance in the production of films and documentaries, participation of ACP artists in European cultural events, and the production of documentaries to raise awareness in Europe of development issues.

[18] See: http://www.europea.eu.int/comm/development/body/theme/human_ . . . /pol_culture_1_en.htm.

[19] OJ [2000] L 317/3.

[20] Ibid., at p 355. See also draft of the Partnership Agreement between members of the Group of African, Caribbean and Pacific States and the European Community and its Member States, COM (2000) 324.

adds to the dimensions of cultural cooperation found in Article 27 by seeking to place such cooperation, as the Lomé Convention had, in the context of the development strategies of the ACP countries. The economic importance of culture is to be emphasized, although it is recognized that the 'economic openings are indirect'.[21] Hence, the requirement that the cultural economy issue be broached in a sectoral approach.

As for future cultural cooperation activities, the Compendium envisaged studies, research, and measures in two areas (the cultural aspects of taking into account the cultural dimension of cooperation and the promotion of cultural identities of the ACP peoples and inter-cultural dialogue) and the promotion of cultural exchanges. As for the resources to be allocated to such cooperation, it must be pointed out that the primary objective of development aid is now poverty alleviation.[22] Within this overarching objective six priority areas were decided on by the Commission in 2000 and culture does not feature in any of these.[23] Although the greater concentration of Community aid is to be commended, the question has been raised about the future of policy areas outside the six priority areas. A suggestion has been made that the official aid could be concentrated on the six areas, with limited financial support being provided to proposals from non-state actors who seek to use the decentralized management procedures outlined in the Cotonou Agreement.[24] Early indications of the impact of the new approach to the allocation of aid introduced by the Cotonou Agreement suggest that resources are being allocated to capacity building among non-state actors.[25]

Whilst it is too early to state that the advances in cultural cooperation witnessed in the final years of the Lomé relationship will continue under the partnership for development established by the Cotonou Agreement, the omens are promising. This optimism stems from the outcome of the first

[21] OJ [2000] L 317/3, para 124.

[22] See http://europa.eu.int/comm/development/lex/en/council20001110_en.htm for details of the joint statement of the Council and the Commission.

[23] The six areas are: the link between trade and development; support for integration and regional cooperation; support for macro-economic policies that have a direct link to poverty reduction strategies; transport; food security and sustainable rural development; and the strengthening of institutional capabilities. There are to be four cross-cutting themes—human rights, the environment, gender, and good governance.

[24] 'Concentrating EU AID: What about other Priorities?—The Case of Cultural Cooperation', in *Mainstreaming Participation*, Cotonou Newsletter No 2 (Maastricht: ECPDM, 2001), available at http://www.ecdpm.org/en/cotonou/cn2_gb.htm.

[25] 'Major Trends in programming in the 9th EDF', in *Putting Policies First*, Cotonou Newsletter No 3 (Maastricht: ECPDM, 2001), available at http://www.ecdpm.org/en/cotonou/cn3_gb.htm.

meeting of the ACP Ministers of Culture held in Dakar in July 2003.[26] The aim of the meeting, according to the ACP Secretary-General, was to 'examine the issues affecting the role of the ACP countries' cultures in their development policies and . . . seek the ways and means of promoting the cultures and cultural industries of the ACP States and regions'.[27] The resulting Declaration committed the ACP to formulate an agreed cultural policy, taking into account existing national and regional policies. This policy would include cultural heritage, cultural cooperation and partnership, capacity building, and the promotion and adoption of measures conducive to the development and establishment of all forms of cultural industries in ACP states.[28] According to the accompanying Action Plan, these cultural policies would be integrated into development strategies, which in turn would recognize the cultural sector as a priority area.[29] If implemented, this will fulfil the aims of cultural cooperation as identified in Article 27 of the Cotonou Agreement, and should therefore ensure Community support for the Action Plan.

(b) Europe

Beyond Lomé, the 1992 Council conclusions on the future of European cultural cooperation also highlighted the Community's relationship with the countries of the European Free Trade Area. One reason for this was that the agreement on the European Economic Area contained a Declaration on the strengthening of cultural links between the two areas, which records the Parties':[30]

> . . . intention to strengthen and broaden cooperation in the area of cultural affairs, in order to contribute to a better understanding between peoples of a multicultural Europe and to safeguard and further develop the national and regional heritage that enriches European culture by its diversity.

The 1992 conclusions also called for special attention to be paid to the countries of Central and Eastern Europe, especially as these countries were potential

[26] The meeting had been prompted by the Santa Domingo Declaration of the ACP Heads and Governments in November 1999 (http://www.acpsec.org/gb/summit2, para 42 and para 13 of the Plan of Action) and the Nadi Declaration of the ACP Heads of State and Government in July 2002 (http://www.acpsec.org/fiji, paras 71–73 and Decision 3/III).

[27] See http://www.acpsec.org/gb/press/sgspeak.dak.htm.

[28] Available at http://www.acpsec.org/gb/council/decldakareng.htm.

[29] Available at http://www.acpsec.org/gb/council/actiondakeng.htm.

[30] OJ [1994] L 1/3, Declaration 16. Declaration 17 records the parties intention to cooperate against illegal traffic in cultural goods.

members of the European Union.[31] This point was recognized at the European Council meetings in Copenhagen in June 1993 and in Essen in December 1994.[32] Pending their accession the relations between these countries and the Community would be governed by a series of Association Agreements, usually referred to as the Europe Agreements.[33]

With respect to cultural cooperation, the provisions of the Europe Agreements state:[34]

> The Parties undertake to promote cultural cooperation. Where appropriate, Community's cultural cooperation programmes, or those of one or more Member States may be extended to the [applicant country] and further activities of interest to both sides developed. This cooperation may notably cover: literary translation, conservation and restoration of monuments and sites (architectural and cultural heritage), training for those dealing with cultural affairs, the organization of European-oriented cultural events.

The next paragraph encourages cooperation in the promotion of the European audio-visual industry, through the participation of the applicant countries in the Community's MEDIA programme. The Europe Agreement was the first aspect of the pre-accession strategy for these countries agreed at the Essen European Council. As for the financing of this strategy, the Phare programme would be of pivotal importance.[35] This programme, designed to help in the adoption by the applicant countries of the Community *acquis*, has two main priorities—institution building and investment financing. Resources would be allocated through accession partnerships, which would identify the priority areas in which the Community *acquis* is to be adopted, the programming

[31] The Parliament had previously passed a Resolution on cultural relations between the Community and Central and Eastern Europe (OJ [1991] C 267). The Resolution recommended that cultural relations be developed in nine areas: information; language and translation; training; the audio-visual sector; art; publishing; libraries; the architectural and cultural heritage; and town twinning.

[32] Negotiations began in March 1998 with Cyprus, the Czech Republic, Estonia, Hungary, Poland, and Slovenia, and with the remaining applicants in February 2000.

[33] Europe Agreements have been concluded with the following countries Bulgaria (OJ [1994] L 358), the Czech Republic (OJ [1994] L 360), Estonia (OJ [1998] L 68), Hungary (OJ [1993] L 347), Latvia (OJ [1998] L 26), Lithuania (OJ [1998] L 51), Poland (OJ [1993] L 348), Romania (OJ [1994] L 357), Slovakia (OJ [1994] L 359), and Slovenia (OJ [1999] L 51). Association Agreements of longer standing exist for Cyprus (OJ [1977] L 133), Malta (OJ [1971] L 61), and Turkey (OJ [1964] B 217/3685).

[34] Beyond this provision, the Preamble noted the desire of the Parties to establish cultural cooperation and develop exchanges of information, and Article 1(2) of each Agreement lists the promotion of cooperation in cultural matters as one of the aims of the Agreement.

[35] The Phare programme was established by Regulation 3906/89 (OJ [1989] L 375/11) and does not cover Cyprus, Malta, and Turkey. Pre-accession aid to Cyprus and Malta is governed by Regulation 555/2000 (OJ [2000] L 68/3) and to Turkey by Regulation 390/2001 (OJ [2001] L 58/1).

of financial assistance, and the terms applying to this assistance.[36] The 1999 Berlin European Council decided to double pre-accession aid from 2000.[37]

Further progress on cultural cooperation with the applicant countries was made as a result of a 1995 Council Resolution in which it was recognized that their participation in various Community programmes was 'of major importance for their integration into the Union and for their future accession'.[38] The resolution highlighted three areas in which the associated countries considered the initiation of cooperation to be important. First, the development of a legal, administrative, and management environment conducive to the expansion of cultural and audio-visual activities and exchanges in those countries. Secondly, the establishment of effective distribution channels within cultural industries such as publishing, records, and film. Lastly, the conservation, restoration, and enhancement of the cultural heritage. It is interesting to note that Community cooperation with these countries would be complementary to such cooperation occurring at bilateral levels. As for what the Community contribution was expected to be, the Resolution invited the Commission, *inter alia*, to make a study of the financial arrangements that could be used to fund projects in the cultural industry.[39]

The day before the Council passed the 1995 Resolution there had been a joint meeting of the Council and the Ministers for Audio-visual and Cultural Affairs with six of the applicant countries, which had explored the priorities for action and specific areas of cooperation. Speaking at the end of the discussions the President of the Council summarized the proceedings and concluded that 'we now have the conditions to start pragmatic and tangible cooperation around the cultural values which we all share'.[40] A year later, a similar meeting expressed the desire of the Central and Eastern European countries to participate in the Kaleidoscope programme, the soon to be adopted Ariane and Raphael programmes, and the MEDIA II programme, as part of the alignment of their legislation in this area with the Community *acquis*.[41] In a subsequent Resolution in June 2001, the Council stated that this alignment

[36] Regulation 622/98 (OJ [1998] L 85/1). On the accession partnerships of Cyprus and Malta, see Decision 2001/802 (OJ [2001] L 304/17); and of Turkey, Decision 2001/235 (OJ [2001] L 85/13).

[37] See Regulation 1266/99 (OJ [1999] L 161/68).

[38] OJ [1995] C 247/2. The Resolution noted the existing scope of cooperation, which included cultural events, heritage, books, and reading.

[39] The European Bank for Reconstruction and Development, the European Investment Bank, and the Phare programme were specifically highlighted in this regard.

[40] Details of the meeting were recorded in the minutes to the 1841st Council Meeting. Details of this meeting are available on the Europa website, http://www.europa.eu.int.

[41] Ibid., 1936th Council Meeting.

was still not complete, and it stressed the need for a reinforced and increased exchange of information and experience between the EU and its Member States and the candidate countries in the audio-visual field.[42] The Resolution underlined the importance of participation in Community programmes, such as the MEDIA II programme, as an integral part of the pre-accession strategy for these countries. However, it did point out that such participation could occur only once their legislation was sufficiently aligned with the audio-visual *acquis*.[43]

Following the successful conclusion of accession negotiations, which focused on the adoption of the 'Television Without Frontiers' Directive,[44] the countries of Central and Eastern Europe have participated in the Culture 2000 programme.[45] This emphasizes the special position naturally occupied by these countries in the external dimension of the Community's cultural policy; a position that is given added value as a result of their participation in the cultural activities of the Council of Europe.

(c) *The Mediterranean*

Provisions supporting cultural cooperation exist in the agreements concluded with the countries of the Mediterranean under the Euro-Mediterranean partnership. For example, Article 69 of the Euro-Mediterranean Agreement with Tunisia instructs the Parties to conduct regular dialogue on any social matter that is of interest to them.[46] The list of issues deserving special mention include schemes and programmes to encourage mutual knowledge of cultures and civilizations. Cooperation in cultural matters is specifically provided for

[42] OJ [2001] C 213. See also the Council Resolution on the exchange of information and experience on the conditions for professional artists in the context of the EU enlargement, in the same issue. The resolutions are also available on the Europa website, n 40 above.

[43] Point 13 of the Resolution. On the alignment of the legislation of the applicant countries with the Community's audio-visual *acquis*, see Commission Reports COM (1998) 700–711, COM (1999) 69 and 501–13, and COM (2000) 701–713.

[44] For details of the negotiations, see http://www.europa.eu.int/comm/enlargement/negotiations/chapters/chap20/index.htm.

[45] See COM (2001) 128. See also Decision 2001/802 (OJ [2001] L 304/17—Decision of the EU-Romania Association Council adopting the terms and conditions for the participation of Romania in the Culture 2000 programme).

[46] OJ [1998] L 97/2. For a further example, with near identical wording, see the Euro-Mediterranean Agreement with Morocco, OJ [2000] L 70/2. The Agreement with the Palestinian Authority (OJ [1997] L 187/3) is different from other agreements. With respect to culture, Article 57 of the Agreement provides: 'The Parties shall promote cultural co-operation. The area of co-operation may include Community activities concerning, in particular, translation, exchange of works of art and artists, conservation and restoration of historic and cultural monuments and sites, training of persons working in the cultural field, the organization of European-oriented cultural events, raising mutual awareness and contributing to the dissemination of information on outstanding cultural events.'

in Article 74, which promises to provide a firmer footing for lasting cultural dialogues and continuous cultural cooperation. Although no field of activity is excluded, special emphasis is to be placed on young people, written and audio-visual means of expression and communication, protection of heritage, and the dissemination of culture, in putting together cooperation projects and programmes and in carrying out joint activities. Such projects, programmes, and activities will be financed under the MEDA Regulation, which also extends beyond bilateral funding to regional funding.[47]

Although Euro-Mediterranean Agreements have not yet been concluded with all the relevant countries, cooperation can still occur through the Barcelona process. This process established three pillars of Euro-Mediterranean cooperation: political dialogue, a Euro-Mediterranean Free Trade Area, and social dialogue.[48] A greater understanding between cultures forms part of the third pillar and dialogue in this area is seen as contributing to the peace, stability, and development of the region. The Work Programme attached to the 1995 Barcelona Declaration with respect to dialogue between cultures and civilizations lists five particular areas where concrete action should be taken. These are: cultural and creative heritage, cultural and artistic events, co-production (theatres and cinemas), translations and other means of cultural dissemination, and training. A separate part of the Work Programme urges closer interaction between the media as a means to promote cultural understanding.

Reviewing progress on the Work Programme at the second Euro-Mediterranean Ministerial Conference, it was recommended that cultural aspects should be taken into account in other actions taken within the framework of the partnership.[49] Reference was also made to the first Euro-Mediterranean Ministerial Conference on Cultural Heritage, which had been held in Bologna in April 1996. The resulting Declaration from this Conference stated that all joint actions in the cultural domain would have the following priorities:[50]

- the development of human resources;
- the transfer of know-how;

[47] See Regulation 1488/96 (OJ [1996] L 189/1), as amended by Regulation 2698/2000 (OJ [2000] L 311/1). See also Decision 96/706 (OJ [1996] L 325/20) on the guidelines for the use of MEDA funds on a bilateral and regional basis. The funds currently available under MEDA are €5350000000.

[48] See http://www.europa.eu.int/comm/external_relations/euromed/doc.htm for the Barcelona Declaration and all subsequent declarations under the Partnership. See also *Euromed Report* No 10 (June 2000) for the Common Strategy in the Mediterranean adopted by the European Council meeting in Fiera in June 2000.

[49] See website, n 48 above, for the recommendations of the Malta Ministerial Conference.

[50] The Declaration of the Euro-Mediterranean Meeting of Ministers of Culture is available at http://www/europa.eu.int/comm/external_relations/med_mideast/euro_med_p.../culture.html.

- training in culture related skills;
- the establishment of joint systems of information and communication;
- the use of new technologies; and
- the promotion of sustainable development.

Joint cultural action would be promoted bilaterally, multilaterally, or through participation in internal Community programmes. The Declaration went on to set broad guidelines for projects aimed at conserving and enhancing cultural heritage using the usual techniques of cultural cooperation: stocktaking, exchange of experience, information, and know-how, and training for those in the sector.[51] These broad guidelines would later be translated into the Euromed Heritage Programme, which would become operational in September 1998.[52]

In 1998, shortly after the second Euro-Mediterranean Ministerial Conference, another Conference of the Ministers of Culture was held in Rhodes.[53] In addition to reaffirming the objectives agreed in Bologna, the Conference Conclusions urged the speedy implementation of the first Euromed audio-visual regional programme. It would be launched later that year, but did not begin effective operation until 2000. This was despite the recognition of the Euro-Mediterranean Foreign Ministers meeting in Malta in 1997 that audio-visual cooperation was a priority area. Projects forming part of the programme include MEDEA (a support fund for the pre-production of films about to be co-produced), EUROPACINEMAS (support for the distribution and circulation of films in both Community and Mediterranean countries), and EUROMEDIATOON (support for the establishment of a studio to produce a series of cartoons). As for the impact of the Euromed Audio-visual Programme, one of the main conclusions of the second Audio-visual Conference of the Euro-Mediterranean Partnership held in Rabat in September 2000 was the desire for 'the continuation, development and

It is interesting to compare these priorities with those identified in the Council Conclusions of 17 June 1994 on the drawing up of a Community Action Plan in the field of cultural heritage, OJ [1994] C 235/1.

[51] These broad guidelines emerged from a series of preparatory workshops on *Identity and Conservation of the Cultural Heritage in the Euro-Mediterranean Context* (Arles, 9 and 10 February 1996), *Access to the Cultural Heritage* (Berlin, 23 and 24 February 1996) and *Cultural Heritage as Factor in Sustainable Development* (Amman, 22 and 23 March 1996).

[52] See http://europa.eu.int/comm/external_relations/med_mideast/intro/index.htm for further details of the Euromed heritage scheme.

[53] The Conclusions of this second Conference of the Ministers of Culture are available at http://www/europa.eu.int/comm/external_relations/med_mideast/euro_med_. . . /culture2.html.

strengthening' of that Programme.[54] The November 2000 Euro-Mediterranean Conference of the Ministers of Foreign Affairs that was held in Marseilles recommended that existing programmes should be built up, indicating that there would be a Euromed Audio-visual II and further development of the Euromed Heritage Programme.[55]

Indeed, the second phase of Euromed Heritage was launched in 2001, with the resources allocated to the programme being increased from €17.1 million to €30 million. As in the new Cotonou Agreement, future funding will be determined in accordance with the Joint Declaration of the Council and Commission in November 2000 on the Principles and Objectives of Community Development Cooperation Policy.[56] As the primary objective of development aid is now poverty alleviation, a question arises about the future funding of cultural cooperation. An answer to this question is provided by the Regional Strategy Paper (2002–2006), which outlines the regional indicative programme for the next two years and notes that one of the more important challenges for the region is to 'foster greater mutual knowledge and understanding between its cultures'.[57] Cultural cooperation has been included within one of the five priorities established for the regional MEDA support programme—bringing the partnership closer to the people. The regional indicative programme will concentrate on Euromed Audiovisual and Euromed Heritage in the hope of enhancing the visibility of cultural cooperation.[58] This will be enhanced as a result of the sixth Meeting of the Euro-Mediterranean Foreign Ministers, held in Naples on 2–3 December 2003, which endorsed the establishment of a Euromed Foundation to promote the dialogue of cultures and civilizations.[59] It is also hoped that heritage protection will form part

[54] See http://europa.eu.int/comm/avpolicy/extern/culdi_en.htm. for the conclusion of the Conference. See also Euromed Special Feature No 24 (26 July 2001), *Euro-Mediterranean Co-operation in the Audiovisual Sector*, for further discussion of the programme.

[55] See above n 48 for the conclusions of the Marseilles Conference.

[56] See above n 22 for details of this statement.

[57] Available at http://www.europa.eu.int/comm/external_relations/sp/index.htm, p 13.

[58] The recent broadcast in Israel, the West Bank/Gaza, and Jordan of 'Sesame Street' stories, partially funded by the Community under the MEDA programmes, has increased the visibility of cooperation. See http://www.europa.eu.int/comm/external_relations/med_mideast/news/ip03_1411.htm.

[59] Details of the final Declaration of the Meeting are available at http://www.europa.eu.int/comm/external_relations/euromed/publication/euromed_report71b_en.pdf. See also the report of the high level Advisory Group established by the Commission President to examine this issue. Entitled 'Dialogue Between Peoples and Cultures in the Euro-Mediterranean Area', it is available at http://www.europa.eu.int/comm/external_relations/euromed/publication/euromed_report68_en.pdf. The Foundation would seek to involve civil society in all areas of inter-cultural dialogue. For details see http://www.europa.eu.int/comm/external_relations/news/ip03_1391.htm.

of the bilateral programmes, although examination of these latter programmes indicates that this hope has not been realized.[60]

(d) Latin America and Asia

The example provided by the inclusion of a provision on cultural cooperation in the Lomé IV Convention in 1990 was repeated as the Community concluded agreements with other countries throughout the 1990s.[61] For example, Article 35 of the 1991 Framework Agreement for cooperation between the Community and Mexico indicated that the parties would 'act jointly in the fields of information and communication in order to further the cultural links which already exist between the Parties'.[62] The measures anticipated included exchanges of information on matters of common cultural interest, studies and assistance for the preservation of cultural heritage, the organization of cultural events and cultural exchanges, and the translation of literary works.[63] The Joint Declaration and Action Plan emerging from the first ever summit of the Heads of State and Governments from Latin America, the Caribbean, and the European Union in Rio de Janeiro in June 1999 established a strategic partnership between the two regions. Greater inter-regional cultural cooperation was subsequently identified as one of 11 key priorities.[64] The Community is

It should be noted that a similar proposal was made to the equivalent 2002 meeting (SEC(2002) 159, p 7). It would be funded by a €1 million contribution from each Member State and the Commission, and by voluntary contributions from each Mediterranean partner; the existing cultural cooperation programmes would continue and the Culture 2000 and MEDIA Plus programmes could also be used. As for the existing involvement of civil society, see the report of 8th Euro-Mediterranean Civil Forum, which addressed the issue of the *Dialogue between Cultures and Civilisations*, the details of which are available at http://www.euromedcivilforum.gr/eng-files/eng_index.htm.

[60] See above n 57, e.g., the programmes for Egypt and Jordan reveal that the specific objectives set in the national indicative programmes do not include cultural cooperation.

[61] See, as examples, the Agreements with Uruguay—Article 16 (OJ [1992] L 94/2), Paraguay—Article 13 (OJ [1992] L 313/72), Brazil—Article 25 (OJ [1995] L 262/54), Mercosur and its members—Article 21 (OJ [1996] L 69/4), Chile—Article 26 (OJ [1996] L 209/5), the Andean Community and its members—Article 28 (OJ [1998] L 127/11), and the Central American Common Market and its members—Article 30 (OJ [1999] L 63/39). The provisions of the Cotonou Agreement cover the Caribbean members.

[62] OJ [1991] L 340/2. The latest Agreement with Mexico (OJ [2000] L 276/45) provides for cooperation on tourism that will safeguard and maximize 'the potential of natural and cultural heritage' (Article 25.2(b)).

[63] In the latest Agreement with Mexico, above n 62, Article 31.1 states that 'The Parties agree to promote cultural co-operation, that duly respects their diversity, in order to increase mutual understanding and the spreading of their respective cultures'. Measures to achieve this include cultural exchanges and joint initiatives, and other activities which will be defined 'in due time'.

[64] See http://www.europa.eu.int/comm/external_relations/la/rio/sum_06_99.htm for further details.

already active in each of these priority areas and the Commission has pointed out, with respect to cultural cooperation, that financial commitments of €6.6 million had been made for the period 1995–99 in both Latin America and the Caribbean on cultural heritage and cultural forums.[65] This area was not identified by the Commission as a priority area for immediate action; instead, it was to be incorporated over the longer term into the established bilateral and sub-regional dialogues. However, it must be noted that cultural cooperation had already been provided for in the agreements with countries and regional organizations in Central and Latin America throughout the 1990s, and in the recent Political Dialogue and Cooperation Agreement concluded with the Andean Community and its Member States.[66]

Agreements concluded with Asian countries throughout the 1990s also include provisions on cultural cooperation. One of the earliest examples is the 1994 Cooperation Agreement on Partnership and Development concluded with India, which was designed, *inter alia*, to facilitate better mutual understanding and to strengthen ties in cultural matters.[67] Article 15 of the Agreement provides that such cooperation may include:

i) exchange of information of matters of cultural interest;
ii) preparatory studies and technical assistance in the preservation of cultural heritage;
iii) cooperation in the field of media and audio-visual documentation;
iv) organizing cultural events and exchanges.

However, there is no uniformity of approach with respect to agreements concluded with countries in this region; some contain provisions broadly equivalent to those contained in the Indian Agreement, whilst others are much less specific.[68] Irrespective of the nature of the cultural cooperation provision, and like the agreements concluded with Latin America, financial support for cooperation does not emerge from a specific programme.

The final area of cooperation is that resulting from the 1996 Asia-Europe Meeting (ASEM), at which it was agreed to promote cultural, intellectual, and

[65] COM (2000) 670, *Follow-up to the First Summit between Latin America, the Caribbean and the European Union*, Annex 2.

[66] Available at http://www.europa.eu.int/comm/external_relations/andean/pol/agreement.pdf, Article 40.

[67] OJ [1994] L 223/24. See also similar agreement with Sri Lanka (OJ [1995] L 85/33).

[68] Those with equivalent provisions include the Agreements with Korea—Article 17 (OJ [2001] L 90/46) and Laos—Article 13 (OJ [1997] L 334/15); whereas agreements with Kazakhstan (OJ [1999] L 196/3), Kyrgyzstan (OJ [1999] L 196/48), and Uzbekistan (OJ [1999] L 229/3) are much less specific.

people-to-people exchanges between Asia and Europe. No formal cooperation agreement exists in this respect, and cooperation in this area is promoted through the Asia-Europe Foundation (ASEF).[69] With the French Government, ASEF co-sponsored the 1998 Asia-Europe Cultural Forum, which included among its objectives discussion of new and innovative ways to promote greater inter-regional cultural cooperation.[70] As for the outcome of the Conference, seven projects ready to be implemented were identified, as was the future scope of cooperation. The Cultural Exchange aspect of ASEF concentrates on cultural forums, ASEM cultural events, and a programme of activities in the following three areas: cultural industries, cultural heritage, and artistic creation. As examples of activities, there has been a workshop on Copyright Trading for Book Publishers, a number of Asian and European film festivals, and seminars on cultural heritage training.

(e) An evaluation

Since the inclusion of a cultural cooperation provision in the Lomé IV Convention in 1990, numerous agreements concluded by the Community have included such a provision. What do such provisions tell us about the external dimension of the Community's cultural policy? Unsurprisingly, there is a remarkable degree of convergence between the internal and external aspects of that policy. For example, there is a great concentration on cultural heritage, the dissemination of information, the exchange of experience, and the training of those involved in the cultural sector. However, the integration of cultural policy into other areas of cooperation remains problematic. For example, there is little evidence from Lomé to suggest the integration of projects into general development efforts.

One of the complaints made by the European Foundation of Arts and Heritage of the Treaty provisions on culture was that their inclusion did not yield increased financial support for cultural activities.[71] Criticisms relating to funding can also be made with respect to external cultural cooperation activities. Projects must be initiated by the non-Community partners and form part

[69] This not-for-profit organization was established in 1997 in Singapore and is funded through contributions from the ASEM partners. The Community has contributed €3.5 million out of a total of pledged contributions of €20 million.

[70] For details see the ASEF website at http://www.asef.org.

[71] See various position papers of the Foundation, available at http://www.efah.org. See e.g., the EFAH Proclamation to the European Parliament on the European Campaign for Arts and Heritage suggesting that culture should receive an equitable share of the Union budget, 'namely at least 1 Euro per capita as a final objective to reach in 2004'.

of a national or regional indicative programme. Given the limited financial resources available for cooperation activities, it is not surprising that cultural activities do not rank high on the list of projects for funding. Moreover, as the primary objective of Community development aid is now poverty alleviation, what hope is there for the future of these cultural cooperation provisions? Perhaps the model of the Asia-Europe Foundation should be replicated in other areas of external cultural cooperation.

3. Globalization

According to the first recital of the Culture 2000 decision:[72]

> Culture has an important intrinsic value to all people in Europe, is an essential element of European integration and contributes to the affirmation and vitality of the European model of society and to the Community's influence on the international scene.

One of the problems with discussion of cultural policy is that such discussion occurs without an accepted definition of what constitutes culture.[73] Despite the existence of Article 151 EC, there is still no generally accepted definition of culture that seems to pervade Community action. This has the advantage of allowing the Community to respond creatively to new developments. One development necessitating a Community response is increasing globalization, and especially the globalization of culture. Two particular matters will be examined: the need to preserve cultural diversity in audio-visual services, and the need to ameliorate some of the consequences of globalization by allowing for cultural considerations to be taken into account in the Agreement on Agriculture.

(a) Audio-visual services

The nature of the globalization of culture is a matter of some dispute. It appears not to be the case that there is an increasing knowledge of all cultures,

[72] OJ [2000] L 63/1.

[73] Recommendation 1216 (1993) adopted by the Council of Europe's Parliamentary Assembly on European Cultural Cooperation defined 'culture' as 'quality of life and preparation for it. The field includes education, youth, sport, the media, leisure activities as well as the arts, literature, architecture and the cultural heritage.' The following, more extensive definition is given in the Preamble to the 1982 Mexico City Declaration on Cultural Policies: 'in its widest sense, culture may now be said to be the whole complex of distinctive spiritual, material, intellectual and emotional features that characterise a society or a social group. It includes not only the arts and letters, but also modes of life, the fundamental rights of the human being, value systems, traditions and beliefs.' Available at http://www.unesco.org/culture/laws/mexico/html_eng/page1.shtml.

but rather there appears to be a global core culture. In film and television, for example, that core culture is American, despite the fact that it is not the world's largest producer of films. Schlesinger has pointed out:[74]

> . . . it could fairly be said that the real common currency of the European audio-visual space is actually American television output from the US. It is producing moving images that most easily traverse any European national barriers.

At least in music, the global core culture appears to be bi-polar; this time the position of the United States is shared with the United Kingdom. As a result the language of the global culture is now English—the world's new *lingua franca*. Attempts have been made to stop what is regarded as a form of cultural imperialism; the Television Without Frontiers Directive is a classic example. However, one question that arises is whether this process of the globalization of culture can be arrested given the increasing globalization of trade managed through the World Trade Organization (WTO) and, in particular, the General Agreement on Trade in Services (GATS)?

The negotiation of the GATS during the Uruguay Round brought the Community into conflict with most members of the GATT.[75] A Working Group on audio-visual services was established as part of the GATS negotiations. The question before it was whether the special cultural considerations of this sector could be specifically addressed in a special annex to the Agreement, or whether it should be excluded from the scope of the Agreement entirely. Supporting the need for a cultural exception, some negotiators argued that this sector provided an important function in terms of the promotion of indigenous languages, national histories, and cultural heritage. The Community had argued throughout the negotiations for a cultural clause that would allow it to exclude audio-visual services from the scope of the GATS, and thus maintain its Television Without Frontiers Directive. The United States (US), supported by others, opposed the idea of a general exclusion and a special annex, arguing that cultural identity was not capable of definition given the multinational nature of television and cinema. An attempt to reach a bilateral solution between the Community and the US failed. At the end of the Uruguay Round negotiations in December 1993, the controversy remained unresolved and the GATS did not include any provision relating to

[74] Schlesinger, J, 'Wishful Thinking: Cultural Policies, Media and Collective Identities in Europe', *Journal of Communication*, 43 (1993), 6, at 12.

[75] For a discussion of the GATS negotiations, see e.g., Reyna, J V, 'Services', in Stewart, T (ed), *The GATT Uruguay Round: A Negotiating History (1986–92)* (The Hague: Kluwer, 1993), Vol II, 2335.

audio-visual services, although commitments were made by some WTO members in this sector.[76]

The Community and its Member States made no commitments on audio-visual services and, indeed, they added five exemptions to the application of the most-favoured-nation clause in the Agreement.[77] Under Article XIX GATS, negotiations for further commitments began in 2000, and the guidelines adopted for the negotiations indicated that there would be no '*a priori* exclusion of any service sector or mode of supply'.[78] An early indication of the approach of the Community to these negotiations was given by the Council meeting in October 1999, when it was noted:[79]

> During the forthcoming WTO negotiations, the Union will ensure, as in the Uruguay Round, that the Community and its Member States maintain the possibility to preserve and develop their capacity to define and implement their cultural and audio-visual policies for the purpose of preserving their cultural diversity.

To prepare for the negotiations, the Commission engaged in a wide-ranging consultation exercise. One of the results of this exercise was the Statement of Prague, which emerged from a seminar on audio-visual policies and cultural diversity in an enlarged Europe that brought together the Member States of the Community, all the applicant countries, and Switzerland. The final point of the Statement affirmed that 'the capacity to define and develop national and Community policies to safeguard and to promote European cultural diversity should be rigorously promoted within multilateral bodies'.[80] Similar sentiments had been expressed a month earlier at the September 2000 Audio-visual Conference of the Euro-Mediterranean Partnership. One of the main conclusions of this Conference was to call on all 27 participants 'to rally together in order to rigorously defend cultural diversity in the framework of the negotiations of the WTO'.[81] It was noted that the overwhelming majority of WTO members shared this position.

[76] It should be pointed out, however, that 22 of the 141 WTO members have made commitments in this sector.

[77] See http://gats-info.eu.int/gats-info/nwtosvc.pl?COUNTRY=European_Community&MFN=00 for the details of the Community's exemptions.

[78] See also the Doha Ministerial Declaration initiating a new round of trade negotiations, WT/MIN(01)/DEC/W/1, para 15.

[79] Cited at http://www.europa.eu.int/comm/avpolicy/extern/gats_en.htm.

[80] Statement available at http://europa.eu.int/comm/avpolicy/extern/culdi_en.htm.

[81] Ibid., point II.3. The conclusions from one of the three workshops at the Conference was that 'the existence and development of regulatory and financial mechanisms to support the audio-visual sector should not be put into question by the application to this sector of the GATS disciplines within the framework of the WTO' (at 7–8).

However, as part of the GATS negotiations, communications have been received from three WTO members that seek to include audio-visual services within the scope of the GATS. The communication from Brazil recognized the need to 'promote the progressive liberalisation of this important sector while ensuring at the same time governments' autonomy to preserve and promote cultural identity and cultural diversity'.[82] Brazil proposed a subsidy scheme aimed at achieving cultural policy objectives, to allay fears arising from the progressive liberalization of this sector.[83] The Swiss negotiating paper endorsed the idea of subsidies, arguing for a common understanding between WTO members on the disciplines governing such subsidies.[84] Beyond this, a cultural diversity safeguard would be the subject of discussion, as would the concept of public service broadcasting and the need to regulate illicit content.[85] The end-point for these discussions could be an Annex to the GATS on audio-visual services.

The final negotiating proposal emerged from the US, who began by noting that the audio-visual sector was significantly different now from that which formed the focus of the Uruguay Round negotiations.[86] In contrast to the position adopted during the Uruguay Round, the US was not arguing for an all-or-nothing approach. Instead it pointed out that the GATT and the GATS provide a number of Articles that could be used to take the special cultural qualities of this sector into account.[87] Its negotiating proposal has three inter-related elements:[88]

- a clear understanding of where the different facets of the audio-visual sector are classified;
- negotiated commitments for audio-visual services using existing GATS disciplines; and
- devising rules to allow circumscribed subsidy use for specifically defined cultural purposes.

[82] WTO Document S/CSS/W/99, Communication from Brazil—*Audio-visual Services* (9 July 2001), para 1.

[83] Ibid., para 12.

[84] WTO Document S/CSS/W/74, Communication from Switzerland—*GATS 2000 Audio-Visual Services* (4 May 2001), para 12.

[85] Ibid., paras 11, 13, and 14.

[86] WTO Document S/CSS/W/21, Communication from the United States—*Audio-visual and Related Services* (18 December 2000).

[87] The particular provisions that the US has in mind are Article IV GATT, which is a specific exception to the GATT national treatment rule for cinematic films, and the more general exceptions in Article XX(a) GATT and Article XIV(a) GATS allowing for exceptional measures to be taken to protect public morals. These particular measures would be in addition to the positive measures that could be taken under the GATS, e.g., the funding of audio-visual services.

[88] See above n 86, para 10.

The response of the Community and the Member States to these proposals has not led to a specific Communication. Instead the general Communication of the Community and the Member States emphasizes that the overall objective for the negotiations is:[89]

> . . . to increase the number and quality of market access and national treatment commitments made by Members across services sectors and modes of supply with a view to achieving a progressively higher level of liberalisation.

In addition, the comprehensive negotiations should not exclude any sector or mode of supply *a priori* and should ensure that WTO members can adequately protect their national policy objectives. For the Community and its Member States, the core of the negotiations will be market access and national treatment rather than the extension of the GATS to include audiovisual services. The injunction provided by Article 151 EC to preserve cultural diversity within the Community mandates this conclusion, which has been confirmed by the conditional offer from the Community and its Member States, which was submitted in accordance with the Doha Declaration by 31 March 2003.[90] This Article may also suggest that the Community should take up the proposal made at the 2000 Rabat Conference of establishing an international instrument that 'would permit the respect and promotion of cultural diversity, in order that globalisation result neither in a trivialisation of cultures, nor the domination of some cultures over others'.[91]

(b) Agriculture

Beyond the GATS, one of the other major achievements of the Uruguay Round was the Agreement on Agriculture that would for the first time establish commitments in the areas of market access, domestic support, and export subsidies. Parties to the Agreement would be expected to increase market access, through tariff reductions and the adoption of the process of tariffication for existing non-tariff barriers. The level of support offered by domestic agricultural policies would be calculated and reductions would have to be made in certain areas. Aspects of such policies were categorized in terms of

[89] WTO Document S/CSS/W/15, Communication from the EC and their Member States, *Overall Approach to Services Negotiations* (30 November 2000), para 1.

[90] See http://europa.eu.int/comm/avpolicy/extern/gats2000/consultdoc_en.htm for further discussion arising out of the Commission's 1999 consultation on audio-visual services. Details of the offer are available at http://www.europa.eu.int/comm/trade/issues/sectoral/services/wto_nego/index_en.htm, pp 107–09 list Article II (MFN) exemptions for audio-visual services.

[91] See above n 80, at 8.

boxes. There were three boxes: a Blue Box, which excluded certain measures from the reform process; an Amber Box of policies that would be subject to reductions; and a Green Box, which, subject to certain conditions, exempted various policies from the reduction commitments. Lastly, budgetary restraints and quantitative limitations would be placed on export subsidies.

Under Article 20 of the Agreement on Agriculture, the negotiation of a new agreement, which began in 2000, will seek to achieve improvements in the areas of market access and further reductions in the levels of domestic support and export subsidies, whilst addressing non-trade concerns. Article 20(c) of the Agreement does not define these concerns and only two particular non-trade concerns are identified in the Preamble to the Agreement, namely, food security and the need to protect the environment. However, paragraph 13 of the Doha Declaration takes note of 'the non-trade concerns reflected in the negotiating proposals submitted by Members' and confirms that these will be taken into account as provided for in the Agreement on Agriculture.[92] The questions are: what are these concerns, and how will they be addressed in the negotiations?

In a discussion paper presented by the European Commission to an International Conference on Non-Trade Concerns in Agriculture held in Norway on 2–4 July 2000, the Commission assessed the contribution of agriculture to environmentally and culturally related non-trade concerns.[93] Of the four non-trade concerns identified, the third was the 'preservation of cultural features, including historical remains on farmland and land uses of cultural significance'.[94] The Commission noted:[95]

> The significance of these non-trade concerns depends on the values placed on them by society. Such values reflect to a certain degree clear and generally accepted thresholds. They can, however, also be a function of history and culture. Thus, one society may value highly the continued existence of a species of wild plant that appears insignificant to outsiders; another society may place emphasis on cultural features, which, again, are not valued to the same extent by other societies.

The conclusion offered was that care was needed to identify legitimate objectives that may be pursued to avoid abuse of the concept. The argument presented by the Commission was that the narrow economic focus of modern

[92] See above n 78, at para 13.

[93] G/AG/NG/W/36/Rev 1, Discussion Paper 4.

[94] Ibid., para 6. The Commission later noted that 'Historical farmland features include archaeological remains, whether under the soil of farmed land or at field margins, as well as field patterns and living remnants of ancient forests. Some features, which society particularly values, may be comparatively recent, such as the century-old field and farm barns which characterise many landscapes in Europe and North America' (para 26).

[95] Ibid., para 7.

agriculture had resulted in various negative consequences for the cultural landscape.[96] As for the future, if identified as a legitimate non-trade concern, then farmers should receive compensation for the additional costs (or revenue foregone) associated with the preservation of this particular public good.

These non-trade concerns would be incorporated into the Agreement on Agriculture through the Green Box, which is provided for in Annex II of the Agreement.[97] The fundamental requirement for these policies is that they have no, or at most minimal, trade distortion effects or effects on production.[98] The preservation of the cultural landscape, if recognized as a legitimate non-trade concern, could be accommodated within the Green Box. The Community's negotiating position recognizes the need to retain the Green Box, although it advocates a re-assessment of the criteria used for Green Box measures so as to ensure that such measures are well-targeted, transparent, and cause minimal trade distortion.[99]

Another Community proposal that seeks to introduce another non-trade concern of a cultural nature, is that on Animal Welfare.[100] This proposal recognizes that there are limits to the ways in which the Community should produce its food, but it does not envisage that this will lead to the introduction of new types of non-tariff barriers. WTO members would not be able to hamper trade in agricultural products because of animal welfare issues. Rather, the Community's objective is to promote high animal welfare standards, particularly in relation to those products emerging from highly intensive and industrialized production methods. So, WTO members that apply high animal welfare standards should have the right to maintain them. As for how this issue should be addressed, the Community identifies three potential solutions.[101]

[96] The negative consequences of the economic focus of modern farming were identified (para 35) as being concentration, specialization, intensification, and marginalization. As for the impact on the non-trade concerns identified by the Commission, see paras 10–28.

[97] Green Box policies are divisible into two categories: general services, such as public stockholding for food security purposes and domestic food aid, and direct payments to producers, such as payments for relief from natural disasters and payments under environmental or regional assistance programmes.

[98] In addition, all such policies must conform to the following criteria: (a) the support in question shall be provided through a publicly-funded government programme (including government revenue foregone) not involving transfers from consumers; and (b) the support in question shall not have the effect of providing price support to producers.

[99] G/AG/NG/W/90, *EC Comprehensive Negotiating Proposal*, para 15.

[100] G/AG/NG/W/19, *Animal Welfare and Trade in Agriculture*.

[101] These are: the development of multilateral agreements dealing with the protection of animal welfare; appropriate labelling, compulsory or voluntary, as provided for under Article 2.2 of the Technical Barriers to Trade Agreement; or the development of appropriate mechanisms under Article XX GATT and/or Article 20 of the Agreement on Agriculture.

The preferred solution is that, in recognition of the likely competitive impact of increased costs associated with high animal welfare standards, the Community would consider it legitimate to provide compensation to producers. Animal welfare would therefore become a Green Box policy. As in the case of the protection of the cultural landscape, animal welfare payments will necessarily have an impact on production and trade, for example, by supporting particular production methods and by increasing the funds available to the producer for use in his or her business. Despite the fact that the Community's negotiating position on animal welfare has not attracted widespread support from other WTO members,[102] it has been incorporated into the proposed draft modalities for a new Agreement on Agriculture.[103]

4. Conclusions

> . . . the people of Europe have a duty to preserve and promote what makes them different one from the other, in view of the wealth represented by that pluralism of cultural expression, and at the same time to be aware of the concept of European culture when it comes to both its heritage and its future, and of its irreplaceable value for Europe's survival and future development.[104]

The duty to preserve and promote difference espoused by the Council of Europe lies at the heart of its approach and that of the Community to cultural cooperation within Europe. Similarly, it also informs the external dimension of the Community's cultural cooperation.[105] The 1992 Commission Communication on culture, as previously noted, considered that it would be necessary to ensure that the provisions on cultural cooperation in various agreements concluded by the Community with third countries fitted within a coherent framework and that they were actually applied in the concerned countries.[106] Does such a framework exist, and are these provisions actually applied?

[102] See, e.g., G/AG/NG/W/164, Statement by Cuba, Honduras, and the Dominican Republic at a Special Session of the Committee on Agriculture on 6 April 2001: 'Concepts have been introduced which, as far as we are concerned, are nothing more than a pretext for continuing with the distortions in the agricultural sector, such as the multifunctionality of agriculture, the non-trade concerns of the developed countries, like environmental protection, animal welfare, and so on.'

[103] TN/AG/W/1/Rev 1, Attachment 8, para 6, Modification of scope of para 12 of Annex II.

[104] Declaration of the Council of Europe's Sixth Conference of European Ministers responsible for Cultural Affairs (April 1990) on Multicultural society and European cultural identity.

[105] See, e.g., Principle 8 of the 1982 Mexico City Declaration on Cultural Policies, n 73 above, which states that 'the international community considers it its duty to ensure that cultural identity of each people is preserved and protected'.

[106] COM (92) 149, *New Prospects for Community Cultural Action*, 16.

As for the existence of a framework, analysis of the provisions on cultural cooperation reveals a remarkable degree of convergence, for example, on issues such as cultural heritage. The problem remains one of application and, in particular, the funding of cultural cooperation. The concentration of Community development aid on poverty alleviation in developing countries poses a threat to the future of these cultural cooperation provisions. A suggestion was made earlier that the ASEF model should be replicated in other areas of external cultural cooperation and the Commission has recently taken this up. The 2003 Meeting of the Euro-Mediterranean Foreign Ministers took such a step by endorsing the Commission proposal for a Euro-Mediterranean Foundation to promote cultural dialogue. There is no reason why a similar approach could not be taken to the countries of Latin America at the next summit of Heads of State and Governments from Latin America, the Caribbean and the European Union, which is scheduled for 2004 in Mexico. One of the advantages of such an approach is that it emphasizes the basic principles of the Community's development cooperation policy of local ownership of development strategies, public-private partnership, and decentralized management.

Such an approach would also recognize the emerging international consensus on the importance of the cultural dimension of development, evidenced by, for example, the Action Plan agreed at the 1998 Stockholm Intergovernmental Conference on Cultural Policies for Development.[107] Principle 7 of this Action Plan noted that:

> New trends, particularly globalisation, link cultures even more closely and enrich the interaction between them, but they may also be detrimental to our creative diversity and to cultural pluralism; they make mutual respect all the more imperative.

The establishment of Forums or Foundations to support the external dimension of the Community's cultural cooperation will lead to greater interaction between cultures, thus promoting mutual respect. The issue of globalization presents a different challenge, one which it is suggested could be met by an international instrument that would permit and promote cultural diversity. Two mechanisms suggest themselves.

First, the development of a cultural exception either generally through an amendment of Article XX GATT, or specifically in each of the WTO Agreements, such as GATS and the Agreement on Agriculture. With respect to Article XX, provision already exists for Members to take measures necessary

[107] See http://unesco.org/culture/laws/stockholm/html_eng/actionpl1.shtml. See also the Mexico Declaration, n 73 above, Principles 10–16.

to protect public morals (paragraph (a)) and to impose measures for the protection of national treasures of artistic, historic, or archaeological value (paragraph (f)). The scope of neither paragraph is clear, as they have not been the subjects of a dispute in over 50 years. However, it must be pointed out that Article XX is an exception and has been very narrowly construed. A similar approach would undoubtedly be taken to a cultural exception contained in any of the more specific agreements. Moreover, as the discussion above illustrated, the possibility of the inclusion of a cultural clause in the GATS caused considerable friction between the negotiators during the Uruguay Round.

Although there is merit in proposing the incorporation of a culture-specific provision in each of the WTO Agreements, it may be more advantageous to adopt the second mechanism, which is the development of a multilateral agreement dealing with the protection of cultural diversity. The 1972 UNESCO Convention concerning the Protection of the World Cultural and Natural Heritage, suitably amended, could serve as a model here.[108] The Convention would define cultural diversity and would allow each party to the Convention to identify aspects of that diversity that it wishes to protect and promote. Of the various forms of protection, measures that restrict trade could be taken on condition that they do not constitute a means of arbitrary or unjustifiable discrimination, or a disguised restriction on trade. Of the various forms of promotion, support policies could be implemented provided that they are the least inconsistent measures with the party's international trade obligations that can be taken.

To conclude, the external dimension of the Community's cultural policy has emphasized the need to promote cultural pluralism. The establishment of Forums or Foundations to support that dimension will increase the visibility and effectiveness of such cooperation and, it is hoped, promote development. It only remains for the Community to respond positively to the impact of globalization on culture to promote and preserve differences.

[108] See http://www.unesco.org/whc/world_he.htm.

From Regional to Global Freedom of Trade in Audio-visual Goods and Services? A Comparison of the Impact on the Audio-visual Sector of the Preferential Trade Zones Established by the European Communities and the World Trade Organization

*Olaf Weber**

1. Potential synergies and conflicts between free trade and culture

This chapter is concerned with the international trade in audio-visual goods and services. Today, audio-visual content in the form, for example, of television programmes or movies is often produced in one state and sold in another. It is transmitted either as an 'intangible' service, be it via satellite, terrestrial airwaves, or (increasingly) over the Internet, or as a 'tangible' product in the form of videos or DVDs. Technological and economic obstacles to such trade have eased in recent decades due to the development of cheaper and faster communication technologies such as broadband and satellite. Traditional media such as the telephone, the printed press, television, and radio are said to be converging in the light of these new technological capabilities.[1]

* LL M (Edinburgh), Rechtsanwalt in Germany. Thanks to Rachael Craufurd Smith. Critique is welcome at olafwe@yahoo.de.

[1] See European Commission, *Green Paper on convergence of the telecommunications, media and information technology sectors, and the implications for regulation*, COM/97/623 (3 December 1997).

National legal systems traditionally bound commercial operators to a single jurisdiction and sought to exclude competition from foreign services—and they still hinder trade in the audio-visual sector to a considerable extent. A number of legal instruments in the cultural field[2] do, however, serve to partially remedy this problem: the International Telecommunications Union allocates satellite slots and regulates certain technical aspects,[3] while the Council of Europe added a Convention on Transfrontier Television[4] to its European Convention for the Protection of Human Rights and Fundamental Freedoms (ECHR).[5] But it is preferential trade zones such as those established by the World Trade Organization (WTO)[6] or the European Communities (EC) at a regional level which are likely to have the greatest impact on domestic rules relating to audio-visual goods and services in the future.[7]

Legal regimes based on free trade affect culture in two ways: on the one hand, different communities can exchange their culture more easily. From the earliest of times the development of human civilization has benefited from such communication, as is illustrated by the Mesopotamian art found on ancient Egyptian sites. Contemporary free trade regimes help members of the creative community to spread their ideas and art—and consumers to receive them—virtually everywhere. Whoever wishes to do so can enjoy a live broadcast of an opera from Milan's La Scala even if he or she lives in Tokyo.

[2] For a catalogue, see Oppermann, T, 'Cultural Agreements', *Encyclopaedia of Public International Law*, vol 1, 885.

[3] See Barendt, E M and Hitchens, L, *Media Law: Cases & Materials* (Harlow: Longman, 2000), 334 *et seq.*

[4] Convention of 5 May 1989, European Treaty Series No 132, amended in October 1998; see also European Convention on Copyright Law and Neighbouring Rights in the Framework of Trans-frontier Broadcasting of 11 May 1994, European Treaty Series No 153; see Barendt, E M, *Broadcasting Law* (Oxford: Clarendon, 1993), 222 *et seq.*; for a comparison to Community law, see Hoffmann-Riem, W, *Broadcasting: A Comparative Study* (New York and London: Guilford Press, 1996), 276 *et seq.*

[5] On the Convention of 4 November 1950: Ovey, C and White, R, *Jacobs and White: The European Convention on Human Rights*, 3rd edn (Oxford: OUP, 2002); Frowein, J A and Peukert, W, *Europäische Menschenrechtskonvention*, 2nd edn (Kehl: Engel, 1996).

[6] On the WTO: Beise, M, *Die Welthandelsorganisation* (Baden-Baden: Nomos, 2001); Jackson, J H, *The World Trading System: Law and Policy of Economical Relations*, 2nd edn (Cambridge, Mass: MIT Press, 1997); Fraser, C, 'The Final Act of the Uruguay Round, the World Trade Organization, its Framework and Purpose', in *Yearbook of Media and Entertainment Law*, (1996), 247; Qureshi, A H, *The World Trade Organisation: Implementing International Trade Norms* (Manchester and New York: Manchester University Press, 1996).

[7] On trade zones and culture: Neuwirth, R J, 'The Cultural Industries and the Legacy of Article IV GATT', Conference on Cultural Traffic: Policy, Culture and the New Technologies in the European Union and Canada of 22–23 November 2002, available at: http://www.carleton.ca/ces/papers/november02/Neuwirth.pdf.

Conversely, Europeans may find Japanese manga comic strips for sale in their local shop. Free markets, thus, can foster a diversity of cultures, readily accessible for individuals everywhere.[8] These benefits of cultural dialogue through trade are acknowledged by international agreements such as the Florence/Nairobi Agreements. Both texts contain an exception under which national culture can be preserved.[9]

On the other hand, global trade also carries with it dangers for culture. Opening borders to international trade can place the viability of smaller cultures in jeopardy,[10] because foreign cultural products may gradually replace traditional domestic ones.[11] Even national identity may be eroded, supplanted by a European[12] or a cosmopolitan one. There is a fear of 'cultural imperialism'.[13] As markets expand geographically there is also a greater incentive for concentration among companies which produce and distribute cultural goods and services. Large industrial players may be able to outgun small, independent artists as creators of culture, which, in the long run, can lead to a unified mainstream culture.[14] The biggest threat, however, is posed by the fact that all preferential trade regimes—intellectually—are founded on economic considerations. Due to such structural advantage, economic interests may gain priority over all other values, however important, including cultural ones.[15] It is not surprising, therefore, that there is a lively debate as to whether, and if so how, trade and the goal to preserve a diversity of cultures should be balanced.[16]

[8] Bernier, M, 'Establishing a New Instrument on Cultural Diversity', invited lecture, Korean National Press Centre (2002), available at: http://www.screenquota.org/data/dboard3/uploadfiles/Conf%20Seoul%202002%20.doc, p 10.

[9] The Florence Agreement of 17 June 1950, UN Treaty Series No 1734, fostered free circulation of educational, scientific, and cultural materials. Its 26 November 1976 update, the Nairobi Protocol, UN Treaty Series No 18222, then comprised audio-visual goods as well. Compare UNESCO, Beirut Agreement for Facilitating the International Circulation of Visual and Auditory Materials of an Educational, Scientific and Cultural Character of 10 December 1948.

[10] Compare de Witte, B, 'Trade in Culture: International legal regimes and EU constitutional values', in Scott, J and De Búrca, G (eds), *The EU and the WTO* (Oxford and Portland, Oreg: Hart Publishing, 2001), 238, 240.

[11] Bernier, n 8 above, p 10.

[12] Bakir, V, 'An Identity for Europe? The Role of the Media', in Wintle, M (ed), *Culture and Identity in Europe* (Aldershot, Brookfield: Ashgate, 1996), 177 *et seq.*; Boxhoorn, B, 'European Identity and the Process of European Unification: Compatible Notions?', ibid., 133 *et seq.*

[13] Roach, C, 'Cultural Imperialism and Resistance', *Media Culture Society*, 19 (1997), 47; Trautmann, C, 'L'exception culturelle n'est pas négociable', *Le Monde*, 10 October 1999, p 14; Allègre, C and Moscovic, P, 'Plaidoyer pour l'Europe des cultures', *Le Monde*, 1 June 1999, p. 17.

[14] Roach, n 13 above, 47.

[15] Cf. Zouari, F, 'Synthèse des rapports', for *l'Agence inter-gouvernementale de la Francophonie*, http://confculture.francophonie.org/TrvxPrep/pdf/synthese.pdf.

[16] See UNESCO Declaration on Cultural Diversity of 2 November 2001; UN/UNESCO World Commission on Culture and Development, 'Our Creative Diversity: 1995 World Report'.

In order better to understand the mechanisms by which preferential trade regimes can affect the flow of cultural goods and services between countries, this chapter considers the legal frameworks for trade established by the EC and the WTO, focusing in particular on their impact on the audio-visual sector. This sector has been selected not only because it develops rapidly and thus forms one of the biggest threats to culture in the analysis of Adorno and Horkheimer,[17] but also because it is regarded as an influential mechanism through which culture is both reflected and changed.[18] The EC is one of the oldest and most integrated regional zones.[19] EC legislation,[20] the Commission,[21] and the Court of Justice (ECJ)[22] seem sensitive to both culture and national cultures. The global instrument WTO,[23] a 1994 evolution of the 1947 General Agreement on Tariffs and Trade (GATT), now features binding rules of international law. Its substantive trade rules appear not unlike those in force in the EC—especially Articles III and XI GATT 1947 in relation to Article 28 EC.[24] It therefore seems promising to compare the EC (section 2.) and WTO (section 3.) regimes, considering the impact of each in turn on the audio-visual sector.

[17] Adorno, T and Horkheimer, M, 'The Culture Industry: Enlightenment as Mass Deception' and 'Le Prix du Progress', both from *Dialectic of Enlightenment* (New York: Continuum,1993). (Originally published as *Dialektik der Aufklärung*, 1944.)

[18] For the high impact of television, see the judgment of the European Court of Human Rights of 23 September 1994, *Jersild v Denmark*, App No 15890/89, (1994) 19 EHRR 1, para 31.

[19] On other preferential zones, see Samtleben, J, 'Der Südamerikanische Gemeinsame Markt MERCOSUR und seine neue Verfassung', *Wertpapier Mitteilungen* 1996, p 1997; Marceau, G, 'The dispute settlement rules of the North American Free Trade Agreement: A thematic comparison with the dispute settlement rules of the WTO', in Petersmann, E U (ed), *International Trade Law and the GATT/WTO Dispute Settlement System* (London: Kluwer, 1997), 487.

[20] e.g., Article 151 EC; Protocol No 32 to the EC Treaty ('Public Broadcasting in the Member States').

[21] EC Commission, *Communication on certain aspects relating to cinematographic and other audio-visual works* (COM/2001/534 final of 26 September 2001) and *Communication on principles and guidelines for the Community's audio-visual policy in the digital age* (COM/1999/657 final of 14 December 1999).

[22] See Cases 7/68, *Commission v Italy (Artistic Treasures)* [1968] ECR 633, 642; C-368/95, *Familiapress v Heinrich Bauer* [1997] ECR I-3689; C-6/98, *ARD* [1999] ECR I-7599.

[23] Marrakesh Agreement of 15 April 1994; displayed in WTO (ed), *The Legal Texts: The Results of the Uruguay Round of Multilateral Table Negotiations* (Cambridge: Cambridge University Press, 1999).

[24] Fanfara, 'Art. 30 ECT', in Quadri, R, Monaco, R, and Trabucchi, A (eds), *Trattato istitutivo della communità economica Europea* (Milan: Giuffrè Edizione, 1965), vol I, 175–6; Mégret, J, Louis, J V, Vignes, D, and Waelbroeck, M, *Le Droit de la Communauté Economique Européenne*, I, Art 25 (Brussels: Presses Universitaires de Bruxelles, 1970), 83.

2. The EC framework for the audio-visual sector

The EC Treaty pursues a variety of socio-economic goals, which are set out in Article 2. The primary mechanism for achieving these goals has been the establishment of a common market under which all tariff barriers to intra-Community trade have been removed.[25] Non-tariff barriers have been tackled by the four basic freedoms and through harmonizing secondary legislation. In this way, the EC has developed a rather detailed set of regulations for the audio-visual sector.[26]

(a) Free movement of goods in the EC

Of considerable importance for trade in culture are the Treaty provisions on free movement of goods. Article 28 EC targets non-tariff impediments to trade, that is, quantitative import restrictions and measures having equivalent effect.[27] Article 29 EC mirrors this clause for exports. These two trade provisions form the Archimedean point for the Community's own activity in the cultural sphere and its influence on national cultural policy.

(i) The objective scope of Article 28

Article 28 EC applies only to 'goods' in the sense of the heading before Article 23 EC. Arguably, items of cultural value might constitute *res extra commercium*, goods not subject to trade and thus the EC Treaty.[28] This was the position taken by Italy in the *Art Treasures* case,[29] which concerned the imposition by Italy of an export duty on all goods of archaeological value. Yet Article 30 EC makes specific, though admittedly defensive, provision for cultural goods of artistic, historic, or archaeological value, which suggests that cultural goods in general were not intended to fall outside the scope of Article 28. In consequence, the ECJ did not exempt cultural goods but rather held that all goods 'having a monetary value, [which] as such may be the object of commercial

[25] Article 25 EC. For tariff rules, see Article 90 EC *et seq*.

[26] On the development of an EC cultural policy: McMahon, J, *Education and Culture in European Community Law* (London: Athlone Press, 1995), 121 *et seq*.; Barendt, n 4 above, 213 *et seq*.; Collins, R, *Broadcasting and Audio-visual Policy in the European Single Market* (London: John Libbey, 1993).

[27] For a comprehensive analysis of Article 28 EC, see Mojzesowicz, K, *Möglichkeiten und Grenzen einer einheitlichen Dogmatik der Grundfreiheiten* (Baden-Baden: Nomos 2001), 28 *et seq*.

[28] The expression originates in canonical law; it negates property titles in cultural objects and, thus, excludes them from trade.

[29] Case 7/68, *Commission v Italy (Artistic Treasures)*, n 22 above, 642.

transactions' were subject to Article 28 EC.[30] As later case law shows, this definition comprises even goods without a legal market[31] and objects traditionally not traded, such as waste.[32]

Even if no sharp line can be drawn between goods and services,[33] Article 28 EC *et seq.*, which relate to goods, and Article 49 EC *et seq.*, which relate to services, establish two different legal regimes: a distinction with specific importance in the rapidly evolving audio-visual sector.[34] As a general rule, the services regime is subsidiary to that of goods,[35] but that does not rule out parallel application of both sets of rules:[36] television broadcasting, for instance, is characterized as a service in that the relevant signals do not transfer any tangible objects.[37] Yet restrictions on television advertising also touch the sale of the product advertised: both EC goods and services rules hence are at stake. Audio-visual products expressed in physical form, such as DVDs or video cassettes, constitute goods.[38] The performance of CDs or videos, however, is treated as a service.[39]

(ii) Non-tariff barriers comprised by Article 28 EC

Article 28 EC's prohibition of 'quantitative import restrictions' and 'measures having an equivalent effect' is thus of great importance for the audio-visual sector.[40] More than the former, which addresses quotas and total import bans, the latter notion is subject to interpretation. In *Dassonville*, the ECJ opted for

[30] See von Plehwe, T, 'European Union and the Free Movement of Cultural Goods', *European Law Review* 1995, 431; Leible, S, 'Art. 28 EC', in Grabitz, E and Hilf, M (eds), *Das Recht der Europäischen Union: Amsterdamer Fassung*, vol 1 (Munich: C H Beck, 2002), para 45.

[31] Case 120/78, *Rewe-Zentrale AG v Bundesmonopolverwaltung für Branntwein (Cassis de Dijon)* [1979] ECR 649.

[32] Case 2/90, *Commission v Belgium (Walloon Waste)* [1992] ECR I-4431, 4480. Only money in the sense of legal currency seems to form an object that is excluded from Article 28 EC: Case 7/78, *Thompson* [1978] ECR 2247; Case C-416/93, *Bordessa* [1995] ECR I-361, 383.

[33] For lottery tickets as services, see Case C-275/92, *Schindler* [1994] ECR I-1078, paras 24–25; for electricity as a good, see Cases C-393/92, *Gemeente Almelo* [1994] ECR I-1477, 1516 and C-158/94, *Commission v Italy (electricity imports and exports)* [1997] ECR I-5789, para 14.

[34] The Court's first test case was Case 155/73, *Sacchi* [1974] ECR 409, 428.

[35] Leible, above n 30, para 53; Müller-Graff, P C, 'Art. 30', in Groeben, H, Thiesing, J, and Ehlermann, C D (eds), *Kommentar zum EU-, EG-Vertrag* (Baden-Baden: Nomos, 1997), paras 273 *et seq.*

[36] Joined Cases C-34–36/95 *et seq.*, *De Agostini et al v Konsumentenombudsmanen* [1997] ECR I-3890, paras 39, 48.

[37] Case 352/88, *Bond van Adverteers* [1988] ECR 2085.

[38] Case 260/89, *Elliniki Radiofonia Tiléorassi* [1991] ECR I-2925.

[39] Case 395/87, *Tournier v Sacem* [1989] ECR 2565.

[40] Measures having equivalent effect are 'le plus délicat': Mégret et al., n 24 above, 101.

the broadest possible definition: measures having an equivalent effect encompass 'all trading rules enacted by Member States which are capable of hindering, actually or potentially, directly or indirectly, intra-Community trade'. In consequence, a rule's mere potential to impede cross-border trade triggers Article 28.[41] While the ECJ never accepted a *de minimis* defence,[42] it let pass measures with a too indirect or unlikely effect on trade.[43] This wide scope of Article 28 EC also explains its inherent tension with cultural measures: culture-oriented rules are likely to affect trade.[44]

There are numerous reasons why states want to control the trade flow in culture. The main state aim, ironically, is the protection of culture itself: states want to preserve domestic culture.[45] States therefore restrict imports using instruments such as quotas, obliging operators to broadcast a certain minimum content of 'national' programmes.[46] Conversely, an interest in preventing exports is likely only where unique cultural items are concerned.[47] But in most cultural fields, especially the audio-visual sector, states support exports, for instance by means of subsidies or organizations set up to promote national culture, such as the Goethe institute.[48] Other interests invoked by the states when attempting to regulate trade in culture are 'ordre public', or, more specifically, fair competition, the protection of consumers and children, and the preservation of morality and public health. The audio-visual sector is often affected by rules on product safety or labelling which relate to advertisements. Article 28 EC applies to all these domestic rules which potentially hinder trade in culture: it assists the Member States in furthering cultural exports, but restricts them in protecting their own culture.

[41] Case 8/74, *Dassonville* [1974] ECR 837, para 5; cf. Case 124/85, *Commission v Greece* [1986] ECR 3935, 3948; Leible, n 30 above, paras 12–15.

[42] Express refusal of 'de minimis': Cases 16/83, *Prantl* [1984] ECR 1299, 1326; 126/91, *Yves Rocher* [1993] ECR I-2361, 2396; cf. Mojzesowicz, n 27 above, 39.

[43] Case C-266/96, *Corsica Ferries France* [1988] ECR I-3949, para 31; C-69/88, *Krantz* [1996] ECR I-594, paras 10–11.

[44] See de Witte, n 10 above, 238.

[45] Free trade easily collides with 'culture' in a wide sense: traditional Spanish regulations, e.g., prescribed that Rioja wine had to be bottled in the region. See Case C-47/90, *Delhaize v Promalvin* [1992] ECR I-3669. France tried to justify discriminating between 'aperitifs' and 'digestifs' by reference to the culture surrounding eating: Case 168/78, *Commission v France (taxation of spirits)* [1980] ECR 347.

[46] For quotas, see Filipek, J, 'Culture Quotas', *Stanford Journal of Int Law*, 28 (1992), 147.

[47] EC Directive 93/7/EC, 'Return of cultural objects', OJ [1993] L 74/74, addresses some of these problems.

[48] Cases 248/81, *Commission v Ireland (Buy Irish)* [1982] ECR 4005 and 113/80, *Commission v Ireland (Souvenirs)* [1981] ECR 1625 outline the borders of EC law for such promotion.

(iii) Limitations to the scope of and defences to Article 28 EC

Article 30 EC establishes explicit limits to the free movement of goods. In addition to these limits the Court, in *Keck* and *Cassis de Dijon*, has created further tools to restrict Article 28 EC.[49]

The *Keck* formula was introduced in order to narrow down Article 28 EC's range of application. 'Selling arrangements' that 'apply to all affected traders operating within the national territory' and which 'affect in the same manner, in law and in fact, the marketing of domestic products and of those from other Member States' were henceforth excluded from the broad *Dassonville* formula.[50] In *Hübnermund*, the Court subsumed generally applicable restrictions on the advertising of pharmacies under the term 'selling arrangements'.[51] Such exclusion of national advertising rules from the scope of Article 28 EC clearly had the potential to affect significantly the commercial media. In *Mars*[52] and *Clinique*[53] the Court clarified that product-specific provisions still fell within the domain of Article 28 EC. *Keck*, in this light, serves only to exempt measures which are not product-specific. Member States thus may maintain general provisions relating to the circumstances of sale, such as video store access for minors or opening hours.[54] Community oversight is maintained in relation to those state measures capable of impeding the market access of audio-visual products.

The aims listed in Article 30(1) EC can be relied on to defend state policy measures infringing Article 28 EC only where they do not result in 'arbitrary discrimination or a disguised restriction of trade'. As an exception to the Treaty freedoms, Article 30 EC is to be interpreted narrowly: any measure taken must be adequate, necessary, and not disproportionate.[55] Applying these requirements to the exception for 'national treasures possessing artistic,

[49] Cases 120/78, *Rewe (Cassis de Dijon)*, n 31 above; C-267–8/91, *Criminal proceedings against Keck and Mithouard* [1993] ECR I-6097. While Article 30 EC provides for a list of justifications and Keck narrows down the scope of Article 28 EC, the proper place of *Cassis* in this categorization is not clear: cf. Case 261/81, *Rau* [1982] ECR 3961 to Case C-368/95, *Familiapress*, n 22 above; and see Leible, n 30 above, para 20.

[50] Case C-267,268/91, *Keck*, n 49 above, para 16; Craig, P and De Búrca, G, *European Union Law*, 3rd edn (Oxford: OUP, 2002), 641–57.

[51] Case C-292/92, *Ruth Hübnermund v Landesapothekerkammer Baden-Württemberg* [1993] ECR I-6787, para 21.

[52] Case C-470/93, *Verein gegen das Unwesen in Handel und Gewerbe Köln v Mars* [1995] ECR I-1923, paras 12–13.

[53] Case C-315/92, *Verband Sozialer Wettbewerb v Clinique* [1994] ECR I-330, para 13.

[54] Cf. cases concerning Sunday trading rules: Case C-69, 258/93, *Punto Casa* [1994] ECR I-2355, paras 13 *et seq.;* Case C-418/93 et al., *Semeraro Casa Uno* [1996] ECR I-2975, paras 14–28.

[55] Leible, n 30 above, paras 3, 8.

historical or archaeological value' indicates that only unique, or at least rare, items of national value are meant.[56] Especially the word 'treasure'[57] implies that not every copyrightable artistic product is privileged by the clause,[58] which mainly targets export restrictions and has limited relevance in the audio-visual context.[59] Another exception listed in Article 30 EC, 'public morals', is more appropriate to preserve national culture and may clearly have an impact on the trade in cultural goods and services. Differing moral standards can create obstacles for the audio-visual sector necessitating, for example, different versions of a particular movie to be produced for different countries. The ECJ has upheld general bans on pornographic content, but does not allow states to discriminate on the basis of the origin of the product.[60] Surprisingly, litigation relating to the public morals exception before the ECJ has been rare,[61] whereas it has been quite frequent in Strasbourg.[62] Last, but not least, Article 30 justifies national intellectual property regimes to a certain

[56] This view is supported by the preamble of EC Dir. 93/7/EC, 'Return of Cultural Objects', n 47 above; Merryman, J, 'Cultural Property: International Trade & Human Rights', *Cardozo Journal of Arts and Entertainment Law*, vol 19 (2001), 51, 54; Pescatore, P, 'Le commerce de l'art et le marché commun', *Revue trimestrielle de droit Européen*, vol 21 (1985), 451.

[57] The German version's notion 'Nationales Kulturgut' is tailored to unique items such as the Guthenberg Bible; it certainly does not comprise mass-reproducible goods. See Leible, S, 'Art. 30 EC', in Grabitz and Hilf, n 30 above, para 18. Comprehensive coverage is provided in Mußgnug, R, 'Europäischer und nationaler Kulturgüter-Schutz', in Mußgnug, R and Roellecke, G (eds), *Aktuelle Fragen des Kulturgüterschutzes* (Heidelberg: C F Müller, 1998), 11 *et seq.*; Streinz, R, *Internationaler Schutz von Museumsgut* (Opladen: Leske und Budrich, 1998); Bila, J, *Nationaler Kulturgüterschutz in der EU* (Bonn: Dissertation, 1997); Hipp, A, *Der Kulturgutschutz in der Bundesrepublik Deutschland im Gefüge des europäischen Binnenmarktes* (Berlin: de Gruyter, 2000).

[58] Yet Cahn, S and Schimmel, D, 'The Cultural Exception: Does it Exist in GATT and GATS Frameworks? How Does it Affect or is it Affected by the Agreement on TRIPS?', in *Cardozo Arts and Entertainment Journal*, XV (1997), 281, 284, want to stretch the like-worded Article XX(f) GATT that far as to comprise every item which is eligible for copyright protection.

[59] The clause, to date, has not been used: see Case 7/68, *Commission v Italy (Artistic Treasures)*, n 22 above, 642.

[60] See Case 121/85, *Conegate* [1986] ECR 1007 and Case 34/79, *Henn and Derby* [1979] ECR 3795.

[61] Case 275/92, *Schindler*, n 33 above, concerns public policy justifications in relation to state control of lotteries.

[62] Judgment of 20 September 1994, *Otto-Preminger-Institut v Austria*, App No 13470/87, (1994) 19 EHRR 34, concerned an Italian ballet based on Oskar Pannizza's book *Das Liebeskonzil*, which, ironically, had been banned already in 1895 on charges of blasphemy; Judgment of 7 December 1976, *Handyside v UK*, App No 5493/72, (1976) 1 EHRR 737, concerned the so-called 'little red school book' imported from Sweden into the UK; Judgment of 24 May 1988, *Müller v Switzerland*, App No 10737/84, (1988) 13 EHRR 212, concerned extreme 'art'. None of the respondent states was an EC member at the time of the facts. See Ovey and White, n 5 above, 207–16.

degree as impediments to trade in culture, at least in the absence of Community legislation in the area.[63]

But Article 30 EC does not cover all legitimate state aims, and the ECJ in its *Cassis de Dijon* opinion accepted a general rule of reason.[64] This defence to Article 28 applies in the absence of specific Community rules (that is, harmonization) and where the measure is equally applicable to foreign and domestic goods.[65] Such mandatory requirements in the general interest must be, again, necessary, adequate, and proportionate.[66] The ECJ has been prepared to include general cultural policy objectives within the scope of this rule of reason.[67] Also, more specific goals, such as media diversity[68] and the demands of the ECHR, especially its Article 10,[69] have been recognized. The rule also acknowledges non culture-based aims, such as the protection of minors and consumers.

In the absence of harmonizing legislation, it is the ECJ's task to find the proper balance between trade and countervailing legitimate interests.[70] Because of the economy's preference for low production costs, decisions which are too liberal on trade may lead to the 'Delaware-effect': the lowest protective standard will set the benchmark. Too lenient a stance on national measures, however, will restrict trade in culture unduly. Cultural interests, as we have seen, can weigh on both sides of the scales. Article 95(3) EC indicates that the Community, despite its trade-liberal basic order, seeks to guarantee a high level of protection for particular non-trade interests. Nor can the Court be said simplistically to favour free trade over other aims. For instance, it respects Scandinavian caution towards commercials targeting children to a certain degree.[71] On the other hand, in cases such as *Clinique* or *Mars*, it rejected Germany's standard of consumer protection as too strict.[72] This balanced approach, in the absence of secondary legislation, results in certain

[63] Council Regulation (EC) No 40/94/EC of 20 November 1993 on the Community trade mark, OJ [1994] L 11/1; EC, First Council Directive 89/104/EEC of 21 December 1988 to approximate the laws of the member states relating to trade marks, OJ [1989] L 40/1.

[64] Case 120/78, *Rewe (Cassis de Dijon)*, n 31 above, para 8.

[65] On the recent discussion as to whether *Cassis* should be applicable to discriminatory measures, see Chapter 3 by Niamh Nic Shuibhne in this volume; Mojzesowicz, n 27 above, 124 *et seq.*

[66] See Stuyck, J, *European Economic Law* (Leuven: Acco, 1997), 25.

[67] See Case 60/84, *Cinéthèque* [1985] ECR 2605, 2626 for the freedom of services, and Case C-288/89, *Gouda* [1991] ECR I-4009; cf., however, Case 229/83, *Leclerc* [1985] ECR 1, 35.

[68] Case C-368/95, *Familiapress*, n 22 above, para 27.

[69] Case 260/89, *ERT*, n 38 above, paras 43–44.

[70] Cf. Article 95(3) EC.

[71] Joined Cases C-34–36/95, *De Agostini*, n 36 above.

[72] E.g., Cases C-315/92, *Clinique* [1994] ECR I-330, para 13; C-470/93, *Mars* [1995] ECR I-1923, paras 12–13.

obstacles to trade in culture still remaining: the Member States keep options to further their cultural goals at the domestic level.

(b) *The freedom to provide services*

For the audio-visual sector, the freedom to provide services established in Article 49 EC[73] is equally as important as the free movement of goods, in that television broadcasting is classified as a service. The EC Treaty in Article 50 defines a service as a performance which is, in general, remunerated and not covered by the other freedoms. Article 49 comes into play when the service has a cross-border element, that is, where the service provider, recipient, or both, travel to another state to provide, or receive, the service.[74] It is also applicable, as in the case of broadcasting, where only the service crosses the border.[75]

As with the Treaty provisions on goods, Article 49 EC has a broad scope. It prohibits, first, distinctions on the basis of nationality or the place of establishment. EC operators cannot be treated less favourably than domestic ones.[76] These discriminatory measures can be justified only within one of the limited written exceptions set out in Article 46 read in conjunction with Article 55 EC.[77] Restrictions that apply indiscriminately to domestic and non-domestic service providers, at least in an import scenario, also fall within the scope of Articles 49 and 50 EC.[78] In particular, there is no category of excluded 'selling arrangements' along the lines established by *Keck* in relation to goods.[79] For indiscriminately applicable measures the Court employs a *Cassis*-style rule of reason approach which enables additional general interest justifications to be put forward.[80] In any case, account must be taken of the level of supervision already undertaken in the home state.[81] Due to the

[73] See generally Craig and De Búrca, n 50 above, 800 *et seq.*

[74] Case C-154, 180, 198/89, *Commission v Greece (Tourist guides)* [1991] ECR I-659, 709, 727.

[75] See Stuyck, n 66 above, 31 *et seq.*

[76] Case 33/74, *Van Binsbergen* [1974] ECR 1299; this rule applies both to export (in parallel to Article 29 EC) and import scenarios: Randelzhofer, A and Forsthoff, U, 'Art. 49/50 EC', in Grabitz and Hilf, n 30 above, paras 67–71.

[77] Cases 352/88, *Bond van Adverteers* [1988] ECR 2085, para 32; 211/91, *Commission v Belgium (cable TV access)* [1992] ECR I-6757; cf. Case C-6/98, *ARD* [1999] ECR I-7599, para 50.

[78] Cases C-76/90, *Säger and Dennemeyer* [1991] ECR I-4221; C-34–36/95, *De Agostini*, n 36 above.

[79] Case C-384/93, *Alpine Investments* [1995] ECR I-1141, para 33 states this explicitly for the export context. Some scholars argue pro *Keck* concerning import restrictions, see Randelzhofer and Forsthoff, n 76 above, para 54. Yet such argument is in spite of cases such as Joined Cases C-34–36/95, *De Agostini*, n 36 above, where the Court did not adopt a *Keck*-based reasoning even though it had had the opportunity to do so.

[80] Craig and De Búrca, n 50 above, 814–18; Case C-76/90, *Säger*, n 78 above.

[81] Case 279/80, *Webb* [1981] ECR 3305.

non-application of *Keck* in the service context, the Court subjects a wider range of measures to its scrutiny than under the goods regime. Nevertheless, Luxembourg is more likely to accept policy goals here, since rules for services vary more markedly within the EC than product rules. In consequence, the traditionally heavily regulated audio-visual sector remains subject to considerable national legislation.

(c) *The freedom of establishment*

Article 43 EC's freedom of establishment[82] is also relevant for the audio-visual industry. Companies, including media, can rely on Article 43 EC in order to establish themselves in the country with the least onerous regulations, or found a subsidiary there. They may, under certain conditions, even shift their head office abroad.[83] The law of the host state may not discriminate against companies properly established in another Member State.[84] However, the Court has held that it is 'not inconceivable that overriding requirements relating to the general interest, such as the protection of the interests of creditors, minority shareholders, employees and even the taxation authorities, may . . . justify restrictions on freedom of establishment'.[85] Yet such justification is 'subject to certain conditions', most likely necessity and proportionality.[86] An outright denial of legal capacity for the purpose of legal proceedings to a company properly established in another Member State with its registered office there, however, does not seem justifiable.[87] As thus defined, the freedom of establishment even applies in the absence of a real and continuous link to the economy of the Member State seeking to regulate.[88] Television operators can and do employ it to their benefit. In *De Agostini*, a company broadcasting to Sweden used, largely successfully, a UK licence to avoid the stricter Scandinavian advertising regulations.[89]

(d) *Specific Treaty provisions concerning culture*

While trade liberalization without any accompanying policy framework may further the race to the bottom, the EC system contains such a policy framework

[82] Generally Craig and De Búrca, n 50 above, 772–99.

[83] Case 81/ 87, *Daily Mail* [1988] ECR 5483, paras 2–4 (transferring head office to The Netherlands).

[84] See Case C-212/97, *Centros* [1999] ECR I-1459; Case C-208/00, *Überseering BV* [2002] ECR I-09919.

[85] Case C-208/00, *Überseering* BV, n 84 above, para 92.

[86] Ibid., paras 92 and 84.

[87] Ibid., para 93. It has to be tested, though, whether this general line can be upheld in cases where the admission of a claim could harm the other party, e.g., the present risk that the claimant falls bankrupt during the trial.

[88] The Court rejected this claim by the Spanish Government explicitly: ibid., paras 74, 75.

[89] Joined Cases C-34–36/95, *De Agostini*, n 36 above, para 11.

for intervention in the cultural field—albeit limited in scope. Article 3 EC sets out the specific areas of activity in which the EC can engage and specifies, in Article 3(q), the development of cultural life in the Member States. The impact of this clause should not, however, be overrated: it is only a regulatory goal with no clear legal effect. Nevertheless, it serves to underline the standing of culture within the EC regime and also justifies the existence of a specific Directorate General for culture (and education) within the European Commission.

According to Article 151 EC,[90] the EC is to contribute to the development of the Member States' cultures while preserving national and regional diversity. Moreover, the common cultural heritage is to be promoted. In the audiovisual and several other sectors, the EC can support trans-border cooperation and, to a lesser degree, cultural activities within a Member State. Article 151(5) EC grants the Community very limited competence for supportive legislation and precludes harmonization.[91] The Council is, however, authorized to make recommendations. Most importantly, Article 151(4) urges the Community to respect cultural aspects where it harmonizes legislation using a legal basis which is not culture-specific, such as Articles 94 or 95 EC. This extends the focus in such contexts from trade to culture. Lastly, Article 87(3)(d) EC makes state aid for cultural purposes eligible for exemption. This acknowledges the fact that, apart from commercially viable art, there are many artistic activities which depend for their survival on support which is not commercially oriented, in many instances of a public nature.

(e) Harmonization: the 'Television Without Frontiers' Directive

Article 151 EC provides neither a genuine basis for legislation, nor a bar to the application of harmonizing competences such as Articles 94, 95, or 55 in conjunction with 47(2) EC. As previously shown, the basic freedoms can have a significant impact on national cultural measures. Nevertheless, primary Community law, through its various exceptions and derogations, still leaves considerable space for divergent national legislation. Harmonizing legislation remedies these remaining trade barriers while further reducing the states' regulatory options. Article 151(4) EC, with its requirement that cultural concerns be taken into account when applying other Treaty provisions, should help to ensure that cultural considerations are not neglected in the legislative process.

[90] For a discussion of this clause, see McMahon, n 26 above, 164.

[91] This is discussed in more detail by Rachael Craufurd Smith in Chapter 2 of this volume.

In the audio-visual sector, the Television Without Frontiers Directive (TWF) is the key harmonizing instrument relating to the content of television broadcasting.[92] It is based on Articles 55 and 47(2) EC, the competence for harmonization of services. The scope of the Directive can be gauged from the following brief overview of its main provisions.

Article 2 TWF establishes a system of 'home state control' to ensure compliance with the Directive's minimum standards;[93] it replaces the receiving state's control in the coordinated areas. Home states are free to enact stricter legislation than that in the Directive for the television operators under their control. Article 2(3) TWF determines which state supervises which operator. The main link now is the head office and the place where editorial decisions are taken. A system of tie-breakers comes into operation when the places of targeted audience, headquarters, and main business activities diverge.

Article 4 TWF introduces a 'soft' minimum European quota: broadcasters must reserve for European works[94] 50 per cent of their transmission time excluding news, sports, games, and advertising.[95] Member States must ensure that the proportion of European content does not fall back below the 1988 average. Broadcasters must also ensure that at least 10 per cent of their programming budget or transmission time is spent on programmes produced by independent European producers (Article 5 TWF). In 'good' European tradition—see agriculture—internal impediments to trade have been transferred to the external borders of the EC, restricting not only US but also independent Asian, African, and South-American movies.

Articles 10 to 20 TWF deal with advertising, tele-shopping, and sponsorship. First, the interruption times and technical modalities of such commercial breaks are regulated. Articles 12 to 16 TWF further introduce content-based rules for them. Advertisements for tobacco products and prescription drugs are

[92] Directive 89/552/EEC of 3 October 1989, OJ L298, 23, as amended by Directive 97/36/EC of 30 July 1997, OJ [1998] L 006, 43. See Keller, P, 'The New TWF Directive', *Yearbook of Media and Entertainment Law*, (1997/98), 177; Hitchens, L, 'Identifying European Community Audio-visual Policy in the Dawn of the Information Society', *Yearbook of Media and Entertainment Law*, (1996), 45, 47; Barendt, n 4 above, 229 *et seq.*; Harcourt, A, 'The EU Commission and the Regulation of the Media Industry', *Cardozo Journal of Arts and Entertainment Law*, (1998), 425, 434–40; Donaldson, J D, 'TWF: The Continuing Tension between Liberal Free Trade and European Cultural Integrity', *Fordham International Law Journal*, vol 20 (1996), 90.

[93] See Article 3(1) TWF, n 92 above; home state control can encompass stricter rules.

[94] This term comprises Council of Europe members; see Article 6 TWF, n 92 above, for a definition.

[95] See Harrison, J and Woods, L, 'Television Quotas: Protecting European Culture', *Entertainment Law Review*, vol 12 I (2001), 5.

totally banned, while alcohol advertisements are restricted. In addition, there are minimum requirements to ensure the protection of children.

The TWF also introduces in Article 22 content-based rules for television programmes, albeit in the limited area of protection of minors and public order. Article 22a TWF prohibits footage inciting hatred on grounds of race, sex, religion, or nationality. Article 23 grants a right to reply in cases of incorrect information, if legitimate interests have been disregarded by the broadcaster.

In the areas covered by the Directive, the receiving state has to live with foreign broadcasts which conform to the minimum standards. Theoretically, higher standards could be introduced for home operators, but such rules can increasingly easily be circumvented by relocation. Even in cases of inefficient home state control, receiving states are restricted in policing the minimum standards. They have to employ the EC judicial procedures, that is, recourse to the Commission or the Court.[96] Unilateral measures taken by the receiving state are only possible in cases where there have been manifest infringements of the youth protection or public order requirements in Articles 2a(2), 22, or 22a TWF, and only after prior discussion with the Commission.

As the *De Agostini* case exemplified in the context of consumer protection,[97] not all obstacles to cross-border broadcasting have been removed by the Directive. In those areas which are not covered by the Directive, the receiving states are free to regulate within the limits set by primary Community law. The TWF, nevertheless, regulates a broad part of trans-frontier broadcasting and strongly influences the audio-visual sector.

(f) *The audio-visual sector and other aspects of EC law*

Several other aspects of EC law, which cannot be explored in detail here, concern the audio-visual sector. One of these is competition law, in the context of which the operating activities and even legitimacy of public service broadcasters have proved to be major issues.[98] However, Protocol No 32 to the EC Treaty acknowledges that public service broadcasters perform a distinct and valuable role,[99] a role acknowledged by the judiciary by and large,[100] even if

[96] Proceedings can be directed against the state of control (Articles 226 or 227 EC), or against the Commission (Article 232 EC) in order to take the appropriate measures against a non-fulfilling Member State.

[97] Joined Cases C-34–36/95, *De Agostini*, n 36 above.

[98] See for more details see Chapter 6 by Josh Holmes in this volume.

[99] Protocol No 32 to the EC Treaty on public broadcasting in the Member States.

[100] See Case C-6/98, *ARD* [1999] ECR I-7599.

particular judgments question certain aspects of public operations.[101] Of importance in this context, but also for cultural sponsorship in general, is the question of state aid. Whilst Articles 87 to 89 EC target such assistance, Article 87(3)(d) EC makes cultural aids eligible for exemption.[102]

Another area which has been subjected to the EC's scrutiny is that of media ownership. Given the failure of the Commission to propose a legislative instrument establishing specific ownership limits, the matter has been addressed primarily, if somewhat indirectly, through the Community merger regime.[103] Article 82 EC seeks to control the activities of those with dominant market positions. Under certain conditions, 'essential facilities' of dominant players have to be opened by means of compulsory licences to the benefit of those market participants in need of such facilities.[104] Even if the courts have been careful not to stretch this rule too far,[105] it seems relevant for those seeking fair access[106] to key communication networks and associated services. There are also a number of other general harmonizing measures which influence the capacity of the media to cross borders, for instance regulations in the field of intellectual property[107] and consumer protection.[108]

(g) Summary EC

The EC trade system has strongly influenced the audio-visual policies of its Member States. The basic trade freedoms have a broad scope and easily extend to cover domestic regulations in the media sector. However, *Keck*, *Cassis*, and Article 30 EC provide tools which can be used to distinguish purely protectionist from genuinely culture-promoting state measures. An

101 Especially the Court of First Instance takes a firm pro-competition stance: see Joined Cases T-185/00 et al., *Métropole Télévision ('Eurovision') et al* [2002] ECR II-305.

102 See McMahon, n 26 above, 161.

103 Council Regulation (EC) 139/2004 of 20 January 2004, OJ [2004] L 24/1. See 1992 EC Commission, *Green Paper, Pluralism and Media Concentration in the Internal Market*, COM (92) 480 final, 23.12.1992, and the follow-up in COM (94) 353 final; see Hitchens, n 92 above, pp 45, 46.

104 Cases C-241/91 et al, *Radio Téléfis Eireann ('Magill')* [1995] ECR I-743; T-504/93, *Tiercé Ladbroke* [1997] ECR II-923; C-481/01 P (R), Order of the President of the Court, *NDC Health v Commission and IMS Health* [2002] ECR I-3401; C-418/01, conclusions by AG Tizzano of 2 October 2003, *IMS Health v NDC Health* (n.y.r.).

105 Case C-7/97, *Oscar Bronner v Mediaprint* [1998] ECR I-7791.

106 For the fair access debate, see Lichtenberg, J, 'Foundations and Limits of Freedom of the Press', in ead (ed), Democracy and the Mass Media (New York: Cambridge University Press 1990), 102 *et seq.*

107 See n 63 above.

108 See Article 153 EC and Council Directive 84/450/EEC of 10 September 1984 relating to the approximation of the laws and administrative provisions of the Member States concerning misleading advertising, OJ [1984] L 250/17–20.

overview of primary Community law thus reveals sufficient space for national cultural policy, whereas discriminatory measures are banned by and large. Harmonization measures of secondary law, however, have the potential to streamline national cultural policy in the audio-visual sector to a much greater extent. As noted, the TWF Directive assimilates the Member State regimes with regard to advertising times, 'problem products', and European content. Nevertheless, even secondary law is far from being comprehensive and in certain areas, such as child protection, the Directive's open language serves to accommodate widely divergent domestic approaches. Lastly, it is necessary to bear in mind the 'horizontal' impact of Article 151(4) EC, which requires the Community, across the whole spectrum of its activities, to identify and show sufficient sensitivity towards cultural concerns.

3. The WTO

Based on the 1994 Marrakesh Agreement, the WTO was established as an international organization on 1 January 1995.[109] Contrary to the 1947 GATT, which allowed states latitude in signing up to the different agreements, creating a complex mosaic of commitments ('GATT-à-la-carte'), the WTO obliges its members to accept a core package of 'multilateral' agreements.[110] Substantially, this includes GATT 1994, the General Agreement on Trade in Services (GATS), and the Agreement on Trade-related Aspects of Intellectual Property Rights (TRIPS). Procedurally, the Dispute Settlement Understanding (DSU) sets up compulsory panel trials, a standing second instance Appellate Body ('AB', Article 17 DSU), and an enforcement procedure.

(a) The WTO's goods regime: GATT

The dominant instrument of the WTO is still the GATT in its updated 1994 version. Complemented by some specific agreements, it serves a similar purpose as the free movement of goods provisions in the EC Treaty: market access for foreign products. However, the WTO is no customs union: import tariffs—despite being subject to negotiation and subsequent commitment—remain legal (see Article II GATT). Major progress has been achieved in lowering tariffs since 1947. Furthermore, the most-favoured-nation clause of Article I GATT grants the lowest tariffs enjoyed by any other member to all

[109] On the WTO in general, see n 6 above.

[110] Accession to so-called 'plurilateral' agreements is still not obligatory.

the contracting states. Regional trading areas, such as the EC, are exempt from this rule under Article XXIV GATT.

(i) The scope of the GATT

As in the EC context, the respective scope of the goods (GATT) and services (GATS) provisions are a matter for interpretation. DVDs and video cassettes, as 'physical products',[111] are covered by GATT, while television broadcasting is regarded as a service. Most scholars deny the relevance of GATT for large parts of the audio-visual sector, and especially for television.[112] This is in spite of the comparable case law in the EC context which points to parallel application.[113] De Witte has noted that the WTO members negotiated the audio-visual sector in the Uruguay round in the context of GATS. Such subsequent state practice may be considered to constitute a source of law.[114] Deselaers and König fine-tune this idea by pointing to the WTO's own classification system, which includes audio-visual activities under the heading of communication services.[115] This argument undoubtedly has some weight. However, there is no evidence that the enacting of GATS narrowed the scope of GATT: as Hahn explains, the Uruguay talks left Article IV GATT,[116] a provision dealing with cinematographic films, and hence the audio-visual sector, unchanged.[117] Nor does the application of GATS to audio-visual services necessarily exclude them from the scope of GATT. Indeed, the DSU organs, in parallel to the ECJ,[118] have accepted that both agreements may be relevant in the context of magazines.[119] The significance of advertising for market access, in particular, would seem to support the application of GATT to broad parts of the audio-visual industry, including television.

[111] AB Report, *Canada—Periodicals*, WT/DS31/AB/R [1997], para 52. (Reference to WTO decisions is made by means of the official WTO Document number. All the WTO decisions are available free of charge on the website http://docsonline.wto.org. Hardcopy reports are published by Cambridge University Press, but this series is not yet a standard feature of most libraries.)

[112] See the pre-WTO opinion of Barendt, n 4 above, 221.

[113] Joined Cases C-34–36/95, *De Agostini*, n 36 above.

[114] See Article 31(3)(b) of the Vienna Treaty Convention; de Witte, n 10 above, 245–6.

[115] Deselaers, W and König, M, 'The WTO Millenium Round and the AV Sector', *International Trade Law and Regulation*, 5 VI (1999), 147–8; WTO Council for Trade in Services, AV Services Background note of the WTO Secretariat of 15 June 1998, p 2, classifies AV services as subsector D of (2) Communications Services. Sub-categories: a) motion picture and videotape production and distribution, b) motion picture projection, c) radio and TV, d) radio and TV transmission, e) sound recording, and f) others.

[116] On Article IV GATT, see Neuwirth, n 7 above, 5 *et seq*.

[117] Hahn, M, 'Eine kulturelle Bereichsausnahme für die WTO?', *Heidelberg Journal of International Law*, 56 (1996), 315.

[118] Joined Cases C-34–36/95, *De Agostini*, n 36 above.

[119] Panel Report, *Canada—Periodicals*, n 111 above, para 5.17; AB Report, *Canada—Periodicals*, ibid., para 58.

(ii) Guarantees of GATT

To facilitate market access, the GATT contains two major guarantees: national treatment for foreign products (Article III GATT), and the abolition of quantitative measures (Article XI GATT).

Article III GATT is too complex to be treated here in detail, but its main implications are fairly straightforward: 'like products' from another contracting state must not be discriminated against, at least not in order to protect domestic production. The product part of the audio-visual sector is certainly affected by this rule. Thus, DVDs in a store cannot be made subject to restrictions because of their origin. But the clause may reach further: for example, it seems clear that a law obliging radio stations to play national or national language music has an influence on which records are sold in music stores. Clearly, foreign cultural products are denied equitable market access and Article III GATT is therefore implicated. With audio-visual content, however, this equation is not so easy. It is not clear whether a screening quota for national television has a similar influence on movie DVD sales. Nevertheless, a certain relevance can be ascribed to GATT in this context and, consequently, its potential application to the audio-visual sector seems undeniable. The relevance of television advertising rules for the free movement of goods has already been identified. To date, these questions have not been addressed in dispute settlement proceedings.

Article XI GATT provides that 'no prohibitions or restrictions other than [tariffs] . . . shall be instituted or maintained by any contracting party on the importation of any product of the territory of any other contracting party or on the exportation'. Due to the GATT's role as a model for the later Treaty of Rome, this clause is similar to Article 28 EC. Yet it does not cover explicitly 'measures having an equivalent effect'. On the other hand, its language is not restricted to 'quantitative restrictions'. The GATT dispute settlement cases decided so far, however, show that Articles XI and III GATT have not developed the same dynamic as Article 28 EC; even if there is potential for a more wide-ranging application, their scope has to date been restricted mostly to cases of import quotas and direct discrimination.

(iii) Defences and their relevance to cultural goods

The GATT, like the EC Treaty, acknowledges certain defences to infringements.

Written exceptions to the GATT

Article IV GATT contains a specific justification for cinema screen quotas. A dynamic interpretation of this clause might encompass television content quotas. Yet the GATS talks, and the explicit disagreement there over the inclusion of such a clause for television, rule this option out on the basis of subsequent state practice.[120] The importance of Article IV, therefore, has to be assessed as rather low.

Article XX GATT,[121] just like the subsequently drafted Article 30 EC, explicitly lists state aims which can be relied on to defend restrictions on free trade. Article XX(f) GATT allows for measures to protect 'national treasures of artistic, historic or archaeological value'. While the temptation exists to stretch this provision to a more general cultural exemption, such an interpretation would clearly depart from its intended meaning. The term 'treasures', as already indicated in the context of Article 30 EC, applies only to exceptional goods.[122] Article XX(a) GATT also endorses 'public morals' as a ground for justification. This clause, indeed, allows for cultural protectionism, since morality cannot be defined without a cultural background. Different countries, therefore, are likely to use this clause to defend quite different values. Conflicting approaches can be anticipated in cases of extremist religious or political messages, or in relation to openly sexual or violent content. Apart from this, the impact of Article XX(a) GATT will remain limited: the clause is not broad enough to support cultural policies reaching beyond the essentials of morals. Lastly, Article XX(d) and the TRIPS Agreement accept intellectual property rights as a barrier to trade. States, hence, are at liberty to reward creativity with commercially exploitable monopolies.

The dispute settlement organs' general construction of Article XX GATT—because of Article 3.2 DSU[123]—has to stay close to its literal wording. An 'aim and effects' test to distinguish pure protectionism from reasonable policy, as necessary as it may be, has not been accepted.[124] The Appellate Body (AB), however, has used Article XX GATT's '*chapeau*'—that is, the general rule before the brackets which applies to all specific elements of the clause—to achieve a similar result. This *chapeau* states that measures cannot benefit from any of the listed exceptions if they are 'applied in a manner which would constitute a means of arbitrary or unjustifiable discrimination between countries, where the same conditions prevail, or a disguised restriction on international trade'. According to the AB, the national policy interest here

[120] See Article 31(3)(b), Vienna Treaty Convention.

[121] Klabbers, J, 'Jurisprudence in International Trade Law: Article XX of GATT', *JWTL* 26 (1992), 63 *et seq.*

[122] See the parallel discussion above, nn 57 and 58.

[123] Article 3.2(2) DSU reads: 'Recommendations and rulings of the DSB cannot add or diminish the rights and obligations provided in the covered agreements.'

[124] Hudec, R, 'GATT / WTO Constraints on National Regulation', *Int. Lawyer*, 32 (1998), 619 et seq.

must outweigh the trade restriction applied.[125] This approach is to be welcomed in that it ensures an acceptable equilibrium between trade and competing values in the fields covered by Article XX GATT. However, cultural considerations are encompassed neither by Article XX, nor by any of the other written exemptions, such as Articles IX.2, XIX, or XXI GATT.[126]

No Cassis-*type rule-of-reason exception*

In the EC, the *Cassis* decision bridged that gap, establishing a rule-of-reason. In the WTO regime, as indicated, no such general exception exists, and neither does a specific 'cultural exception'. Judicial restraint is the DSU's primary imperative.[127] Thus, the first-round panels, and even more so the AB, have been at pains to apply a strictly text-based interpretation, refraining from adopting a 'rule-of-reason' test. As long as an aim of national policy is mentioned in Articles XX GATT, the AB has been quite willing to accept public policy considerations such as environmental policy.[128] Also, standards set in treaties outside the WTO framework have been taken into account, at least if they are of universal character.[129] Some international treaties do contain specific cultural provisions[130] and even exemptions to free trade.[131] Still, DSU organs have not yet used such an external peg to enhance their consideration of cultural matters.

(iv) Case law on GATT and culture: Canada Periodicals

The status of cultural measures in the WTO is illustrated by the *Periodicals* case.[132] The New York based editorial board of *Sports Illustrated*, a Time Warner magazine, transmitted its content electronically to Canada for printing. Unaltered in its editorial part, but complemented with Canadian advertisements,

[125] AB Report, *USA—Gasoline*, WT/DS2/AB/R, see n 111 above; cf. Hudec, n 124 above, 619, 637 *et seq*.

[126] Neuwirth, n 7 above, 14 *et seq*.

[127] See n 123 above.

[128] See Article XX(b) and (g) GATT; AB Report, *USA—Gasoline*, n 125 above; AB Report, *USA—Shrimps*, WT/DS58/AB/R, see n 111 above.

[129] Reports regularly refer to the general instruments such as the Vienna Treaty Convention; see *USA—Sec. 301–310*, WT/DS152/R, para 7.21, n 111 above.

[130] See, e.g., the Paris Agreement on the Protection of World Heritage of 23 November 1972, 1037 UN Treaty Series 151; Instrument establishing a Preparatory Educational, Scientific and Cultural Organisation of 16 November 1945 and UNESCO Constitution, UN Treaty Series Vol 4, p 275; Articles 13 and 15(1)(a), International Covenant on Economic, Social and Cultural Rights of 19 December 1966, UN Treaty Series, Vol 993, p 3.

[131] See the Florence/Nairobi context, n 9 above.

[132] Discussed by James, C P, 'Trade, Culture and Technology: A Test of Canada's Cultural Mettle', *Entertainment Law Review*, 8 VII (1997), 253; Tawfik, M J, 'Competing Cultures: Canada and the WTO—Lessons from Sports Illustrated', *Canadian Yearbook of Int Law*, 36 (1998), 279; Carmody, C, 'When Cultural Identity was Not at Issue: Thinking about Canada— Periodicals', *Georgetown Journal of Law and Policy in International Business*, 30 (1999), 231.

the journal then was printed there, thus avoiding import duties for hard-copies. Canada subsequently established an 'excise tax' for domestically printed periodicals with content produced abroad. A WTO panel classified such 'split-run' magazines as 'like products' to Canadian ones. The measures, hence, did not meet the national treatment requirement of Article III:2, s 1 GATT. Concerning culture, the panel observed that the cultural identity of a WTO member was 'not at issue'.[133] They found not only Article III, but also Article XI:1 GATT, the non-tariff barriers clause, to be violated.[134] Only the Article III GATT finding was appealed. The AB found that the facts established by the panel did not suffice to prove 'like products' in the sense of Article III.2, s 1. Nevertheless, the tax applied at least to some products in direct competition. This afforded protection to domestic production in the sense of Article III:2, s 2.[135] This clause, thus, was held violated on appeal.[136]

The case revealed that the Canadian measures were protective of economic rather than cultural interests in that they took into account neither the market strength of domestic producers, nor the actual content of the publication in question. As a result they potentially benefited big Canadian players and discouraged foreign publications, even if they contributed an outside view on Canadian culture. The WTO Report prohibited neither cultural sponsorship nor genuine cultural policy measures, but it removed arbitrary discrimination and opened the Canadian market to foreign publications, thus giving consumers the freedom to decide what they wanted to read. The outcome of the case, therefore, was correct.

Yet the decision's reasoning is dangerous, for it did not incorporate a balancing test between culture and trade. It is instructive to contrast it with the ECJ's opinion in the *Familiapress* case, where the *Cassis* 'rule of reason' test was applied.[137] In *Familiapress*, Austria, just like Canada, feared that it would be swamped by publications from media giants located in its bigger neighbours (here, Germany). Austria did not establish a general barrier to all foreign productions, but directed its measures more specifically towards big players: the

[133] Panel Report *Canada—Periodicals*, n 111 above, para 5.26; AB Report, *Canada—Periodicals*, ibid., paras 81–82.

[134] Panel and AB do not need to find a 'violation'. Articles 26 DSU and XXIII GATT, instead of a concept of legality, provide for a different standard: 'nullification and impairment of any benefit accruing directly or indirectly under the treaty'. It includes 'non-violation' claims. See Roessler, F, 'The Concept of Nullification and Impairment in the Legal System of the World Trade Organization', in Petersmann, n 19 above, 123.

[135] AB Report, *Canada—Periodicals*, n 111 above, paras 73–88 and 91–97.

[136] See n 134 above for the concept of nullification and impairment.

[137] See text accompanying n 64 above.

legislation, framed in general terms, targeted prize competitions in magazines. Such prize draws tend to shift readers to the financially more powerful publishers because smaller operators are unable to afford them. The ECJ accepted that legislation can properly seek to promote the diversity of the media, even if such a rule hampered the distribution of German magazines in Austria. The question of the rule's necessity, a mandatory element of the *Cassis* approach, was here left for the national court to decide.[138]

Consequently, it appears that the WTO is not sufficiently able to take into account important general interest objectives and balance them against the interest in trade. Although measures which apply equally to national and foreign products are treated with greater tolerance by the WTO, the existence of a threat to rules preserving cultural diversity cannot be denied. In future cases, where genuinely culturally motivated rather than purely protectionist measures are at stake, the panels and AB might—and definitely should—rethink their approach. The absence of a general rule of reason not only is felt in cultural matters, but clearly has a much wider impact. As indicated, international agreements outside the WTO could prove to be a vehicle for the dispute settlement organs to remedy this problem.

(v) GATT and audio-visual measures

To sum up, contrary to popular belief, GATT is relevant to the audio-visual sector and may have a parallel application to GATS. While, on the one hand, the reach of GATT is not as extensive as that of Articles 28 and 29 EC, especially as far as non-discriminatory measures are concerned, on the other hand a general rule of reason has not been recognized alongside the written exemptions. Culture, therefore, remains unprotected. The GATT's potential impact on the audio-visual sector should consequently not be underestimated.

(b) GATS

By contrast, GATS[139] is perceived as having a potentially great influence on the audio-visual sector.[140] According to Article I, GATS applies to all measures

[138] Case C-368/95, *Familiapress*, n 22 above.

[139] Generally on the GATS: Kennett, W, 'The European Community and the General Agreement on Trade in Services', in Emiliou, N and O'Keeffe, D (eds), *The EU and World Trade Law after the GATT Uruguay Round* (Chichester, New York: John Wiley & Sons 1996), 136 et seq.; Morrison, P K, 'WTO Dispute Settlement in Services: Procedural and Substantive Issues', in Petersmann, n 19 above, 375 *et seq.*; Sauvé, P, 'Assessing the GATS—Half Full or Half Empty', *JWTL*, 29 IV (August 1995), 125.

[140] Flint, M, 'GATS 2000 and the European AV Industry', *Int. Media Law*, 17 VI (1999), 41; Deselaers and König, n 115 above, 147.

affecting trade in services. As modes of supply, the GATS recognizes true trans-border services as well as service receivers or suppliers travelling abroad.[141] Remarkably, a commercial presence in another Member State will also bring GATS into play, so that it overlaps in terms of scope with the EC's freedom of establishment provisions. One important exception to the operation of GATS, of relevance for the audio-visual sector, concerns services 'supplied in the exercise of governmental authority': Article I.3(b) and (c) GATS. Such services differ strongly from the EC's concept of a public undertaking.[142] The WTO's concept is narrower: public services are defined as being supplied neither 'on a commercial basis', nor 'in competition' with private suppliers. Major disputes about the scope of this clause are to be expected.[143] In the audio-visual sector, public broadcasting, as exercised in most parts of Europe, would not seem eligible to profit from this exception, in that even if such stations do not operate commercially, they nevertheless face private competition. This problem arises even for public service monopolies as are in force in Austria or Switzerland, since Article 10 ECHR forces them to tolerate competition to a certain degree.[144]

Article II GATS, in parallel to GATT, provides for most-favoured-nation treatment (MFN).[145] However, Article II.2 GATS allows the members to derogate from this requirement for listed services, provided the rules of the Annex on Article II are met. The operation of these exemptions is in general, by virtue of para 6, restricted to a maximum of 10 years. The EC has excluded most of the audio-visual sector from Article II.[146] Article V privileges zones of service integration, such as the EC, in relation to Article II. Preferential audio-visual regulation within the EC, therefore, is not prohibited per se. But privileged treatment of Council of Europe states as agreed under the

[141] Chang, P, Karsenty, G, Mattoo, A and Richtering, J, 'GATS—The Modes of Supply and Statistics on Trade in Services', *JWTL* 33 III (June 1999), 93–4.

[142] Article 2 of Directive 80/723, OJ [1980] L 195/35, as amended by OJ [1985] L 229/20; see Case 188–190/88, *France, UK, Italy v Commission (Transparency Directive I)* [1982] ECR 2545, paras 25–26.

[143] Kennedy, M, 'Services Join GATT: An Analysis of the General Agreement on Trade in Services', *Int. Trade Law and Regulation,* 1 I (1995),11, at 14 *et seq.*

[144] European Court of Human Rights, Judgment of 24 November 1997, *Informationsverein Lentia v Austria,* App No 13914/88 (1993) 17 EHRR 93; annotated by Craufurd Smith, R, 'Do Human Rights Require Private Broadcasting?', *Maastricht Journal of International and Comparative Law,* II (1995), 63; Judgment of 5 November 2002, *Demuth v Switzerland,* App No 38743/97.

[145] Sapir, A, 'The GATS—From 1994 to 2000', *JWTL,* 33 I (February 1999), 51, 57; Kennedy, n 143 above, 11, 16.

[146] See Final List of 15.4.1994, WTO-Document GATS/EL/31; see n 111 above.

Trans-border Television Convention seems problematic. For now, such preferential treatment is covered by the wide-ranging exemptions taken by the EC under Article II.2. In consequence, the MFN principle has to date played a minor role in the audio-visual sector.

National treatment is not automatically a feature of the GATS.[147] It is granted only where specific commitments have been accepted by a member (Article XVII.1 GATS). Only on these terms is equal market access granted (Article XVI.1 GATS).[148] For the audio-visual sector, few countries have made such specific commitments. The EC has not. At present, therefore, national treatment does not influence the audio-visual sector at all. However, the negotiations for the GATS 2000 are in process.[149] The position of the EC Commission is it not to give any specific commitments there, while the US pursues open markets.[150]

Just like Article XX GATT, Article XIV GATS makes provision for general exceptions. Public morals are again included. Some new grounds for defence are introduced, such as public order, even if a footnote limits the application of this to 'serious threats' to 'fundamental interests' of a society. Also contained is a privacy and data protection clause, Article XIV(c)(ii), which could justify national measures such as defamation and privacy laws that impede the media's freedom to report. Additionally, Article XV restates some security exceptions. But just as in GATT, no anchor is found to which the AB could tie a rule of reason in favour of culture.[151]

While the justification block of GATS is almost equal to that of GATT—a 'cultural exception' does not exist either—the initial guarantee for the freedom of trade in services is far less elaborated. Moreover, due to extensive exceptions, states can restrict its impact to a minimum, especially in the audio-visual sector. The threat posed by GATS today is thus of commitments being exacted in the future.

(c) *Harmonization and the role of other multinational treaties*

A final point should be noted. In the EC, owing to the recognition of general interest exceptions to the Community freedoms, a considerable number of

[147] See on national treatment and GATS in general, see Mattoo, A, 'National Treatment in the GATS—Cornerstone or Pandora's Box', *JWTL*, 31 I (February 1997), 107.

[148] Sapir, n 145 above, 51, 58; Kennedy, n 143 above, 11, 16.

[149] Sapir, n 145 above, 51, 62.

[150] See Allègre and Moscovich, n 13 above, 17.

[151] Cahn and Schimmel, n 58 above, acknowledge that the Uruguay round's non-agreement on AV-measures could serve to a certain degree as such a peg. Bernier, n 8 above, 16, talks about an exception only *de lege ferenda*.

obstacles to trade—and national options to regulate culture—potentially remain. However, EC harmonization has removed these possibilities in many fields. The WTO has no such competence. It could enact measures of this type only by means of amendments to primary law requiring a strong majority.[152] Furthermore, states can exit the WTO by means of Article XV. This option does not exist in the EC context yet, but is envisaged by the European Convention's draft for a Treaty Establishing a Constitution for Europe in its Article 59. It thus seems rather unlikely that any such rule could come into force against the will of a major player. Harmonization at the WTO level therefore is not to be anticipated. A fact, by the way, which strengthens the impact of dispute settlement decisions. As previously noted, however, the quasi-judicial WTO organs do take into account substantive rules of other multinational organizations in the trade context[153] and make reference to general international law. The named existing culture-related agreements[154] consequently should have an influence on the WTO regime; the adoption of a specific treaty under UN auspices could help to nail the issue down.[155]

(d) Subsidies and other questions

In the WTO, competition law is undoubtedly an issue, as several cases show,[156] yet there is no world competition authority, and no comprehensive competition law code. The only area that is regulated is subsidies.[157] Furthermore, the so-called non-violation claims of Article XXIII GATT guarantee a minimum levelling of the playing field. Functioning as a sort of *clausula rebus sic stantibus*, they had been used already under the GATT 1947 by panels to target measures by contracting states which granted unfair competition advantages to their operators. These issues are, again, too complex to be treated within the scope of this chapter. As a general rule, however, it may be noted that the subsidies agreement is not that tightly worded, providing ample space for 'non-actionable subsidies' (see Article 8, Agreement on Subsidies).

[152] Compare Articles IX and X, especially Articles X.5 and X.2 WTO.

[153] The TRIPS incorporating WIPO rules is the best example for this. In the GATS, Article 7 Annex on telecommunications explicitly acknowledges rules of the ITU; see Kennedy, n 143 above, 11, 15. Other WTO rules refer to Codex Alimentarius, the World Standard, and the World Health Organization.

[154] See n 9 and n 130 above.

[155] Neuwirth, n 7 above, 17 *et seq.*

[156] See Panel Report, Japan—*Measures Affecting Consumer Photographic Film and Paper* (*Kodak / Fuji*), WT/DS44/R (1998); see n 111 above.

[157] See Agreement on Subsidies, Annex to the WTO agreements.

(e) Summary WTO

The GATT constitutes a sharp sword for free trade which strikes at national cultural policies, since it does not acknowledge a rule of reason for culture. Nevertheless, the key GATT freedoms do not reach as far as those of the EC. As for GATS, this is very much a *quantité négligeable*—at least at present.

4. Conclusions: the impact of GATT/WTO and the EC on the audio-visual sector

Both preferential trade regimes discussed here feature a cultural and an economic dimension. A purely economic analysis would focus on David Ricardo's doctrine of comparative benefits,[158] on which both the EC and the WTO are based intellectually. This doctrine chiefly criticizes protection of domestic industry.[159] Nevertheless, states have always employed Listean[160] protectionism for their 'infant' domestic industries. Interestingly, even Karl Marx concurred with Ricardo, pointing to the damaging socio-economic consequences of protectionism.[161] Protectionism today is perceived to hinder national industries both by denying them export opportunities and by saving them from competition, which renders them ineffective in the long run. Some examples drawn from the European audio-visual industry seem to confirm this purely economic view: European films, as a cliché, disregard the mass market and focus on a rather intellectual audience. They are said to be, in general, funded by subsidies rather than by entrepreneurship. And ARTE, an important Franco-German cultural television project, could probably not survive outside the fishbowl of public funding, owing to its barely existent audience. From this merely economic point of view an even more vigorous removal of market barriers would consequently seem fruitful.

However, the case for such a purely economic assessment has never been made. Preferential trade zones raise the danger that economic principles will

[158] Ricardo, D, *On the Principles of Political Economy, and Taxation* (London: Murray, 1817).

[159] Hudec, n 124 above, 619.

[160] List, F, *The National System of Political Economy* (London: Cass, 1982; first published as *Das nationale System der politischen Oekonomie*, 1837/1842).

[161] Marx, K, *Das Kapital* (Stuttgart: Kroener 1957; first published 1867, 1885, 1894), 386: 'protectionism may be a means to shorten the transition from ancient to modern ways of production by force', yet the price to be paid for that are negative consequences for the national economy, e.g., 'state debts, enormous taxation, protection, trade wars and so on . . . ' (translated by the author).

be applied to all sectors of life, including the cultural. Yet do interactions between two people necessarily have to be categorized as between buyer and seller? Is it not possible for people, especially in the cultural domain, to communicate without a commercial goal, from citizen to citizen? The view is perfectly defendable that commercial operations are nothing but a vehicle to allow human beings their cultural activity. The cultural perspective, hence, should not be neglected when passing judgement on the two preferential trade zones at issue. In consequence, equating cultural regulation with protectionism is unjustified.

Nevertheless, not all protectionist measures in the name of culture are founded on solid cultural considerations. As stated before, cultural exchange itself is an important cultural consideration. Even though Heinrich Heine claimed that customs borders cannot hinder trafficking in thoughts,[162] open borders clearly support cultural dialogue. An individual's right of access to cultural diversity also militates in favour of free trade in culture. Some state measures, such as import or minimum national content quotas, may ultimately impede a broader freedom both of information and of expression, and so curtail the very cultural diversity they seek to achieve. It is for individuals to choose their own culture and not for the state to order one. Article 10 ECHR underlines this individual entitlement.

Measures designed to exclude foreign influence are often taken in the fear of cultural imperialism, or the sorrow of losing domestic culture.[163] But these consequences can be avoided if states commit themselves to supporting domestic and independent culture without excluding foreign influences. Only two examples of such active cultural policy measures will be given. First of all, competition law or specific ownership rules should be employed to remedy the abuse of market dominance in the cultural industries and to avoid too strong a concentration of the media. As a result, a greater number of smaller players will exist. Such policy will help to achieve a wider cultural diversity. While quotas impede all foreign art— Cuban Salsa music, movies by African aborigine communities, or books by Chinese dissidents are affected in the same way as American pop music, Hollywood films, and novels by Stephen King—competition-based rules can contain media giants, be they foreign or domestic. And just by the way, Vivendi and Bertelsmann are European firms, even if they certainly are just as dangerous to small and independent operators as AOL Time Warner, Disney, or Viacom. A further tool of competition law,

[162] Heine, H, *Deutschland—Ein Wintermärchen* (Frankfurt: Insel, 1968; first published 1844), Caput II.

[163] See nn 12 and 13 above.

fair access rights to infrastructure in the hands of dominant players,[164] will help to give independent artists an outlet.

Another promising trade-neutral policy is the provision of state aid to independent domestic artists. Article 87 *et seq*. EC therefore grant a certain latitude to the states in financing cultural projects. Of course, public funding may not suffice to compete with large commercial players in terms of production and advertising budgets. Furthermore, if there is a market for a certain domestic cultural activity, private companies for sure will serve it. 'Les Visiteurs', 'Der Schuh des Manitu', and 'Resident Evil' are productions which exemplify that there is a commercially viable European movie market that definitively cannot be said to be too intellectual. Public start-up assistance thus may be enough to open new commercial segments in the cultural market. Still, some creative output will always require financial support beyond that provided by the marketplace. It is here that the states should focus their support. Such aid will keep small creative companies and independent artists viable and, at the same time, will not preclude customers from their access to the culture they wish to enjoy, albeit commercial, mainstream, or foreign.

To sum up, culture should have standing alongside economic considerations in preferential trade regimes. But there are forms of protectionism which cannot be justified by either of these values. The WTO and EC, therefore, should be judged by their capacity to differentiate between purely protectionist measures and those that foster valuable cultural interests in the audio-visual sector.[165] This chapter has shown that both regimes have influence on state measures concerned with culture in the audio-visual sector. Comparing them, the EC, by far, provides a more detailed regulatory system for the audio-visual sector than the WTO, yet it is more sensitive to culture at the same time. However, a common pattern of conflict between culture and trade emerges as well, and this tension can arise on three distinct levels:

- First, when determining the scope of the guaranteed rights or entitlements. Here, the EC goes further than the WTO: not only does it abolish all duties, it also employs the wide-ranging concept of non-tariff barriers. The entitlements established under the WTO regime are consequently more limited in scope than the basic freedoms of the EC. But even inside the WTO regime, there is an enormous difference between the impact of Articles III and XI GATT and the GATS. The latter does not require comprehensive national treatment. This explains the attempts by supporters of

[164] See text accompanying n 104 above.

[165] On which see the discussion by Nic Shuibhne in Chapter 3 of this volume.

cultural measures to shift cases from the GATT to the GATS. Within the EC there is not such a big difference between the goods and services regimes.

- Secondly, when determining the scope of exceptions to those rights. The written catalogues of exceptions in the WTO and the EC are comparable. Unlike the ECJ in some areas, the AB seems willing to afford these clauses a broader meaning.[166] However, a general rule of reason is missing in the WTO. Also, unlike NAFTA,[167] the GATT and GATS agreements do not contain an explicit cultural exception. The AB, hence, is unlikely to accept culture-based justifications for obstacles to trade. The only possible way for the judicial organs to do so is through reliance on treaties outside the WTO. In this respect, the ECJ's approach is more sensitive to culture.
- Thirdly, in the context of harmonization. Here, the EC has considerable scope for regulatory intervention and influences national policies the most. The WTO, in comparison, has almost no options for secondary legislation.

To conclude, both the EC and WTO seek to advance economic objectives in the audio-visual sector. While the EC regime has the widest reach, encompassing both discriminately and indiscriminately applicable measures and with the potential for harmonization, it also affords cultural concerns greater standing than the WTO. The WTO regime is not as intrusive as that of the EC and, without the option of harmonization, its impact on the audio-visual sector is potentially much lower. The danger of this system lies in its lack of flexibility towards cultural considerations. There are some international agreements in existence which vaguely touch on the issue of culture. Yet a more specific treaty agreed outside the WTO,[168] or an amendment to include culture in Article XX GATT and Article XIV GATS respectively, could provide the DSU organs with a peg on which to hang cultural considerations. But since other legitimate political interests face similar problems, the adoption within GATT and GATS of a comprehensive general rule of reason along EC lines would seem preferable—a proposal which, in terms of *realpolitik*, must for the time being be considered rather utopian.

[166] See, however, AB Report, *EC—Hormones*, WT/DS26,48/AB/R (1988); see n 111 above. There, considerations stemming from the SPS and the TBT Agreements led to a narrower interpretation of Article XX GATT by the AB.

[167] Article 2005. Exemption except for matters specifically regulated: Maule, C, 'Rhetoric and Reality—The Debate over Trade and Culture', (2002), 3: http://www.carleton.ca/economics/cep/cep02–02.pdf.

[168] Canada proposed an 'International Agreement on Cultural Diversity' in September 2002, available at http://www.dfait-maeci.gc.ca/tna-nac/documents/sagit_eg.pdf; see Neuwirth, n 7 above, 18.

Part VI

Concluding Observations

13

Culture and EU Law: The Exploration of an Interface

*Paul Kearns**

The object of this short chapter is to provide by way of conclusion an overview of the theme of this book, to draw together miscellaneous but connected strands, and, at the same time, to complement the preceding material by adding supplementary information that makes the text more complete on the chosen theme of EU law and culture. To these ends, I offer, after a brief introduction: observations on the contemporary nature of culture, especially in the light of EU legal and political objectives; a short overview of the relationship between EU law and culture using the theory of autopoiesis, which is particularly suited to interfacial issues of the type with which we are dealing; a necessarily succinct commentary on Article 151[1] and selected associated case law; a reflection on EU legal subjects deemed relevant to culture that have, for the most part, featured in this book; and, lastly, conclusions forming an assessment of the relationship between EU law and culture, having regard both to the law's apparent aims and the synthesis in practice of law and culture. That this is a somewhat mixed bag serves to underline the difficulties and complexities which arise when two not obviously compatible entities are fused in a juridical structure lacking not only a clear focus but also any specific design for their particular interrelation.

1. Introduction

Given the economic priorities of the incipient EC, it is unsurprising that culture did not feature as an EC concern from the outset.[2] As the European

* Lecturer in Law, University of Manchester.

[1] The complete text of Article 151 is set out in the frontispiece to this volume.

[2] The area is still little-covered in even standard textbooks such as that of Craig, P, and De Búrca, G, *EU Law: Text and Materials*, 2nd edn (Oxford: OUP, 1998), and does not feature in

Community developed, however, culture began to gain in prominence, emerging as a new EU concern at Maastricht. It is also possible to identify other arguably related initiatives: the notion of citizenship found a place in the treaty law, also at Maastricht, and human rights, *inter alia*, gradually infiltrated the *acquis communautaire*. Cultural protection was originally allied to both these evolving fields in an attempt to fit it under an appropriate existing umbrella for practical purposes, if not conceptually ideal ones.[3]

The notion of cultural rights, however, evolved slowly in the EC framework in contrast to other culture-related measures such as the provision of cultural aid, for example, for regional festivals and their ilk, which fell within the scope of the structural funds and well-established legal categories, and was therefore more easily assimilated into an existing pattern. Arguably, though, some of this funding did not actually have a legal base but was pushed through by the Parliament using its budgetary powers in a way which would now be considered unconstitutional. The current Cultural Title XII, initially established at Maastricht, nevertheless promised a more sound and pronounced role for culture as a distinct and legitimate EU concern, not least because founding such additional policy initiatives in existing EU law by the treaty route is historically something of a successful mechanism for the object concerned.[4] However, in the case of citizenship there was a Community precedent in the form of the free movement of persons, which paved the way for the more all-embracing idea to become a legal reality. No comparable avenue pre-existed for culture and, in this way, it can be better compared to human rights in EU law, which were a somewhat residual EU concern, only gradually assimilated into EU law[5] as it broadened its socio-political as well as economic horizons. It is indisputable, though, that EU measures in the realm of culture have been seen as a less necessary and less pressing concern than adequate provision for basic freedoms and concomitant obligations.[6]

Glockler, G, Junius, L, Scappucci, G, Usherwood, S, and Vassallo, J, *Guide to EU Policies* (London: Blackstone Press Limited, 1998).

[3] See, further, Ross, M, 'Cultural Protection: a Matter of Union Citizenship or Human Rights?', in Neuwahl, N and Rosas, A (eds), *The European Union and Human Rights* (The Hague: Kluwer, 1995).

[4] From the time of its inclusion in a EU treaty, a given EU purpose is built upon and expanded with little fear for its future contraction, given the current constraints of unanimity.

[5] Through the mechanism of unwritten general principles of EU law established in Case 29/69, *Stauder* [1969] ECR 419.

[6] This is also a political reality in individual Member States.

2. General perspectives on culture and EU law

The autonomy of culture as a concern within the EU reflects sociological conditions. As Clement Greenberg has said:

In societies below a certain level of economic development everybody works; and where this is so, work and culture tend to be fused in a single functional complex. Art, lore and religion then become barely distinguishable, in either intention or practice, from the techniques of production, healing and even war. Rite, magic, myth, decoration, image, music, dance and oral literature are at one and the same time religion, art, lore, defence, work and 'science'. Five thousand years of civilisation have separated these areas of activity from one another and specialised them in terms of their verifiable results, so that we now have culture and art for their own sake, religion for the sake of things unknowable (or, like art, for the sake of states of mind) and work for the sake of practical ends. It would seem that these things have now become separated from one another forever.[7]

This sense of fragmentation of different spheres is a typically postmodern phenomenon.[8]

Postmodernism has many distinct features but it follows a scheme of fragmentation, compartmentalisation, assimilation, then integration. These traits are discerned in the various celebrated works of Fredric Jameson, including his 1991 monograph, *Postmodernism*.[9] The term 'integration' appears for the first time in the EU's formal development in the debates prior to the Treaty of Nice, so politico-legal practice is here shadowing theory and implicitly calling for reconciliation of theory and practice. The specific recognition of cultural trends in the EU regime suggests an appeal for closer associations[10] between Member States at a grass-roots inter-human level, an area for expansion under the Committee of the Regions. The specialized juridification of culture is, though, not assisted by the lack of a suitable precedent to show the ways in which culture could be judiciable; the issue of human rights, by way of contrast, was clearly a justiciable field prior to the EU's *sui generis* regulation of it. Moreover, the controversial legal, notably judicial, application of the principle

7 Greenburg, C, *Art and Culture: Critical Essays* (Boston: Beacon Press, 1989), 32–3.

8 Postmodernism occurs after modernism, as its name suggests, and embraces at least the last 50 years; its more precise timing is a matter of controversy. See, further, Kearns, P, *The Legal Concept of Art* (Oxford: Hart Publishing, 1998), 185–92.

9 Jameson, F, *Postmodernism* (London: Verso, 1991).

10 For a critique of the difficulties of closer cultural cooperation in the cultural sphere, see, further, Weatherill, S, 'Finding Space for Closer Co-operation in the Field of Culture' in De Búrca, G and Scott, J (eds), *Constitutional Change in the EU: from Uniformity to Flexibility* (Oxford: Hart Publishing, 2000), 237–57.

of subsidiarity could prove problematic for juridical applications of EU law's central institutional cultural conceptualizations at the local level.

It was always unlikely that EU law's regulation of culture would be holistic. When the wheel of EU law turns, it takes with it, in each of its relevant separate segments, a particular dimension of culture; the type of cultural concern regulated will depend on which branch of EU law is at play. Despite the rubric of the cardinal EU culture provision, Article 151,[11] discussed later, this leaves a picture like crazy paving, with random regulation of unspecified but allegedly culturally-related factors which fail to unite under the one titular head of culture in a conceptually convincing way. Because there is no precise conceptual parameter to, or apparent constraint upon, the definition of culture, it would be naive to assume that forthcoming cultural regulation will be strictly confined to the loosely-expressed areas and processes specified in Article 151. European cultural integration is ready to be manipulated as a disguised political phenomenon as much as an explicitly legal one.

'Culture' means cultivation or the result of cultivation; the state of being cultivated; refinement in manners, thought, taste, etc.; loosely, the arts; a type of civilization; the attitudes and values which inform a society.[12] A definition of 'civilization' is the state of being civilized, but civilization can be defined as exactly synonymous with culture.[13] In his *Notes Towards the Definition of Culture*,[14] T S Eliot also tends to make the two concepts of culture and civilization interchangeable throughout his analysis.[15] In addition, he tells us that culture is 'what is worthwhile' in a society.[16] If this is an acceptable conception of culture, as I would venture, then its implications are very interesting. To consider something 'worthwhile' cannot be construed as being other than a judgement of positive value; culture, accordingly, cannot embody other than commendable quality. Is this the meaning of culture we will find developed in EU law? That remains to be seen. Sometimes mere customary practice as a way of life does not invite evaluation as positive or negative but can nevertheless be described as 'cultural'. Let us then first explore further what culture denotes in cultural theory.

B Robbins has recently observed that

> Never have the moral consequences of laying claim to membership in a culture, or accepting someone else's claim to such membership, seemed so far from self-evident. As a result, many are now wondering in some bewilderment how culture could ever

[11] See the frontispiece to this volume.

[12] *The Chambers Dictionary* (Edinburgh: W & R Chambers Limited, 1995). [13] Ibid.

[14] Eliot, T S, *Notes Towards the Definition of Culture* (London: Faber & Faber Limited, 1983).

[15] Ibid. [16] Ibid., p 27.

have been allowed to expand until there was no one it didn't appear to include, nothing it didn't appear to explain—until it had become . . . everything.[17]

Mulhern and Kuper, in different studies, one in the area of literary studies,[18] the other in the area of anthropology,[19] offer evidence that the concept of culture is itself experiencing cultural fatigue. This is a far cry from Raymond Williams's classic account of the idea of culture, which was a concept invented only at the end of the eighteenth century, and which was essentially a standard against which industrial modernity could be judged. There has been a dramatic growth in metaculture, which is discourse about what culture is or does, in the last half-century, which concludes counter-intuitively that culture is indeed everything. Gone are the antiquated but refined notions of C Geertz that culture is the epitome of values that rule in a society, embodied most immaculately in the revered religious rites and high art of an elite.[20] Postmodernists are much more concerned with the forging of extreme relativism and acute popularism in cultural analysis, which is undoubtedly the tenor and reflection of the age.

Kuper's scholarship does not indicate great hope for European Union political integrationists committed to common cultural identification. He distinguishes the German, French, and English approaches to cultural thinking. According to him, the German is romantic and ethnic, the French is civilized, and the English is a synthesis of the other two. More worryingly for Europhiles, Mulhern insists that the concept of culture is, always was, and always will be, generative of a narrow nationalism. J Tusa is more optimistic. He says that

[d]efining European cultural identity is a challenge of its own. Even without too specific a definition, thinking about the contribution that existing cultural experience makes to the political task of forging a new Europe is worthwhile, if only because it forces us to raise our horizons beyond our own seemingly ever-present [national] miseries.[21]

Tusa also has a more negative opinion on the limited use of the power of culture as a unifying force:

From Lithuania in the Baltic to Slovenia in the Adriatic, the new democracies of the former socialist bloc are desperate to become members of the European Union . . . As Eurocrats wrestle with the task of creating true adherence to the European Union in the countries of Central and Eastern Europe, the notion that a millennium or so of

[17] Robbins, B, 'No Escape' (1 November 2001), *London Review of Books*, 34.

[18] Mulhern, F, *Culture/Metaculture* (London: Routledge, 2000).

[19] Kuper, A, *Culture: the Anthropologist's Account* (New York: New York University Press, 2000).

[20] Mulhern, n 18 at p 35.

[21] Tusa, J, *Art Matters: Reflecting on Culture* (London: Methuen, 2000), 36.

European cultural activity might be a good way of reinforcing and popularising the widening and deepening Europe has not featured strongly in what has been an overwhelmingly politicised process.[22]

He believes, further, that 'Europe's sheer cultural homogeneity might be used to build European identity'.[23] J Pietrse provides a definition of Europe's homogenous cultural backcloth:

Europe is formed by the . . . community of nations which are largely characterised by the inherited civilisation whose most important sources are: the Judaeo-Christian religion, the Greek-Hellenistic ideas in the fields of government, philosophy, arts and science, and, finally, the Roman views concerning law.[24]

Drawing on this extensive corpus of basic cultural unity could prompt in EU citizens a more profound feeling of European, as opposed to mere national, cultural identification.

If culture were used more habitually in the politico-legal arena, it is arguable that it would also bring with it a livelier and more dynamic sense of European status. A feeling for specifically European culture could stop local cultures being introspective by placing them on a broader European footing while ensuring that they did not become submerged in a global quagmire and lose their identity. Time could be spent isolating truly European traits in the arts—European classical composers have always written to common rules of structure and harmony; European playwrights have regularly drawn on Greek drama; there have always been distinctively European visual-artistic canons.[25] There is now a wariness of fake internationalism[26] and the associated uniformity resonant in commercial brands utilizing globalization, but it is indubitable that occidentally-inspired international consumerism has reinforced a specifically European allegiance more effectively than dry political allegiances and purely legal ambitions. The seeming paradox of cultural diversity in a legal homogeneity designed to foster cultural identity is, in reality, practicable. This is the case despite the fact that the horizons of culture are far wider than the horizons of law. Culture clearly transcends the legal notion of jurisdiction, EU or otherwise, and is inherent in all societies, though it is not confined to merely societal culture. The 'worthwhile' permeates nature as well as civilization, and, though culture and civilization can be synonyms, culture is not restricted to human enterprise. Culture also exists, for example, in the animal

[22] Tusa, J, *Art Matters: Reflecting on Culture* (London: Methuen, 2000), p 37.

[23] Ibid. [24] Pietrse, J, 'Fictions of Europe', *Race and Class*, vol 32, 3.

[25] See, further, Tusa, n 21 above, at p 42. [26] Ibid., p 36 *et seq.*

kingdom.[27] One school of thought[28] might consider that it would be undesirable for EU law to discriminate between cultural forms as a matter of EU priority because it cannot grip the diverse nature of local or national culture by institutionally-centralized, remote, and unwanted selectivity; if EU law were to attempt to establish discriminatory prescriptive requirements for culture, the Europe that would evolve would be in that very discriminatory action already more penurious in cultural terms.

3. Autopoiesis, culture, and EU law

It is instructive to attend to the more theoretical ramifications of the relationship between culture and EU law using the concept of autopoiesis[29] to enlighten us. Autopoiesis is useful to us because it is concerned with both the idea of the autonomy of systems and their interface. This can very pertinently illumine the EU law/culture relation when EU law attempts to juridify in any way the system or notion of culture. It also provides an intellectual overview.

Autopoiesis comes in several forms but all of them have the same fundamental features. The legal theory of autopoiesis derives essentially from the work of the late German theorist, Niklas Luhmann, who utilized the work of the South American biologists, Maturana and Varela, who saw biological systems as entities which regularly reproduced their elements from their own elements in a self-generating way, in so doing becoming autonomous, and intrinsically insularized from their environment. Luhmann was responsible for divorcing autopoiesis from these biological origins and applying it to social systems. He defined social systems as systems of meaning, with communication at their heart. For cells and organisms, Luhmann substituted communications; and an autopoietic system for Luhmann constituted a representation of society within society. Each social system became a system of meaning-production.

Some see autopoiesis as an attempt by lawyers to impose their closed systems approach on the open systems view favoured by social science, but law is, of course, a more nuanced entity than the caricature this misconception

[27] The underestimation or dismissal of animals' complex cultural systems is beginning to be reassessed, albeit somewhat belatedly.

[28] The author's opinion is that this school's opinion is too exaggeratedly locally defensive.

[29] See, further, Luhmann, N, 'Autopoiesis, handlung, and kommunikative Verstandigung', *Zeitschrift für Soziologie*, 11 (1982), 366; Rottleuthner, H, 'A Purified Sociology of Law: Niklas Luhmann on the Autonomy of the Legal System', *Law and Society Review*, 23 (1989), 779.

engenders. According to autopoietic theory, law's components are self-constituted in self-referential cycles, and together become a hypercycle of self-reference; self-sufficiency and self-governing operations are therefore intrinsic to an autopoietic system. If external elements enter the realm of legal communication, they are transformed by law in a manner which permits their transmutation into identities recognizable as legal communications. Our specific theoretical enquiry is how EC law appears to, or attempts to, perform this operation on culture.

Essentially, autopoiesis as a legal theory offers valuable insights into the operation of the legal system and its relationships with other social systems, including the cultural. Applied to our study it raises important questions, namely, whether the EU legal system is firmly closed to all external influences to defend and perpetuate a traditional hegemony (and to assert a potent form of legal positivism) and the way in which culture 'threatens' such a regime. Culture may do so by being all-embracing: it surrounds the traditional legal hegemonic area, influencing law from inside and without, saturating law with its ubiquity. We will test the accuracy of this suggestion in autopoiesis's specialized terms.

The conclusion of most recent systems theory is that the openness of legal and cultural systems is an essential prerequisite for equilibrium in the context of wider society. Autopoiesis, rather than using an input-output model, emphasizes the internal operations in a given system of self-production, seeing that system as a system of meaning rather than as a group of people. Culture will exist within the system of EU law only according to the meaning that the EU system assigns to it is the basic autopoietic premise. But is culture too broad and unmanageable for that, too all-infusing? Will culture in EU law be simply, in Teubnerian[30] terms, a 'semantic artefact'? No: because it will interconnect with the remainder of its conceptualization outside the EU system uninterruptedly, a process which is part of its own pervasive autopoietic system. EU law will reproduce within itself its version of the external social environment which culture permeates, amplifying the environmental complexity it has to master.

The test of EU law's degree of autopoietic self-sufficiency depends on how that system manages to constitute its own components and identity in a self-referential cycle. Culture threatens this cycle because EU law is just one part of culture's own hypercycle, a cog in culture's larger wheel. Another difficulty for EU law is that, in its interaction with culture, it may be forced to receive

[30] Gunther Teubner is a leading authority on autopoiesis. See, further, King, M, 'The Truth about Autopoiesis', *Journal of Law and Society*, 20 (1993), 218.

and produce non-legal communications, which it may be ill-equipped to do and a consequence of which may be the thwarting of its regulatory function and its legal autopoietic independence. However, once culture is in the EU legal domain, it is arguable that culture is likely to be transformed or reconstructed by EU law in ways which allow for its conversion into data recognizable as EU legal communications. But this is not inevitable, not least because EU law's role regarding culture is primarily facilitative rather than unduly prescriptive or punitive, and very largely unconcerned with the dichotomy of legal and illegal. Culture is, though, 'shadowed' in the EU legal system when any of its facets are integrated into rules, as in EU customs law, under which art is non-dutiable. A counter consideration is that EU law can never have autonomous operation but is moulded by culture in its social environment. Culture will no doubt influence the content of legal communications, but the question becomes: can it determine legal communications in any direct way, or in a way that is possible to predict? If the answer to this is 'yes', EU law ceases to be an autopoietic system because it is not then *normatively* closed. It is no threat to its autopoietic character, though, if it is simply *cognitively* open, which, in its relationship with culture, *inter alia*, it clearly has to be, for effective decisions to be made in relation to it. EU law then reconstructs cultural objectives as EU law in keeping with its autopoietic remit. There is no problem with the EU law being motivated by 'external' initiatives since that does not compromise its cycle of self-reference in EU-legal terms.

If cultural issues *are* reformulated by EU law, they are reconstructed within EU law's system of meaning. This can seem dehumanizing when culture involves as epistemic units personal dimensions, and neutralizing when EU law processes creative and vital cultural versions of reality. Any parallel conclusive definition of culture by law suggests comparable power in the conceptual realm. The application of such power is perhaps inevitable in a formalist regime but, as we have seen above, it cannot be assumed that culture will be easily reduced to one of EU law's reality constructs, not least because its sheer multi-dimensionality and ubiquity may resist such formal reductivism. There also remains the hierarchical issue that EU law may be simply one element in culture's autopoietic hypercycle: depending on how broadly we configure culture, it may be that EU law's autopoietic character is of relatively minor stature in systemic terms. After all, is culture capable of being autopoietically confined by a legal regime when (a) culture's definitional parameters are so elastic and potentially all-inclusive, and (b), as a consequence, its alleged central fabric is so endlessly contentious?

4. Culture and EU case law

Prior to the development of a treaty provision for cultural purposes in the form of Article 151,[31] it was easy to be negative about the EU law approach to culture. Critics have claimed that until that development European cultural identity was an essentially residual idea based on a precept of what Europe was not.[32] In particular, the original Treaty of Rome can be blamed for cultural stagnation given the paucity of references to culture within it.[33] Even the national treasures derogation from the free movement of goods in Article 30[34] can be interpreted as a way of achieving the economic goal of the internal market at the expense of leaving national culture static, underdeveloped, or repressed. The more conventional interpretation of the effect of the current Article 30 is that it actually performs the positive function of protecting 'national treasures possessing artistic, historic or archaeological value'.

The rather incidental inclusion of cultural matters in the original treaty law of the EC, such as that pertaining to the restriction of the movement of national treasures, implicitly indicates a lack of interest in cultural matters as a complete genus in EU law's early history. The first signal of a real concern for cultural issues *per se* came in 1969, when the Heads of Government of the Member States recognized the need to preserve Europe as an exceptional seat of development, culture, and progress. The institutions of the EU nevertheless remained apathetic until, in 1977, the EU Commission issued a document called *Community Action in the Cultural Sector*, which it followed up, lamentably slowly, with another in 1987 ironically and self-consciously entitled *A Fresh Boost for Culture in the European Community*. In the early 1990s one Regulation and one Directive involved cultural subject matter.

The position of the rather arbitrary treatment of cultural issues by the EU persisted until the scope for EC action in the area of culture was augmented at

[31] For the full text, see the frontispiece to this volume.

[32] This original exclusive approach is partly explained by the then lack of sufficient development of supra-national institutions in Europe.

[33] The marriage of culture and EU law was obviously but lamentably not a perceived priority at this incipient stage of predominantly economic EC development.

[34] Article 30 provides that: 'The provisions of Articles 28 and 29 shall not preclude prohibitions or restrictions on imports, exports or goods in transit justified on grounds of public morality, public policy or public security; the protection of health and life of humans, animals or plants; the protection of national treasures possessing artistic, historic or archaeological value; or the protection of industrial and commercial property. Such prohibitions or restrictions shall not, however, constitute a means of arbitrary discrimination or a disguised restriction on trade between Member States.'

Maastricht. Current Article 3(q)[35] indicates that the activities of the Community will now include a contribution to education, training of quality, and the flourishing of Members States' cultures. The rubric of Article 3(q) actually uses the term 'flowering' instead of flourishing, the poeticity of which has been subsequently much-criticized for its vagueness. 'Flowering' does, though, have an appropriately artistic appeal and captures the flavour of creative activity. The Article's linking of education, training, and culture suggests that the first two terms are not self-evidently included in the last, a situation which prefaces the definitional problems EU law ineluctably confronts in its attempted juridification of the term 'culture(s)'. It also anticipates the practical drafting technique that spells out different manifestations of culture whenever a given EU provision aims to assist or regulate one specific form or forms of culture in particular. Another treaty reference to culture appears in an amendment to former Article 87, which permits the granting of state aid to promote culture and heritage conservation. Again, we notice that heritage conservation is specified independently of culture, which could definitionally include it, because, somewhat obviously, the law's main objectives in the amendment have to be concretized rather than left at the mercy of imprecise inference. Nevertheless, an unwanted tautology occurs when the word 'culture' itself is juxtaposed with terms for one aspect of culture as if they were separate things. Such an approach also begs the question what is included within, and what is excluded from, the often residual generic term 'culture' in these contexts.

As mentioned previously, the principal dramatic development in EU law's treatment of culture occurred with the coming into force of what is now Article 151, set out in full in the frontispiece to this volume. A number of things are immediately noteworthy about this provision. In Article 151(1) there is a sensible appeal to appreciate that within the EU there are both common and individual cultural phenomena in the Member States. The homogeneity sought is not a uniform, bland EU conformism, it is a richness of detail in a complex holistic picture that is European in its parameters. Article 151(2) spells out Community action regarding the type of cultural activities that are designed to be encouraged between Member States in their interaction; the Article also envisages Community action beyond those aims, though the specific nature of such additional action appears to be confined to

[35] Article 3(q) provides that: '[For the purposes set out in Article 2], the activities of the Community shall include, as provided by this Treaty and in accordance with the timetable set out therein] . . . a contribution to education and training of quality and the flowering of the cultures of the Member States.'

the activities already enumerated in the Article's second paragraph despite the broad enterprise conceived of in the first. Article 151(3) is an outward-looking provision that urges cooperation between the Community and Member States, presumably disjunctively and conjunctively, and third countries and apt international bodies. The Council of Europe is specifically mentioned as such a competent organization. This is unsurprising since the Council of Europe is centrally involved in both cultural and rights issues, and is a fellow European organization with similar distinctive European cultural goals explicit and implicit in its activities. Article 151(4) is a provision that is important but not easy to interpret. It envisages the Community taking cultural matters into account when acting under other provisions of its treaty law, with the added emphasis that such measures should respect and promote the diversity of its cultures. There is an invitation here for the principle of subsidiarity to be utilized to its fullest extent. Article 151(5) is a mainly procedural measure that involves in part consultation with the Committee of the Regions to achieve the substantive objective of incentive measures. A reasonable assumption, taking Article 151(4) and Article 151(5) together, is that there will be the promotion of much cultural activity at a local level in accordance with the subsidiarity principle, and, optimally, the work of the Committee of the Regions, which has local concerns central to its remit. This militates somewhat against the fear that cultural uniformity is behind the EU's programme of cultural law.

In *Cinéthèque v Fédération Nationale des Cinémas Français*,[36] it was said that cultural aims may justify certain restrictions on the free movement of goods provided that those restrictions apply to national and imported products without distinction, that they are appropriate to the cultural aim which is being pursued, and that they constitute the means of achieving them which affects intra-Community trade the least. From this case, it is evident that the protection of at least motion visual art can be added to the *Cassis de Dijon*[37] list of mandatory requirements. In *Groener v Minister for Education*,[38] in the context of the free movement of persons, it was pronounced that the EEC Treaty does not prohibit the adoption of a policy for the protection and promotion of a language of a Member State which is both the national language and the first official language. However, it was said, the implementation of such a policy must not encroach upon a fundamental freedom, such as that of the free movement of workers. Consequently, the requirements deriving from measures

[36] Cases 60 & 61/84, *Cinéthèque v Fédération Nationale des Cinémas Français* [1985] ECR 2605.

[37] Case 120/78, *Cassis de Dijon* [1979] ECR 649.

[38] Case 379/87, *Groener v Minister for Education* [1989] ECR 3967.

intended to implement such a policy must not in any circumstances be disproportionate in relation to the aim pursued and the manner in which they are applied must not bring about discrimination against nationals of other Member States.

In *Stichting Collective Antennevoorziening Gouda v Commissariaat Voor De Media*, it was stated, with a rare explicit reference to policy, that a cultural policy may indeed constitute an overriding requirement relating to the general interest which justifies a restriction on the freedom to provide services.[39] It was additionally held in this case that restrictions may be imposed in order to protect consumers against excessive advertising or, as an objective of cultural policy, in order to maintain a level of programme quality. Also in the context of the provision of services, the Court has held in *Commission v Italy* that the general interest in consumer protection and in the conservation of the national historic and artistic heritage can constitute an overriding reason justifying a restriction on the freedom to provide services.[40] In *Commission v France*, it was said somewhat differently that the general interest in the proper appreciation of places and things of 'historical interest' *and* the widest possible dissemination of knowledge of the artistic cultural heritage can also constitute an overriding reason justifying a restriction on the freedom to provide services.[41] Another variation on this theme arose in *Commission v Greece*,[42] where it was considered, along *Commission v Italy*[43] lines, above, that the general interest in the proper appreciation of the artistic and archaeological cultural heritage of a country and in consumer protection can constitute an overriding reason justifying a restriction on the freedom to provide services. However, despite the above rulings relating to three EU traditional freedoms, namely goods, persons, and services, the Court of Justice has not yet thoroughly examined the impact of cultural policy on competition law or other such prominent areas of EU law. It is incontrovertible, though, that in due course cultural concerns will infiltrate most dimensions of EU activity and prompt further related litigation and judgments.

The Court of Justice has thus acknowledged, albeit scantly, the notion of cultural policy in its nomenclature, and culture *per se* as an important concern of Member States; and it is such judicial activism in this area that will ultimately determine the precise rules that will apply where any 'cultural policy' is a central issue. The comparative paucity of relevant EU legislation on the

[39] Case C-288/89, *Stichting Collective Antennevoorziening Gouda v Commissariaat Voor De Media* [1991] ECR I-4007.

[40] Case C-180/89, *Commission v Italy* [1991] ECR I-709.

[41] Case C-154/89, *Commission v France* [1991] ECR I-659.

[42] Case C-198/89, *Commission v Greece* [1991] ECR I-727.

[43] See n 40 above.

subject, and the fact that there is not really a discernible EU cultural policy to serve as a guide or blueprint, despite exiguous references to one in the Court's case law, will not assist the Court in its deliberations. This lacuna does not help culture and law prepare to marry in the EU law context, and Article 151[44] is not a firm enough foundation or even signpost for this exercise, despite being *lex lata* with a prospective vision. R Lane has said of Article 151 that '[it] cannot be said to be an example of the draughtsman's finer arts'[45] on the grounds that it is not obviously justiciable and the Member States' common cultural heritage is relatively amorphous. My personal animus is that what has happened since Lane's prophetic insight is that, rather than having a doctrinal development of the EU law–culture interrelation, precluded perhaps by culture's non-justiciability, there is currently only a judicial *theme* of cultural awareness dealt with on an *ad hoc* basis. This is not a satisfactory footing for an area lacking related precursors in EU substantive law to suggest the road ahead.

Neither is human rights law or citizenship an apt matrix from which to try to elevate the autonomous concerns of culture as a single monolith. Only the Commission has addressed cultural policy directly, and it treats it as a mediator for integration rather than on its own terms. What emerges from this approach is what Kymlicka has famously coined 'societal culture',[46] and yet, ironically, there is little overlap between culture and EU social policy. Additionally, art and literature, for example, embody cultural value in a way which does not immediately suggest a *societal* dimension except in the sense that they anticipate an audience. Those two entities could be said, rather, to comprise *immanent* or *inherent* culture, of a self-standing variety.

From EU case law on culture we have a very fuzzy impression of what culture is. The Court of Justice is prone to simply citing cultural forms, somewhat arbitrarily, as being linked to the type of culture it has in mind on a particular occasion. Lane, considering education and culture, has warned that

> the Court . . . will have to be on its mettle, both in defining the meaning and breadth of Community education and cultural competence and the subsidiarity and integration provisions, but also for another reason: much of its intrusion hitherto into sensitive national domains has been, and has been accepted as being, justified by the economic interests of the common/internal markets. Education and culture, however, are sensitive

[44] See frontispiece to this volume, above.

[45] Lane, R, 'New Community Competences under the Maastricht Treaty', *CML Rev*, 30 (1993), 939.

[46] See, further, Chalmers, D and Szyszczak, E, *EU Law Vol. 2, Towards a European Polity* (Aldershot: Dartmouth, 1998).

non-economic spheres, of which the Court has had little experience. Its reasoning may therefore be coloured by, and subject to attack on grounds of, not economic analysis but ideology.[47]

Since Lane's observations we have had neither significant judicial insights into culture's definition or nature, even for purely EU purposes, nor prominent dicta on culture's capacity or incapacity for being justiciable, or even being simply *judicialized*—that is, operated on by judges in the way that other relevant factors are habitually treated by judicial process. This is perhaps explained by the particular difficulty of the definitional task and the comparatively recent judicial acquaintance with the issue of cultural appraisal.

The inclusion of culture in the Treaty on European Union was part of a strategy to involve the people of Europe more closely in the process of European integration. Nevertheless, its scope can be perceived as very narrow. The text of Article 151[48] confines the competence in the audio-visual realm to artistic and literary creations, *including* in the audio-visual sector, rather than opening the whole of the audio-visual sector to Community intervention. In addition, the Article's provision that the Council shall adopt incentive measures, excluding any harmonization of the laws and regulations of the Member States, indicates the lack of availability of what can be termed hard law. This arguably results in the European Union being essentially confined to the establishment of financial incentives in the area of culture. A further constraint is that Council decisions in the cultural area are to be taken unanimously as opposed to by qualified majority voting. Another inhibiting factor is that although cultural rights have gained importance, particularly within public international law, they have not acquired the same status in European Union legal vocabulary and instruments, perhaps because they are normally viewed as group rights rather than individual rights; this is the case despite there being cultural issues which fall within Community competence.

Such difficulties for cultural development in the European Union can nevertheless be put in perspective. Until Maastricht, there was no policy for culture but, even within the strictly economic competences of the Community, matters of cultural concern occasionally surfaced. This was most conspicuous when the derogation to the free movement of goods for the protection of national treasures possessing artistic, historic, or archaeological value[49] was periodically invoked. Regulation 3911/92 on the export of cultural goods and Directive 93/7 on the return of cultural goods and objects exported illegally,

[47] Ibid., at p 956. [48] See full text at the frontispiece to this volume.
[49] See text accompanying n 34.

though different in objective from the treasures derogation, also pointed up culture as a Community concern. In addition, the Treaty on European Union introduced into the EC Treaty a derogation from the state aid prohibition for aid which promotes culture and heritage conservation, provided the aid does not affect trading conditions and competition in the Community to an extent that is contrary to the common interest.

Traditionalist commentators, such as the late Mary Whitehouse, have expressed concern that cultural values have been degraded by the promotion of free speech to include all manner of violent and pornographic vulgarity. Many commercial products possess the label of culture without being 'objectively' cultural, is the tenor of their argument. To them, the Television Without Frontiers Directive 89/552, for example, is very disappointing because the European Union promotes the transmission of 'European works' rather than 'European cultural works', the latter term not necessarily equating with the former. The lack of a strong case for 'real' culture is also arguably reflected in the operation of the Treaty competition rules, which, absent the possibly disabling distractions of a cultural law dimension, may lead to the setting aside of the cultural interest in favour of maintaining competition in the internal market. However, this dynamic is not yet sufficiently developed in practice to make firm generalizations. The conservative reservations, and the whole question about the quality of culture promoted by the European Union, are crucial in the areas mentioned and raise evaluative difficulties that are seldom easy to resolve, and which are explored later in this chapter. Is there a justifiable preference for 'high art' standards immanent in EU policy, or do more populist conceptions of cultural worth now dominate? It may be that, in the contemporary Union, decisions on cultural worth are still largely market-driven in accordance with the economic emphasis of the traditional Community; or it may be that such decisions are coloured entirely by the priorities of the specific EU legal area in the course of which they are now made, and are thus simply context-dependent and context-determined. The lack of a sharp, explicit cultural policy in the European Union arguably leaves the matter as one for mere educated inference.

5. Culture-related paradigms in EU law

One of the primary difficulties when addressing the problematic of culture's assimilation by EU law is the fact that there are many arguably culture-related subjects that are branches of EU law but which are not necessarily dealt with under Article 151[50] and which are not embraced by a putative EU cultural policy, explicitly, implicitly, or otherwise. The lack of a policy under which these subjects are, or can be, unified is potentially confusing, as well as unhelpful for the development of a cultural head in EU law. The subjects are either directly or indirectly, firmly or loosely, connected to cultural matters, and the lack of a suitable EU legal definition of culture means that they all have possible relevance to cultural concerns as legally-conceived. There is no EU legal prescription of what is culture and what is not that can help form a unitary cultural identity for otherwise miscellaneous, independent legal categories.

What are these culture-related subjects? Many are covered in this book, but there are also many which are not. They are a wide-ranging group, and include: education, equality and gender, sport, consumer protection, language policy, copyright, the movement of national treasures, external policy, citizenship, human rights, visa and asylum policy, audio-visual policy, customs law as it pertains to art, and artists' resale rights. No doubt this list is not exhaustive.

The perceived links between these areas and culture will be more or less close depending on the definition of culture taken as one's starting point. There was no provision for, or allusion to, education in the EEC Treaty, only 'vocational training' under former Article 128. Following the Treaty on European Union amendments, the development of education falls expressly, albeit with significant constraints, within the Community's competence. There is little doubt that education has cultural dimensions. Matters of equality and gender have become central parts of Union activity, the law having moved on a great deal since the days of simply equal pay for equal work. In this respect, identity of a personal nature impacts on culture. A more doubtful cultural entity is sport. Kicking a football between players in a game does not seem intrinsically cultural but is, rather, more of a leisure-time pursuit, which could also be said of all other forms of mere entertainment and participation in it. What we retain of primary value from Ancient Rome includes literature and philosophy but only peripherally details of antics in the amphitheatre. There is arguably a durable aspect to 'real' culture and something beyond the merely interactive and prosaic. In contrast, the movement of national treasures is of essential cultural importance because art is indubitably a cultural concern. External policy, citizenship, human rights, and visa and asylum policy all have human issues involved that are linked, rather like gender and equality, to cultural concerns, albeit relatively loosely. They are clearly not as

[50] See the frontispiece to this volume.

self-evidently cultural as, for example, high art. Similarly, it can be argued that audio-visual policy impacts on popular culture, in particular, but is really only contingently cultural, as a vehicle only, and only incidentally a vehicle for culture. Customs law deals in cultural distinctions because art passes through customs controls duty-free, and a question often arises as to what is art for these purposes, which is a cultural enquiry. The legal area of the resale rights of artists is probably a legal category even more central to truly cultural issues. So, one can make such distinctions as to the degree of cultural import in a particular EU legal field, but only on the firm understanding that the criteria employed are inevitably somewhat contestable, and thus need to be clearly articulated, even though they may be difficult to justify objectively. Nevertheless, despite the lack of such objective justification, they might strike a chord of integrity in many, and might be relevant when considering how to shape an EU *cultural* policy that merits that title.

Since they have not received separate coverage in this book, let us briefly profile EU customs law pertaining to art, and the EU law on artists' resale rights, to see to what degree they have cultural relevance. This exercise can be seen as an assessment of these legal sectors that prefigures the consideration of whether they, for example, should in principle be included within an EU cultural policy that deserves the dignity of that name.

First, EU customs law pertaining to art.[51] EU customs law has evolved within the Customs Union and the Common Customs Tariff. The Customs Union has regulated the common customs area's internal market and the Common Customs Tariff has regulated the external trade of the EU, with the Common Commercial Policy as a partner in this role. Customs duties within EU territory are eliminated as is desired by any customs union between Member States. The basic rule is that all art passes through customs control duty-free. Since art has been more privileged duty-wise than other items, there has been substantial litigation over its definition when used in this particular context, and it is evident that EU customs law often penalizes innovative forms. By 'works of art', the customs tariff sense refers only to the fine arts and not to the useful, mechanical, industrial, or commercial arts. In ascertaining whether an object can be considered a work of art, the Court has not only had recourse to whether its appearance meets some definition of one of the fine arts, but has also examined the occupation of the person creating it and/or the purpose for which it was made. The EU customs approach can favour too strongly a commercial characterization of an object over its habitual

[51] See, further, Kearns, P, *The Legal Concept of Art* (Oxford: Hart Publishing, 1998), 159–70.

artistic designation. Whereas pop art has transcended the commercial character barrier and escaped customs duties, paperweights, irrespective of their having appeared in art exhibitions, have not, because of appearing functional. All art-works have an incidental commercial potential because their artistic work gives them the possibility of commercial significance. If an object can be regarded as a work of art, it is arguable that any concomitant commercial potential it might have should not decree that it is placed outside the 'works of art' head for customs classification purposes. A contrary view renders the purpose of customs duty exemptions applicable to art unjustly jeopardized by giving inappropriate weight to factors inimical to the fiscal privilege, specifically conferred on art for reasons which go beyond the usual commercial rationale for customs duties. The centrality here of cultural concerns militates clearly in favour of bringing EU customs law under the aegis of a cultural policy, which could resolve some of the inherent problems of art identification in this area by directions on artistic character and quality.

Now, concisely, artists' resale rights in EU law.[52] In April 1996, the European Commission presented the European Council with a proposal for a European Parliament and Council Directive to harmonize national laws relating to artists' resale rights. The subsequent legislative progress was complex and slow, and remains problematic following the lack of conciliation between the Parliament and the Council. However, the so-called 'Common Position' was adopted by the Council in June 2000 providing, *inter alia*, that the resale right is inalienable and incapable of waiver. It applies only to a resale of an 'original work of art' that is subsequent to the first transfer of the work by the artist. The term 'original works of art' is defined and the phrase is said to embrace even numbered, signed, or otherwise duly authorized copies. A royalty is payable to the 'author', or, after his death, to those entitled under him. The term of the right is the same as the copyright term, which is the case for moral rights in certain Member States including the United Kingdom, but in principle the latter is opposed to such an artists' resale right.

It is clear that, with the concern for artists at its heart, the EU position on the artists' resale right is of fundamental cultural concern. It joins the EU provisions on the national treasures derogation from the free movement of goods as an area of law intrinsically connected with art, which is indubitably a matter of cultural relevance. Like the EU customs law pertaining to art, the artists' resale right has fundamental and direct financial significance for artists, and it indirectly promotes, on a practical level, artistic productivity.

[52] See, further, Stokes, S, *Art and Copyright* (Oxford: Hart Publishing, 2001), 65–86.

6. Conclusions

There are a number of observations that one can make in general terms about the EU and cultural policy. The first is that a distinct explicit policy is not apparent from the current state of EU law. This causes obvious difficulties for the legal management of the area. There are too many diffused strands of law relating to culture that are in no way anchored together, and this is attributable to straightforward EU disorganization. Secondly, it is difficult to evaluate the efficacy of EU legal measures on culture when there are such vague and generalized cultural objectives set, when set at all. Thirdly, it is evident that the EU's general vision of culture is not an elitist one containing solely high art or fine art matters; EU cultural interest appears to accommodate sport and television as readily as national treasures and artists' moral rights. The overall cultural perspective of EU law is not classical but, rather, incorporates popular culture, which is to be expected given the removal of hierarchies in, and the eclectic nature of, the postmodern era[53] in which the law is operating. This approach requires overt pronouncement in terms of policy objectives.

What are currently perceptible in EU law are different concepts of culture co-existing not necessarily inconsistently, just diversely. What is problematic is the lack of a collation of these concepts in a mainstream policy, which would be a very broad-ranging one if we simply inferred the policy from the facts of current cultural regulation in EU law. But, one could urge, a policy should be a dynamic forerunner of events, explicit not inferred, actively not passively constructed. At the moment, the theme of cultural regulation in EU law is infused somewhat haphazardly throughout the law. Something needs to be done to congregate disparate elements pertinent to culture into a reservoir where they can be collectively analysed and from which a policy can deliberately emerge. This book and its ilk may prove a catalyst for this process.[54]

EU cultural policy is not definite, let alone coherent, and is open-ended. The autopoietic model elaborated earlier in this chapter shows that culture's relative immunity to justiciability means that it cannot be operated on as tightly as human rights or citizenship, which were both legal phenomena that benefited from clear internal or external legal precedents for EU law to follow. Culture has an elasticity in EU law that has the subtle advantage of seeming unpolitically-determined, except, perhaps, when the law is obliged to

[53] For a critical guide to postmodernism see, further, Kearns, n 51 above, at 185–92.

[54] There is ample room for additional scholarship on the EU's approach to the regulation of culture that could potentially assist the more coherent development of the law in this area.

regulate a matter that is not self-evidently cultural, but which someone has to decide is cultural for one legal reason or another, which could have the colour of a subjective political decision. This is also likely to be the case when authority has to be expressed on cultural quality matters, including appropriate value judgements, which may be deliberations for which EU legal personnel are not particularly apt, and concerning which they are undoubtedly insufficiently expert.

Contemporary EU cultural policy should provide direction, and a nexus for culture-related law. Currently, any such policy is at best inchoate, has no apparent stamp of allegiance, no tendency to constructive selectivity, and no conceptual parameters with which to close its field of application. In its vagueness and variable incidence, it is near to being regarded an uncoordinated non-event. That situation must be remedied by proactive EU institutional synergy of a concerted and effective nature in order to clarify EU cultural goals in the legal arena.

INDEX

Lightning Source UK Ltd.
Milton Keynes UK
UKHW010622231118
332646UK00009B/558/P

9 780199 275472